ORDINARY
LANGUAGE CRITICISM

Rethinking Theory

GENERAL EDITOR

Gary Saul Morson

CONSULTING EDITORS

Robert Alter
Frederick Crews
John M. Ellis
Caryl Emerson

ORDINARY LANGUAGE CRITICISM

Literary Thinking after Cavell after Wittgenstein

Edited by

Kenneth Dauber and Walter Jost

With an afterword by

Stanley Cavell

Northwestern University Press
Evanston, Illinois

Northwestern University Press
Evanston, Illinois 60208–4210

Printed in the United States of America

10 9 8 7 6 5 4 3 2 1

ISBN 0-8101-1957-9 (cloth)
ISBN 0-8101-1960-9 (paper)

Library of Congress Cataloging-in-Publication Data

Ordinary language criticism : literary thinking after Cavell after Wittgenstein / edited by Kenneth
   Dauber and Walter Jost ; with an afterword by Stanley Cavell.
       p.   cm.
   Includes bibliographical references and index.
   ISBN 0-8101-1957-9 (cloth : alk. paper) — ISBN 0-8101-1960-9 (paper : alk. paper)
   1. Literature, Modern—History and criticism.   2. Criticism—History—20th century.
3. Cavell, Stanley, 1926–   4. Wittgenstein, Ludwig, 1889–1951.   I. Dauber, Kenneth, 1945–
II. Jost, Walter, 1951–
PN695 .O73 2003
801'.95'0904—dc21   2002152188

Austin E. Quigley's article first appeared in *New Literary History* 19 (1988): 209–37; Edward Duffy's
in *University of Toronto Quarterly* 65 (1996): 561–83; Martha Nussbaum's in *New Literary History* 26
(1995): 731–53; Anthony J. Cascardi's in *New Literary History* 19 (1988): 403–17; R. M. Berry's in
Philosophy and Literature 21 (1997): 61–76; Gerald L. Bruns's in Bruns, *Tragic Thoughts at the End of
Philosophy: Language, Literature, and Ethical Theory* (Evanston: Northwestern University Press, 1999),
133–63; Richard Eldridge's in Eldridge, *The Persistence of Romanticism: Essays in Philosophy and Literature*
(Cambridge: Cambridge University Press, 2001), 229–45; William Day's in *Philosophy and Literature* 19
(1995): 292–307.

Contents

Abbreviations

"AF"   James, Henry. "The Art of Fiction." In *The Art of Criticism: Henry James on the Theory and Practice of Fiction*. Ed. William Veeder and Susan M. Griffin. Chicago: University of Chicago Press, 1986.

BB   Wittgenstein, Ludwig. *The Blue and Brown Books*. New York: Harper and Row, 1965.

BGE   Nietzsche, Friedrich. *Beyond Good and Evil: Prelude to a Philosophy of the Future*. Trans. Walter Kaufmann. New York: Random House, 1966.

BT   Nietzsche, Friedrich. *The Birth of Tragedy*. Trans. Walter Kaufmann. In *The Portable Nietzsche*. New York: Viking, 1954.

CH   Cavell, Stanley. *Conditions Handsome and Unhandsome: The Constitution of Emersonian Perfectionism*. Chicago: University of Chicago Press, 1990.

CPR   Kant, Immanuel. *The Critique of Pure Reason*. Trans. Norman Kemp Smith. New York: St. Martin's, 1965.

CR   Cavell, Stanley. *The Claim of Reason: Wittgenstein, Skepticism, Morality, and Tragedy*. New York: Oxford University Press, 1979. Reprint, Oxford: Oxford University Press, 1982 [chapter footnotes show which edition cited].

CV   Wittgenstein, Ludwig. *Culture and Value*. Ed. G. H. von Wright, trans. Peter Winch. Chicago: University of Chicago Press, 1980.

CW   Emerson, Ralph Waldo. *The Collected Works of Ralph Waldo Emerson*. 5 vols. Ed. Robert E. Spiller, Alfred R. Ferguson, et al. Cambridge: Harvard University Press, Belknap Press, 1971–.

DK   Cavell, Stanley. *Disowning Knowledge in Six Plays of Shakespeare*. Cambridge: Cambridge University Press, 1987.

"DK"   Cavell, Stanley. "Disowning Knowledge." In *Six Plays of Shakespeare*. Cambridge, Mass.: Blackwell, 1996.

DQ   Miguel de Cervantes. *Don Quixote*. See, for example, translation by J. M. Cohen. Harmondsworth: Penguin, 1950.

EL   Emerson, Ralph Waldo. "Self-Reliance." In *Essays and Lectures*. Ed. Joel Porte. New York: Viking Press, 1983.

GH	Wittgenstein, Ludwig. *Geheime Tagebuche, 1914–1916.* Ed. Wilhelm Baum. Vienna: Turi und Kant, 1991.
"GM"	James, Henry. "Guy de Maupassant." In *The Art of Criticism: Henry James on the Theory and Practice of Fiction.* Ed. William Veeder and Susan M. Griffin. Chicago: University of Chicago Press, 1986.
HD	Beckett, Samuel. *Happy Days.* New York: Grove Press, 1970.
IQ	Cavell, Stanley. *In Quest of the Ordinary: Lines of Skepticism and Romanticism.* Chicago: University of Chicago Press, 1988.
JS	Proust, Marcel. *Jean Santeuil.* Paris: Gallimard, 1971.
"KA"	Cavell, Stanley. "Knowing and Acknowledging." In *MW.*
LA	Wittgenstein, Ludwig. *Lectures and Conversations on Aesthetics, Psychology and Religious Belief.* Comp. Yorick Smythies, Rush Rhees, and James Taylor. Ed. Cyril Barrett. Berkeley: University of California Press, 1966.
LEC₁	Wittgenstein, Ludwig. *Wittgenstein's Lectures: Cambridge, 1930–32.* Comp. John King and Desmond Lee. Ed. Desmond Lee. Chicago: University of Chicago Press, 1989.
LEC₂	Wittgenstein, Ludwig. *Wittgenstein's Lectures: Cambridge, 1932–35.* Comp. Alice Ambrose and Margaret Macdonald. Ed. Alice Ambrose. Chicago: University of Chicago Press, 1989.
M	Eliot, George. *Middlemarch.* Ed. Bert G. Hornback. New York: Norton, 1977.
"M"	James, Henry. "Middlemarch." Review of *Middlemarch,* by George Eliot. In *The Art of Criticism: Henry James on the Theory and Practice of Fiction.* Ed. William Veeder and Susan M. Griffin. Chicago: University of Chicago Press, 1986.
MPWL	Perloff, Marjorie. *Wittgenstein's Ladder: Poetic Language and the Strangeness of the Ordinary.* Chicago: University of Chicago Press, 1996.
Mul.	Mulhall, Stephen, ed. *The Cavell Reader.* Cambridge, Mass.: Blackwell, 1996.
MW	Cavell, Stanley. *Must We Mean What We Say? A Book of Essays.* Cambridge: Cambridge University Press, 1969 [essay authors use various editions of this standard text; chapter footnotes show which edition cited].
NYUA	Cavell, Stanley. *This New Yet Unapproachable America: Lectures after Emerson after Wittgenstein.* Albuquerque, N.M.: Living Batch Press, 1989.
OC	Wittgenstein, Ludwig. *On Certainty.* Trans. Denis Paul and G. E. M. Anscombe. New York: Harper, 1969.

"OE"   Taylor, Charles. "Overcoming Epistemology." In *After Philosophy: End or Transformation*. Ed. Kenneth Baynes, James Bohman, and Thomas McCarthy. Cambridge: MIT Press, 1987.

OLC   ordinary language criticism

"OM"   Austin, J. L. "Other Minds." In *Philosophical Papers*. 2d ed. Ed. J. O. Urmson and G. J. Warnock. Oxford: Clarendon Press, 1970.

PD   Danto, Arthur. *The Philosophical Disenfranchisement of Art*. New York: Columbia University Press, 1986.

PI   Wittgenstein, Ludwig. *Philosophical Investigations*. Rev. ed. Trans. G. E. M. Anscombe. 1953. Reprint, Oxford: Blackwell, 2001 [essay authors use various editions of this standard text; chapter footnotes show which edition cited].

PO   Wittgenstein, Ludwig. *Philosophical Occasions, 1912–1951*. Ed. James Klagge and Alfred Nordmann. Indianapolis: Hackett, 1993.

PP   Cavell, Stanley. *A Pitch of Philosophy: Autobiographical Exercises*. Cambridge: Harvard University Press, 1994.

PP2   Wittgenstein, Ludwig. *Remarks on the Philosophy of Psychology*. Vol. 2. Ed. G. E. M. Anscombe and H. H. von Wright. Chicago: University of Chicago Press, 1980.

RM   Monk, Ray. *Ludwig Wittgenstein: The Duty of Genius*. New York: Macmillan, 1990.

RTP   Proust, Marcel. *A la recherche du temps perdu*. 8 vols. Paris: Gallimard, 1954.

SP   Frost, Robert. *Selected Prose of Robert Frost*. Ed. Hyde Cox and Edward Connery Lathem. New York: Holt, Rinehart and Winston, 1949.

SW   Cavell, Stanley. *The Senses of Walden: An Expanded Edition*. San Francisco: North Point Press, 1981.

T   Cavell, Stanley. *Themes Out of School: Effects and Causes*. Chicago: University of Chicago Press, 1984.

TC   Danto, Arthur. *The Transfiguration of the Commonplace: A Philosophy of Art*. Cambridge: Harvard University Press, 1981.

TLP   Wittgenstein, Ludwig. *Tractatus Logico-Philosophicus*. Trans. D. F. Pears and B. F. McGuinness. London: Routledge and Kegan Paul, 1961. Reprint, trans. C. K. Ogden. London: Routledge and Kegan Paul, 1981 [chapter footnotes show which edition cited].

WCT   Heidegger, Martin. *What Is Called Thinking?* Trans. J. Glenn Gray. New York: Harper and Row, 1968.

WJ   James, William. "What Pragmatism Means." In *The Writings of William James: A Comprehensive Edition*. Ed. John J. McDermott. Chicago: University of Chicago Press, 1977.

Z   Wittgenstein, Ludwig. *Zettel*. Ed. G. E. M. Anscombe and G. H. von Wright. Berkeley: University of California Press, 1970.

Introduction:
The Varieties of Ordinary Language Criticism

Kenneth Dauber and Walter Jost

The volume in hand extends the friendship of an argument, by way of a collection of examples, on behalf of a critical reflection and practice to which we have given, with some misgivings, the name of ordinary language criticism (OLC). In our view no intellectual clique or school can claim exclusive possession of this title as a rubric around which to organize itself. Since the ambition of ordinary language criticism is to return criticism to its grounds in the "ordinary" or natural language we all speak, it is hardly even a rubric and offers little hope for systematic organization. We might go so far as to say that all criticism is really ordinary language criticism, that is, when criticism *is* criticism as opposed to something else (quasi-scientific theory, or ideology, or even nonsense). Naming a sort of intensification of the familiar grammar of our speech, a heightening of those connections and associations that Wittgenstein calls "the possibilities of phenomena"[1] and that others call the tacit, the prosaic, the dramatistic, OLC is a term that might appropriately be used by any reader to signify almost any critical practice that sees texts as speaking to him or to her with a certain directness. Still, we narrow the field for two reasons, one historical and one polemical. First, we mean OLC to take as its point of departure the so-called ordinary language philosophy deriving especially from Ludwig Wittgenstein in the early twentieth century. More important, we mean to register by it a departure from what we take to be the dead end of contemporary critical theory, much of which, in contemning the ordinary and familiar, proceeds in the direction of what is almost programmatically abstract and remote.

This is a situation that previous generations of what were arguably ordinary language critics never faced or had to face in the way that our contributors are trying to face it. For while criticism has never not been theoretical, at least in the sense that every particular reading implies a position or consequential way of reading, nevertheless the attempt by some contemporary theorists to use theory as a means of mitigating or undoing reading altogether is what OLC critics would specifically oppose. Accordingly, where theorists today use theory to distance and even separate themselves from texts that they seem to feel too narrowly constrict them, OLC would employ theory to enable a fuller inhabitation of texts in a variety of ways. OLC shares theory's interest in exposing textual assumptions and raising self-consciousness, even in laying bare the categories, in Kant's term, of our perceptions, what Wittgenstein and Cavell call the "criteria" of our reading and writing. But the goal of ordinary language critics is not the rather facile one of sophisticated disengagement through the construction of a theoretical overview from which we may observe our lives at a comfortable remove from them, but rather reengagement at the level of our lives themselves. In our view the criteria in which OLC is interested are nothing more than the names we give our engagements; but they are also nothing less than the terms of our various narratives, concepts, arguments, conversations. In naming these we come to see "what counts" by seeing it in relation to other things that count. But in another, perhaps more important, sense, what we see—at least, the work of art that we see—simply does not, as Kant also said, fall under concepts at all; so that, in effect, OLC reverses direction from removal to reinvestment, to a seeing from the inside, where theory, no longer meta-explanation, elaborates what we *are* invested in, for better or worse, in all the richness and complexity of that investment.

To put this in other terms, ordinary language criticism challenges the present-day rule of theory not because it is "against theory" but because it is against rules. That is, it is against theory that conceives of knowledge as knowledge of formulas or rules, or that establishes itself on the basis of a set of abstract axioms and logical methods. Investing itself in works rather than in disciplinary knowledge, OLC resists abstraction altogether, not, again, to secure a new consciousness about theory but to renew our collective conscience about criticism. Holding fast to the world that our thinking constitutes in all its methodological variety, ordinary language critics might even claim the mantle of "pluralists," if that term were not (to our ear) too flat-footed and honorific to be of much use. We might say, a little awkwardly, that OLC is "pluralist-committed," for that term breaks rank with the current obsession with imposing yet one more master method on texts from which it would therefore render us free. Instead, it construes freedom as commitment to the circumstances of judgment—even or especially aesthetic judgment. Hence it is committed to an intimacy with the experience of texts in all of experience's provisionality and potential for unforeseen reversal and projection.

What is ordinary language criticism? The answer to this question is more surprising and less ordinary than one might expect, but then real things usually do surprise us. It continues to be a misapprehension of ordinary language philosophy that it enshrines commonsense beliefs and is politically conservative, as if, by refusing a higher perspective, it held us to distinctions without any difference. Yet if OLC observes the uses of words and common beliefs, it does so not to enshrine but to illuminate. It distinguishes not to trivialize but to register and test, and this is a matter not of conserving but of making available such words and beliefs as we have for a wider range of significances than most current "theoretical" approaches, with their reduction of meaning to the bounds of closed systems of signification, allow. Getting in touch with what Wittgenstein and Cavell have called the "ordinary" and "obvious" is not a matter of confirming one's "worst" inclinations or reproducing one's "best" self. Indeed, getting to understand oneself and one's world is rather like getting to understand one's children. One gives what one has, the heart is spent. But just when everything seems in order, love returns tenfold or a hundredfold, the initially simple having proved far more rich and generous in its turn than one's own poor self. Loving a work of literature is akin to loving one's friends. It is something *you* must do. But it is also something that you can never quite do for yourself, since it is something half given to you by the recipient of your gift, in constant need of rejuvenation by your own personal contact. The trick is a kind of heightened attention or consideration of what one is doing. And indeed the special difficulty with which OLC is concerned is the difficulty of staying alert to the thoughts one is always in danger of thinking one knows only too well.

In this respect the tendency of OLC critics to speak without any specialized jargon is deceptively pacific. As even a cursory reading of the pieces we have collected makes clear, OLC critics tend to put their questions in terms less technical than is usual in current academic discourse. Their styles, typically free of catchwords and metadiscursive jargon, seem to cover an impressive but indefinite ground. Their overall projects, less bonded to principled disciplines and theories, may seem amorphous or overdetermined, at times even uncritical. OLC critics tend to focus on concrete cases, particular examples of some more general problem or claim or argument never foregrounded perfectly clearly. Yet if such argument by example too often makes it appear as if OLC were following a round that criticism has followed too often to get us anywhere, then perhaps what it demonstrates is that we have arrived already. For the aim of such criticism is not to re-create the works it criticizes in the terms of a doctrine that may be serviceable to some higher position or politics, but to discover how they are *already* serviceable and, *for that reason*, in need of being shown why they require ongoing inquiry into their nature and implications. Thus, like any good critical approach, OLC is not content to leave what it criticizes unchallenged or unchanged. It is concerned that in reading, writing, and talking, as Wittgenstein puts it, "we do not command a clear view of the use of our words," that we require "perspicuous representations" of the grammar of specific language-games in particular cases not by seeking stricter logical controls—say via definition and inference, or by reference to some overarching a priori—but by "seeing connexions" (*PI*, §122) among our concepts and the circumstances of their employment. For in OLC the aim is to see rather than know, or rather to see what, in some senses, we know already. It is to see what we *do* say, for this enables us to determine what we are willing to keep on saying about the lives we live and therefore how they might or ought to be changed in words and deeds. And here the seeming pointlessness of some ordinary language criticism is just the point.

As anyone familiar with Wittgenstein's *Philosophical Investigations* knows, even a perspicuous representation can grow cloudy in its upper reaches. Wittgenstein at his best seems to say nothing superfluous. He is spare in his choice of words, free of merely decorative flourish, and the result is a kind of gnomic quality elusive of the impatient reader's grasp or penchant for straightforward conceptualization and deduction. In a quite different way, Stanley Cavell prefers the long line to Wittgenstein's apothegms. His sentences are crafted, his phrases intensely deliberated, and in his deliberateness and the weight of his words and the train of their associations he becomes as difficult to summarize as Wittgenstein is to paraphrase. Wittgenstein, as we might put it, says what he means. Cavell means what he says. But if—as seems the case—what makes the meanings of Wittgenstein or Cavell or other ordinary language critics difficult to grasp is their locating meaning *in* the circumstances of saying rather than always just beyond saying, in some founding supposition either unsayable or too reductive to be worth saying, then therein lies the virtue of OLC. For the weight of OLC resides in no more than its attunement to what it criticizes, and such attunement cannot become the stuff of political agendas or schools of thought. Both Cavell's dancing roundaboutness and Wittgenstein's gnomic twinkling refuse those loyalty oaths that turn literature and its criticism into mere staging areas for systematic theory. Accordingly, over and against the temptations of master formulations, OLC does not so much dismiss the excitement of the last two decades of literary theorizing as it reminds all of us involved in theorizing that individual works, like lives, are not the same thing over and over but one thing after another, and to be treated as if our lives depended upon them.

This is not merely an academic issue, though it has wide implications for the academy, in which an ersatz sophistication of too many professors has shorted the circuit between literary works and the real lives of those reading and teaching them. The exigencies of the problem confront us daily. A student hands in a paper that will not do. It is not that he cannot think but that, lacking all conviction in thinking, he does not bother. "Whatever," in the postmodern vernacular, he seems to say. But why, an instructor might wonder, have you placed this particular word here, that sentence there? Perhaps we ought to say, "You do not say what you mean or mean what you say, for you have not attended to the saying of it." Except that, too often lacking conviction ourselves in the efficacy of attention to words, we hear instead, over our own shoulders, voices remonstrating at us from the marketplace of critical theory, and we grow impatient. For how do you teach that words matter except by a labor too intensive for your doubts about literary labors to bear? How do you demonstrate such mattering except by giving examples, by patiently showing it to yourself and to students so caught up in the skepticism you have taught them that they have lost even the faith necessary for working their skepticism through? It is not easy to think in this way, to read and grade papers in this way. It costs time and money. And it is risky, too, for it means exposing the authority of your response to students who have as good reason to question as to listen to it. It means testing such faith as what you say may command on your saying's very grounds, on the grounds of a certain mastery of words ungrounded except in a faith in words themselves.

"Theory," so-called, as the ordinary language critic knows, will not suffice here. A fast doctrine, as we should have learned from the rapidity with which doctrine has lately been superseding doctrine, is what you can only teach your students to pretend to mean. But even worse is the theory that teaches that you cannot possibly mean what you say even when you try to be patient. We may justify ourselves by claiming that we really are teaching because of the formal difficulty of what we make our students learn. We may make them labor to master a certain skeptical technique. But such mastery does not take even skepticism seriously, because, once learned, it obviates skepticism's very significance, its ethical imperative patiently to choose what you say and to keep on choosing in every word you speak. Such labor as the academy now too often demands is only "theoretical" labor. It is labor *with* words, but not a labor *for* or *of* words. For words do not serve theory. They are the language of theory themselves. They are not techne. They are the world. And it is in this world of words that the ordinary language critic would live.

This, then, is the ordinariness of ordinary language criticism: that it would reconnect us to our words, with which, increasingly, we have been losing connection; that it would bring language back from the *"abyme"* in which we have somewhat hastily concluded it can only circulate to the life which it constitutes all too meaningfully; that it would think not the inadequacy of the grounds on which speaking and writing are established but the kinds of grounds, beyond adequation, that speaking and writing establish in practice; that it would explore not contradictions we take to be inevitable in a novel or a poem or a play as it confronts its own limits before the larger world, but the limits of such a world beyond which this novel or that, this poem or that play, will not go; that it is concerned not with where words break down but with the experiences that these words or those can and cannot reach. Ordinary language criticism is a modest kind of criticism, interested in linguistic particularities, wary of linguistic generalizations. Or better, it is interested, warily, in describing the limits of the variety of generalizations that can be made about a variety of particulars. So while it is as skeptical in its interrogation of the grammar of languages as any grammatology, yet because the grammars it interrogates are not forms of form but forms of life, it puts its own life on the line that its skepticism would draw, and its "mental make-up," in the phrase of William James (to whom Wittgenstein went to school in formulating his own version of skepticism), might be compared to grammatology's in the shape of a kind of Jamesian catalog of representative traits:

Grammatology	OLC
general	particular
deep	superficial
theoretical	empirical
objective	experiential
playful	dogged
aporetic (breaking down)	connective ("going on")
paradoxical (either/or)	paratactic (both/and)
dialectical	dialogic
formalistic	anthropocentric
metaphysical	ethical
aesthetic	literary

Not all of the ostensibly attractive characteristics line up under OLC, and those that do are subject to corruption. Being playful is a happier condition than being dogged, and experience can lapse into the most arrant relativism. Metaphysics may be recondite, but, unlike ethics, speaking about it is not so embarrassing. Moreover, not all of our pairs will seem like opposites. The sense in which formalism and anthropocentrism or aestheticism and literariness conflict needs to be clarified by an investigation of what Wittgenstein calls the "phenomenology of the word," of the whole world or worlds of words in which each particular word participates. Even more significantly, not all of the traits in either column will be common to all of the intellectual habits of all of that column's thinkers. One can be particular without being empirical and both particular and empirical without being dialogic. At most, such terms connect by a kind of "family resemblance" or preponderant associativity, which is all the connection on which any serious skepticism, at least since Hume, has been able to rely. Still, it may be useful to sketch out some sense of the significance of the terms of that associativity to serve as a kind of reference, a map of the terrain that follows.

Ordinary language criticism is particular. This is not to say that, even as it relies on cases and examples, OLC eschews larger formulations. We have said that ordinary language criticism is wary of generalizations. It begins with details rather than concepts and propositions. Yet it is concerned with concepts and propositions. Without them we have no way of determining what any example is an example of. It is only that "of," here, means not "dependent on" but "constituting." That is, for OLC, concepts and propositions are coterminous with their cases and examples, and there are potentially as many of the one as there are of the other. As Wittgenstein puts it, meaning is "meaning as." What matters is the relation of cases or examples to each other. So that, in arriving at a concept or proposition, we arrive not at the case or example's "real" meaning but only at a certain relation of example to example. Which is to say that

Ordinary language criticism is superficial. This is because it does not attempt to reduce or to simplify. It does not attempt to get back to what is behind or before. It takes it that words do not refer to things but are things. Things, propositions, words, and cases are not deeper than each other; they are explanations of each other. And the interest of OLC, accordingly, is in following the round of such explanations. Which is why

Ordinary language criticism is empirical. What counts as an explanation cannot be derived a priori. You must look and you must listen. Explanation is not a formula but a language. Or even if you hold, as most ordinary language critics do, that you will find in particular instances of a language certain regularities, yet in keeping with ordinary language's radical sense of particularity, such regularities are only as regular as they are in the particular instances in which you do find them. This is the way in which ordinary language's skepticism in never finished and done with, why its formulation of things, only as good as the next case it can confirm, requires almost too exquisite a paying of attention to how people explain in fact. To put a finer point on it, in OLC even "empiricism" is not a theory. Or rather, the place of empiricism in ordinary language criticism differs from its place in the theory-construction of the "human sciences." For in the latter, the particular case is taken to ground a theory into whose explanations it then, however, disappears, while in OLC, explanation theorizes the particular case. For there is never knowing in advance in what language a case should be explained, never any telling except by looking and listening to the whole train of someone's explanations (and perhaps not even then). And this is why

Ordinary language criticism is experiential. It trusts to the explanations people actually give of what they are looking at and listening to and not to any master explanation. Because OLC associates meaning and saying so closely, its role is not to correct but to clarify, or to correct by holding up to someone who says something what it is precisely he or she is saying. As Cavell reminds us, if traditional philosophy has asked how a world is or how a world so much as comes to be conceived, what its conditions are, hence what are its fundamental concepts, yet "con-ditions" are not transcendental categories but rather what we speak with, the language with which we articulate a world, which is therefore fundamental through and through. "[T]he issue is one of placing the words and experiences with which philosophers have always begun in alignment with human beings in particular circumstances who can be imagined to be having those experiences and saying and meaning those words. This is all that 'ordinary' in the phrase 'ordinary language philosophy' means, or ought to mean."[2] Thus OLC does not abandon judgment. It does not proscribe disagreement with what someone says. And certainly it does not hold that one explanation may not be better or worse than another. On the contrary, mastery of language may be better or worse; but the measure of better and worse is as much authenticity, or even truthfulness, as it is accuracy. It defines accuracy as a kind of authenticity, as the range of application to the variety of his or her experiences of what someone says, the degree to which it carries over into other situations, the way in which it comports with his or her other sayings. So that

Ordinary language criticism is dogged. First, this is because it will not let you escape from what you are saying. It will not let you assume that since what you say doesn't mean anything anyway, you may say whatever you want. Rather it holds you to yourself, leaving no room for pretend saying, for saying what you cannot possibly mean if, elsewhere, in the life you lead outside your saying this or that, you say and mean something else. Here, too, this does not mean that you may not correct yourself. It does not mean that "you" are somehow fixed and invariable, that you may not choose to be someone different, to try on the experience of another, attempt some better experience or some better self. But it does mean that you must make that self your own, that you must return it to yourself, testing its reality as one you would actually live. That is to say that OLC is dogged because, insisting on that return, it does not let you get very far. But neither does it allow you the luxury of doing nothing and getting nowhere. It holds that language is not a holiday in which you play but a life in which you work. Which is also to say that

Ordinary language criticism is connective. It is concerned with "going on" rather than with jumping to the end or, because we never do get to the end, with breaking down. Somewhere is where you are when something has been said. Somewhere else is where you get to whenever you respond to what has been said. Nor is there any end to saying and responding, no shortcut to working out each step of the way, which is why Wittgenstein emphasizes the importance of "finding and inventing intermediate cases" (PI, §122). Politically, this probably means that ordinary language criticism is, for many, insufficiently radical, that it tends to be ameliorative rather than utopian. But it also means that it is antihierarchical and even democratic, because it holds that without an end, almost anyone may go on in almost any way, that anyone's going on in the way that he or she does has the authority of the life which going on in that way constitutes, and that no one way of going on can recommend itself over another a priori but only for the way that it does go on, for what it makes possible. Which is why

Ordinary language criticism is paratactic rather than paradoxical, or, at any rate, it sees parataxis where other modes of skepticism only see paradox. Since there are many equally supportable ways of responding to a particular statement, the fact that some of those ways may carry in different directions than others does not necessarily betoken self-contradiction. In writing, as in the life which is writing, one does not go on by syllogism. One proceeds not by deduction but by a kind of induction, more by experience than logic, and the "logic" of a particular way of going on is what you establish by giving a truthful account of your experience. So that

Ordinary language criticism is dialogic, not "dialectical." It holds that to say this or that you must not necessarily be unsaying that or this. Not every thesis must be the antithesis of some other. Rather, insofar as to say anything means to respond to some other saying, there is always, in anything that is said, a history of sayings, the copresence of numbers of speakers with numbers of experiences in numbers of situations. This is the explanation of OLC's penchant for qualification, its habit of second thought, asking questions of the answers it has just given. Because OLC does not establish itself by confuting what it would interrogate but by going on from it, in effect it incorporates into itself the presence of an interlocutor or a number of interlocutors, of voices in conversation with each other, which are not always easy to sort out. This is another reason why the point of any ordinary language critique may be difficult to get. Yet the ability to sort out various voices in more or less full ways is just what OLC would teach, for happily such sorting is an activity in which not only intelligence but education counts, in which education, as an exposure to different experiences, produces intelligence, giving something of a hope, for those of us who teach being wary of language, that our skepticism might rather be useful than solipsistic. To put it another way,

Ordinary language criticism is anthropocentric. It teaches language for the sake of its uses. It teaches that language *is* use, the whole history of its use by users who will thus find, in studying in an ordinary language mode, neither a system that constrains nor a system to overthrow but, all unsystematically, examples for use, instruction, and further invention. In this sense OLC participates in the postmodern project of the "dissemination" of language, of loosing it from the authority of some centering *theologos*. But in the deposing of such authority it sees not the death but the liberation of the author, the multiplication of authorial possibilities. We might say, in contemporary parlance, the author's multiplication in gender, in race, in ethnicity, and the like, except that that is a very limited sort of multiplication. For OLC would not replace the constraint of some one putatively perfect formal system of language with a series of many but equally constraining systems. Defining language as humanity's condition, as we have said, it denies that language is humanity's prison, denies the constraint of the formalistic altogether, and defines the study of language and of the human condition, therefore, as the study, in Kantian terms, of "what concerns our freedom." Which is to say that

Ordinary language criticism is ethical. OLC is about the ways in which, reading and writing, people dispose their freedom, or fail to dispose it, or dispose it badly. It is about whom they would reach with their readings and writings, whom they would exclude, what experiences they link together—the world or worlds their writing and reading constitute. In a larger sense it is about ethos, insofar as writers and readers may form a community of writers and readers. But OLC denies that the foundations of any such ethos is metaphysical. Writing is neither "meta"—that is, it does not transcend the writers and readers who do write and read, as if their writing and reading were expressions of a community that existed somehow prior to their writing and reading it; nor is it "physics"—that is, nothing inherent in the acts of writing and reading necessitates (even "mentally" or cognitively) any particular way of writing and reading. Accordingly, ordinary language criticism is also ethical in the force it grants to the ways writers write and readers read. Or, as we might put it,

Ordinary language criticism is literary. OLC regards tropes as truth-capable. Or it might be better to say that it displaces the fruitless battle between tropes and truth onto terms which are mutually constitutive not antagonistic. In hermeneutics these are referred to as "horizont" and "applicatio"; in Burkean pragmatism "idea" and "image"; in deconstruction "trope" and "symbol"; and in ordinary language philosophy "criteria" and "circumstances." But in whatever terms, truth is not a matter of the correspondence of words to things but of the illumination of words by words. Truth is tautologous. Yet, because OLC sees such tautology as announcing itself from the start, it offers its criticism in the attitude not of hermeneutical suspicion but of what used to be called the willing suspension of disbelief and what we have called attentiveness, a willingness to look and listen. The work of OLC is not the revelation of absence but the exercise of what in elitist times was termed "taste" and what we, more democratically, would term "good judgment." Judgment is not a matter of knowledge of aesthetic rules. To invoke Kant once more, it is that for which no rule can be given. It is a matter of experience, of what appears more or less capacious, more or less useful, of what is arguably more or less "right." The feeling of rightness in its own turn is not something that can be proven or disproved by correspondence or rule. It is demonstrable not by reason but by rhetoric, that is by topics and tropes, which returns us, tautologously, to literature and to the literary judgments, experiences, tautologies of the essays that follow.

These essays, now that we have said our word of argument for them as a group, must recommend themselves on the basis of their individual merits. The reader is likely to find them variously compelling. The editors, too, differ in their favorites, much as the essayists will be found to disagree among themselves and sometimes even to slide right by each other in formulations of worlds neither quite parallel nor exactly intersecting. Accordingly, our arrangement is intended to facilitate a certain amount of at least local association among the pieces and to provide, especially for readers unfamiliar with the territory, an access not exactly gradual but, as it were, self-orienting.

So we begin with Austin E. Quigley on Wittgenstein and Edward Duffy on Cavell laying out what they take to be the inheritance of ordinary language for its use in literary study. These essays understand the implication of that inheritance in ways that might be complementary but that also suggest significantly different tempers of mind for how reading should be carried on. The one, we might say, is a liberal construction (one of the editors thinks too liberal) of the implications of ordinary language philosophy for agreement, even among those who disagree about the meaning of a text. The other is a radical account (the other editor thinks too radical) of the independence with which anyone constructs meaning. Together, however, they constitute a kind of frame, the poles of the readings that come after. These continue with Martha C. Nussbaum's analysis of independence and agreement in a so-called stream-of-consciousness novel by Virginia Woolf. Nussbaum's reading, indeed, makes the case for the necessity of independence *for* agreement and demonstrates a kind of assent to a kind of not-knowing within knowing as critical for human relations. Nussbaum's essay is followed by Walter Jost's kindred reading of the rhetoric of personhood, of meeting and avoidance, in one of Robert Frost's most powerful poems, in which the tragedy of saying and knowing is played out with a severe pathos that is at once both philosophical and literary. And they are in turn followed by Stephen Mulhall, who raises overtly the issue of literary modality as thought in representations of thinking by Cavell and Heidegger. Here the distinctions between philosophy and literature are usefully complicated, Mulhall thus opening the way for Anthony J. Cascardi, who discusses aesthetic thinking in general as the rendering of an account, quite literally a counting, of the particulars of a field, linking them together in narrative and exemplified in *Don Quixote*. In turn, William Flesch, addressing himself to the phenomena of quotation and canonicity, takes on at once, more specifically, the limit case of narration that he calls citation and, more generally, the mode of thinking that is narration itself even in the absence of the thing narrated. What is, in effect, a debate on the person who does narrate—the narrator's authority, what he or she may claim to know and the kind of performance, for better and worse, that knowing might be said to be—is then the burden of the pieces by Garry L. Hagberg, championing Cavell's deployment of the autobiographical person, and Charles Altieri, castigating it. And next is a group of pieces quasi historicizing the question of personhood and literature or, perhaps better, raising the question of personhood as central to modern conceptions of philosophy and literature. These begin with a brief by Marjorie Perloff for Wittgenstein's ostensible antiaesthetics as rather an appreciation of aesthetics as an ethics of literary judgment. And they continue with articles by R. M. Berry on Henry James, whom he places against a certain modernist crisis about the status of judgment in reading and telling a story; Gerald L. Bruns on language poetry, which he sees as re-creating the idea of the subject as ethical reader; and Richard Eldridge, who offers a discussion of romantic responsibility, of self-understanding in the protomodernist condition of skepticism. The volume then concludes with William Day, who extends ordinary language considerations of responsibility—of taking stock of the world and letting it go—to the language of the movies, and to Kenneth Dauber's analysis of thinking in scripture as world creating, as a kind of continual beginning from the beginning—with which we end.

The editors find the arrangement productive. The whole gains strength from the ways in which the various pieces "neighbor" each other, to use a word of Thoreau's taken up by Stanley Cavell, to whom we extend our thanks for his encouragement of the project and whose Afterword offers a reflection on his own neighboring of the essays collected. A more wayward perusal of the volume's contents, however, or a direct turning to writers and issues with which the reader may already be concerned, might better suit the tastes of some readers. The pieces, as we hope, provide a context of support for each other. But they will also stand on their own.

Notes

1. Ludwig Wittgenstein, *Philosophical Investigations*, 3d ed., trans. G. E. M. Anscombe (New York: Macmillan, 1958), 199e; hereafter cited in text as *PI*, with Wittgenstein's numbered sections, or "remarks," indicated by the symbol § and page numbers by "p."

2. Stanley Cavell, *Must We Mean What We Say?* (Cambridge: Cambridge University Press, 1969), 270.

ORDINARY
LANGUAGE CRITICISM

Wittgenstein's Philosophizing and Literary Theorizing

Austin E. Quigley

Among the well-known thinkers whose ideas have achieved prominence in modern literary theory, Wittgenstein strikes many as the most problematic. It is often difficult to get any precise sense of what the fuss is about. Literary theorists with a Wittgensteinian turn of mind seem firmly convinced about their position but betray little of the inclination, so common in literary theory today, to advertise noisily or display graphically the origins of their intellectual labors. Direct recourse to Wittgenstein's writings often seems no more satisfying. His major work, *Philosophical Investigations,* is a peculiar aggregate of loosely related paragraphs which offers no detailed statement of intended goals, no sustained elaboration of a narrative thread, and no triumphant summary of achieved conclusions. Although the author's preface to this enigmatic work registers his awareness of what might appear to be missing, he seems at best to be only semiapologetic about it:

> It was my intention at first to bring all this together in a book whose form I pictured differently at different times. But the essential thing was that the thoughts should proceed from one subject to another in a natural order and without breaks.
>
> After several unsuccessful attempts to weld my results together into such a whole, I realized that I should never succeed. The best that I could write would never be more than philosophical remarks; my thoughts were soon crippled if I tried to force them on in any single direction against their natural inclination.—And this was, of course, connected with the very nature of the investigation. For this compels us to travel over a wide field of thought criss-cross in every direction.—The philosophical remarks in this book are, as it were, a number of sketches of landscapes which were made in the course of these long and involved journeyings. [1]

The absence of a conventional narrative coherence and the absence of inflated claims are thus not accidental. Wittgenstein's concern for finding an appropriate structure is explicitly linked to what he feels are the demands of the ideas he has to offer. The book is finally, he suggests in his preface, "only an album," by means of which we can get "a picture of the landscape" which he repeatedly traverses in his intellectual "journeying" (*PI*, p. ix).

We should, of course, be alert to the implications of the image of an album for a philosopher whose initial reputation was established by arguments in favor of a picture theory of meaning. His earlier attempts to establish for every proposition a definitive picture are superseded by later attempts to sketch out "tolerable" pictures whose application extends beyond the sentence and whose value depends on neither their singularity nor their singleness. His declining interest in establishing definitive scenes is accompanied by a growing interest in sketching emerging landscapes, whose complicated contours require repeated journeys from one imprecise locale to another. Journeying is, indeed, one of the favorite images employed in the text. Language, we are told, is "a labyrinth of paths" (*PI*, §203); a philosophical problem has the form "I don't know my way about" (*PI*, §123); and "a rule stands there like a sign-post" (*PI*, §85), offering us helpful guidance but not explicit instructions. The journeys seem fraught with danger, the map of the terrain imprecise at best, and the destination not clearly known.

The concern that Wittgenstein exhibits for the structure of his book is evidently related to the images used within it and to the nature of the investigations he is conducting. To recognize this is to recognize one of the reasons why the book has seemed philosophically obscure and why it is nevertheless possible to locate via its obscurities an appropriate mode of participation in what it has to offer. The repeated images of journeying, of failing to get under way, of getting lost when under way, and of arriving at the wrong destination are intriguing enough in themselves, but the difficulty that confronts us is figuring out which journey Wittgenstein might wish us to take and at which destination we might thereby arrive. His constant wanderings from point to point, from paragraph to paragraph, and from image to image have led many to question whether Wittgenstein actually has a philosophical position to offer us, whether he has indeed a summarizable set of philosophical beliefs, and whether there is or could be a Wittgensteinian approach to things in general.

This is of major consequence, of course, to anyone wishing to use Wittgenstein's work in literary theory or interpretative practice. If we compare his work to, say, that of Kant, Hegel, Marx, Freud, Jakobson, or Lévi-Strauss, or to that of many other thinkers whose work has been of major consequence in the modern era, we can get some sense of what the problem is. Wittgenstein offers us no clearly defined system of analysis, no elaborate set of theoretical distinctions, and (apart from a sprinkling of characteristic metaphors) no highly developed technical vocabulary. While a Freudian analysis of a literary text instantly declares itself to be so, it can be difficult to identify as such a Wittgensteinian analysis. There is no elaborate jargon to give the game away, no set of presuppositions to be posited and illustrated, no characteristic goals that pronounce themselves in advance. The question then arises whether there is or could be a Wittgensteinian theory of art or of interpretation or, indeed, of anything else. And this question is of the same order as those which register doubts about whether Wittgenstein can, in any conventional sense, be said to have a philosophy.

Wittgenstein himself is keen to offer support to those who might entertain such doubts. Rejecting the ambitions of his youth, Wittgenstein warns us, as he warns himself, that "we may not advance any kind of theory" nor any kind of final "explanation" (*PI*, §109), nor any definitive "method" (*PI*, §133). Nor is there to be any attempt to make a breakthrough to some underlying foundation or transcendent goal: "We feel as if we had to *penetrate* phenomena: our investigation, however, is directed not towards phenomena but, as one might say, towards the *'possibilities'* of phenomena" (*PI*, §90). His argument is directed less toward final discovery than toward local equanimity; the satisfactory result is regarded less as a matter of resolving an issue than of rendering it harmless: "The real discovery is the one that makes me capable of stopping doing philosophy when I want to.—The one that gives philosophy peace, so that it is no longer tormented by questions which bring *itself* in question" (*PI*, §133). The resistance Wittgenstein displays to the temptation to offer any kind of totalizing, all-embracing theory is a resistance to the recurring consequences of such efforts—the gnawing doubts and ultimate frustrations that confront those determined to absorb multiple phenomena into unifying frameworks. At a time when literary theory is itself riddled with such doubts, at a time when Derridean deconstruction has dramatized what followers of Wittgenstein have long known, at a time when one of the major journals of literary theory finds it necessary to precipitate a debate on the viability of literary theory,[2] there is reason to reconsider what Wittgenstein had to say about the nature of theory and what he was able to display as a possible alternative.

The word "display" is carefully chosen. It relates both to Wittgenstein's characterization of his book as an album and to the potential dilemma of the antitheorist. As many would be quick to point out, to argue for or against theory is to make a theoretical argument, and there is little for anyone to gain in involving themselves in an inadvertent self-contradiction. Wittgenstein's alternative to existing theory is not an antitheory, any more than his alternative to existing philosophy is an antiphilosophy. It is instead a philosophical procedure displayed in action, a philosophical technique variously exemplified, a philosophical process that refuses to become a reified product. Though Wittgenstein warns us against our "craving for generality" and our "contemptuous attitude towards the particular case,"[3] his aim is not to substitute the particular for the general but to locate a relationship between the two that prevents them or us from coming to a final and definitive resting point. Such refusal of final resting points is not, however, a refusal of all resting points.

One of the recurring images in Wittgenstein's writing is of philosophy as a form of therapy: "The philosopher's treatment of a question is like the treatment of an illness" (PI, §255). The human mind, like the human body, exhibits recurring weaknesses and is prone to recurring illnesses. Some forms of treatment will correct the problems, but as they will not rule out the possibility of recurrence, we need both to keep the remedies at hand and to try to ward off renewed dangers before they strike. Habits of mind, like habits of the body, are, however, very hard to break, and it takes persistent intellectual effort to prevent ourselves from lapsing into habits we thought we had transcended. For Wittgenstein, many philosophical problems arise from habits of this kind, and he is prepared to characterize his own philosophical procedure as one of "assembling reminders for a particular purpose" (PI, §127). Such reminders are to be assembled in the light of, are to establish their viability and gain their function from, "the philosophical problems" that generate philosophical activity (PI, §109). And the philosophical activity about which he is most concerned in Philosophical Investigations is that precipitated primarily by problems that emerge when we attempt to explain to ourselves the nature of our language and the nature of our knowledge.

Such issues are, of course, of major consequence to current literary theory. There are few areas of concern more central to literary activity than inherited assumptions about the nature of language and few issues more likely to activate the illnesses that Wittgenstein's therapeutic techniques are designed to treat. To rehearse some of Wittgenstein's arguments on these issues is to cover well-trodden ground but also to remind ourselves of reminders that modern literary theory seems often to have forgotten. More important, however, is that in doing so, we will encounter in action aspects of Wittgenstein's thinking that can only be encountered in action. Knowing, in Wittgenstein's later philosophy, is not easily separated from doing.

The first voice we encounter in Philosophical Investigations is not that of Wittgenstein, but that of Augustine. The second is that of Wittgenstein offering clarifications and corrections to the views of Augustine. More often Wittgenstein plays both roles, alternately offering the view that inherited habits of mind encourage and the view that a more enlightened mind might offer instead. Stanley Cavell describes these as the voice of temptation and the voice of correctness, but, as others have remarked, it would be more accurate to call the second voice the voice of correction.[4] Indeed, Cavell himself points out that it is not easy to abstract from the conflicting voices a summary of what is wrong or right about either position.[5] Wittgenstein's is not a philosophy of correct positions but of corrections to positions that might most readily be adopted. By exposing the unsatisfactoriness of particular philosophical stances, Wittgenstein absolves them from the need to answer the unanswerable questions they repeatedly generate. Thus Wittgenstein responds to Augustine's description of how we learn a language (through elders pointing out objects and naming them) not by arguing that the description is wrong but by summarizing it, indicating its limitations, and then illustrating its shortcomings:

> These words, it seems to me, give us a particular picture of the essence of human language. It is this: the individual words in language name objects— sentences are combinations of such names.—In this picture of language we find the roots of the following idea: Every word has a meaning. This meaning is correlated with the word. It is the object for which the word stands.
>
> Augustine does not speak of there being any difference between kinds of word. If you describe the learning of language in this way you are, I believe, thinking primarily of nouns like "table," "chair," "bread," and of people's names, and only secondarily of the names of certain actions and properties; and of the remaining kinds of word as something that will take care of itself.
>
> Now think of the following use of language. . . . (*PI*, §1)

Wittgenstein opposes Augustine's illustration of language acquisition with an illustration of language use, an illustration designed to demonstrate that we use the words "five," "red," and "apple" in different ways, and that any attempt to base a theory of language acquisition or linguistic meaning on any one of them is to fail to do justice to the others and to the fact that there are many "kinds of word" that function in many ways. Just as important is his readiness to use a local example (sending someone shopping) to oppose the example Augustine uses to cover language in general. Wittgenstein opposes Augustine's big picture with a small picture whose consequences are disruptive but whose implications seem, initially at least, much more local. Here, at the outset, we see the beginnings of the assembling of Wittgenstein's album, of his set of philosophical reminders that function as corrections to misleading habits of mind.

The particular habit of mind Wittgenstein initially addresses is, of course, carefully chosen. It is not the only possible example, but it is one with far-reaching implications. The conviction that the meaning of a word is the object for which it stands is a conviction that dies hard. But one of the reasons for its persistence is its entanglement in a pattern of assumptions about the nature of language and the nature of knowledge. Wittgenstein points out, again by example, that our tendency to confuse the bearer of a name with the meaning of a name is a tendency that presents us with insurmountable problems: "When Mr. N. N. dies one says that the bearer of the name dies, not that the meaning dies. And it would be nonsensical to say that, for if the name ceased to have meaning it would make no sense to say 'Mr. N. N. is dead'" (*PI*, §40). But he is well aware that this is not simply a theoretical commitment on our part. After years of having it pointed out to us that the same word can be used to refer to different objects (for example, "I," "that," "it"), that the same object can be referred to by various words (for example, John F. Kennedy," "the husband of Jacqueline Bouvier," "the president assassinated in Dallas"), and that many words do not refer (for instance, "afterwards," "hello," "exciting"), we continue to be tempted by the most primitive forms of signifier/signified vocabulary.[6] Augustine's words, Wittgenstein argues, provide a particular picture of language; they are embedded in and inseparable from a way of thinking whose consequences are much more widely dispersed. Wittgenstein's concern is not so much with the theoretical correctness of an alternative theory of meaning but with the intractability of certain presuppositions about the ways in which our language functions. To correct such habits of mind we need therapy, and not just theory, and the therapy must address the many facets of the problem and not just its most visible manifestation.

What is primarily at issue in the reference theory of meaning is that it offers a comforting and apparently commonsense explanation of the principles of control that enable our language to function. And assumptions about that mode of functioning persist, even among those most aware of the problematic status of reference. Though there are many variations on the theme, Wittgenstein is less concerned with addressing any particular variant than with correcting an intractable and misleading habit of mind. Characteristic of that habit of mind are the assumptions that the object world provides language with a firm external foundation, important rules of use, a major privileged function, and an obvious preeminent form. It is these larger implications as well as the local issue of meaning that Wittgenstein is seeking to confront.

The foundation, first of all, has long been regarded as empirical: "the individual words in language name objects. . . . [The] meaning is . . . the object for which the word stands" (*PI*, §1). Second, the important rules have been those of referential logic, the kind of logic taken to an extreme by positivist philosophers. Third, the privileged function (to cite Bertrand Russell) has been regarded as follows: "The essential business of language is to assert or deny facts"[7] (the primary function, coincidentally enough, of philosophical propositions). And last, the preeminent form has been, of course, the form of the statement, the assertion, the philosopher's true/false proposition.[8] Wittgenstein had, at one time, shared many of these convictions and, early in his career, had recorded in a notebook that "my whole task consists in explaining the nature of the proposition."[9] But a key strategy of his later work is to dismantle the whole conceptual apparatus that had so arranged this set of assumptions that they seemed to provide each other with mutual support.

As far as the proposition is concerned, he is now prepared to reconsider its status and its importance: "Why," he asks, "do we say a proposition is something remarkable?" (*PI*, §93). Well, he answers, partly because of the enormous importance philosophers have habitually attached to it and partly because "a misunderstanding of the logic of language, seduces us into thinking that something extraordinary, something unique, must be achieved by propositions" (*PI*, §93). Wittgenstein's readiness to reconsider the importance of the proposition is accompanied by an interest in upgrading various other forms of language. He asks us to imagine languages without propositions, such as a language consisting only of orders and reports in battle, or of questions designed simply to elicit the answers "yes" and "no" (*PI*, §19). And he once suggested, as Norman Malcolm records, "that a serious and good philosophical work could be written that would consist entirely of jokes (without being facetious). Another time he said that a philosophical treatise might contain nothing but questions (without answers). In his own writing he made wide use of both."[10]

Having queried the status of the supposedly preeminent form of language, Wittgenstein moves steadily along to question whether language is primarily in the business of asserting and denying facts and to suggest that it has a multitude of equally important functions embedded in a multitude of language-games that we regularly play (*PI*, §23). And this leads logically enough to his efforts to dismantle once and for all the empirical foundation of language by contrasting meaning as reference with meaning as use in a language-game.

Though it is important to recognize the habits of mind Wittgenstein is opposing, it is just as important to note the techniques of correction he adopts. Wittgenstein is not interested in substituting another set of privileged elements for those he is now trying to dismantle. His aim is not just to revalue one mistakenly privileged form of language but to remove the notion that there is or should be a single privileged form. He likewise wishes to do away with the notion that there is or should be a single primary function for language; he resists the temptation to replace one set of comprehensive rules for language use with another set; and he displays no interest in offering a new foundation for language to replace the one he is dismantling. "Philosophy," he argues, "may in no way interfere with the actual use of language; it can in the end only describe it. For it cannot give it any foundation either. It leaves everything as it is" (*PI*, §124). Philosophical problems are solved "not by giving new information, but by arranging what we have always known" (*PI*, §109).

It is this concern for rearranging what we have always known that leads Wittgenstein to rely less on conventional philosophical argument and more on illuminating reminders.[11] Rhetorical presentation and philosophical procedure merge in the focus on exemplary instances. Rather than relying on philosophical assertion, Wittgenstein regularly resorts to illuminating examples. If we are inclined to think, for instance, that all words function in the same way, he asks us to imagine a text in which punctuation marks are typed out as words ("comma," "period," and so forth) (*PI*, §4). The possible confusion between ordinary words and punctuation marks would be, he suggests, a confusion no less significant than the one that occurs because our various word types (noun, adjective, and so on) are not always distinctively marked, with the result that we regard their typographical similarity as registering a functional similarity (*PI*, §11). He asks us to think of the diversity of tools in a toolbox and offers this example as a reminder that they cannot all be equated just because they are all tools. He asks us to think of the control handles in a steam locomotive, which all look more or less alike (because they are all meant to be handled): "But one is the handle of a crank which can be moved continuously (it regulates the opening of a valve); another is the handle of a switch, which has only two effective positions, it is either off or on; a third is the handle of a brake-lever, the harder one pulls on it, the harder it brakes; a fourth, the handle of a pump: it has an effect only so long as it is moved to and fro" (*PI*, §12). The images multiply and we can add our own. Today we might conceive of a control panel at NASA, where pressing one button activates a television screen, pressing another sets off a fire alarm, another opens a door, another launches a rocket, and so on.

It is, of course, open to us to construct our own examples, for Wittgenstein's use of multiple examples registers a clear refusal to establish a single definitive example. He does not try out several and then recommend the best one, nor does he circumscribe the task and the examples needed to complete it. Each example sheds one kind of light on an issue, and that is then supplemented by others. None covers all aspects of an issue and none achieves a uniquely privileged status; and this is, of course, in keeping with the antifoundational thrust of Wittgenstein's ongoing therapeutic activities.

Wittgenstein's album of examples is designed to replace any privileged picture (like Augustine's) that we might be allowing not only to guide but to govern our thinking about language. Examples as he wishes to employ them cannot constitute a closed set or a privileged series. Their function is designedly therapeutic; they address our persisting ills and contribute to our continuing health. And one of the key ways in which they do so is by their very multiplicity. Many of the philosophical problems that we encounter, he argues, arise because of our tendency to nourish our imaginations with only one kind of example (*PI*, §593). Wittgenstein's technique is to offer us examples of many kinds so that we can see by the light of their variety and thus resist the tendency to absorb the multiplicity of language into some reductive explanatory schema. For one of the key reminders that he is trying to accommodate and to share is the reminder that the multiplicity of language is not the multiplicity of a fixed state but the multiplicity of an evolving organism, in which the uses of words, sentences, and modes of discourse are constantly open to extension and revision and will constantly outrun our capacity to unify them: "How many kinds of sentence are there? Say assertion, question, and command—There are *countless* kinds: countless different kinds of use of what we call 'symbols', 'words', 'sentences'. And this multiplicity is not something fixed, given once for all; but new types of language, new language-games, as we may say, come into existence, and others become obsolete and get forgotten" (*PI*, §23).

This emphasis on existing and emerging multiplicity is characteristic of Wittgenstein's argument about language; it dictates the structure of his text, explains the function of multiple examples in his chosen mode of discourse, and clarifies the role that example making plays in the philosophical discourse he illustrates and incites. And it is important to recognize that the procedure his work exemplifies is a procedure that invites emulation rather than replication. It is a procedure that redirects thinking, rather than one that compels thinking to travel in any particular direction or to arrive at any particular goal.

Exemplary instances, rather than achieved conclusions, thus play a key role in Wittgenstein's argument, and they function not by offering comprehensive coverage but by supplying local correction and larger guidelines. Cumulatively, they register not a philosophical position but a philosophical process of positioning. And to recognize that is to recognize that Wittgenstein's interest in assembling reminders for particular purposes is something more than a diverting variant on in-house skirmishing between professional philosophers. To ask whether Wittgenstein has a philosophy or not, or whether he has a theory of language or not, is to register presuppositions about the possibilities of philosophy and theory that he does not share. Wittgenstein's aim is to reconceive the nature of philosophy and of theory. His interest is in philosophizing as a form of philosophy, in learning how to move around rather than in how to arrive, in showing how to continue an intellectual journey rather than how to end it prematurely. As a result, his philosophizing becomes of interest and consequence to anyone with any kind of personal, social, or professional concern for understanding how language works. In a narrow sense, it is true, he does not have a "philosophy" to offer at all: There is little in his later work that is reducible to a systematic array of beliefs or rules of procedure. What he offers is a philosophical technique displayed in action. What he is able to demonstrate is less a philosophy, or a theory, or a position, than a technique of philosophizing, theorizing, positioning—a technique based not upon postulates and propositions but upon images, examples, and models.[12] And it is a technique that we are invited not just to learn, but to develop. As Wittgenstein puts it in his preface, "I should not like my writing to spare other people the trouble of thinking. But, if possible, to stimulate someone to thoughts of his own" (*PI*, p. vi).

These emphases upon multiplicity and creativity have served for some to locate Wittgenstein in the camp of the philosophical skeptics rather than in the camp of the system builders. Indeed, so brilliantly has Wittgenstein displayed the multiplicity and contingency of language that followers of the current strategist of skepticism, Jacques Derrida, seem uncertain whether to regard him as an ally or as an adversary. Seduced by the siren song of continuous contingency, deconstructionists have a great deal of difficulty locating any clear goal beyond it.[13] But Wittgenstein's exploration of contingency is designedly therapeutic—it refuses us one kind of closure while opening up access to others. To argue that "the method that Wittgenstein is teaching is precisely the method of destabilisation"[14] is to recognize the anticredulity strain in Wittgenstein's work but to overlook the strain that is, as Charles Altieri points out, just as strongly antiskeptical.[15]

Wittgenstein's technique of positioning does not imply the endless deferral of locating a position. The very fact that he went on to write a manuscript on the viability of "certainty" is indicative of his interest not just in dismantling premature conviction but also in dismantling premature doubt. A philosopher who wishes to describe and not simply prescribe must not only expose the premature but also find a place for conviction and doubt in language-games. Wittgenstein's images are thus characteristically double-edged: they respect the unity and variety of concepts, the repetition and revision of language-games, the replication and renovation of meaning.

If it seems difficult to conceive of entities that are both single and multiple, Wittgenstein's most famous images display those features repeatedly and register the vital importance of both. Indeed, his two most characteristic voices diverge on precisely this point of the viability of attempts to reconcile unity and variety. But it is important to recognize the direct connection between attempts to reconcile unity with variety and attempts to mediate between foundationalism and skepticism. What is very much at issue in this conflict of voices is whether Wittgenstein's concept of language-game (or form of life) inadvertently supplies what he has been seeking to avoid: a new foundation to replace the one he has so determinedly dismantled.

> Here we come up against the great question that lies behind all these considerations.—For someone might object against me: "You take the easy way out! You talk about all sorts of language-games, but have nowhere said what the essence of a language-game, and hence of language, is: what is common to all these activities, and what makes them into language or parts of language. So you let yourself off the very part of the investigation that once gave you yourself most headache, the part about the *general form of propositions* and of language."
>
> And this is true.—Instead of producing something common to all that we call language, I am saying that these phenomena have no one thing in common which makes us use the same word for all,—but that they are *related* to one another in many different ways. And it is because of this relationship, or these relationships, that we call them all "language." (*PI*, §65)

It is in this context of unity and variety that the most famous of Wittgenstein's images emerges, but what is also at stake is a concerted effort to accommodate both contingency and control.

As is well known, Wittgenstein's description of the variety of games we play with the word "game" generates an image of "family resemblances" to indicate the way in which various similarities serve to unify this otherwise disparate grouping. It is not necessary that specific similarities run across the whole group or that the various similarities form a closed set. The continuities serve to supply what other conceptual approaches cannot—a due observance of the unity and variety of the concept. And it is important to note how quickly Wittgenstein moves on from this image to another in which *continuity* is the most visible feature: "Why do we call something a 'number'? Well, perhaps because it has a—direct—relationship with several things that have hitherto been called number; and this can be said to give it an indirect relationship to other things we call the same name. And we extend our concept of number as in spinning a thread we twist fibre on fibre. And the strength of the thread does not reside in the fact that some one fibre runs through its whole length, but in the overlapping of many fibres" (*PI*, §67). At another point Wittgenstein uses the image of language "as an ancient city" whose multiform organization provides an evolutionary record of the various forms of architecture, transportation, and community living that have created it (*PI*, §18). In one image after another, it becomes apparent that continuity is Wittgenstein's key to reconciling the competing claims of unity versus variety, foundationalism versus skepticism, and certainty versus doubt. We repeatedly encounter images of unity, continuity, and multiplicity, each of which Wittgenstein is at pains to incorporate into his album of reminders.

What is important is that we recognize that the stability invoked in these images of contingency is a stability that is neither feeble nor foundational but provisional and historical. Wittgenstein's examples repeatedly display patterns of similarities that invoke chains of similarities. Concepts don't just have a use, they have a history of use, and though we are free to revise it, we are not free to ignore it. There is a principle of control as well as a principle of contingency exemplified in these various images: the variety exemplifies the contingency and the continuities the control. The much abbreviated slogan about meaning that Wittgenstein almost casually offers—"the meaning of a word is its use in the language" (*PI*, §43)—is a phrase that invokes not just use, but "use in the language." As Wittgenstein's examples repeatedly indicate, as his insistence upon offering reminders repeatedly exemplifies, language is a historical phenomenon and signs are "souvenirs."[16] To use them is to invoke their history of use in the language—a history of combining with and contrasting with other words in language-games made up of words, things, events, processes, and actions which constitute, in another of Wittgenstein's famous phrases, "forms of life" (*PI*, §23).

Henry Staten finds the latter term either metaphysical if applied strongly or misleading if applied weakly.[17] And it is in their differing estimates of the power, importance, and diversity of historical constraint that Derrida and Wittgenstein most strongly diverge. It is helpful in this respect to bear in mind a comment made by philosopher William James when defending his philosophy of pragmatism and pluralism against charges that it offered no principles of control beyond situational expediency. In matters involving change of belief we are in general, he argues, "extreme conservatives." Acceptable novelty, he goes on, "preserves the older stock of truths with a minimum of modification, stretching them just enough to make them admit the novelty, but conceiving that in ways as familiar as the case leaves possible. An *outrée* explanation, violating all our preconceptions, would never pass for a true account of a novelty. We should scratch round industriously till we found something less eccentric. . . . New truth is always a go-between, a smoother-over of transitions."[18] The past as a series of forms of life, as a set of residues of earlier community activity, is alive in us and in our language. It provides us with regulative principles and also with points of departure, and to fail to do justice to both is to fail in general to establish *"a clear view* of the use of our words" (*PI*, §122). To lose contact with the regulative principles is to fall prey to the very philosophical skepticism Wittgenstein is at pains to avoid. Such skepticism fails to command a clear view of the role that doubting plays in our discourses of assertion and belief. To lose touch with regulative principles, to fail to establish an adequate account of them, is to give ourselves, as Wittgenstein puts it, "a false picture of *doubt.*"[19] Paradoxically enough, the false picture of doubt must be adjusted not just to rescue the viability of certainty but to lend credibility to the process of doubting itself.

Recognizing that his activity of explaining by example is never complete, never definitive, and therefore always subject to doubt, Wittgenstein seeks to re-draw our picture of doubt and its role in language-games. When skeptical philosophers deal with doubt, he notes, they tend to convert it into an unending process, one that destabilizes everything. Yet, he argues, in ordinary use no explanation "stands in need of another—unless *we* require it to prevent a misunderstanding. One might say: an explanation serves to remove or to avert a misunderstanding— one, that is, that would occur but for the explanation; not every one that I can imagine" (*PI*, §87). He argues against the notion that "secure understanding is only possible if we first doubt everything that *can* be doubted, and then remove all these doubts" (*PI*, §87). Furthermore, he notes, it is folly for us to say that "we are in doubt because it is possible for us to imagine a doubt" (*PI*, §84). These remarks and others which register the antiskepticism stance of *Philosophical Investigations* are subsequently picked up and extended in *On Certainty*, a book which goes on to ask the key question about philosophical skepticism: How is doubt introduced into language-games and consequently how is it controlled? (*OC*, §458).

Once again Wittgenstein employs his characteristic technique of showing that philosophers tend to ask words (in this case, "doubt" and "certainty") to perform tasks that are inconsistent with their ordinary language uses. To say we "know" something is, for Wittgenstein, to be "familiar with it as a certainty" (OC, §272). But certainty does not necessarily reside either in our having investigated the issue or in our having had the issue proved to us or in our having had all imaginable doubts about it addressed and discounted. Many things count as certain to us because of the forms of life we have experienced. And such forms of life are necessarily historically based:

> There are countless general empirical propositions that count as certain for us.
>
> One such is that if someone's arm is cut off it will not grow again. Another, if someone's head is cut off he is dead and will never live again.
>
> Experience can be said to teach us these propositions. However, it does not teach us them in isolation: rather, it teaches us a host of interdependent propositions. . . .
>
> If experience is the ground of our certainty, then naturally it is past experience.
>
> And it isn't for example just *my* experience, but other people's, that I get knowledge from. (OC, §§273–75)

For someone to come along and imagine ways in which we might doubt such certainty is to disturb our quiet but not to disturb our conviction. And it is just such a role that radical skepticism has come to play in literary theory. Once again Wittgenstein resorts to an example to embody the point at issue. We are asked to imagine a pupil who will not accept anything said to him and who constantly interrupts the teacher with doubts about the existence of things, the meanings of words, the uniformity of nature, and other such issues. The teacher eventually cuts him off by telling him to stop interrupting and by pointing out that "your doubts don't make sense at all" (OC, §310). The pupil, Wittgenstein argues, has not learned how to ask appropriate questions, he has not learned the range and role that doubt has earned in this language-game. These illustrative doubts are deliberately extreme, but they serve to force radical skeptics to come to terms with the difference exhibited—not just in our practice, but in their own practice—between doubts that are reasonable and doubts that are unreasonable and also to consider how they and we differentiate between the two.[20]

The impracticality of doubting everything is obvious enough, but Wittgenstein's point is stronger. There is built into every language-game a role for doubt and a role for certainty, and we learn what they are as we learn the language-game. But if this is so, are language-games, whose evolution Wittgenstein had earlier insisted upon, suddenly locked once more in place? Does every language-game have, after all, a fixed and unchallengeable foundation? Has Wittgenstein, in his efforts to restrict doubt, done so only by reintroducing the very unmoving foundation that he had sought to dismantle in *Philosophical Investigations*? Wittgenstein is quick to address this problem. If there are such things as reasonable doubt and reasonable certainty, we must nevertheless take into account the fact that "what men consider reasonable or unreasonable alters" (OC, §336). Wittgenstein seeks to maintain the distinction between reasonable and unreasonable doubt, to accommodate the fact that the distinction can change, and nevertheless to retain it as a form of control that prevents contingency from sliding into chaos.

Wittgenstein's solution to this problem is a subtle one and a crucial one. Instead of linking unity with fixity and variety with change, he reverts once more to the possibilities of continuity that had been implicit in his earlier image of extending a concept as if we were weaving a thread. But now the image of continuity switches from that of a thread to that of a river—a river that exhibits not just unity and variety but two contrasting speeds of change. The two contrasting speeds of change register two differing kinds of continuity that characterize two separable but not separate components.

I did not get my picture of the world by satisfying myself of its correctness; nor do I have it because I am satisfied of its correctness. No: it is the inherited background against which I distinguish between true and false.

The propositions describing this world-picture might be part of a kind of mythology. And their role is like that of rules of a game; and the game can be learned purely practically, without learning any explicit rules.

It might be imagined that some propositions, of the form of empirical propositions, were hardened and functioned as channels for such empirical propositions as were not hardened but fluid; and that this relation altered with time, in that fluid propositions hardened, and hard ones became fluid.

The mythology may change back into a state of flux, the river-bed of thoughts may shift. But I distinguish between the movement of the waters on the river-bed and the shift of the bed itself; though there is not a sharp division of the one from the other. (OC, §§94–97)

This image of two different speeds of change, of the riverbed moving more slowly than the river waters, registers Wittgenstein's ability to accommodate our competing convictions about unity and variety without allowing either to substantiate claims about foundationalism or skepticism. The possibility of further variety leaves room for doubt to function; the actuality of inherited stability prevents doubt from having unlimited play. Things stand fast for us without needing to stand permanently. What is certain and what is doubtable are separable without being separate. We are not in doubt just because we can imagine a doubt; a doubt needs to impress us as a useful doubt, and to do so it must reveal its own certainties so that we can indeed regard it as a doubt worth taking seriously. As Wittgenstein puts it, "If I wanted to doubt the existence of the earth long before my birth, I should have to doubt all sorts of things that stand fast for me. And that something stands fast for me is not grounded in my stupidity or my credulity. . . . A doubt that doubted everything would not be a doubt. . . . Doubt itself rests only on what is beyond doubt" (*OC,* §§234, 235, 450, 519).

The process of locating the appropriate role of doubt in a language-game serves to clarify both the role of doubt and the role of certainty without making the former unlicensed and the latter unchallengeable. Things stand fast for us because we learn with particular language-games the slowly evolving relationship between reasonable and unreasonable doubt.

It is tempting, of course, to ask for the criteria that enable us to distinguish reasonable from unreasonable doubt, but this is once again to ask in general terms more of the local stabilities in our language than they can be expected to deliver. "Our talk," says Wittgenstein, "gets its meaning from the rest of our proceedings" (*OC,* §229), and we cannot look for final grounds: "As if giving grounds did not come to an end sometime. But the end is not an ungrounded presupposition: it is an ungrounded way of acting" (*OC,* §110). If it is not possible to give our actions final grounds, it is nevertheless possible to characterize the constraints that guide action without governing it. Things stand fast for us not because of external grounds but because of a conventional history of use, because of established forms of life, because of inherited characteristics of discourse, because of recognizable generic constraints, because of all those things we have learned to exempt from doubt in order to investigate things it seems more fruitful to doubt. Since the riverbed of thought does change, it is possible to imagine situations in which anything can be doubted. But this does not make everything equally worth doubting, and it does not remove from doubt the necessity of leaving something exempt from doubt if the word "doubt" is to function at all.

To the skeptical mind, this may still prove too likely to leave us trapped in inadequate systems of belief. But it also forces the skeptical mind to acknowledge and account for the certainties that circumscribe its own doubts. Wittgenstein's insistence on the stability and continuity of language and knowledge, as well as on their contingency and multiplicity, leaves us free to make a variety of cases for reasonable doubt and also free to offer a variety of defenses against unreasonable doubt. More important, it reminds skeptics and believers alike that they have to find ways of accommodating both fixity and change. If some certainties are presupposed in particular language-games, it makes no sense to doubt them, for one is not then engaging the language-game in play: "I really want to say that a language-game is only possible if one trusts something," says Wittgenstein. "It may be for example that all enquiry on our part is set so as to exempt certain propositions from doubt, if they are ever formulated. They lie apart from the route travelled by enquiry" (OC, §§509, 88).[21] The caveat about formulating such propositions is, of course, an important one, for there is much that governs our actions that cannot be summarized but only displayed. This is one of the reasons why an inability to describe definitively the typical case is not to be equated with an inability to recognize untypical ones (OC, §27). And Wittgenstein's concern for what can only be displayed is registered in his insistence upon actions, events, journeys, and multiple images. As a consequence of these concerns, he brings forward to *On Certainty* several of the techniques he employed in *Philosophical Investigations*. The latter is, however, a more finished work, while the former is an assemblage from notebooks, so it is difficult to assess its overall form.[22] But the concern for multiple images and the concern for what can only be shown take us back to the form of *Philosophical Investigations* and to the consequences of both books for the status and function of literary theory.

What sort of procedure, we might ask, will enable us to make the key distinction between reasonable and unreasonable doubt if the language-game in question, if the very concept of language-game itself, is neither clearly defined nor firmly bounded? How are we guided in our playing of games that do not have complete and exhaustive rules? Well, says Wittgenstein, putting this question to himself, "How should we explain to someone what a game is? I imagine that we should describe games to him, and we might add: 'This *and similar things* are called "games."'" And do we know any more about it ourselves?" (*PI*, §69). The answer, of course, is that we do not. And Wittgenstein's elaboration of this point is also an elaboration on both the technique of positioning that his philosophizing exemplifies and the structure of the book he writes to exemplify it.

> One gives examples and intends them to be taken in a particular way.—I do not, however, mean by this that he is supposed to see in those examples that common thing which I—for some reason—was unable to express; but that he is now to *employ* those examples in a particular way. Here giving examples is not an *indirect* means of explaining—in default of a better. . . .
>
> . . . Isn't my knowledge, my concept of a game, completely expressed in the explanations that I could give? That is, in my describing examples of various kinds of game; showing how all sorts of other games can be constructed on the analogy of these; saying that I should scarcely include this or this among games; and so on. (*PI*, §§71, 75)

The mode of definition may well be inexact, but, in another of Wittgenstein's famous phrases, "'inexact' . . . does not mean 'unusable'" (*PI*, §88). Indeed, such inexactness is a necessity for usability. There is no point in trying to establish exact definitions for concepts whose history of use exemplifies their multiplicity and open-endedness. It is like asking which shade of green is the real green; or precisely how old is someone who is middle-aged; or trying to decide how sharply defined we wish to make a photograph of a speeding car. We offer examples as modes of orientation, recognizing that any other mode of orientation can be misunderstood, too. Working against "our craving for generality" and our neglect of "the particular case" (BB, 18), Wittgenstein searches for particular cases in the light of which we can characterize sets of particular cases. And it is in this context that judgments about reasonable and unreasonable doubt are made. But it is important to recognize that the exemplary instance can only characterize and not prescribe the possibilities of a language-game, and this reminds us once again of the need for several such instances, and not just one.

To recognize this is to recognize the importance of one further implication of Wittgenstein's use of examples that bears directly upon his concerns for multiplicity, for reminders, for provoking further thought, and for provoking others to thoughts of their own. And it is an implication with large consequences for those interested in linking Wittgenstein's techniques to literary theory. Discussing the various examples he has invoked, Wittgenstein points out that one of the reasons they are neither definitive nor foundational is that they are meant to function as an array of orientating images. The examples of language-games he has employed serve not to conclude investigation but to help it continue.

> Our clear and simple language-games are not preparatory studies for a future regularization of language—as it were first approximations, ignoring friction and air-resistance. The language-games are rather set up as *objects of* comparison which are meant to throw light on the facts of our language by way not only of similarities, but also of dissimilarities.
>
> For we can avoid ineptness or emptiness in our assertions only by presenting the model as what it is, as an object of comparison—as, so to speak, a measuring-rod; not as a preconceived idea to which reality must correspond. (*PI*, §§130–31)

Wittgenstein's album of exemplary pictures, of characterizing reminders, thus functions also as an array of measuring rods, a series of investigative instances in the light of which we can perceive, by way of similarity *and* difference, the key characteristics of particular cases. And it is in this context that we can perceive the larger implications of Wittgenstein's philosophizing for what we might now wish to conceive of as literary theorizing rather than literary theory.

What we have long conceived of as literary theory has taken many forms, but it has constantly sought to locate the appropriate relationship between general principles and particular cases. The current revulsion against literary theory is in part a revulsion against the totalizing imperative, visible in endeavors as various as those of high structuralism, vulgar Freudianism, and (old) historicism—an imperative that compels us to subordinate particular cases to general patterns. Whether the complaint arises from those defending the aesthetic integrity of unique texts, or from those who argue that literary study is unusual in seeking to grapple with language-games that are played only once,[23] or from poststructuralists committed to exposing the instability of all system building, the complaints register a widespread concern. It is not, however, a concern that is readily addressed by conceding the case for irreducible particularity or by capitulating to continuous contingency, for such concessions generate further revulsion against theoretical arguments. Yet efforts to get beyond the particular seem so quickly to impose on us the reductive commitments of the imperialistic general. And it is here that Wittgenstein's mode of positioning can exemplify a procedure that allows general and particular to interact to the benefit of both.

Wittgenstein's reliance upon the evocative example places him in one major modern tradition, and it is important to recognize how he resolves one of the dilemmas with which it is confronted. Theorists in many disciplines have been seeking in recent years to come to grips with the recognition that our activities of speaking, thinking, and knowing are grounded in figurative concepts rather than empirical data. One of the widely recognized consequences of such activities is that any framework of inquiry, whether it is psychological, sociological, anthropological, or (otherwise) figurative, tends to become both departure point and destination. The same is also true of literary inquiry. If, in literary criticism, critics invoke psychological neuroses as a point of departure, they often end up discovering what they began by positing. If they rely on archetypes as their point of departure, they usually end up discovering yet another exemplification of an archetype. Mythic patterns, dream structures, hermeneutics of desire, New Critical ironies and paradoxes, structuralist binary oppositions, and deconstructive chasms and abysses constantly remind us, in the achieved conclusions, of a critic's initial presuppositions. As everyone recognizes, figurative language as a ground for interpretative activity has the capacity to serve as a mode of orientation, a mode of characterizing the particular. But does it also have the capacity to serve as a means of investigation, as something that offers not just a ground upon which to stand but a point of departure from which to proceed? Can the figurative mode of orientation also function as a means of discovery; can it help us locate the unexpected and not just uncover what figuration presumes to be there?

What so often happens when we apply our investigative metaphors is that "seeing something in terms of X" degenerates into "seeing something as X" and then finally into simply "seeing X." The figurative mode of orientation becomes not the means of discovery but the thing to be (re)discovered. What we need to establish is that there is a possibility of discovery even when what we see is constantly encountered in the context of presuppositions about what we are likely to see.

The question that faces us is how our figurative means of knowing can provide access to knowledge that is neither given in some ontologically prior form nor fully codified by us in advance of our encounter with it. To recognize the function of Wittgenstein's album of orientating examples is to recognize what theorizing can offer that theory in its more global forms cannot. The choice we often force upon ourselves of discovering either what we presuppose or the real facts out there independent of presupposition is an unnecessary one; and it emerges from a recurring erroneous assumption—that our mode of inquiry should consist of a single, unified, harmonious set of procedures. And it is this assumption that Wittgenstein's multiply constituted philosophical album most visibly opposes.

Wittgenstein's insistence upon the model as measuring rod, on the example as an object of comparison, and on the importance of multiple measuring rods and multiple perspectives are all means of insisting that the mode of measuring is also measured. And only if the mode of measuring is itself subject to measure can it function as an instrument of discovery. Wittgenstein's concern for similarities *and* differences prevents us from converting the investigative example into "a preconceived idea to which reality *must* correspond. (The dogmatism into which we fall so easily in doing philosophy.)" (*PI*, §131). Such dogmatism is not restricted to philosophers. Literary theorists and theorists in other domains are also prone to the error of "[predicating] of the thing what lies in the method of representing it. Impressed by the possibility of a comparison, we think we are perceiving a state of affairs of the highest generality" (*PI*, §104). The difficulty here lies in maintaining control of the instrument of investigation, the mode of inquiry, the means of understanding, so that it does not convert into something that controls us.

When we ask ourselves what is being measured by the theoretical model and whether it is simply the things the model posits or the things in themselves beyond the model, we force ourselves to choose between two unpalatable options. What is being perceived beyond what a particular model posits is related data seen from a related point of view. The measured data are neither completely inside the model nor completely outside it. What the model measures and what measures the model is something seen in terms of another model or another component of the same model. This is neither to be trapped in a hermeneutic circle nor to be free of hermeneutic circles, but to participate in a polysystemic process of discovery in which the various modes of orientation function as a polysystemic means of discovery. Wittgenstein's album of exemplary reminders is itself both an example and a reminder of our need to establish, whatever our field of inquiry, an armory of investigative instruments.

In the field of literary criticism, that armory of investigative instruments cannot be elevated to the level of grandeur that literary theory, in its more ambitious forms, has sought to grant it. It remains important for us to characterize as best we can literary conventions, genres, and periods, for these are some of our major instruments of investigation. It also remains important that we remember the difference between characterizing such things and rigidly defining them. We must overcome our tendency to forget that conventions, genres, and periods are irreducibly multiple and also our competing tendency to dismiss these instruments as unwieldy once we remember their multiplicity. As Ralph Cohen has demonstrated in persuasive detail, an acknowledgment of the historical complexity of genres is not incompatible with a recognition of their various continuities, and an appropriate understanding of the relationship between continuity and change restores to genre study its credibility and viability.[24] What we must bear in mind in describing these investigative instruments is that our descriptions of them are always tentative and approximate and that appropriate use of such descriptions always involves treating them as provisional points of departure rather than as necessary destinations. We recognize the particularity of a text by locating it in the context of a set of related but unsynthesizable generalities. Whether we use actual instances of literature as exemplars or whether we use descriptive summaries, the provisional nature and investigative function of the exemplary models remain the same. Such exemplars serve to characterize the continuities that make the form of a text recognizable and thereby provide access to the discontinuities that make it individual and unusual.[25]

Literary theory can suitably multiply the armory of instruments: it can invite us to appropriate the most advanced forms of thinking in related fields such as psychology, sociology, philosophy, linguistics, and anthropology. But it must resist the urge to elevate any one of these to privileged status or to try to synthesize them into an all-embracing model. It must also resist the urge to convert *those* recognitions into an acknowledgment of an empty pluralism or into a metaphysics of multiplicity, irreducibility, and iterativeness. When theory has had its say, there remains a great deal of practical work to be done, but if theorizing has done its work appropriately, the practical work is neither untidy nor unlimited.[26]

Theory goes most sadly wrong when it seeks to govern rather than guide acts of literary interpretation, when it tries to replace rather than regulate the kinds of evidence that literary scholarship provides. Its role is not to replace or dismantle historical evidence but to guide our use of it, to help us sort out issues of relevance, priority, and persuasiveness. This is, of course, a much more humble role for theory, because such theorizing is, in many ways, a matter of problem solving rather than field defining. While local issues can thus be resolved, it is not necessarily the case that definitive rules of procedure will consequently emerge. This is not, however, an unacceptable loss, and an adjustment of literary theory to a more humble role may well be long overdue. It has always been apparent that if we ever found a grand schema that incorporated all of literature and which guaranteed that interpretation would have predictable results, we would instantly lose interest in literature. A grandiose supertext of our culture that could mean only one thing is about as interesting as the notion of a pitiful multitext that can mean anything. We need to find our way back to the aggregate of constraints supplied by the past, to the continuities that provide novelties with their appropriate context and significance. This is not a return to historicism but to the recognition John Ellis supplies when he characterizes literature as a set of modern archaic texts whose conventions are neither old nor new but repeatedly renewable. In such a context, literary theorizing and literary interpreting become parallel rather than sequential activities. Together they confront not certainty or doubt but certainties and doubts whose reasonableness or otherwise is weighed in the light of the conventionality and novelty of language-games that accommodate the continuities of our culture.[27]

Without appropriate attention to such continuities, we are, of course, likely to lose our way. It is in the nature of literary language-games, as it is in the nature of other language-games, that many things neither proven nor susceptible to proof are to be taken as givens. To refuse assent to their givenness can be to refuse to acknowledge appropriate conventions and thus to refuse to play. The investigative urge to doubt whatever it is possible to doubt is constrained by the certainties our language-games supply—not absolute certainties but certainties that are "as certain as such things are" (OC, §184). These certainties, these regulative principles, provide the conventional riverbed through which meaning flows. Though never fully formulatable, they are nevertheless there, in particular circumstances, to be exemplified and invoked. And the context in which they are invoked is one in which "consequences and premises give one another mutual support" (OC, §142).

What we are appropriately unwilling to doubt is that which our experience of literary language-games has shown it is unlikely to be productive to doubt and what our related modes of measuring suggest should not be doubted in this case. As Wittgenstein points out, we do not evaluate doubt on a piecemeal basis. Our convictions belong to a nest of convictions, and some doubts run counter to too much of what we are satisfied that we know. J. Hillis Miller may well be right to argue that good strategies of reading must surely include "the elementary assumption that the text being read may say something different from what one wants or expects it to say or from what received opinion says it says,"[28] but we should be very wary of converting "may" into "must." Indeed, if studying literature involves, as Ellis and others have argued, a study of the continuities of our cultures and our communities, we should be very wary indeed. The concern of interpretation is not the rediscovery of diverting facts about the peculiar instability of language structure, nor the rediscovery of the metaphors that guide interpretative procedures, but the discovery, through a variety of modes of orientation, of valued possibilities of structuring that particular texts have sustained and can disclose.

Knowing when to stop interpreting is as important as knowing where to begin and knowing how to proceed beyond one's starting point. To err on any of these is to fail to engage the language-game that is in play.

The difficulty, of course, is that knowledge of the appropriate parameters of interpretive behavior is not knowledge that can be converted into explicit theory. It can be registered in exemplary theorizing and displayed in exemplary interpreting, but it cannot be wholly reduced to explicit rules. As Wittgenstein puts it, "Not only rules, but also examples are needed for establishing a practice. Our rules leave loop-holes open, and the practice has to speak for itself " (OC, §139). To conceive of literary theorizing as both a practice and a guide to practice is to help restore elements of action and multiplicity to literary theory, which has long seemed unable to establish stability without degenerating into reductiveness nor to incorporate contingency without collapsing into chaos. To restore mobility and multiplicity to literary theory is to maintain in the means of inquiry features that are indispensable when that which is being inquired into is itself mobile, multiple, and elusive. We have long known that we misconceive the nature of literature when we treat it as an object containing a message instead of as an event with an experience to share. The function of interpretation is not to provide paraphrases, nor to abstract messages, nor even to summarize meaning (though it may make use of any of these); its function is to provide access to an experience that is always more than and other than the interpretation can incorporate. The function of interpretation is to provide us with an orientation, a point of departure, a means of access, a set of signposts for a journey we must make on our own. To have read a successful interpretation is to have learned principles of access, not to have received the final results of such access; the appropriate feeling is not that we have arrived but that we have learned how to go on by ourselves.

Though it would be possible to abstract many principles from Wittgenstein's philosophizing, few are more important to modern literary theory than those that relate to our capacity to control our own investigative procedures. Wittgenstein's aggregate of philosophical reminders reactivates our awareness of the problematic status of our investigative instruments. If we ignore their inexactness, we become prematurely certain of results that overlook counterevidence. If we overemphasize their inexactness, we become convinced that all possible doubts are necessary doubts. To maintain control of our figurative modes of knowing, I have elsewhere suggested two principles to guide interpretive practice and investigative theory. First, no interpretive practice or investigative theory is persuasive if it offers no general principles or procedures for constraining doubt, for preventing possible doubt from converting into necessary doubt. Second, no interpretive practice or investigative theory is persuasive if it succeeds only in rediscovering in the data its own origins in figurative language, if it displays no general procedures for preventing possible certainty from converting into premature certainty.[29] In both cases the model as measuring rod is misused, and the means of discovery dissolves into the problematics of the mode of investigation.

It thus becomes apparent that the premature doubts of interpretive procedure are part of the same problem as those of premature certainty. In both cases the mode of orientation fails to function as a means of discovery and is judged by that failure. Only to the misguided metaphysicians is the loose and multiple structure of languages and texts endlessly worth rediscovering, and only to their alter egos does interpretation require a precision and finality to which it can never aspire. As Wittgenstein's album of illustrative reminders and exemplary measuring rods repeatedly displays, appropriate therapy consists of guidelines to action—not guarantees to certainty. When we rely, as we must, on images, examples, metaphors, models, case studies, instances, and so on, as the figurative basis of our hermeneutical activities, we rely on their status as multiple approximations; it is folly to lament their individual inexactness and folly to rely unjustifiably on their individual precision. What we need is an acknowledgment of and repeated reminders of their status as various and mutually measuring approximations—approximations that help us confront the mobility of signs and their complex but controllable modes of signifying. In the context of convention-based language-games, we confront reasonable and unreasonable doubt, reasonable and unreasonable certainty, and seek to distinguish between them by locating them in the variedly moving riverbed of historical continuity and historical change. Though such pictures of the linguistic landscape remain considerably complex, we can, as a consequence of Wittgensteinian philosophizing and literary theorizing, view such complexities with equanimity, for the models we use to measure can also be measured, and the historically grounded instruments of investigation can indeed function as means of discovery.

Though there is, of course, no fixed set of rules for distinguishing valuable from valueless discovery, any more than there are final rules for distinguishing reasonable from unreasonable doubt, the investigator using examples to investigate some body of data is himself providing an example of what it is like to use examples in an appropriate way. Our decision to model our activity upon his has no higher court of appeal than the forms of life, forms of discourse, forms of discovery, and forms of community that are invoked by it and follow from it. Wittgenstein's album of exemplary reminders provides a set of signposts that guides us through the "labyrinth of paths" that constitutes our language, and it does so without diminishing the labyrinth or disguising the paths. To follow Wittgenstein's example is not to be constrained by an inherited picture but to be educated into a process of picturing—one that invites us to find our way toward the future by judiciously representing to ourselves characteristic examples of the shareable past (*PI*, §122).

Notes

I am grateful to my colleague Michael Levenson for helpful discussion of several of the issues raised in this essay.

1. Ludwig Wittgenstein, *Philosophical Investigations*, 3d ed., trans. G. E. M. Anscombe (New York: Macmillan, 1958), p. ix; hereafter cited in text as *PI*, with Wittgenstein's numbered sections, or "remarks," indicated by the symbol § and page numbers by "p."

2. See the collection of essays from *Critical Inquiry* in *Against Theory*, ed. W. J. T. Mitchell (Chicago: University of Chicago Press, 1985).

3. Ludwig Wittgenstein, *The Blue and Brown Books* (New York: Harper and Row, 1965), 18; hereafter cited in text as *BB*.

4. Stanley Cavell, *Must We Mean What We Say?* (Cambridge: Cambridge University Press, 1976), 71. These are the characteristic voices in Wittgenstein's improvised dialogues, but they by no means exhaust the voices of the text.

5. Ibid., 70 n. 13.

6. In spite of Saussure's insistence that both signifier and signified are included within the sign, there is still a widespread tendency to think of meaning in terms of names and objects. More recently, recognition of the lack of such obliging objects has led to much loose discussion about free-floating signifiers and to a peculiar readiness to elevate the absence of appropriate objects to a significant status. To convert a mistaken presupposition into a lost possibility is very misleading, and nothing but confusion can follow from attempts to speak of the absence of something that has no potential for presence. To go further and conceive of signifiers that have lost their accompanying signifieds is even more confusing, for a signifier without a signified would not be recognizable as a signifier. We also need to recognize that a signified that lacks visible presence is not usefully characterized as absent. What is at issue is one kind of presence versus another, as W. Haas clearly established many years ago in "The Theory of Translation," *Philosophy* 37 (1962): 208–28.

7. Bertrand Russell, introduction to *Tractatus Logico-Philosophicus*, by Ludwig Wittgenstein (London: Routledge and Kegan Paul, 1969), x.

8. This has seemed self-evident to many, and Noam Chomsky takes it for granted in his transformational-generative grammar, which has dominated recent American linguistics. Transformations convert the statement form into such derived forms as questions and commands. The possibility of another basic form or of several basic forms has rarely been elevated to the level of discussion.

9. Reported by Georg Henrik von Wright in Norman Malcolm, *Ludwig Wittgenstein: A Memoir* (Oxford: Oxford University Press, 1970), 7.

10. Ibid., 29.

11. It is often the case that Wittgenstein reminds us of what we have so far

known only operationally rather than conceptually; that is, he can help us recognize what we have been doing with language, even if we had never conceptualized it before. This is not unlike the process by which children can recognize, years after they have learned to talk, the accuracy of a grammatical description of what they have been doing when speaking.

12. In an impressive study of Wittgenstein's mode of writing, Timothy Binkley describes Wittgenstein's philosophizing as "thinking as it happens, not the results ordered, packaged, and neatly labelled." See Timothy Binkley, *Wittgenstein's Language* (The Hague: Martinus Nijhoff, 1973), 201. In terms of Wittgenstein's procedure of composition, this is not, of course, an accurate description, but it is a useful indication of the importance of action rather than result in Wittgenstein's thinking, and also of the priority of process over product. Binkley also offers valuable clarifications of the relationship between "use" and "usage" and of the status of the notion of "ordinary language" in Wittgenstein's philosophizing (94–102). Though there are many commentaries on *Philosophical Investigations*, Binkley's views on Wittgenstein's style of writing seem most steadily consistent with the techniques of the original, and his ideas parallel my own in several important respects.

13. This is not to say that the urge to do so is not there. But deconstructionists, having first assented to that prejudicial label, having encouraged a great deal of iconoclastic rereading of canonical texts, having demonstrated considerable flexibility in construing meaning, and having established themselves on the intellectual scene by defining themselves against texts which make foundational claims, now find themselves in trouble. The reconstructive aspect of deconstruction has never been as strong as the deconstructive aspect (as the prominence of the term *deconstruction* confirms). Consequently, it is proving much harder for deconstructors to establish their position against that of radical skepticism than it was to establish their position against that of various forms of foundationalism. There seems no doubt that they do not wish to function as radical skeptics, and there is no doubt that Derrida and the more persuasive of his followers do, at one stage of their work, read texts very carefully indeed (in terms that the authors might well approve). But that is only one stage of the process, and it is rarely clear that the constraints upon subsequent deconstruction register anything of more general implication than the limited ingenuity of the deconstructor.

There is, however, an ambivalence on the issue of generalizable controls in the otherwise happily heterogeneous field of deconstruction, as one recent public manifestation of it indicates. J. Hillis Miller used the forum of the 1986 presidential address at the Modern Language Association convention to offer an aggressive denunciation of those who have failed to do justice to the intentions of the authors of deconstructive critical texts: "The misrepresentation of what Derrida or de Man says about history, politics, and the positive role of the humanities

would be incredible if it did not so patently derive from the anxiety of the ac-
cusers." This rhetoric of grievance continues with accusations of a "blind refusal
to read" and a "blatant and consistent violation of [a] basic ethical obligation."
This is scathing commentary on the reading habits of others, but there is not
the slightest awareness of possible inconsistency when Miller, in the very same
paragraph, accompanies his attack on those who would misread the sacred texts
of deconstruction with a reminder of something characteristic of all good reading
but fundamental to deconstructive reading strategies—that careful, patient, and
scrupulous reading must surely include "the elementary assumption that the text
being read may say something different from what one wants or expects it to say or
from what received opinion says it says." This is in turn followed by a (yet another)
definition of deconstruction that confirms that what is regarded as indefensible
when addressed to approved-of texts is still regarded as essential when addressed
to others: "'Deconstruction' is the current name for the multiple and heterogeneous
strategies of overturning and displacement that will liberate your own enterprise
from what disables it." (See J. Hillis Miller, "The Triumph of Theory, the Resistance
to Reading, and the Question of the Material Base," *PMLA* 102 [1987]: 284, 291.)

   To anyone conversant with the complexities of deconstruction, it is evident
enough how these seeming inconsistencies might be reconciled. But the failure of
those making such claims to recognize that they might be perceived as inconsistent
registers the increasing need for partisans of deconstruction to make as visible and
as public what stands fast for them as they have made visible and public what does
not. For his part, Wittgenstein has, of course, already done so.

   14. Henry Staten, *Wittgenstein and Derrida* (Lincoln: University of Nebraska
Press, 1984), 75. Wittgenstein would, of course, be reluctant to be regarded as the
teacher of a method.

   15. Charles Altieri, "Wittgenstein on Consciousness and Language: A Challenge to Derridean Literary Theory," *Modern Language Notes* 91 (1976): 1397–423.
The general line of Altieri's argument is persuasive, but his attempt to convert the
residue of ongoing action into an "irreducible ontological base" (1409) involves
an unfortunate turn of phrase, as does the argument that "the irreducible bases for
human certainty are a variety of ways of acting" (1418). Though one recognizes
the remarks of Wittgenstein from which Altieri is extrapolating, such formulations
invite the kind of riposte that Staten is quick to supply: "Is there any more thoroughly *metaphysical* concept than this?" (*Wittgenstein and Derrida*, 75). Unless there
is an ongoing interplay between action and the history of action such that the
history of action continues to evolve, action becomes as static as empiricism.

   16. Haas, "Theory of Translation," 223.

   17. Staten, *Wittgenstein and Derrida*, 75–79.

   18. William James, *Pragmatism: A New Name for Some Old Ways of Thinking*,
in *"Pragmatism" and "The Meaning of Truth"* (Cambridge: Harvard University Press,

1978), 35. Though recent work in the history of science and elsewhere confirms that there are nevertheless moments of radical change in our thinking, it remains the case that these moments occur in spite of, rather than because of, character- istic attitudes toward radical novelty. Even after seemingly radical change, efforts continue to rehabilitate the problematic past.

19. Ludwig Wittgenstein, *On Certainty*, trans. Denis Paul and G. E. M. Ans- combe (New York: Harper, 1969), §249; hereafter cited in text as *OC*.

20. This is, of course, the only way that authors of the texts of deconstruction can themselves make claims about being appropriately or inappropriately read.

21. Wittgenstein's renewed concern for propositions in *On Certainty* arises from his interest in grappling with G. E. Moore's arguments in "Proof of an External World," *Proceedings of the British Academy* 25 (1939): 273–300, and "A Defence of Common Sense," in *Contemporary British Philosophy*, ed. J. H. Muirhead (London: Allen and Unwin, 1925), 193–223. Note that Wittgenstein is not arguing that all modes of inquiry share the same common ground or that propositions ground all language-games. In some language-games, presupposed propositions play a role "like that of rules of a game," while in those games and others there may also be other kinds of rules that provide the stability of the game. Note also Wittgenstein's comment that "the same proposition may get treated at one time as something to test by experience, at another as a rule of testing" (*OC*, §§95, 98).

22. For a useful study of the evolution of *Philosophical Investigations* and for some stimulating ideas about the relationships among Part I, Part II, and *Zettel*, see Georg Henrik von Wright, "The Origin and Composition of Wittgenstein's *Investigations*," in *Wittgenstein: Sources and Perspectives*, ed. C. G. Luckhardt (Hassocks, Sussex: Harvester Press, 1979), 138–60.

23. An issue E. D. Hirsch raises to illustrate the appeal and the inadequacy of arguments for unique language-games in his *Validity in Interpretation* (New Haven, Conn.: Yale University Press, 1967), 70.

24. Ralph Cohen, "History and Genre," *New Literary History* 17 (1986): 203– 18.

25. I have explored this process at greater length in *The Modern Stage and Other Worlds* (New York: Methuen, 1985).

26. Paul Armstrong summarizes a set of procedures for maximizing the possi- bilities of pluralism in "The Conflict of Interpretations and the Limits of Pluralism," *PMLA* 98 (1983): 341–52.

27. John M. Ellis, *The Theory of Literary Criticism: A Logical Analysis* (Berkeley: University of California Press, 1974), 147–54. Current interest in a new historicism is one response to the historical inadequacies of structuralism and poststructural- ism, but Edward Pechter has devastatingly displayed the ease with which new historicism collapses into old historicism in "The New Historicism and Its Discon- tents: Politicizing Renaissance Drama," *PMLA* 102 (1987): 292–303. As Ellis has

argued, inadequate notions of the nature of history constantly distort attempts to bring history, literature, and language into appropriate relationship and undermine attempts to establish appropriate modes of generalizing about literature (*Theory of Literary Criticism,* 211–32). Efforts to develop a new literary history predate by many years, of course, the activities of the new historicists.

28. Miller, "Triumph of Theory," 284.

29. I have discussed these points in more detail in "Taking the Measure of Theoretical Models," *University of Hartford Studies in Literature* 17 (1985): 1–12.

Stanley Cavell's Redemptive Reading: A Philosophical Labor in Progress

Edward Duffy

Although Stanley Cavell opens *The Senses of Walden* with the self-deprecating shrug, "what hope is there in a book about a book," it soon becomes clear that, far from undervaluing the pages he has readied for the hands of his reader, he is claiming their worthiness to do spiritual battle with our all-too-average and depressed estimate of what reading counts for in the economy of what we do and in the substance of things we let ourselves hope for.[1] Finding himself in receipt of the burden of Thoreau's song that those he addresses are dead to the world, Cavell labors toward an account of the writing of *Walden*, which would resubmit that book's claim that the reading of the "bulk of these pages" is gathering toward the advent of a scripture, now (if anytime) at hand, and big with either (as *Walden* puts it) the dumps or a budding ecstasy. Like William Blake, Cavell says to his reader, "Mark well my words! they are of your eternal salvation."

As if this were not offense enough for one professor of philosophy, Cavell persistently claims that what he is doing is not literature or religion. It is philosophy, just as *Walden* is "the major philosophical text in my life—other than [Wittgenstein's] *Philosophical Investigations*."[2]

If Cavell's career in professional philosophy finds itself drawn to aggressively therapeutic and redemptive claims, that career commences in (and never completely abandons) the very different offense Cavell notes as so often taken at "the ferocious knowledge the ordinary language philosophers will claim to divine by going over stupidly familiar words that we are every bit as much the master of as they" (*IQ*, 161). With the likelihood of offense its only apparent constant, the progress of this professional philosopher is from John Austin's crisp precisions to these impassioned claims of Cavell's later work: that Wittgenstein is a prophet for our dark time; that *every* (Cavell's repeated emphasis) word of Thoreau and Emerson is calling for redemption; that, in turn and as a continuing inheritance of these writers who (he repeatedly testifies) found thinking for America, every one of Cavell's own words must be about this same redeeming business.

Given the stark difference at least of style between Cavell's professional beginnings and his present voice in our culture, the first necessary business of this essay is to track how this self-styled "philosopher in American life" (*IQ*, 3) has found himself taking steps along a little explored and idiosyncratically posted route, which is somehow "beyond, or through, the ordinary language philosophy of the later Ludwig Wittgenstein and J. L. Austin."[3] My working intuition in tracking this "hobo of thought"[4] is that, first and last, he has set his heart on what our human form of life has found to say to and for itself. Cavell's unhedged investment in how we have worded the world will subsequently turn toward the "grammar" and criteria of Wittgenstein and toward the complex and encompassing forms of literary art, but by Cavell's own testimony this commitment commenced when, as a listener and reader of Austin on "what we would say when," he found himself "being read" in a way that left him struck and even stricken with how little he knew of the terms of his own existence.

A Claim and Fervor of Reason

John Austin is a writer very different from either Thoreau or the later Cavell, but for every word on which each of these thinkers trains his close philosophical attention, the task is, as Cavell says, to raise it "up to the light" (*SW*, 28) so as "to let it speak for itself; and in a way that holds out its experience to us, allows us to experience it, and allows it to tell us all it knows" (*SW*, 16). If Austin's practice of "linguistic phenomenology" serves to remind us of the way we use such familiar words as "believe" and "know," and if a recurrent outcome of this activity of recollection is that we are surprised that we have just learned something about our world by learning something about our words, "perhaps," writes Cavell, "it is because we forget that we learn language and learn the world *together*, that they become elaborated and distorted together, and in the same places."[5] Unearth the consequences of our words and "with each turn [we] seem further to unearth the world."[6]

   If Jacques Derrida is set on disclosing the deferred and differential "structurality of the structure" of *langue*, Austin concentrates on the occasionality of that form of life of us talkers which is speech or utterance, Saussure's *parole*. As either writers or talkers, our words occur (and endlessly recur) to us as our occasions call for them, and as listeners and readers we are well practiced in what is differently meant, on their differing occasions, by an identical sequence of words. Because "The coffee is hot" may be (among other possibilities) an observation, a hint, or a warning, what these four words in that order mean is not identical with what, on their differing occasions, is meant by these words (*IQ*, 131). But this distinction between the grammar and the rhetoric of a phrase is not a cue for a predictable deconstructionist set piece on undecidability. Rather, it unmelodramatically indicates something (logically) needed if someone is to be counted a competent user of the language: "Words come to us from a distance; they were there before us; we were born into them. Meaning them is accepting that fact of their condition. To discover what is being said to us, as to discover what we are saying, is to discover the precise location from which it is said; to understand why it is said from just there, and at that time" (*SW,* 64).

With little apparent effort and as part of our initiation into the form of life of our shared language, we competent users of English have learned both to pick up on the pragmatic implications of others' speech and to take responsibility for our own. Because this mastery of pragmatics is a condition of the form of life of us talkers, one of the driving forces of early Cavell is toward the increasingly solid conviction that in sufficiently imagined or described cases he (but he no more than anyone else) has the authority to say that if we say X then we *must* mean Y. To a science-bewitched objection that the use of the first person plural in the "must we mean what we say?" formula of Cavell's first book is presumptuous and empirically unwarranted mind reading, he responds that the question is not asking for the empirical evidence of a head count or for the magic of a *pre*-diction. Rather it is appealing to, or bringing to mind, our presently shared diction. And for such things, Cavell insists, we speakers of the language do not need, and could not benefit from, evidence. We are the evidence as we go about patiently asking ourselves what we should say when (*MW,* 4).

The inescapable and incalculable pertinence of asking "what we should say when" accounts for how Austin's work must be a philosophy of examples, must include the literariness of staging little dramas whose protagonists are "know" and "believe," or "mistake" and "accident." By their copious and pertinent specificity of detail, Austin's examples repeatedly drive it home that "the sounded utterance is only a salience of what is going on when we talk" (*MW,* 33) and that the rigorous matching of words such as "mistake" or "accident" to the goings-on around them is a philosophical labor yielding its practitioners not just a more finely articulated inheritance of their native language but also, and *through* this process of imaginative articulation, a disclosure of what these quite real things of mistakes and accidents *are* in our world, what for us (in a Cavellian master tone) "count" as mistakes and accidents.

Austin's philosophical example to Cavell on his way to Wittgenstein was that if we but avail ourselves of its distinguishing criteria, such an expression as the word "mistake" can tell us about ourselves and our world "through mapping the fields of consciousness lit by the occasions of [that] word" (*MW,* 100). Cavell will retain Austin's tenaciously nuanced attention to individual words; he will testify that it was Austin who knocked him off his horse. But precisely as "thus grounded,'"[7] precisely as an "ordinary language" philosopher given to this way of going on in philosophy, he will find his interest and his investigations gravitating toward the most common of our words: words more common and more indivisible than even "mistake"; words so common that they seem to have come to be as they are not by the dictates of the kind of criteria unearthed in Austin's philosophical practice but by the workings of those incalculably more basic (and hence routinely unnoticed) "Wittgensteinian" or "grammatical" criteria by which, as a matter of course and at an unfathomable depth of confidence, we call *this* that is happening in us our "pain," or *this* routine bodily posture in reference to *this* most ordinary piece of furniture "to *sit* on a *chair*."

Cavell's turn from Austin's to Wittgenstein's concept of a criterion is most thoroughly rehearsed in the first part of *The Claim of Reason*, entitled "Wittgenstein and the Concept of Human Knowledge." There Cavell characterizes his and Wittgenstein's "concept of knowledge" as "the human capacity for applying the concepts of a language to the things of a world" (*CR*, 17), where such application of concepts is both prompted and regulated by criteria that are constantly in play throughout the most common passages of our life with one another and with objects. The question Cavell wants this chapter to bring into focus about Wittgensteinian criteria is: As opposed to the manifest (but perhaps philosophically trivial) usefulness of Austinian criteria for purposes of identification, what is the good of Wittgensteinian criteria? "What," he writes "is the force of *his* [Wittgenstein's] habitual claims and questions about what a thing is called?" (*CR*, 66).

For Cavell, philosophy begins when "we 'don't know our way about,' when we are lost with respect to our words and the world they anticipate" (*CR*, 34). Wanting to understand something about which we suddenly feel at a loss (for example, "opinion," "faith," "see," "certain"), we remind ourselves of what kinds of statement we make about it; we perform what in remark 90 of the *Investigations* Wittgenstein calls a "grammatical investigation." Wittgenstein acknowledges that in such straits we will "feel as if we had to *penetrate* phenomena," and then declines to go that route, turning instead to an act of overt self-presentation: "[O]ur investigation, however, is directed not towards phenomena but, as one might say, towards the *'possibilities'* of phenomena. We remind ourselves, that is to say, of the *kind of statement* that we make about phenomena. . . . Our investigation is therefore a grammatical one" (all Wittgenstein's emphases).[8]

Wittgenstein seeks not a parting of the phenomenal veils to reveal the "thing-in-itself" but a persistent explication of the tissue of possible statements that would "establish the position of the concept of an 'object' in our system of concepts" (*CR*, 76), that would leave "explained, unwrinkled before us" (*CR*, 78) the texture of assertion whereby we "[relate] various concepts to the concept of that object" (*CR*, 73). To effect these unwrinkling investigations, we are peremptorily told "don't think, but look!" (*PI*, §31)—and look not at anything calling itself hard and resistant reality, but look at what we *say* about the phenomena in question. Because "*Essence* is expressed by grammar" (*PI*, §116; Wittgenstein's emphasis), it is just such superficially pedestrian but endlessly alert and painstakingly complex tracking of our grammar that will tell us "what kind of object anything is" (*PI*, §116).

As tracked by Wittgenstein, criteria bring up to the light our most common and unremarkable concepts and thus lay out in "perspicuous representation" the endlessly specific details of all we are in agreement on as our shared language. "It is," writes Wittgenstein, "what human beings *say* that is true and false; and they agree in the *language* they use. That is not agreement in opinions but in form of life" (*PI*, §88; Wittgenstein's emphasis). As the provider of the conditions for our knowing, saying, or proving anything at all, forms of life are not themselves a matter of opinion. They are neither to be verified nor falsified. They are to be accepted or acknowledged, received or trusted. They are the given, the unconditioned. And their obscurely recurring good is that they give us the world, secure it to us in (and as) a net of conceptual articulation.

In Cavell's account of modern philosophy, Wittgenstein's *Investigations* "go on" from what he calls the Kantian "settlement," a settlement of philosophy ventured in response to the threat of skepticism and condensed into the axiom that "the conditions of the *possibility of experience* in general are at the same time the *possibility of the objects* of experience" (*NYUA*, 102).[9] As continually remembered and reassessed in Cavell's work, this settlement, which famously represented itself as a Copernican revolution that would understand "the behavior of the world by understanding the behavior of our concepts of the world," is to be "radicalized, so that not just twelve categories of the understanding are to be deduced, but every word in the language" (*IQ*, 38). And we are so to deduce every word—we are, for example, to unknot "the conditions . . . in human thinking controlling the concept of condition" (*IQ*, 38)— in a way that will not bargain away the world for the mixed solipsistic pottage of sense data and the categories of the understanding, but will instead claim Thoreau and Emerson as "inheritors of Kant's transcendentalism [who write] out of a sense of the intimacy of words with the world, or of intimacy lost" (*IQ*, 170).

To a Cavell progressively more convinced that criteria do not "limit" but "constitute our access to the world,"[10] the persistent trackings of Wittgensteinian grammatical investigations cleared the way toward a new "space of investigation" (*NYUA*, 81) in Thoreau and Emerson, where he could even more confidently go on with the effort of his earlier philosophical days to "identify Wittgenstein's *Investigations* (together with Austin's practice) as inheritors of the task of Kant's transcendental logic, namely, to demonstrate, or articulate, the a priori fit of the categories of human understanding with the objects of human understanding, that is, with objects (*NYUA*, 80). But because the going price for the Kantian settlement of human knowledge had turned out to be the positing of some necessarily unknowable (but still unappeasably sought) "thing-in-itself," Cavell found at least a piece of himself responding to this offer with a sardonic "thanks for nothing"

(*IQ,* 53). To Cavell, Kant's recuperation of human knowledge was itself in need of recuperation, and coming to its rescue Cavell sees Thoreau and Emerson "working out . . . the problematic of the day, the everyday, the near, the low, the common, in conjunction with what they call speaking of necessaries, and speaking with necessity" (*NYUA,* 81). But as Cavell retrospectively maps this eccentric philosophical itinerary, he does not envisage a complete break with the Kantian teaching of our conditionedness. Instead, he proposes and speaks for his representative human need to recover from (or get out of the grip of) this giant Kantian hand's *"picture"* of the thing-in-itself (*IQ,* 47) as irretrievably withheld behind an unbreachable epistemological line dividing appearances from whatever they are the appearances of. Moreover, he can find it in himself to sight the prospect of this recovery from within his own Wittgensteinian inheriting of Kant. He sights it in Wittgenstein's pressure to turn the skeptic's self-defeating rhetorical question, "([H]ow) can we know what there is in the world?" into what Cavell wants to get in place as the very real question, "[W]hat makes our knowledge *of* a world of objects at all?" (*CR,* 225; Cavell's emphasis).

If human knowledge has limiting conditions, either Kantian or Wittgensteinian, then as a species we are fated to dissatisfaction with those conditions and hence fated to overreach ourselves with what Kant calls the "transcendental illusion" that we can "know what transcends the conditions of possible knowledge" or with what Wittgenstein speaks of as "the illusions produced by our employing words in the absence of the (any) language game which provides their comprehensible employment" (*MW,* 65). As positioned within what Cavell calls the "argument of the ordinary," the skeptic represents a never finally stilled voice within each of us that will seek a way of leaving or repudiating the game whenever our criteria are found to disappoint. And disappointing they will always be found because, as ours and only ours, they must at times strike us as arbitrary or merely conventional.

The originality of the *Investigations'* necessarily incessant response to skepticism is the way the book "takes [philosophy's] drift toward skepticism as the *discovery* of the everyday, a discovery of exactly *what* it is that skepticism would deny" (*IQ,* 170; Cavell's emphases), that is, the everyday "home" (*NYUA,* 32ff.) of our ordinary concepts as they deliver a world of "objects" to us within those human forms of life "which grow language" (*CR,* 170) and which "alone provide the coherence of our expression" (*MW,* 61). For Cavell, ordinary language philosophy rightly does not seek to *refute* skepticism. Instead it takes its stand in the necessity for an always renewed *response* to the skeptical "threat of world-consuming doubt by means of its own uncanny homeliness, stubbornly resting within its relentless superficiality" (*IQ,* 176). Cavell calls for "an acknowledgment of human limitation which does not leave us chafed by our own skin, by a sense of powerlessness to penetrate beyond the human conditions of knowledge" (*MW,* 61), and the form this acknowledgment will have to take is "the form not of philosophical construction but of *the reconstruction or resettlement of the everyday"* (*IQ,* 176; emphasis added).

The skepticism that pictures its rough handling of human knowledge as a scrupulously impartial critique Cavell sees another way: as a coconspirator in a mode of "Western conceptualizing" for which (in both Heidegger and Emerson) the clutching human hand emblematizes a "kind of sublimized violence" (*CH,* 39). When Cavell summarizes this region of Kant (the region of only sense percepts received and intellectual concepts only synthesized) as "no intellectual intuition" and adduces, as its knowingly aversive counter, Emerson's "all I know is reception" (*NYUA,* 80), he urges us to be receptive to what counts as any given object or concept in the grammar and criteria of our ordinary language. From within this recuperation of our philosophical history, Cavell sees philosophical skepticism powering its way toward the disappearance of the world not on the nice epistemological rigor of its own accounting but on "some other power, less genteel, call it repression" (*IQ,* 47). Call it, in one of Cavell's titles, a disowning of knowledge, a refusal to know what we cannot just not know.[11]

To disown the knowledge encoded in our agreements in forms of life is a form of repression because, on the Wittgensteinian principle that concepts follow interests, everything given us in the counts and recountings of our shared language traces what has mattered to us. We count only what counts or matters, and we count according to an "aesthetics and economics of speech" (*CR,* 94–95), according to which we shear out a continually reforming "constitution" of words, which is not arbitrary but *natural.* For if we follow Cavell's example and take Wittgenstein's central concept of "form of life" as principally directed to the biological or "vertical" differentiation of the form of our life as talkers (both [horizontally] Greek and Jew but neither plant nor animal), the yield is of an intuition as to what (in Cavell's polemically unfashionable emphases) *naturally* draws our "form of life" to construct for itself, in whatever language and with whatever refinements of distinction, such conceptual underpinnings and verbal spaces as are expressed in words such as "hope" and "expectation," "horror" and "home," "intention" and "excuse," "chair" and "pain" (*NYUA,* 41ff.). Any social grouping will have to fix into place a multitude of conventions for its common business, but by the level of his address to the concepts of *criterion* and *agreement,* Wittgenstein would have his others and interlocutors consider "attunements" which, as evidence of our "natural history," go deeper than the more or less explicit adjustments any one cultural or historical grouping will call its conventions. He would have us consider what we settle on as a consequence of the "human fix itself" (*CR,* 110).

Our attunements expressed through criteria and gathered into a language (to imagine which is to imagine a form of life) witness to what we have found *worth* saying. They are, before all else, agreements in valuing—agreements about "how we individuate things and name, settle on nameables, why we call things as we do—questions of how we determine what *counts* as instances of our concepts, this thing as a table, this as a chair, this other as a human, that other as a god. To speak is to say what counts" (*IQ,* 86; Cavell's emphasis). For any thing in our world to *be* a thing of our world, we must beforehand have settled on it as worth the candle of conceptualizing. We must care about it, take such interest in it as to drive it into what Heidegger calls "unconcealment."

Because the "idea of valuing is the other face of asserting" (*CR,* 94), Cavell regularly finds himself pondering "what we have it at heart to say," an expression that strikes my ear as a remembering of the kerygma that where we have laid up our treasure, there will we find what we have set our heart on. Where we have laid up our conceptual treasure (as in the keeping and gathering of Heidegger) is, case by case, the evidence of something that has counted for us, mattered to us. And because a word or concept is both the expression of our interests and a schema of connectedness with other concepts, the issue is always how we are to settle (with) these words of ours as they endlessly call for a way to voice their proper individual interests and still "come to terms with" their others in a newly trued basis of constitution. This is what the bringing-our-words-back-home of ordinary language philosophy comes to or from. It is a response to what, by Cavell's account, stands at the heart of Thoreau's "book of losses," where "it is no set of desired things he has lost, but a connection with things, the track of desire itself" (*SW,* 51). And if these lost words of ours call out to be resettled, the venue for this mission is what, following Thoreau, Cavell calls writing or the second ("reborn") inheritance of language, when the slapdash mouthings of the mother tongue give way to the "father tongue" and its autonomously "reserved and select expression" in which every written word preserves its integrity under the pressure of differing occasions but still allows itself (and each of its fellows) to exit into and be adjusted by the company it keeps on each of these occasions (*SW,* 34).[12]

The father language of writing is "not a new lexicon or syntax at our disposal, but precisely a rededication to the inescapable and utterly specific syllables upon which we are already disposed" (*SW,* 16). Language so conceived and taken on is not a banner raised on high in order to *enforce* the unity of a human group. It is the standard of an attunement which is already there, only lost and tattered in the dark wood of our words as we are ordinarily given to blather them. If every word is a sign of (and a motion toward) bonds which we are always already violating, and if increasingly in Cavell our faithlessness to these commitments presents itself as the allegorical "first blight" for the legion of all our other forms of dereliction, then against this condition of chronic backsliding, the "writer's faith" stakes its hopes on the furthering and rational good that will come of recollecting the bearings of *every word* we find we have had it at heart to enter into the account of our condition. The aspiration of this faith is that, place by place and time after time, we may yet labor toward a fullness of term and so bring (back) to life-signaling circulation and currency whatever portions of our commitments and conditions have become dead and lost within us.

If Cavell's conviction in the hiding places of power to be found in our word-ings of the world takes fire from the flinty Austinian mask of superficiality, what becomes of this abiding conviction in later Cavell is a very un-Austinian ambition still to raise our words up to the light and still thereby, as Heidegger's *What Is Called Thinking?* puts it, "to let the truth happen" (*NYUA*, 3) of ourselves and our worlds, but now letting truth happen in the service of nothing less than the saving of the human as it now stands in need of what Cavell calls the second creation of a deliverance or a redemption. As provoked and deepened by the *Investigations*, Cavell's philosophical vision comes to see that what is all too commonly lost on us in our most ordinary words amounts to nothing less than a pit of perdition, from which the only promise of an exit is what *The Senses of Walden* is already calling not just a "rescue" but a "redemption" of language (*SW*, 63, 92). While remaining an American philosopher committed to the procedures and promises (and something of the stinting self-denials) of the ordinary language school, Cavell migrates from the Oxford don making virtuoso distinctions in the common room to the prophet crying in the wilderness. As the animus of his writings increasingly betrays its inspiration in the underlying current of moral fervor that he makes such a point of in Wittgenstein, Heidegger, and Emerson, one cannot help but be struck at the way the later Cavell requires that the attending *to* his words be reconceived as attendance *at* his words (as in attendance at some public and sacred enactment), the way he demands that—as in his "lectures after Emerson after Wittgenstein"— the reading of his readings be not just an intellectual engagement but a spiritual exercise. In this spiritual exercise, the interlocked reader and writer are to take steps toward a wording of human condition, the success and profit of which will be less tallied up in the coin of instruction than proved experientially in such modes of responsiveness as his readers must learn to call *deliverance* (as from bondage) or *recovery* (as from an illness) or *redemption* (as from perdition).

A Writer's Testament and Faith:
Staying with Wittgenstein/Going on with Emerson

"You only need sit still long enough in some attractive spot in the woods that all its inhabitants may exhibit themselves to you by turns." This is a sentence from *Walden's* "Brute Neighbors" reiteratively honored by Cavell as all of the book's healing waters condensed into a few drops. Cavell's most extended draw on it occurs in his contribution to a 1981 symposium on "The Politics of Interpretation" (*T*, 50–51). There, in the course of again claiming Thoreau for philosophy, he brings the stilled sitting counseled by this sentence into close affinity with the therapeutic posture of psychoanalysis. As the persistent reader of *Walden* is to be drawn ever more deeply into its attractive pool of words so that, under the stillness of its gaze, this reader may in turn be read or found (out), so likewise with the dynamics of attraction and discovery at play in psychoanalytic practice. In the talking cure, the aptly named analysand suffers herself (the apposite pronoun in Freud's groundbreaking studies of Dora and hysteria) to be read under the all-gathering, all-inscribing gaze of a resolutely still analyst. By transference to this analyst as the archive of her own history, the patient subjects herself to what has come to settle just there as the text or constitution of herself, the therapeutic aim being to "get the hang of" one's self and hence the freedom or run of one's self, a voice in one's history.

In Cavell's staging of the "talking cure," the resolutely still therapist is "one human being [who] represents to another all that that other has conceived of humanity in his or her life, and moves with that other toward an *expression of the conditions which condition* that utterly specific life" (emphases added).[13] To Cavell, this one-on-one drama of reading and acknowledgment concretizes the philosophical call for our condition(s) to be brought up to the light and thus betrays the aggressively denied Kantian origin for the theory and practice bearing Freud's name. In Cavell's intellectual progress, philosophy and psychoanalysis come to figure as mutually repressed Others. If analysis denies its origins in philosophy, philosophy, particularly in American universities, clearly wants to continue repressing any claims to healing that might have been advanced at its Socratic origins.

If *The Senses of Walden* directly affirms the need for the "redemption" both of our lost lives and of our lost words, the 1981 invocation of Freud presents psychoanalysis as the model for this "redemptive reading": "For most of us, I believe, the idea of redemption or redemptive reading and interpretation will not be credible apart from a plausible model or picture of how a text can be therapeutic, that is, apart from an idea of the redemptive as psychological. . . . I imagine that the credible psychological model of redemption will have to be psychoanalytic in character" (*T,* 51–52). When Cavell conflates psychoanalytic practice both with philosophy as revised in Thoreau and redemption as urged in the prophets, he might be taken as (merely) engaging in a patently "secularizing" example of his constant attempt "to fit together into some reasonable, or say convivial, circle a collection of the main beasts in my jungle or wilderness of interests" (*IQ,* 153). But as Cavell strives to call psychoanalytic practice to its rightful and companionable place at the table of his interests, he seems drawn less to ruining the sacred truths of redemption down into the kind of recovery promised by analysis than to bringing up to the light the unacknowledged religious conditions of what we call psychotherapy. In *The Claim of Reason,* Cavell himself cautions that "nothing is obvious about 'secularization,' especially not whether in a given case it looks like, as one might call it, eternalization" (*CR*, 471–72). I think, then, of what Cavell's words here enact as a (not totally acknowledged) religious analogue to what Cavell will more openly and confidently write about the *philosophical* origins of psychoanalysis in his "Freud and Philosophy: A Fragment."[14]

To return to Cavell's earlier offer of a psychoanalytic model for redemptive reading. He there seems less sure of his ground; he betrays an anxiety about which discourse is to be master, the religious or the psychoanalytic. For his one thing needed of redemptive reading, he clearly wants to appropriate psychoanalytic procedures as a model of great and shareable explanatory power. But he can't seem to do so with the sound of full conviction. The way he clears his throat—"For most of us, I believe"—is just halting enough that it carries with it a whiff of momentarily bad intellectual conscience, as if the speaker knows that what is driving him toward this conversational tic is the sense that, as he prepares to issue a call for redemptive reading, he had better quickly send his audience an ingratiating signal about the like-minded reasonableness known to subsist between them.

What I am taking as (in part) a gambit of accommodation edged with frayed uneasiness is, to my ear, amplified by Cavell's manifest impatience with what he sees as the typical inability of psychoanalytic interpreters to let their reading of texts turn into that experience of "being read," which is his touchstone for an authentic act of (and success in) what he wants reading to become. Addressing himself to psychoanalytic readers of all stripes who programmatically subject the text at hand to the truths of the master discipline, Cavell asserts that too often this routine has "seemed typically to tell us something we more or less already knew, to leave us pretty much where we were before we read." And he goes on to say "that from the point of view of psychoanalytic therapy the situation of reading has been turned around, that it is not first of all the text that is subject to interpretation but we in the gaze or hearing of the text" (*T*, 52).

The signs and wonders of recovery sought by Cavell haunt that region of the Kantian settlement where one is (as Cavell writes of Emerson and Thoreau) called to "the speaking of necessaries, and speaking with necessity" (*NYUA*, 81). Some of Cavell's (mostly) Wittgensteinian pictures of this region are *forms of life, ground*, the *given*, the *unconditioned*, and the *ordinary*. At the level at which we all have our various and specific ways of going astray from these necessities and thus of darkening ourselves to ourselves, the workings of what analysis would call repression or alienation are so fundamentally a portion of our human fate that the familiarly available grammatical possibilities of the phenomenon we conventionally call "therapy" are miscast as what to these griefs would count as recovery. Indeed, to try to make what we call "therapy" play this role—to let the physiognomy of this word win this audition—strikes me as liable to a variation on Cavell's abiding grief that nothing is so human as this way we mistake our metaphysical finitude for some intellectual lack. It strikes me as letting some contingent developmental mischance stand in for the ground-level given that we are finite, that (as Beckett's Hamm says) "we're on earth, there's no *cure* for that" (*MW*, 129; Cavell's pointed emphasis).

"No *cure* for that," Cavell goes on, "but perhaps there is something else for it—if we could give up our emphasis upon cure. There is faith, for example." But *is* there faith when we do not as yet (or any longer?) have any way of saying how "that faith [could be] achieved, how expressed, how maintained, how deepened, how threatened, how lost" (*CR*, 243), when, that is to say, we are not in command of even the "opening pieces" of this word's grammar as, for example, "that *this* is what we call 'to lose one's faith,'" this to maintain it, and so on? (*IQ*, 136). Because what Cavell is struggling to find words for does not fill the ready-to-hand bill of "therapy" or "cure," he is provoked toward trying on such "religious" caps as "faith" and "redemption"—even as in so doing he becomes more alive to the fact that "we do not understand a word of all this" (*SW*, 59).[15]

If there is no *cure*, then perhaps there is *faith*, and specifically there is what, speaking of Thoreau, Cavell calls the "writer's faith" that "human forms of feeling, objects of human attraction, our reactions constituted in art, are as universal and necessary, as objective, as revelatory of the world, as the forms of the laws of physics" (*SW*, 104). With all the fraudulent dreck and slipshod babble abroad in the world, the abandon with which Cavell expresses his trust in our "constitutions of words" or "our reactions constituted in art" must seem extravagant. But neither Thoreau nor Cavell harbors any illusions about how "before a true gaze" the bulk of our constructions would, in the former's memorable words, "all go to pieces in your account of them." What, on the contrary, Cavell proposes for the expenses of our spirit and the investments of our trust is at hand, for example, in the construction of *Walden* as it newly inhabits or settles our words. What Cavell commends to us is just this edification, the offering or boon of which is its own "primary evidence" that the constituting has happened, that the art of writing is here doing its work of wording the world together. Call this how Cavell, keeping faith with the intuitions of ordinary language philosophy, receives Thoreau's counsel that we are to allow our "anxious wakefulness" (with our words maddening and haunting us) to give way to that "constant awakening" (*SW*, 98) in which "our words need not haunt us. [For] if we learn how to entrust our meaning to a word, the weight it carries through all its computations [i.e., 'as it recurs page after page, changing its company and modifying its occasions'] will yet prove to be just the weight we will find we wish to give it" (*SW*, 34–35).

Cavell acknowledges that his vision of writing assumes a posture toward "every word" that we have come to expect (if at all) only in poetry of the highest scriptural or prophetic ambition. But, like Thoreau, he would shoulder the burden in prose, his every word so pondered as to bear a part, and that a needful part, toward a gathering of itself and company toward a constitution or (justified) city of words. As Virgil famously says about getting *back* from the dead, *hoc opus, hic labor est.* This is the real task and the real undertaking. It is what is called redemption. And redemption not just of our alienated grammar, but also a (continuing) redemption of that world which skepticism's denial of our grammar would deprive us of, but which Thoreau and Emerson as the American "inheritors of Kant's transcendentalism" would recover in their way of writing "out of a sense of the intimacy of words with the world, or of intimacy lost" (*IQ,* 170). What makes our knowledge of a world of objects is (in a phrase from Emerson) "the mysteries of human condition" (*IQ,* 37)—not some thoroughly familiar and constant entity to be called "*the* human condition" but the provisionality of a form of life had only on condition. We are, in other words, to accept and acknowledge that by the terms of human condition, "thought is not confined *by* language (and its categories) but *to* language" (Cavell's emphasis).[16] John Austin's entrustment of ordinary words represents one exemplary posture toward the form of life which is the life of our language; others are the later Wittgenstein and the Heidegger of *What Is Called Thinking* (*CH,* 38). And still another is to be found in Cavell's reading of Emerson as indeed a philosopher, but one whose characteristic call for, and practice of, a radical "abandonment of and to language and the world" (*IQ,* 175), while it earned the unstinting admiration of Nietzsche, has repeatedly provoked his American readers into the denial to him of any serious philosophical standing.

Cavell first testifies to the "writer's faith" in Thoreau, but it is to Emerson that he eventually and then habitually turns for the recurring advent of this faith in what he characterizes as the essayist's own parable for the promptings, character, and bearing of the words he commits to paper and to the hands of his reader: "I shun father and mother and wife and brother, when my genius calls me. I would write on the lintels of the door-post, *Whim.* I hope it is somewhat better than whim at last, but we cannot spend the day in explanation."[17] Cavell draws repeated attention to how the "genius" here calling on Emerson—genius as not some special endowment but the "capacity for self-reliance" (*CH,* 26)—occupies the commanding position of Jesus calling on his disciples to come follow him unconditionally, and how the marking of the lintel reinscribes the discriminating sign which, in Pharaoh's Egypt, warded off the angel of death from the chosen people.

Cavell emphasizes the apparent blasphemy of Emerson's claims for a vocation commenced under the sign of shunning departure and opened toward an exodus undertaken in the hope that it alone is the way to life, freedom, and deliverance. "Emerson," writes Cavell, "is putting the calling and the act of his writing in the public place reserved in both of the founding testaments of our culture for the word of God. Is he serious?" (*T,* 19). The temptation here is too quickly to affirm that Cavell definitely thinks so, no two ways about it. But perhaps the trailer about seriousness should be left there as a real and standing question—one which, far from impeding Cavell's writing, provokes him to a style, which, while often appearing to court offense or dismissal, is deliberately penned in the hope that, at the last, it will indeed be taken to heart as deadly serious—but on the dauntingly estranging terms of a precursor who, in "presenting the credentials of his vocation" (*IQ,* 22), is "submitting his writing to the condition of acquiring whatever authority and conviction is due to it by looking at its countenance and surface" (*IQ,* 23).

By whatever marks of writing Emerson blazes his trail "as from an Intuition of what counts to a Tuition of how to recount it" (*NYUA,* 102), these marks have, for Cavell, no foundation or authority other than themselves. Emerson's writing is not *backed* by anything. It is "fronted by the character of the judger" (*CH,* xxx). There is no guarantee that anyone will take Emerson at his word, no assurance that he will not be laughed out of countenance. That is up, by turns, to each reader of each essay. The writing itself is the "path of [Emerson's] faith and redemption" (*T,* 19), and if the self-reliant inscription of Whim is to prove better than whim at the last, then that will "be proven only on the way, *by* the way" (*SW,* 137; Cavell's emphasis).

To Cavell, the "readings" of Thoreau and Emerson originate from thinkers repressed into amateur status by professional philosophy because, in marked contrast to what is commonly called argument or consecutive reasoning, "they propose, and embody, a mode of thinking, a mode of conceptual accuracy, as thorough as anything imagined within established philosophy, but invisible to that philosophy because based on an idea of rigor foreign to its establishment" (*IQ,* 14). The "foreign rigor" Cavell calls "reading." Coming to this account of reading with a faith that *our* terms constitute the conditions or possibilities of phenomena, Cavell "*sees*" reading "*as*"[18] a process of "being read" (*IQ,* 16) and, like Thoreau, includes within it much more than the literal act of reading: "But while we are confined to books, though the most select and classic, and read only particular written languages, which are themselves but dialects and provincial, we are in danger of forgetting the language which *all things and events* speak without metaphor, which alone is copious and standard. Much is published, but little printed. . . . [The best course of study is] the *discipline of looking at what is to be seen.* Will you be a reader, a student merely, or a *seer?* Read your fate, *see what is before you,* and walk on into futurity" (emphases added). Cavell comments that "what is before you is precisely not, if you catch Thoreau's tune, something in the future; what is before you, if you are, for example, reading, is a text. He asks his reader to see it, to become a seer *with* it. Only then can you walk beyond where you are" (*IQ,* 16; emphasis added). As "writing is a variation of reading, since to write is to cast words together that you did not make so as to give or take readings," so reading is "a variation of writing, where they meet in meditation and achieve accounts of their opportunities" (*IQ,* 18). The lesson from either direction of this writing/reading exchange is: Words are not your private property. They were there before you as your grounding terms or conditions. If you want to walk, you need the friction of this "rough ground"(*NYUA,* 56; *PI,*

107). You need to see that it is the traction-affording grammar of this form of life which is before you as your tract of possibilities and instruction. Only then can you take your own steps beyond where you are. While Cavell insists that for him "philosophizing is a product of reading, the reading in question is not especially of books, especially not of what we think of as books of philosophy. The reading is of whatever is before you" (*IQ*, 18).

And the hoped-for success or "progress" of Cavellian reading is for the reader to become the one read, the one called out. For a preliminary example in Cavell's own practice of reading, consider how he has turned to his own account this sentence from Emerson's "Divinity School Address": "Truly speaking, it is not instruction, but provocation, that I can receive from another soul" (*EL*, 79). Cavell has manifestly found provocation in this call for that "calling out" which reading shares with its related step-by-step activities of writing and thinking. He has placed this sentence at the epigraphic head to the entire enterprise of *The Claim of Reason*. And a full decade later, he confesses that the sentence still "echoes" for him as he asks of this American English, coming from a thinker given like Heidegger to thinking about thinking, "What translation will capture the idea of provocation here as calling forth, challenging?" (*CH*, 37).

If one applies to Cavell's reading of Emerson his interpretation of reading as "being read," then it seems inescapable that this reading of Emerson on the "act and calling" of his writing repeatedly turns up in Cavell's own writing because it constitutes a perpetually renewed opportunity for his own writing to be read and understood in the character of a philosophical precursor who here and now claims for himself the callings of *both* Moses and Jesus. What does it say about Cavell's conception of his own work in progress that he continually returns to this spot in Emerson's writing, where (by Cavell's own account) this writing imagines itself as recounting for itself the two dramas of "calling forth" in which the "founding testaments of our culture" cast the word of God as summoning either the Israelites out of Egypt or all of us out of the body of this death?

My thought here about what might be called the religious conditions of Cavell's philosophical practice is that in his work of "revising mythology" (*IQ*, 53), Wittgenstein and Emerson are drawn on as the two needed characters or heroes of the two founding testaments of our culture, the one handing down, or drawing out, the law, the other polemically proclaiming a "new" instauration of the spirit to fulfill and so succeed the law. This is extremely treacherous terrain, and some cautionary signposts are in order. First of all, the institutional Christian step from so-called Old to New Testament may still enjoy an incalculable cultural privilege, but about the broad intertextual way the one testament has of going on from the other, there is precisely nothing new. As Robert Alter authoritatively puts it, the Hebrew Bible is so much "a set of texts in restless dialogue with one another"[19] that it may rightly claim to have itself taught the writers of its successor testament that their tidings, to have any hope of a hearing, would have, like Second Isaiah, to say, "behold I show you a new thing." When this "Old Testament" prophet calls for and celebrates a New Exodus from a new Egypt, he is clearly as out "to make it new" as the author of *Revelations*. In addition, the religiously charged words saturating Emerson's and Cavell's writing are invariably directed toward what is at hand in the near and the ordinary, and although most of the writers attracting Cavell's attention are (by his own testimony) "bone by bone"(*CR,* 471) reinterpreters of Christianity, "nothing," as already noted, "is obvious about 'secularization,' especially not whether in a given case it looks like, as one might call it, eternalization" (*CR,* 471–72). When, for example, Cavell first finds himself moved to write of Emerson answering the call of his genius and writing "Whim" on the lintel, he hits upon these words: "Something has happened; it is up to us to name it, or not to. Something is wrestling for our blessing" (*SW,* 137). The allusion to Jacob wrestling with the angel could scarcely be more open, but Cavell has turned the onus of naming and blessing around to the self-reliant human agent. Here, the human striver is the one called out to the naming of where, at this juncture and thigh-stressing step of experience, he finds himself. To me, this looks less like a secularization of Jacob with the angel than an "eternalization" of Emerson's (and Cavell's) way with words. [20]

Cavell pictures Emerson and Wittgenstein as bound by a certain trust (and a certain distrust) of words. But if, for Wittgenstein, this trust issues into a call back to the "language of life," for Emerson it provokes a call onward to the "life of language" that can be received in "every word" as a potential vehicle for carrying on what Cavell calls thinking. This thinking attitude toward "every word" Cavell finds epitomized in Emerson's description of the poet as one who "in every word he speaks rides on them as the horses of thought":

> Given that the idea of "every word" is not a generalization but bespeaks an attitude toward words as such, toward the fact of language, the horse suggests that we are in an attitude or posture of a certain grant of authority, such as humans may claim, over a realm of life not our own (ours to own), in view of some ground to cover or field to take. That words are under a *certain* control, one that requires that they obey as well as that they be obeyed, is captured in Wittgenstein's idea that in his philosophizing words are seen to be away and as having to be returned home (to their *Heimat*). What he says is not quite that "what we do is to bring words back," but more strictly that we *lead* them (*führen* die Wörter)—from metaphysical to everyday; suggesting that their getting back, whatever that is, is something they must do under their own power, if not quite, or always, under their own direction. (*CH,* 22; Cavell's emphases)

Emerson's "horses of thought" picture our ordinary language as the "given" of the form of life of us talkers, which, while not ours to own, is nonetheless granted to us with a certain corresponding grant of authority. We don't own it but we have the run of it, and the successful pursuit of our claims on and with it is to be grounded on a life with our language such that our obedient readiness to inherit and "go on" with the words portioned out to us might (as in the ideal of poetry) find one of its exemplars in the posture of the capable equestrian perpetually on the qui vive for every slightest turn in the pulse and flexion of a spirited mount.

But in the very act of singing Emerson's "life of language" as something like Elijah's "horses of fire," Cavell keeps himself in continuing conversation both with the kind of "every word" the European Wittgenstein "in our poverty" typically bears down on and with the even more different kind of "every word" which three decades ago the Harvard grad student witnessed the Oxford don clinically palpating into the natural history of such microscopically intertwined verbal tissue as "inadvertently," "automatically," and so on. Grant to Emerson that "all language is vehicular and transitive, and is good, as ferries and horses are, for conveyance, not as farms and houses are, for homestead" ("The Poet," *EL*, 463), it would still seem to be a condition of any transit to the Emersonian life of language that we get back to the Wittgensteinian language of life. It is from there that, as from a hard bottom with words in place, each "crescive self" may begin to spring its arch toward a "constitution of words" which, in truing itself into its own "due sphericity," would stay ready for whatever, wheel without wheel, it finds to be its newly real needs and (at)tractions along the hard-bottom ground of where we live and what we live for.

This dual (but not divided) allegiance of Cavell's is his way of making his own what he finds common to such heroes of his as Wittgenstein, Thoreau, Rousseau, and Luther: a clearly admired "sensibility" (*NYUA*, 44), the effect of whose provocative "attempts to conserve a project [respectively, philosophy, America, community, Christianity] is to bring on deep revolutionary changes." Quoting Jesus, Cavell trenchantly asserts that "to demand that the law be fulfilled, every jot and tittle, will destroy the law as it stands, if it has moved too far from its origins" (*CR*, 121). This is an old story about the letter that killeth and the spirit that giveth life, a story that gets translated into Cavell's Thoreauvian conception of his writing as a neighborly call upon the reader not to let the dead letter of these offered words evidence a slaying and themselves kill, but rather, with a correspondent and "congening" (*NYUA*, 12) spirit, to take them in and so recuperate them (back) up into the spirit in which they live and move and have their being. (As Thoreau says in the conclusion to *Walden*, "The volatile truth of our words should continually betray the inadequacy of the residual statement. Their truth is instantly translated; its literal monument alone remains.")

The "sensibility" that fulfills the law by destroying it is that of the prophet who takes the "project" he was born into and, instead of consenting to it as it stands, aversively subjects what has come to seem the dead letter of its conventions to a corrosive inquest meant to reveal and make newly alive what these hidebound conventions were originally in service of, in what spirit framed. Any "reading" of where one finds oneself and one's form of life requires what John Keats called a "greeting of the spirit." Without the latter's perpetually renewed advent, any writing "penned" into the residual statement of the dead letter will, for all its monumental bulk, lie stillborn. It will not be (in Cavell's play on words) "expounded" (*IQ,* 126). It will not be raised up into the unseen force and flight of its volatile truth.

Cavell continues to inherit Wittgenstein (and Austin) because, as disclosed in criteria, the bedrock ground or origin (the "home") of our language-games is something we are continually called to acknowledge as positioning us at one of the two Kantian "standpoints," the one that situates the human as subject to, and determined by, the concept of law. As the critic of culture "declining decline" and calling our words back to the language-games in which they are at home, Cavell's Wittgenstein is like a Moses insisting to his backsliding flock that to get back on what Deuteronomy calls the "way of life" they must return to the law given to them. But the tablets of this law are not for Cavell a stone of stumbling and offense to be put behind him once he has come into his own as a faithful receiver of the spirit wafting his way from Emerson. On the contrary, the law retains its claim on this representative *zoon exon logon.* For if the law or home of our language games is bedrock—if this is where, as Wittgenstein repeatedly insists, justifications come to an end and we find ourselves without grounds or reasons and saying "this is what I do"—the story does not just end there. For this bedrock or grounding calls on us to attend to that reiterated Wittgensteinian moment in Cavell when, spade turned and criteria found disappointing, he feels called upon to "remind myself of the sorts of expressions in which Wittgenstein presents what I understand as the background against which our criteria do their work; even make sense" (*CR,* 83). At such junctures, Wittgenstein calls for (or reminds us of) the posture of acceptance or acknowledgment that alone provides the background against which criteria can be criteria, the law can be the law: "What has to be accepted, the given, is—so one could say—forms of life" (*CR,* 83, quoting *PI,* §226; Wittgenstein's emphasis). Such backgrounding expressions are not handed down as the law inscribed in stone. They are voiced, rather, as appeals toward a specifically human capacity for response and acknowledgment. They intimate that if we withhold the greeting spirit of acknowledgment—if we refuse to count—then our criteria go dead, all the breath gone out of them. "Words [then] have no carry. It is like trying to throw a feather; for some things, breath is better than strength; stronger" (*CR,* 84).

If it is within the breath of our acknowledgment alone that our criteria can live and move and have their all too human being, then, in addition to being the subjects of the law, we are, in what may be successive acts of lively origination, the bringers of the law. As a "stupendous antagonism" (*EL,* 953), we each of us constitute a scene for the playing out of the polarity of Emerson's Man Thinking as the latter finds himself positioned at both Kantian standpoints as a common subject of the law and the inventor of the game, the lordly claimant of autonomy. For Cavell, Wittgenstein is the self-described tenant of "the darkness of this time" (*PI*, p. x), remanding him back to the "rough ground" traction of our language-games, but as just such an exponent of the possibilities of phenomena, he also affords his American successor a way of "going on" from him. He provokes Cavell into a posture toward the given fact of language such that, in the face or reception of this fact, neither he nor his others need each "imitatively declare our uniqueness (the theme of skepticism)" but may "originally declare our commonness (the theme of acknowledgment)" (*IQ,* 132). In this latter spirit of acknowledgment, Cavell turns to Emerson on the near, the low, and the common; counts this too as a (re)turning to the "language of life"; but also claps, with a rebirth of infantile joy, when he finds that these essays in and of the New World draw him extravagantly on toward the "life of language" as it is constituting itself into the "new, yet unapproachable America" of this writing (*NYUA,* 92).

As it now stands, our culture may profess to understand its self-defining step from an Old Testament (of law) to a New Testament (of spirit) as having been successfully taken a long time ago, but in aversion from this conformist picture of our success, Cavell would, with Emerson, "find the journey's end in every step of the road" (*EL,* 479; *NYUA,* 114). Reiteratively setting out on his own philosophical work in progress, Cavell comes to conceive of this work and progress in the Emersonian terms of "stepping, lasting, grounding, achieving succession." He comes to sense his calling as continually present in the systole and diastole of what he has it at heart to say about our human finitude as called to be both the obedient subject of the law's dictation and the autonomously mastering and spirited bringer of the law's character. In a word—a word he applies to just about every writer he cares about—Cavell "diurnalizes" the passage from Old to New Testament. He makes it an everyday thing, a daily posture of "diurnal devotedness" (*IQ,* 176), a stance toward words that would be fully responsive to their knotted call for *both* a pedestrian taking of legitimately authorized steps *and* an aversively volatile "leaping free of enforced speech, so succeeding it" (*NYUA,* 118). It is, so to speak, the law of a word that its meaning cannot legitimately be "up for decision" (*IQ,* 135). The meaning a word has is not totally (is not at all) at our disposal. But if a verbal concept is "stable," it must also be "tolerant." It must be graced with the "play" required for an "indefinite number of instances and directions of projection" (*CR,* 185). As it deals in the words given to it for its expression, any human form of life only stiffs itself with any stiff-necked try at "an attempted choice of meaning" (*SW,* 64) such as the one perpetrated by the American government when, on the way to civil war, it persuaded itself to pass an abomination called the Fugitive Slave Law, as if "a man is a fugitive who is merely running from enslavement" (*SW,* 64). The alternative to such a forlorn "attempted choice of meaning" will appear subtle only because its demands are so utterly specific and incessant. That alternative is endlessly to take steps toward coming into one's own by acknowledging that it is but one's human due and one's human responsibility to keep going on with "an autonomous choice of *words*" (*SW,* 64; emphasis added).

As the friend and prophet of our finitude and with Emerson as his Virgil of the ordinary, Cavell would discredit all final solutions and, like Emerson,"'[direct] his work against every finality" (*CH,* xvii). His Emersonian call on each of his readers is to stay the course of that defining human activity of "thinking as knowing how to go on, being on the way, onward and onward. At each step, or level, explanation comes to an end; there is no level to which all explanations come, at which all end" (*NYUA,* 116). As against what, in reference to Beckett's *Endgame,* he calls "the greatest endgame" of some eschatological Somewhere or Purpose in which all other purposes do (or do not) find their end and peace, Cavell would take on "the hard Nietzschean alternative" to nihilism: namely, "the task of purposely undoing, reevaluating all the purposes we have known, re-locating the gravity of purpose itself" (*MW,* 150)—relocating it, exempli gratia, to the words here at hand as they carry on what Cavell would announce as an incessantly present (and only present) "[struggle] between the hope and the despair of writing and reading redemptively" (*IQ,* 25).

Cavell's drive toward the dismantling of eschatology complements his participation in contemporary philosophy's more widely trumpeted and more recent animus against foundationalism. And so we readers after Cavell after Emerson find ourselves back with them as on a stair at the outset of "Experience" (or at the outset of "what is called" experience). We find ourselves addressed by an opening interrogative sentence as to where we find ourselves "in a series of which we do not know the extremes, and believe that it has none" (*EL,* 471). The sequence of words opening itself up to us in this essay is a series of steps out to get us on our own way in the progress (or success[ion]) of a life that each step of the way is "always to be found [and] always at the risk of loss" (*IQ,* 132).

Before ever coming to Emerson's "Experience"—or before ever letting this essay come to him and declare its attractions—Cavell had already hedged his stake in Thoreau as a philosopher of our losses and our findings with this epigraph from Martin Luther: "For all our life should be baptism, and the fulfilling of the sign, or sacrament of baptism; we have been set free from all else and wholly given over to baptism alone, that is, to death and resurrection. This glorious liberty of ours, and this understanding of baptism have been carried captive in our day." In the first chapter of his "book about a book," Cavell develops this sense of *Walden's* baptismal ambitions, but right from the book's outset, this epigraph gives fair warning of the pressures Cavell's own writing is bringing to bear on Thoreau's. With these words borrowed from Luther, Cavell declares that he writes in the hope of recovering a sacramental standing for what he hears in the wind as *Walden's* call for "the redemption of language" (*SW,* 92).

But because of the sound or look which Cavell finds philosophy to have achieved in Thoreau (and next in Emerson), the epigraph from Luther is, in turn, opened toward a transfiguring return to the ordinary as the everyday home of what we call death and resurrection. The love of wisdom wafting Cavell's way from Thoreau attracts in him the gathering or summarizing idea of baptismal rebirth, but by this very same condition of attraction, such a redemptive possibility "carried captive in our day" is itself drawn "handsomely" into a transfiguring conversation with "the problematic of the day, the everyday, the near, the low, the common, in conjunction with what they [i.e., Thoreau and Emerson] call speaking of necessaries, and speaking with necessity" (*NYUA*, 810). And this near and this common—this "argument of the ordinary"—is, as Cavell repeatedly emphasizes, here present in *every* word of this writing, which is constantly bringing the "heaven under our feet" (*SW*, 101) up to the light cast there from "a sense of the intimacy of words with the world, or of intimacy lost" (*IQ*, 170). If we are nowadays still to live only for the death and resurrection of baptism, this sign of the human is now to be released into an understanding of itself as a version of covenantal attunement (and covenantal backsliding) which Cavell finds it in himself to propose as a "theology of reading" (*T*, 53).

Because of the urgent "religious" demands Cavell brings to philosophical writing, it is no accident that when he finds his professional footing in Emerson's character of "wisdom [as] . . . to finish the moment, to find the journey's end in every step of the road," he can do no other than contract the fervor of the "moral or religious demand" he repeatedly witnesses in Emerson (and in Wittgenstein and Heidegger) not as "the subject of a *separate* study . . . call it Ethics" but as a pervasive yeastlike agency, a call to its readers to attend to these words, to which they are abandoned and in which they might yet find themselves. Picked out like all of his human semblables to be both the patient bearer of the law and the spirited bringer of that law's impishly protean character, Cavell would be about his philosophical business like the Emerson after and beside whom he would be next in the vineyard. By and on the way of his words, he would let rise the intuitive leaven of what he has it at heart to say, and so take steps to deliver into the hands of his reader the promise of a new birth of our glorious liberty, not here effected once and for all but now confidently to be found "in every word, with every breath" (*CH*, 55).

Notes

1. Stanley Cavell, *The Senses of Walden: An Expanded Edition* (San Francisco: North Point Press, 1981), xiii; hereafter cited as *SW*. (For a bibliography of works by and about Cavell through 1987, see Peter Wasel's "A Working Bibliography on Stanley Cavell," *Bucknell Review* 32 (1989): 322–34; repr. in *The Senses of Stanley Cavell*,

ed. Richard Fleming and Michael Payne (Lewisburg, Pa.: Bucknell University Press, 1989), 322–34. Also, for a more current bibliography of Cavell's published work, see Peter S. Fosl and Michael Payne, "Stanley Cavell: A Bibliography 1958–1994," in *Philosophical Passages: Wittgenstein, Emerson, Austin, Derrida,* by Stanley Cavell (Oxford: Blackwell, 1995), 187–97.

2. Stanley Cavell, *In Quest of the Ordinary: Lines of Skepticism and Romanticism* (Chicago: University of Chicago Press, 1988), 169; hereafter cited as *IQ.*

3. Gerald Bruns, "Stanley Cavell's Shakespeare," *Critical Inquiry* 16 (1990): 612–13.

4. Stanley Cavell, *This New Yet Unapproachable America: Lectures after Emerson after Wittgenstein* (Albuquerque, N.M.: Living Batch Press, 1989), 116; hereafter cited as *NYUA.*

5. Stanley Cavell, *Must We Mean What We Say? A Book of Essays* (Cambridge: Cambridge University Press, 1969), 19; hereafter cited as *MW.* The phrase "linguistic phenomenology" is cited at p. 99; it comes from John Austin, "A Plea for Excuses," *Philosophical Papers,* 3d ed., ed. J. O. Urmson and G. J. Warnock (Oxford: Oxford University Press, 1979), 182.

6. Stanley Cavell, *Themes Out of School: Effects and Causes* (Chicago: University of Chicago Press, 1984), 40; hereafter cited as *T.* One locus classicus for Austin's philosophical practice of excavating the world by excavating words is the alternative stories he weaves around the same set of physical actions as now a "mistake," now an "accident" ("Plea for Excuses," 185).

7. Stanley Cavell, *The Claim of Reason: Wittgenstein, Skepticism, Morality, and Tragedy* (New York: Oxford University Press, 1979) xi; hereafter cited as *CR.*

8. Ludwig Wittgenstein, *Philosophical Investigations,* trans. G. E. M. Anscombe (Oxford: Blackwell, 1953), 42–43; hereafter cited as *PI,* with Wittgenstein's numbered paragraphs, or "remarks," indicated by the symbol §.

9. Immanuel Kant, *Critique of Pure Reason,* trans. Kemp Smith (New York: St. Martin's Press, 1965), A 158, B 197 (Kant's emphases).

10. Stanley Cavell, *Conditions Handsome and Unhandsome: The Constitution of Emersonian Perfectionism* (Chicago: University of Chicago Press, 1990), 22; hereafter cited as *CH.*

11. Stanley Cavell, *Disowning Knowledge in Six Plays of Shakespeare* (Cambridge: Cambridge University Press, 1987); hereafter cited as *DK.*

12. Thoreau on the "father tongue" is to be found in the "Reading" chapter of *Walden;* Cavell takes up the idea in *SW,* 14ff., and *IQ,* 133.

13. Stanley Cavell, "Psychoanalysis and Cinema: The Melodrama of the Unknown Woman," in *The Trial(s) of Psychoanalysis,* ed. Françoise Meltzer (Chicago: University of Chicago Press, 1988), 245.

14. Stanley Cavell, "Freud and Philosophy: A Fragment," *Critical Inquiry* 13 (1987): 386–93. This piece is incorporated into "Psychoanalysis and Cinema."

Even there in his manifest claiming of psychoanalysis for philosophy, Cavell will conclude on a "religious" note. He cannot quite bring himself to end on the speculation that Freud's clinical methods make the task set by Wittgenstein's idea of grammar "concrete." Instead, he goes one (guarded) step further toward the functional identity of this Wittgensteinian grammar with the Logos of John's Gospel: "The matter is to express the intuition that fantasy shadows anything we can understand reality to be. As Wittgenstein more or less puts an analogous matter: the issue is not to explain how grammar and criteria allow us to relate language to the world but to determine what language relates the world to be. This is not well expressed as the priority of mind over reality or of self over the world. . . . It is better put as the priority of grammar—the thing Kant calls conditions of possibility (of experience and of objects), the thing Wittgenstein calls possibilities of phenomena—over both what we call mind and what we call the world. If we call grammar the Logos, we will more readily sense the shadow of fantasy in this picture" (Cavell, "Freud and Philosophy," 393).

15. My use of the ideas of bill filling and cap fitting draws on John Austin's elucidation of "name-giving" and "sense-giving" as two distinguishable directions in a speech act of identification. See John Austin, "How to Talk: Some Simple Ways," in *Philosophical Papers*, 3d ed., ed. J. O. Urmson and G. J. Warnock (Oxford: Oxford University Press, 1979), 142.

16. Stanley Cavell, *Pursuits of Happiness: The Hollywood Comedy of Remarriage* (Cambridge: Harvard University Press, 1981), 78.

17. Ralph Waldo Emerson, "Self-Reliance," in *Essays and Lectures*, ed. Joel Porte (New York: Viking Press, 1983), 262; hereafter cited as *EL*. To underscore the pressure exerted on Cavell by this passage of fewer than fifty common and mostly monosyllabic words, I note the main sites and dates of its many returns: "Thinking of Emerson" (1978) and "An Emersonian Mood" (1980), both in *SW*; "The Politics of Interpretation" (1981), 50, and "The Thought of Movies" (1982), 19, both in *T*; *IQ*, 22; "Hope against Hope" (1985), 134, in *CH*, 55, 65, 79, 97–98.

18. The flamingly ordinary "sees . . . as" is in quotation marks and italics in order to indicate its draw on what, in a long section of *CR*, Cavell discusses as "'seeing something as something' [which] is what Wittgenstein calls 'interpretation' [and] is the principal topic of the chief section of what appears as Part 2 of the *Investigations*" (354). The section is launched under the famous sign of the duck-rabbit and involves what Wittgenstein calls the "dawning of an aspect."

19. Robert Alter and Frank Kermode, eds., *The Literary Guide to the Bible* (Cambridge: Harvard University Press, Belknap Press, 1987), 31.

20. In J. P. Fokkelman's contribution on Genesis in *The Literary Guide to the Bible*, the scene of Jacob wrestling with the angel is brilliantly analyzed as itself an agonistic drama of acknowledgment in which a protagonist whose very name is Fraud is forced to "stand up for himself, take responsibility" (52).

The Window: Knowledge of Other Minds in Virginia Woolf's To the Lighthouse

Martha C. Nussbaum

1

"How, then, she had asked herself, did one know one thing or another thing about people, sealed as they were?"[1] Sitting close to Mrs. Ramsay, "close as she could get" (78), her arms around Mrs. Ramsay's knees, loving her intensely, Lily Briscoe wonders how to get inside her to see the "sacred inscriptions" in her heart, "which if one could spell them out, would teach one everything, but they would never be offered openly, never made public" (79). She searches for a technique by which these internal tablets might be read: "What art was there, known to love or cunning, by which one pressed through into those secret chambers?" (79). The art eludes her, and yet she continues to long for it: "How, then, she had asked herself, did one know one thing or another thing about people, sealed as they were? Only like a bee, drawn by some sweetness or sharpness in the air intangible to touch or taste, one haunted the dome-shaped hive, ranged the wastes of the air over the countries of the world alone, and then haunted the hives with their murmurs and their stirrings; the hives, which were people" (79–80).

People are sealed hives full of bees that both attract other bees and keep them off. In her complex image Lily Briscoe indicates both that knowledge of the mind of another is a profound human wish—it feels as if to have that knowledge would be to be finally at home, in one's own hive—and, at the same time, that this knowledge is unattainable. The hives are sealed. Their sweetness or sharpness lures us—and then all we can do is to hover around the outside, haunting the hive, listening to the murmurs and stirrings that are the signs of vibrant life within. We can never see whether those murmurs and stirrings really come from other bees like ourselves, rather than, say some engine constructed to make beelike noises. And even if we assume there are bees inside, we can never fully decode their messages, can never be certain of what they are thinking and feeling. And yet we pursue the goal obsessively. Knowledge is a project that draws us to one another, and we cannot bear to let that project go.

The first part of Virginia Woolf's *To the Lighthouse* depicts, repeatedly, both our epistemological insufficiency toward one another and our unquenchable epistemological longing. But the first part is also called "The Window." The authorial image of the window stands in tension with Lily's image of the sealed hive, suggesting that Lily is blind to a possibility. And part 1 ends with a scene in which, or so it would seem, knowledge of another mind is attained. Mrs. Ramsay stands close to her husband, who looks at her as she looks out of the window. "And as she looked at him she began to smile, for though she had not said a word, he knew, of course he knew, that she loved him. He could not deny it. . . . She had not said it: yet he knew" (185–86).

Virginia Woolf tackles a venerable philosophical problem. I believe that she makes a contribution both to our understanding of the problem and to its resolution (or perhaps its nonresolution). She may well have discussed this issue with philosophers, and she may well have profited from her philosophical reading. It is not these connections, however, that I wish to investigate. I shall focus here on what is philosophical in the novel itself, both in what it says about the problem of other minds and in the way it says it—for I shall argue that the statement of both problem and "resolution" is made not only by overt statements inside the text but also by the form of the text itself, in its manner of depicting both sealed life and communication.

Woolf's approach to the problem is very different from that of many philosophers who have investigated it, for she suggests that the problem of other minds is not simply an epistemological problem, a problem of evidence and certainty, but, above all, an ethical problem, a problem produced by the motives and desires with which we approach beings who are both separate from us and vital to our projects. Although for many reasons I shall avoid speaking directly of comparisons between Woolf and the thought of Wittgenstein—not least being the knowledge that we would never get started with Woolf if we once tried to get agreement about Wittgenstein on this issue—I shall simply state that her approach can in some respects be fruitfully compared with some interpretations of the later Wittgenstein, particularly that found in Stanley Cavell's *The Claim of Reason,* and with Cavell's own approach to the problem of skepticism.[2] In other ways, as I shall indicate, her approach is intimately related to the portrait of skepticism and jealousy in Proust's *Recherche,* which certainly must count as one of the profound philosophical contributions on the topic. Woolf makes a distinctive contribution, however, through her depiction of the sheer many-sidedness of the problem of other minds, by her indication that it is not a single problem at all but many distinct human difficulties that are in complex ways interrelated. She is distinctive, too, in her insistent focus on ethical character and on the virtues of persons that make knowledge possible.

In pursuing these issues, I shall examine, first, the statement of the problem in part 1 of the novel: Why is it that people are sealed hives to one another? I shall then return to the scene in which Lily Briscoe attempts to know the thoughts and feelings of Mrs. Ramsay, asking how Lily understands the epistemological project and why, so conceived, the project is doomed to failure. I shall then turn to Mr. and Mrs. Ramsay, asking how it comes about that these two people, so deeply dissimilar, so lacking in firsthand understanding of one another's goals and aims, should nonetheless claim, at least, to have solved Lily's problem, communicating and receiving the knowledge of one another's love. On what does Mrs. Ramsay base her claim, and what should we make of it?

2

If one were to stage the overt actions and interactions of *To the Lighthouse* as a play, one would have hardly enough action and dialogue to fill half an hour. Most of the novel is set inside the minds of its various characters, and its drama is a drama of thought, emotion, perception, memory. Very little of this thinking and feeling finds expression in language. The reader is thus constantly made aware of the richness of consciousness and of the tremendous gap between what we are in and to ourselves and the part of the self that enters the interpersonal world. Only the prose of the novel bridges the gap—and this, we are made to feel, imperfectly and incompletely. Thinking about Mr. Ramsay and Mr. Bankes, Lily finds a host of thoughts and perceptions crowding in on her, a few of which the authorial voice manages to pin down—but then suggests the limits even of its own accuracy: "All of this danced up and down, like a company of gnats, each separate, but all marvelously controlled in an invisible elastic net—danced up and down in Lily's mind, in and about the branches of the pear tree . . . until her thought which had spun quicker and quicker exploded of its own intensity" (40–41). The crowd of gnats in the net becomes an explosion of uncountable fragments, and we recognize that even the lengthy summary we have been given—none of which any of the other characters will ever know—is no doubt only a crude pinning down, a linguistic simplification, of processes far more elusive and complex. In this sense, as the novel shows repeatedly, people really are sealed hives—buzzing centers of intense activity, little of which is communicated to any other hive. The novel begins with a single sentence spoken aloud by Mrs. Ramsay. This sentence is followed by a page and a half representing the thoughts of James Ramsay, which is followed in turn by five words spoken aloud by his father, and then one more page from James's thoughts, eleven words aloud from Mrs. Ramsay—and so on. The ratio of internal action to external communication is frequently more lopsided still than this, rarely less so.

What, then, is the problem of access to the other, as the novel presents it? Why are the insides of the hive not made available for the secure grasp of others? First of all, there is the sheer problem of time. The inner world, like the company of gnats, moves extremely rapidly and has many, many small pieces, each complexly connected to the others. If one were to set oneself to communicate everything, one would never be done with it, and one would certainly not be able to get on with life. (In this sense the stance of the authorial voice presents itself as radically detached from the ordinary activities of life: by determining to burrow into consciousness and to record its small movements in language, the novel is taking on a task strangely unnatural in the detachment from ordinary activity that it requires, and hubristically ambitious in its goal—a task that is hardly fit for a human being, that could be completed, perhaps, only by a god.) Lily thinks of Mr. Bankes and Mr. Ramsay: "Standing now, apparently transfixed, by the pear tree, impressions poured in upon her of those two men, and to follow her thought was like following a voice which speaks too quickly to be taken down by one's pencil" (40). Human beings cannot even take down the dictation of their own thought, so rapidly and complexly does it move. How much more difficult, then, is it to communicate this thought to another; how impossible, it would seem, by following the signs given by another, to attain access to the rapid complex inner world that exists inside another body.

But time, rapidity, and complexity are not the only obstacles to communication of the inner world. The novel shows us, as well, that language, the instrument we must use to make ourselves available to one another, is in some ways a very imperfect instrument of understanding. It is, first, a general medium of exchange, its meanings blunt and serviceable. It appears to be too crude to express what is most personal, what is deepest in the individual consciousness. Mrs. Ramsay thinks of the language of daily social interchange as a crude lingua franca that offers uniformity at the cost of suppressing individuality: "So, when there is a strife of tongues, at some meeting, the chairman, to obtain unity, suggests that every one shall speak in French. Perhaps it is bad French; French may not contain the words that express the speaker's thoughts; nevertheless speaking French imposes some order, some uniformity" (136).

This is not a claim that each person has a language of thought that is in its essence private. The fact that all these thoughts are contained in a novel shows that this is not Woolf's view. The claim is, instead, that the meanings of the common language become inflected with the peculiarities of each person's history and character and taste, in such a way that, although in principle language might express the peculiar character of an individual's thought (if we waive for a moment our reservations about time and density), in fact the shopworn common language of daily social interchange rarely does so. We also have here a self-referential claim on behalf of the language of the literary artist, which is able to render individuality in a way that most of us, speaking, cannot.[3]

Because the language of daily life is a blunt imperfect medium, and because each of us has a distinctive history and set of experiences, we find ourselves using the same words in different ways to mean very different things. If we try to gain knowledge of another person's consciousness by listening to his or her words and then asking ourselves what meanings these words conjure up in our own consciousness, we will frequently go wrong. Mr. Ramsay thinks about the universe, with a comfortably self-indulgent fatalism:

> "Poor little place," he murmured with a sigh.
> She heard him. He said the most melancholy things, but she noticed that directly after he had said them he always seemed more cheerful than usual. All this phrase-making was a game, she thought, for if she had said half what he said, she would have blown her brains out by now.
> It annoyed her, this phrase-making, and she said to him, in a matter-of-fact way, that it was a perfectly lovely evening. And what was he groaning about, she asked, half laughing, half complaining, for she guessed what he was thinking—he would have written better books if he had not married. (106)

This highly complex passage reminds us that words, in life, are used to convey meanings that are shaped by an individual history. What Mr. Ramsay means by "poor little place" is not what Mrs. Ramsay would mean if she said something like that about the universe. For her, prone as she is to real depression, such a fatalistic utterance would only be chosen as an expression of despair. To keep herself away from the depression that menaces her, she tries to avoid such phrases. Her husband, by contrast, with his taste for the melodramatic, for "The Charge of the Light Brigade" and other images of courage pitted against disaster, takes a certain delight in characterizing the universe this way. The phrase expresses his image of himself as a courageous solitary voyager pitted against fate. That image pleases him, restores his sense of pride in himself. As she recognizes, the original thought that prompts the phrase is a serious one—he would have written better books if he had not married—but his choice of the quasi-tragic phrase is his way of avoiding the sadness such thoughts might induce, by portraying himself as a victim of fate, to be commended for his courage in sticking it out in a hostile universe. What would for her be a capitulation to depression is his device for keeping depression at bay.

Language, in short, issues from a personal history. It reports the speaker's meanings, which are often highly idiosyncratic, though in principle nonprivate and tellable in the way and to the extent that a novel is told. In some cases we might need a history of novelistic complexity to get at what those meanings are.

Moreover, language also does things to and in that history. The words we use to others are not just reports of the inner world, they are also agents. To understand what Mr. Ramsay is saying here, not only do we need to know how he uses that phrase and phrases like it on many occasions, what actions and other gestures accompany that phrase, but also we need to know or guess why he speaks at all, what he is trying to do with and by the phrase—in this case, to distance himself from real personal loss and guilt by the projection of a beloved image of solitary courage. To understand what he means—if, indeed, Mrs. Ramsay does (and we must always remember that her conjectures are shaped by her own needs and desires and are fallible, as any interpretation is fallible)—she does need to know the pattern of his actions and utterances, his history, but she also needs to know his desires and projects, what he wants, what he is seeking to do to himself and his world. To grasp all this, even in an intimate relationship of long duration, is a formidable challenge. Most people lack such information about themselves.

Suppose that these problems could be overcome—for example, by taking up the supple fine-tuned language of literary art, together with the literary artist's willingness to tell the story of a unique character so that we can get a grip on that character's idiosyncratic meanings and dynamic goals. We do suppose that we know things about the minds of others when we read novels of consciousness, and we suppose so with good reason, given that novels present us with data requisite for adequate interpretation of a human life, data that social interaction frequently denies us.[4] The novel now shows us, however, that these are not the only obstacles to knowledge of another. For so far we have been supposing that people want to make their meanings known to one another. This, for many different reasons, may not be the case.

This novel contains no Iagos, no evil manipulative characters who system-atically deceive, saying one thing and thinking another. In fact, it contains very little dissimulation of a morally blameworthy kind. And yet these characters al-most always resist being known, speak and act in ways that actively impede the encroaching movements of an alien understanding. Social form is one prominent reason for this resistance. The novel is not just incidentally about middle-class English people, who carry with them cultural habits of reticence so long developed that they have become a part of their very character, making it impossible for them to give direct expression to most sentiments, especially deep emotions, especially any socially discordant thought. As Mrs. Ramsay speaks the polite "French" appro-priate to social intercourse, Charles Tansley thinks of the more violent, expressive language he would use with his lower-class friends, "there in a society where one could say what one liked" (136) without worrying about decorum. He "suspected the insincerity" (136) of the social language and thinks of how he will call it "nonsense." But this is not simply a point about English social habits. Any social code, the novel suggests, imposes some discipline on the expression of emotion;

in order to achieve order and uniformity, it teaches people to have at least some reticence, some reluctance to be known.

But there are other, more personal motives for this reluctance. Above all, the novel shows us the strength of shame as a motive for self-concealment. Behind Charles Tansley's anger and his fantasies of denouncing the Ramsays to the people of his class is a profound feeling of embarrassment and inadequacy that he is not like them, does not belong, has nothing appropriate to say. He desperately conceals this insecurity beneath his angry silence. For Mr. Ramsay, the root of shame is not class-linked but personal—the sense of professional failure that underlies all his bluster and his fatalistic assertiveness. As we learn in a passage that is probably set in Lily Briscoe's consciousness (although it follows seamlessly a passage in which Ramsay himself is contemplating his career), we see him depicted as a man who standardly takes refuge in self-consoling disguises:

> But . . . his glory in the phrases he made, in the ardour of youth, in his wife's beauty, in the tributes that reached him from Swansea, Cardiff, Exeter, Southampton, Kidderminster, Oxford, Cambridge—all had to be deprecated and concealed under the phrase "talking nonsense," because, in effect, he had not done the thing he might have done. It was a disguise; it was the refuge of a man afraid to own his own feelings, who could not say, This is what I like—this is what I am; and rather pitiable and distasteful to William Bankes and Lily Briscoe, who wondered why such concealments should be necessary. (70)

Out of shame at what he feels to be a gap in his attainment, Mr. Ramsay conceals himself systematically from others. Of course they guess at this—and we are led to think their guesses accurate. But the real emotions are not honestly "owned."

The case of Mr. Ramsay shows us something else about concealment: that it is a way of getting power. Mr. Ramsay is not just attempting to cover his shame. That already has a strategic role: Covering one's true weakness and vulnerability is one way people have of trying to exert influence over others. But Mr. Ramsay's strategic use of concealment is more complex. His blusterings and his cheerful fatalisms, which conceal from himself and others what he's really worried about, also have the role of soliciting attention and comfort from others in his circle, especially women. The utterance "poor little place" (106)—which Mrs. Ramsay knows to be a way of distancing himself from the thought of his failure—is also a solicitation, a request that she comfort him. She goes to him, as always, asking "what was he groaning about."[5] After Mrs. Ramsay's death, Lily Briscoe feels continually the now unanswered demand for comfort as something "bearing down on her" (221)—"and she pretended to drink out of her empty coffee cup so as to escape him—to escape his demand on her, to put aside a moment longer that imperious need" (219).

Here we arrive at a subtle point. Mr. Ramsay is not only in some respects a concealer; he is also a self-dramatizer. He makes himself more emotionally transparent, in a certain way, than the other characters do, especially in the third part of the novel—but even this transparency is both statement and demand: "Mr. Ramsay sighed to the full. He waited. Was she not going to say anything? Did she not see what he wanted from her? . . . He sighed profoundly. He sighed significantly. All Lily wished was that this enormous flood of grief, this insatiable hunger for sympathy, this demand that she should surrender herself up to him entirely, and even so he had sorrows enough to keep her supplied for ever, should leave her . . . before it swept her down in its flow" (226). Even the apparently frank statement of grief is not to be taken at face value. Mr. Ramsay does feel grief, but he is also putting on a show to get from Lily the sympathy he wants. It may be impossible for him or for anyone else to say to what extent he exaggerates or changes his grief in the process. Emotions don't stand still to be inspected like so many stones or bricks. The act of bringing them to consciousness frequently changes them; the act of expressing them to another almost always does so.

In fact, one might even ask how clear it is that there is a fact of the matter about Mr. Ramsay's grief that his external statements either do or do not render correctly. The inner world is fluid and dynamic, complexly linked up with the strategies and the aims of the outer. Indeed, it is frequently also undemarcated and in flux, a buzzing of confused conflicting feelings and impulses, which cannot be reported in definite language without being changed. In short, even when we have what seems most like frankness, we may have something far more complicated and strategic. The very concept of frank depiction of the inner may itself involve an oversimplification.

Shame and power are not the only sources of concealment and misrepresentation in the novel. The sheer desire for liberty and privacy is another. Mrs. Ramsay, who lives so much for and toward others, protects her few moments of solitude, cherishing these as what is most real, what is most herself:

> She took a look at life, for she had a clear sense of it there, something real, something private, which she shared neither with her children nor with her husband. . . . [I]t was a relief when they went to bed. For now she need not think about anybody. She could be herself, by herself. And that was what now she often felt the need of—to think; well, not even to think. To be silent; to be alone. All the being and the doing, expansive, glittering, vocal, evaporated; and one shrunk, with a sense of solemnity, to being oneself, a wedge-shaped core of darkness, something invisible to others. . . . This core of darkness could go anywhere, for no one saw it. They could not stop it,

she thought, exulting. There was freedom, there was peace, there was, most welcome of all, a summoning together, a resting on a platform of stability. Not as oneself did one find rest ever, in her experience . . . but as a wedge of darkness. Losing personality, one lost the fret, the hurry, the stir; and there rose to her lips always some exclamation of triumph over life when things came together in this peace, this rest, this eternity. (91, 95–96)

Mrs. Ramsay protects her private self. But we notice that it is not the same neatly shaped conscious self that she might communicate to others. Her solitude is not formed for or toward the outer world. We reach here an especially deep difficulty in the way of knowing another mind. What we usually think of as "the mind"—that is, its conscious mental acts, acts that could at least putatively be rendered in language and communicated to another—are only, perhaps, a part of the mind, a part bound up with the outer world of "being and doing," a sort of marshaling of the mind preparatory to communication.

Woolf's depiction thus supports a view of consciousness similar to the one advanced by Nietzsche in *Gay Science*, where he depicts self-consciousness as a relatively late evolutionary arrival, useful only in connection with communication. Most of our mental life, he plausibly stresses, could be carried on without it, at a level of experience and awareness more like that we are accustomed to attribute to other animals.[6] This account has recently received strong support from research in neuroscience and evolutionary biology. Mrs. Ramsay supports this idea; what she feels like in and of herself is something dark, made up of intuition and free-ranging meditation. The more hard, definite, verbalizable parts of her are the parts she associates with being at the disposal of others, not with the core of her self. This may not be true of the identities of all individuals. For example, Mr. Ramsay is almost certainly more fully identified with his consciousness than his wife is. He feels most fully himself when he forms himself into words and concepts. But if we admit that Mrs. Ramsay's account of herself is a true account of many people much of the time, we have a very tough obstacle in the way of our knowledge of others, for the very presentation of self as a possible object for knowledge may be a kind of self-change—or even, as Mrs. Ramsay thinks, a making of a nonself, an internalized artifact of the public realm from which she flees.[7]

Woolf supports this outer-inner distinction, but she also calls it into question, for Mrs. Ramsay's identity for the reader is fundamentally constituted by her care for others, her public doings and actings. When she herself uses the language of the "outer" and the "inner" and associates the core of her selfhood with the wedge-shaped core of darkness, the reader both assents and dissents. We understand this distinction not as a universal metaphysical claim but as a very particular psychological fact about Mrs. Ramsay—namely, that she likes to flee at times from the demands of others and to identify herself with her nonverbal meditations. The point about the significance of the nonlinguistic stands, but it is more complex than Mrs. Ramsay's language initially suggests, for the public realm is a crucial constituent of the self; the meditative realm is both the hidden self and, at the same time, the death of the self. Consider the way the passage goes on: "Not as oneself did one find rest ever, in her experience. . . . Losing personality, one lost the fret, the hurry, the stir." Mrs. Ramsay feels herself at such moments to be very close to, almost identical with, certain inanimate objects, "trees, streams, flowers" (97). But that both is and is not to be Mrs. Ramsay.

3

In the light of all these obstacles in the way of knowledge, it is no accident that the novel is saturated with images of hiddenness and remoteness: the image of a loved child's mind as a well, whose waters are both receptive and distorting (84); the image of thoughts and feelings hidden as if under veils (160); Lily's images of the loved person as hive, as secret treasure chamber (79). The novel's very structure shows us this hiddenness by giving us a miraculous access to thoughts of the characters, an access that they are far from having to one another, though at the same time it is still plainly incomplete—itself too succinct, too strategically plotted, too much a construct of consciousness and language to constitute in itself a full response to its own challenge.[8]

(As we notice the novel's way of solving a problem human beings seem not to solve so well in life, we should recall that this novel represents Woolf's own personal attempt to know the minds of her own parents—that Mr. Ramsay's anxiety and Mrs. Ramsay's depression are conjectures that fill the hives of Leslie Stephen and her beautiful remote mother with definite sounds, as the bee haunts their outsides and uses the power of art to represent what may [or may not] have been within.)

Responding to the fact of hiddenness, Woolf's characters try to solve the problem of knowledge by attempts to invade the chambers of the other, to possess, to grab hold, even to become one with the other's thoughts and feelings. For possession would be, it seems, the most satisfying solution to their epistemological problem. The most elaborate case of this is Lily Briscoe's attempt to know Mrs. Ramsay, in the passage with which I began. We now need to examine this passage at length:

> Sitting on the floor with her arms round Mrs. Ramsay's knees, close as she
> could get, smiling to think that Mrs. Ramsay would never know the reason
> of that pressure, she imagined how in the chambers of the mind and heart of
> the woman who was, physically, touching her, were stood, like the treasures

in the tombs of kings, tablets bearing sacred inscriptions, which if one could spell them out, would teach one everything, but they would never be offered openly, never made public. What art was there, known to love or cunning, by which one pressed through into those secret chambers? What device for becoming, like waters poured into one jar, inextricably the same, one with the object one adored? Could the body achieve, or the mind, subtly mingling in the intricate passages of the brain? or the heart? Could loving, as people called it, make her and Mrs. Ramsay one? for it was not knowledge but unity that she desired, not inscriptions on tablets, nothing that could be written in any language known to men, but intimacy itself, which is knowledge, she had thought, leaning her head on Mrs. Ramsay's knee.

Nothing happened. Nothing! Nothing! as she leant her head against Mrs. Ramsay's knee. And yet, she knew knowledge and wisdom were stored up in Mrs. Ramsay's heart. How then, she had asked herself, did one know one thing or another thing about people, sealed as they were? Only like a bee, drawn by some sweetness or sharpness in the air intangible to touch or taste, one haunted the dome-shaped hives, ranged the wastes of the air over the countries of the world alone, and then haunted the hives with their murmurs and their stirrings; the hives, which were people. (79–80)

Lily's attempt to know Mrs. Ramsay is, we notice, unilateral; it coexists with her own amused pride in her own self-concealment. This suggests that the project of knowing, as she conceives it, has itself something of the desire for power in it, is just as strategic as the desire to protect herself from knowing. I shall later return to that point.

Lily thinks of the project of knowing as, first, a kind of reading: We go (somehow) inside the room of the other mind and we read the sacred inscriptions that nobody else can see. But reading is not intimate enough, after all. It substitutes an internal object for an external object, but it doesn't really yield the grasp of what it's like to be that person, to have that person's thoughts and feelings. It is this, not just propositional book knowledge, that Lily desires. She now thinks of the possibility of becoming fused with the person one loves, "like waters poured into one jar, inextricably the same." She conceives of this possibility in a frankly sexual way—as a union to be achieved by either the body or the mind—"subtly mingling." "Loving, as people called it." In this way she alludes to the pervasive idea that sexual intercourse achieves not just intimate responsiveness but an actual oneness. She attempts, through the very intensity of her adoring thought, to achieve some simulacrum of this union. The attempt fails—she has no illusion that she has become closer to Mrs. Ramsay's mind than she was before. She then asks herself the question with which I began: Given that people cannot be entered and possessed—are, in fact, sealed hives—how in fact can we know one thing or another thing about them? Notice that she abandons the goal of complete fusion and also the goal of complete unmediated access to the "sacred tablets" and substitutes a more modest goal—knowing "one thing or another thing."

There is, I think, a progress here, both epistemological and moral. The goal of complete transparent access to the "sacred tablets" is not just unattainable, it is morally problematic, because it asks that Mrs. Ramsay surrender her privacy and her boundedness before Lily's curious gaze. We note that Mrs. Ramsay is in fact most unwilling to give up her privacy, which she regards as a central constituent of her selfhood; we also recall that Lily herself wishes to be able to conceal her thoughts from Mrs. Ramsay, even while she dreams of removing from Mrs. Ramsay all possibility of concealment. The move from unmediated reading to fusion deepens the problem, for the wish to be fused with Mrs. Ramsay isn't a wish to know her *as other, as Mrs. Ramsay*—as Lily quickly recognizes; it is a wish to incorporate her power, to be that powerful envied presence.[9] But, as Lily soon discovers,[10] having the other person's thoughts and feelings as oneself, in one's own body and mind, is neither necessary nor sufficient for knowledge of the other: not sufficient, because that would precisely be not to know the *other*, the separateness and externality of that life, those feelings; not necessary, because we can conceive of a knowledge that does not entail possession, that *acknowledges*, in fact, the impossibility of possession as a central fact about the lives of persons. That alternative remains to be discussed—and I think that Woolf in many respects anticipates Cavell's argument. But there appears to be wisdom in Lily's shift from the grandiose demand for possession to the modest demand to know "one thing or another thing" about those sealed hives that murmur and buzz as we hover greedily around them. At the very least, Lily's new question involves a more adequate conception of herself—as not a superhuman but a human being, finite in both body and mind, partial and incomplete, separate from other humans of necessity and always.

4

Woolf's image of the window suggests that people are not completely sealed to one another. There is an opening, one can see through or see in, even if one cannot enter. Part 1 of the novel ends with a knowledge claim: "She had not said it: yet he knew" (186). In not a trivial but a central matter—a wife's love—Mr. Ramsay is said by his wife to have gained knowledge. What is the basis for this claim? And to what extent does this case offer a solution to the problems of knowing raised elsewhere in the novel?

Very clearly, Mr. and Mrs. Ramsay do not gain knowledge by any kind of unity or mingling of experience, nor by any violation of one another's solitude and privacy. One of the distinctive features of their relationship is a cautious respect for that which the other wishes to conceal. Mrs. Ramsay senses a good deal about his academic insecurity and his sense of incomplete achievement. But she does not try to get at those insecurities or to show her knowledge of him by dragging them out into the open. Think what it would be for her to demand that he talk about his failures; suppose, in the scene we have examined, she had said to him, "Tell me what's really going on when you say, 'Poor little place'—you aren't worrying about the universe really, are you, you are worrying about your book." We see that such a claim or demand for "knowledge" would be a way of belittling him and asserting ascendancy over him. She shows him respect and love by allowing him his concealment. She doesn't even try to grasp his failure sharply in her own mind—for it would be incompatible with her love to see him as a failure. We might even say that this respect for hiddenness and this reluctance to pry even in imagination are Mrs. Ramsay's ways of knowing her husband's insecurities in the context of his life—of seeing their importance and their role, of behaving in a way that acknowledges their importance and their role. (Notice that this means that knowing is a very individual thing; in another relationship one might be aware that the person was longing to be "seen through," thrived on that particular kind of intimacy.)

On his side Mr. Ramsay, who is accustomed to burst in on the privacy of others, "bearing down" on Lily and the children, is very careful with his wife's solitude.

> He turned and saw her. Ah! She was lovely, lovelier now than ever he thought. But he could not speak to her. He could not interrupt her. He wanted urgently to speak to her now that James was gone and she was alone at last. But he resolved, no; he would not interrupt her. She was aloof from him now in her beauty, in her sadness. He would let her be, and he passed her without a word, though it hurt him that she should look so distant, and he could not reach her, he could do nothing to help her. (100; see also 103)

Mr. Ramsay knows his wife, we might say, in a way in which he knows no other character. What does this mean? It means, I think, that he attends to her more fully as a person separate from himself existing in her own right, rather than as an instrument of consolation for himself. His knowledge of her separate being is expressed in, and perhaps also constituted by, such small episodes of noticing and respecting, of refusing to burst in upon her. He puts her own mind at the center of the stage and subordinates, for once, the imperious demands of his own. All that may be at least part of what it is to know another mind as other.

Nor do Mr. and Mrs. Ramsay know one another by analogy, or by similar and parallel structures of experience. Of course at a very general level they do analogize—they interpret one another as human beings and as sharing with them certain goals and aims characteristic of human life as they know it. But analogy of that sort doesn't go very far, especially in the context of both idiosyncrasy and socially taught gender differences.[11] We know that they are very dissimilar, in thought patterns, in thought content, in patterns of emotional response, in goals and actions, in what they mean by their words. Part of what convinces us that they do have knowledge of one another is the fact that, in case after case, they allow for these differences, they refuse to analogize. He knows that she doesn't want comfort, even though with similar utterances that is exactly what he would be thinking about and wanting. She knows that he is more exhilarated than despairing when he says the words that to her would mean despair. This doesn't even mean that they can vividly imagine what it would be like to be the other person. Sometimes they can, and sometimes they can't. Mr. Ramsay cannot empathetically conceive of her depressed ruminations, though he can learn to respect them; Mrs. Ramsay thinks his mind is strangely different from her own, while recognizing that she cannot really quite imagine what it is like to be him:

> Was it not odd, she reflected? Indeed he seemed to her sometimes made differently from other people, born blind, deaf, and dumb, to the ordinary things, but to the extraordinary things, with an eye like an eagle's. His understanding often astonished her. But did he notice the flowers? No. Did he notice the view? No. Did he even notice his own daughter's beauty, or whether there was pudding on his plate or roast beef? He would sit at table with them like a person in a dream. . . . [T]hen, she thought, stooping down to look, a great mind like his must be different in every way from ours. (107–8)

Here we see that in one sense Mrs. Ramsay has only the most rudimentary knowledge of her husband's mind. She has no idea what he thinks about, nor has she any inclination for the sort of abstract thinking she associates with her vague notion of "the great mind." All she can say about it is what it leaves out; and she herself couldn't think in a way that leaves out those daily things.

How, then, do they know each other, insofar as they do? We might say, they know one another as we know them—by reading. Having lived together for a long time, they have gathered a lot of information about patterns of speech, action, reaction. Among other things, they have learned a lot—partly by making mistakes with one another—about the limits of analogizing, about relevant similarities and differences. They have gathered this information, furthermore, not in the manner of a detached scientist but in the course of interactions to which both ascribe enormous importance. They work hard to "read" the other, to fit the data into a meaningful and predictively accurate pattern, because each loves the other more than anyone else in the world, and it thus matters tremendously that they should get one another right, as far as possible. They spend a good part of their solitude thinking about each other, piecing together what they perceive and think, learning to read not just statements but also gestures, facial expressions, silences. Each learns the idiosyncratic text of the other in the way that one might learn a foreign language—never having a once-for-all guaranteed translation manual but holistically piecing it all together, trying to make the best sense, over time, of all the words and phrases.

The novel suggests that their love for and need of one another plays an important role in making them good readers. Because of this love and need, they hover around one another, they allow signals from the other to pull them out of themselves. When Mr. Ramsay, chuckling at the story of Hume stuck in a bog (which comforts him, on account of its metaphorical relation to his intellectual predicament), notices the way she purses her lips while knitting, he quickly reads a good deal in the expression: "[H]e could not help noting, as he passed, the sternness at the heart of her beauty. It saddened him, and her remoteness pained him, and he felt, as he passed, that he could not protect her, and, when he reached the hedge, he was sad. He could do nothing to help her. He must stand by and watch her. Indeed, the infernal truth was, he made things worse for her. He was irritable—he was touchy. He had lost his temper over the Lighthouse. He looked into the hedge, into its intricacy, its darkness" (98–99). Here love pulls him toward perceptions and reflections that elude him completely in the case of other people. A simple facial expression is read in ways that pull in data from years of knowledge of her sadness—so that he knows, as he passes, not only what she is likely to be feeling but also what he can and cannot do to help. And this leads him to a more accurate reading of himself, since to himself he is a text just as difficult to read correctly as any other mind. Later, at the dinner party, with their focused intensity of mutual concern, the two are able to carry on complicated conversations about the proceedings simply by small gestures and expressions: "And why not? Mrs. Ramsay demanded. Surely they could let Augustus have his soup if he wanted it. He hated people wallowing in food, Mr. Ramsay frowned at her. He hated everything dragging on for hours like this. But he had controlled himself, Mr. Ramsay would have her observe, disgusting though the sight was. But why show it so plainly, Mrs. Ramsay demanded (they looked at each other down the long table sending these questions and answers across, each knowing exactly what the other felt)" (144). Once again, both long familiarity and an intensity of focus inspired by love are at work to make their language vastly more efficient than the clumsy "French" of social interaction. Because they have been in similar situations together and talked about them afterward for many years, each caring what the other feels, the smallest facial sign conveys a history. The theory of truth underlying the knowledge claim is a coherence theory, clearly—they each have no independent unmediated access to the "sacred tablets," either in self or in the other. But there is every reason to feel, here, that the demands of coherence have been well met.

We now need to examine the scene with which "The Window" ends, as it builds up to its final knowledge claim. Mrs. Ramsay watches her husband as he reads a novel of Walter Scott. She reads the meaning of his expressions of pleasure and satisfaction—by combining what she knows of his anxieties about his own work, combined with the likely effect of Charles Tansley's dismissal of Scott at dinner (177). She knows well the persistence and centrality of his worries about whether his books will be read, even though at the same time she doesn't quite know what it is like for him to have those worries ("It didn't matter, any of it, she thought. A great man, a great book, fame—who could tell? She knew nothing about it" [177]). She then thinks in a general way about his truthfulness and outspokenness. "If only he would speak! She had complete trust in him" (178).

This is an important moment, since it reminds us that none of the knowledge either has of the other is immune to doubt, based as it all is on reading and interpretation. They get from coherence to knowledge not by any extra step of grasping or possessing but simply by trusting, by waiving the skeptical questions that could arise even about such a complex and carefully sorted fabric of data. Trust, of course, is itself not blind; she trusts his truthfulness because her experience has shown her that he can be trusted. But experience never really shows this; it never really rules out a refined clever deception. [12] So in allowing her experience of him to have this meaning, to lead all the way to trust, Mrs. Ramsay does add to the evidence an extra ingredient—a willingness, we might say, to be at his disposal, to leave her life open to what he says and does. [13] Roused from her reverie by the sound of her husband slapping his thighs with pleasure, she knows that he is delighted by the fact that Scott's novel holds up and gives delight—and so perhaps his writings have some lasting life in them, and perhaps it doesn't even matter. "Their eyes met for a second; but they did not want to speak to each other. They had nothing to say, but something seemed, nevertheless, to go from him to her" (179).

As she reads a sonnet, she falls into a pleasant trance and feels the peace of a mind swept clean and clear (181). He looks at her, and she feels what he is thinking. The novel itself now shifts rapidly from one center of consciousness to the other so that we can hardly tell who is having what thought, so rapidly and accurately do they communicate: "But she was becoming conscious of her husband looking at her. He was smiling at her, quizzically, as if he were ridiculing her gently for being asleep in broad daylight, but at the same time he was thinking, Go on reading. You don't look sad now, he thought. And he wondered what she was reading, and exaggerated her ignorance, her simplicity, for he liked to think that she was not clever, not book-learned at all. He wondered if she understood what she was reading. Probably not, he thought. She was astonishingly beautiful" (182). If in part the exaggeration of her ignorance is in his mind, it is also, equally, in hers—she knows how he sees her, and perhaps, too, he knows that he exaggerates. (In this odd way, knowledge can be present even when mistakes are clearly being made.) He knows that he finds her beautiful, but she also knows that he finds her beautiful. It is on that account that she puts down her book and responds to his smile. Mrs. Ramsay now mentions the engagement; she wants him to respond, so she tries a joke—"the sort of joke they had together" (183)—another reminder of their long habits of intimate communication.

Mrs. Ramsay now feels the shadow of sadness closing around her. She looks to him, as if to appeal for help, speaking silently. He thinks of Scott and of Balzac, and yet they are responding with ever closer responsiveness and knowledge: "But through the crepuscular walls of their intimacy, for they were drawing together, involuntarily, coming side by side, quite close, she could feel his mind like a raised hand shadowing her mind" (184). The image of the shadowy wall shows us that barriers are never removed—but somehow the walls become more like shadow than like substance, and she can feel the action of his mind as if it stood between her and life, casting protection over her mind. He fidgets, thinking how little he likes her "pessimism." He says, in a sharp tone, "You won't finish that stocking tonight." The words are trivial, but they communicate far more. "That was what she wanted—the asperity in his voice reproving her. If he says it's wrong to be pessimistic probably it is wrong, she thought" (184).

Here we are returned to our earlier point about words and actions—but with a difference. For earlier we observed that people use words to conceal vulnerability and to gain power over others. Here, too, the use of words is strategic, but the strategy is one of comfort. His asperity is protection.

Now she senses that his look has changed. "He wanted something—wanted the thing she always found it so difficult to give him; wanted her to tell him that she loved him" (184). She finds it difficult to put her emotions into words. She recognizes their mental difference here—for him verbal articulation of emotion is natural and easy, for her it is not. Instead, she looks for an action through which she can convey the meaning he wants: "Was there no crumb on his coat? Nothing she could do for him?" (185). She stands by the window with the stocking in her hand; he watches her, demanding an expression of love.

> Then, knowing that he was watching her, instead of saying anything she turned, holding her stocking, and looked at him. And as she looked at him she began to smile, for though she had not said a word, he knew, of course he knew, that she loved him. And smiling she looked out of the window and said (thinking to herself, Nothing on earth can equal this happiness)—
>
> "Yes, you were right. It's going to be wet tomorrow. You won't be able to go." And she looked at him smiling. For she had triumphed again. She had not said it: yet he knew. (185–86)

How is knowledge conveyed? The entire pattern of the marriage is the neces-sary background. A smile, a trivial sentence—all this would mean nothing without the years of intimacy and of daily life that lead up to the moment. In the moment, she conveys her love simply by turning to him and looking at him, only that. It is only after she feels the happiness of knowing that he knows that she says her indulgent words about the weather, healing the slight quarrel that had erupted in the morning. How does he know that she loves him? Only by his experience of her verbal reluctance, her beauty, her willingness to turn to him with her beauty. None of this is beyond skepticism, clearly; and Mr. Ramsay, demanding words, is at times not immune to doubt and the need for reassurance. But here doubts are put aside, and trust, it would seem, enables him to move from interpretation to knowledge. They don't raise doubts not because all grounds for doubt have been extinguished but because that is the way they are, that is the way their marriage is. Skepticism is an attitude, a way of relating, that is just not their way, at least in the context of this history of long intimacy and loyalty.

How far, then, have the problems of knowledge, as the novel presents them, been answered? As fine readers of one another's words, gestures, and actions, the Ramsays have clearly gotten beyond the crudeness of everyday speech as a medium of communication, and they have also come to a refined understanding of the differences in the personal meanings with which each invests words and gestures. They have not, however, found a magic remedy for the deeper issues with which the novel presents us: problems of shame, of power seeking, of the sheer need for hiddenness. They surmount these problems, to the extent that they do—and we feel that this is considerable, though not total—simply by making a continual patient effort to be a certain sort of person in relation to one another, to be willing to put aside shame or pride, to be willing to use the power of marriage generously rather than manipulatively, to be willing to allow their privacy to be qualified by the needs of another. If Mrs. Ramsay triumphs in conveying the knowledge of love, the triumph is one of yielding generosity—for she has allowed him to summon her out of herself. If Mr. Ramsay triumphs in extracting the much-desired communication, it is again a triumph made possible only by his being the sort of person who is ready to come to her aid. Knowledge, in short, is a function of character.

5

As readers of Woolf's novel, we may become aware that our own activity is anal-ogous to that of the Ramsays. We read as the characters read one another, going over the presented features carefully and with emotionally rich attention, trying to develop an interpretation on the basis of both familiarity and concern. The role of novel reading is discussed in this very scene, so that we are invited to explore the parallel. Mr. Ramsay responds to the Scott novel as to a beloved and intimate friend. He allows it to delight him and in a sense he trusts it—he doesn't read it with detachment in the manner of a skeptical theorist of interpretation. We feel that he "knows" Walter Scott not only by virtue of his familiarity with the novels but also by virtue of the vigor, openness, and unsuspiciousness of his response. But in his love of his wife there are also features that novel reading lacks. There is an intense absorption with a particular being who is seen as necessary for one's own life; there is a willingness to be extremely vulnerable toward her, to put much of his life at risk; there is sexual desire; there is, finally, an intense desire to give protection and love to her.

All of these features make personal love in some respects more problematic than novel reading. In the context of these deep needs and vulnerabilities there are ample opportunities for skepticism and jealousy to arise; there are many reasons why one inclined to such love might respond with shame-inspired concealment of self or with projects of possession and incorporation. We don't really see what those possibilities would be in the case of our relation to the literary text. All this led Proust to hold that it was only in relation to the literary text and its author that we could really have knowledge of another mind. All our relations with real people in real life are marred by a possessiveness and jealous skepticism that are the more or less inevitable outgrowths of our sense of ourselves as needy and incomplete.[14] Proust is convinced that this response to our own weakness obscures any accurate perception of the other person, since we make ourselves the construct we need. It also prevents any sort of trust in the evidence with which the other person presents us. We never rule out the possibility that the whole fabric is an elaborate ruse concealing something altogether different. With the literary text, by contrast, we are intensely concerned but not personally at risk. The author is not going to hurt us, and in a sense, we don't really need him. This alone permits us to have what amounts to knowledge of the mind of another living person.

Woolf's response to these points is not exactly epistemological; it is ethical. One can, of course, be the sort of person Proust describes. It is not difficult, in fact, to imagine the Ramsay marriage taking a turn in this direction—if, for example, she had come to feel that his whole relation to her was exploitatively patriarchal, that he underrated her capacity for autonomy, that he was using love and sex to bring about an unequal and unjust division of domestic labor. There is much truth in all these claims, and in some moods I feel she would have been right to focus on them and to be more skeptical of his love. Women frequently buy a kind of domestic harmony at the price of justice; skepticism in circumstances of inequality is a rational response.

On the other hand, one has to grant that a relationship based on this sort of suspiciousness of the intentions of the other could not be a good marriage *and* would yield little of the interpretive knowledge they attain. And I also want to say that the relationship itself, whatever its deficiencies, has excellences—and the Ramsays, as parties to it, have excellences—that can and should be cultivated, whatever else we seek. If they are cultivated sufficiently, Proust's problem can be overcome. The marriage of the Ramsays has yielded a kind of understanding and trust that is admirable as an ethical norm even if we would prefer to see it realized in the context of greater justice—as indeed it could be, given different upbringing and different expectations on the part of the two partners.[15]

But this means that there simply are possibilities for generosity, for the defeat of shame and anxiety, that Proust has not acknowledged. To develop these possibilities would be the theoretical job of an ethics of character, the practical job of parents and teachers of children, and of friendships of many kinds.

It is no surprise that this account of Woolf's novel should end with broader ethical and social speculations. For it is the distinguished contribution of this novel to show how a problem that philosophy frequently cordons off from the messy stuff of human motivation and social interaction is actually a series of human problems of great complexity, many of them ethical and social, which can't really be adequately described, much less resolved (where resolution is possible) without reflecting about emotions and desires, without describing a variety of possible human loves and friendships in their historical and social setting, without asking, among other things, how love, politics, power, shame, desire, and generosity are all intertwined in the attempt of a single woman and man to live together with understanding.

Wittgenstein saw, if Cavell is right, that the problem of other minds had to be investigated in some such way, as part of the history of our acknowledgment and avoidance of one another. But there is little concrete pursuit of that investigation in Wittgenstein, nothing to compare with the rich detail we find in Woolf. This, it would seem, is because the concrete pursuit of that particular philosophical investigation requires narrative depiction of individual lives and their interplay, and this was simply not a task in which Wittgenstein was engaged as a writer. (I leave to others the question whether the joy and generosity displayed in Woolf's narrative approach, and so important a part of her "solution," would have been compatible with his personal response to life.) A narrative approach to this set of problems is present in Proust but in a form that denies the resourcefulness of human generosity and universalizes a primitive longing for comfort as all there really is to love, an obsessive peering at one's own mental constructs as all there is to knowing the loved one. Unlike Wittgenstein, Woolf depicts our searches for knowledge in something like their full human complexity and many-sidedness. Unlike Proust, she does so with an optimism about good character that makes the problem of skepticism a sometimes soluble ethical problem. The mysterious grand problem of other minds thus has, here, a mundane humble tentative answer, or rather answers, whose meaning can only be fully grasped in the context of a narrative as complex as this novel: By working patiently to defeat shame, selfish anxiety, and the desire for power, it is sometimes possible for some people to get knowledge of one thing or another thing about some other people; and they can sometimes allow one thing or another thing about themselves to be known.

Notes

1. Virginia Woolf, *To the Lighthouse* (New York: Harcourt, Brace,1955); hereafter cited parenthetically by page number in text.

2. Stanley Cavell, *The Claim of Reason: Wittgenstein, Skepticism, Morality, and Tragedy* (Oxford: Clarendon Press, 1979), especially part 4; hereafter cited as *CR*.

3. Compare Marcel Proust: "Style for the writer, no less than colour for the painter . . . is the revelation . . . of the qualitative difference, the uniqueness of the fashion in which the world appears to each one of us" (*Remembrance of Things Past*, vol. 3, trans. C. K. Scott Moncrieff, Terence Kilmartin, and Andreas Mayor [New York: Random House, 1982], 931–32). Proust, however, focuses here on the unconscious expression of individuality by the artist in the creation of the work as a whole, whereas Woolf draws attention to the power of the artist consciously to represent individuality in the creation of characters, each with a different texture of consciousness.

4. Note, however, that novels frequently do so by making meanings more definite and coherent than they are in real life. To put a meaning into words is already to impose an interpretation on what may have been an undemarcated buzzing.

5. See also: "But he must have more than that. It was sympathy he wanted, to be assured of his genius, first of all, and then to be taken within the circle of life, warmed and soothed, to have his senses restored to him, his barrenness made fertile" (59).

6. Friedrich Nietzsche, "On the Genius of the Species," in *The Gay Science*, trans. Walter Kaufmann (New York: Random House, 1974), secs. 354, 297–300.

7. We should compare the posing of this problem in Samuel Beckett's *The Unnameable* (New York: Grove Press, 1958), where the attempt to "say myself" is shown to contain a self-contradiction: putting himself into language, the narrator feels himself becoming a public nonself, a generalized "pupil Mahood"; and yet (as with Mrs. Ramsay here) to cease to use the categories of consciousness is in a significant way to cease to be.

8. Part 2 takes on the task of depicting reality from the point of view of nonconscious nature—a paradoxical task, given that the novelist's tools must still

be words and concepts, but a task that shows us Woolf's sense of the importance of a reality that is alive but nonconscious.

9. See the related argument about sexual fusion in Martha Nussbaum, *The Therapy of Desire* (Princeton, N.J.: Princeton University Press, 1994), chapter 5. On Proust's related arguments and their defects, see Martha Nussbaum, "Love's Knowledge," in *Love's Knowledge* (New York: Oxford University Press, 1990), 261–85.

10. See the similar argument in Stanley Cavell, "Knowing and Acknowledging," *Must We Mean What We Say?* (New York: Scribner, 1969), 238–66. See also *CR*, part 4. On the way in which a desire for knowledge can generate a desire for incorporation but then in turn the realization that incorporation would precisely *not* be knowledge, one might fruitfully compare aspects of Hegel's "Master-Slave" dialectic.

11. What this brings out, among other things, is that the common "analogy" solution to the problem of other minds is too crude to be really informative, for what makes all the difference is to say which analogies are helpful and which analogies are not. The novel suggests that there is no single answer to this question— one just has to learn by experience.

12. On all this, see *CR*, especially the reading of *Othello* at the end.

13. Could hate generate knowledge of another? In some respects it might, for it could motivate a close intense focusing on the pattern of the other person's sayings and actions that would make the hater a good reader. On the other hand, if the hatred is mutual and known to be such, skepticism about the evidence would always be a reasonable response and would defeat the epistemological aim. In an asymmetrical hatred—for example, in the relationship of Iago with Othello— perhaps one-way knowledge might be attained, but note that its condition is Othello's openhearted trust in his "friend" and Iago's consequent trust in the evidence with which Othello presents him.

14. See Nussbaum, "Love's Knowledge."

15. Here I have in mind the discussion of love and justice in Susan Moller Okin, *Justice, Gender, and the Family* (New York: Basic Books, 1989).

Ordinary Language Brought to Grief: Robert Frost's "Home Burial"

Walter Jost

It stands to reason that if some image of human intimacy, call it marriage, or domestication, is the fictional equivalent of what the philosophers of ordinary language understand as the ordinary, call this the image of the everyday as the domestic, then the threat to the ordinary that philosophy names skepticism should show up in fiction's favorite threats to forms of marriage, namely in forms of melodrama or tragedy.

—Stanley Cavell,
"The Uncanniness of the Ordinary," in *In Quest of the Ordinary*

It is a question in marriage, to my feeling, not of creating a quick community of spirit by tearing down and destroying all boundaries, but rather a good marriage is that in which each appoints the other guardian of his solitude, and shows him this confidence, the greatest in his power to bestow.

—Rainer Maria Rilke

Introduction: Fronts

"Why can't a dog simulate pain? Is he too honest?"[1] Such questions are characteristic of Ludwig Wittgenstein's intermittently comic line of inquiry about pain and other so-called inner states (intending, expecting, understanding, and so on) in *Philosophical Investigations* (1953). Perhaps part of what Wittgenstein meant when he said that a book of philosophy could be composed entirely of such jokes runs along the following lines. Jokes presuppose a rich sense of what is conventional (part of a form of life) and what would constitute a breach or breakdown of convention in a specific case. For Wittgenstein, John Wisdom, J. L. Austin, and Stanley Cavell, among others, this understanding of convention and its susceptibilities constitutes, I take it, the very problematic of the philosophy of "ordinary" language and accounts in part for its comic relief.[2] For these thinkers, investigating our conventional boundaries in their breaking down, or in their return after their suppression, can free us, as in laughter, to understand and accept our powers and limits.

Of course serious breakdowns of communal conventions often break or at least bend those facing them; if anyone manages to laugh, it is usually only long after he or she (after we) have climbed out of some black hole. For this reason most readers have naturally resisted Robert Frost's famous "Home Burial," feeling the poem's pull on us, its gravity, but trying, unsuccessfully, to sidestep both its pitfalls and pratfalls. Yet in this poem especially, I propose, Frost most fully looks to confide in his readers, relying upon a similar recognition on our part of the significance of conventions (chiefly linguistic) taken by all of us as markers of, boundaries between, obstacles to, limits of, and ultimately bridges across lives and worlds. "Home Burial" places untold confidence in our ability, despite our discomfort, to accept and negotiate the deepest man-made fissures in, and walls around, each human being. (As Frost says elsewhere, "I'm in favor of a skin and fences and tariff walls. I'm in favor of reserves and witholding."[3]) The characters in "Home Burial," by contrast, only fitfully and weakly acknowledge, because they resist and avoid, the linguistic conventions that are normally needed to constitute a self, a marriage, a form of life. They avoid them with good reason, and possibly even to some good effect, being constrained, it may be, from doing otherwise. Yet Frost hands it to us not to dodge their difficulties but to try to articulate the characters' (and our own) situation appropriately. He so positions us that, though we are tempted to mouth platitudes or to go mute altogether (as we often do at real funerals), we must—emphasis on the word "must"—take a dual perspective on each character's plight if we are to understand, and accept, not only their limits but our own. In this way the poet looks to redeem a particular human tragedy as our ordinary human comedy.

On any reading this much is obvious, however: Nothing in the characters' view of their situation in "Home Burial" is laughable *simpliciter.* Amy and her husband suffer terribly together, alone. By contrast, the method of presentation and paradox that Frost employs may usefully be called comic, or "comedic," in Kenneth Burke's expansive sense of the term. For Burke the comedic refers to the engaged but ironic acceptance of human limits or boundaries—much as it does in Wittgenstein and Cavell. If, accordingly, we read "Home Burial" from within the larger situation we readers occupy and in the larger context of other Frost dialogue poems—"West-Running Brook," "Snow," "The Death of the Hired Man," each of which exemplifies different orders of ingenuity and success in speech, or in the context of the romantic interest in ordinary language—the poem can be understood to locate some of the powers and limits of our *own* form of life. For the poem voices, at the scene of the death of a child, the eloquent refusal to remain in a world of speech on the part of one of its parents, quite as though refusal were a live option. And it poses what may happen when the unquestionable framework of our form of life with one another is shaken at ground zero.

In a letter to Louis Untermeyer, Frost records that he insinuated "no villains" into the poems in his second book, *North of Boston* (1914), in which "Home Burial" appears.[4] His observation brings forward a similar remark regarding Robert Browning's purpose in "My Last Duchess," to the effect that the inclination of readers to moral condemnation of the villainous Duke offers the least productive approach to the poem.[5] In "Home Burial" we experience similar temptations to contrast the characters' condition with our own and to judge them harshly; or, conversely, to dissociate ourselves from the suffering and grief and moral failings of the wife and her husband altogether. What, after all, is there to say? Resisting those temptations to dumb commonplaces or to dead silence is not easy, for we are tempted to think that our critical talk is all or nothing. Instead we need to listen to what the poem says and to respond to the characters appropriately. But, then, "The *appropriate* word. How do we find it?"[6] We might begin by asking: How do the characters themselves speak?

Intimations of what I am calling philosophic breakdown, of something perversely gone wrong, may be heard in the husband's tragicomic "I shall laugh the worst laugh I ever laughed" (line 89). Among other things, this is an exclamation of incredulity spoken after his wife harangues him for something ostensibly no more than a breach of etiquette, his bringing his spade into the entryway of their farmhouse. By contrast, his wife speaks as though the coherence of all things in heaven and earth had been broken by his lapse, shall we call it, regarding these most mundane of matters: shoes, stains, a spade, "everyday concerns" (line 86). "Then you came in," she says:

> I heard your rumbling voice
> Out in the kitchen, and I don't know why,
> But I went near to see with my own eyes.
> You could sit there with the stains on your shoes
> Of the fresh earth from your own baby's grave
> And talk about your everyday concerns.
> You had stood the spade up against the wall
> Outside there in the entry, for I saw it.
>
> (lines 81–88)

These contrasting attitudes of husband and wife register the two chief perspectives juxtaposed in the poem: the extraordinary perspective on ordinary things provided by death and grief and the perspective of what can be called everyday life itself, belonging to those not exigently forced to walk along the edge. The husband is actually buffeted between both positions—he sees different things under one or another aspect—hence his inclination to laugh (after all, why get upset over a spade, stains, shoes?) a laugh that would nevertheless be his "worst" (for he seems to suspect, at least, that it might be unforgivable to laugh at such a thing, that is, at such a time; we might say that what he ought to be able to *see*, namely, his wife's pain, he has to *interpret* to be pain, as though he were an inexperienced reader).

A related expression, this time of of self-protective skepticism, can be heard in the wife's more generalized cry of contempt, beset as she is over the death of their firstborn infant son, at the moment she stitches her fate to Fate:

> The nearest friends can go
> With anyone to death, comes so far short
> They might as well not try to go at all.
> No, from the time when one is sick to death,
> One is alone, and he dies more alone.
> Friends make pretense of following to the grave,
> But before one is in it, their minds are turned
> And making the best of their way back to life
> And living people, and things they understand.
> (lines 97–105)

"Friends make pretense of following to the grave" (line 102)—which is to say, they *simulate pain* (grief) with respect to an event they are said not to be able to understand and wish to escape (lines 103–5). The claim marks another moment of the breaking down of conventions and expectations, when the wife redefines a shared ritual as farce, friends as impostors, and the world as evil. Hearing this we would prefer, I think, to distance ourselves, at least, from the indictment it records, handling her contempt either as perfectly explainable rage born of grief or as textbook hysteria. In doing so we fail even to begin to puzzle out the complex argument and role this indictment performs in the poem.

Being able to simulate pain or grief, for example, or to penetrate the masks of simulation in others, as Amy claims to do, presupposes a knowledge of shared pain or grief conventions against which faked speech or behavior can be compared, perhaps exposed as unreal. This is the reason that only human beings are said to be able to simulate pain, whereas we say that dogs not only "don't" but "can't" do so: not because they're too honest (!) but because they fail to engage at least certain complex conventions involved in such an act as simulating. Although we do say, it is true, that dogs "obey" or "disobey" us, we do so because they exhibit the ability to follow or contravene their own rudimentary reactions to some of our more manifest desires. And while they also experience the physical distress of pain, they do not formulate—they can not do anything with—the word "pain," and they can not entertain possible purposes for pretending or playacting or appreciate the occasions on which it might be to their benefit or harm to do so. In sum, they do not, because they *can* not, play "Let's pretend pain."[7]

The point is rather belabored here to highlight the notion of pretense or simulation, including the criteria or conditions for its recognition. The charge of pretense, after all, bubbles up from the lime pit of Amy's rage against her friends and world. Our own particular challenge is not to understand why Amy may be angry, nor to strike a studied pose as though facing her down, but to take up a position as it were *beside* her and her husband. Like a next-door neighbor to the calamity, we must struggle to find a place from which to confront the misery. Only then might we manage to have the poem illuminate our own real, ordinary lives with the breakdown of everything real visited upon these others. That would be an accomplishment both coming and going: refusing ourselves the usual consolation of commonplaces about death and facile judgments of the characters (in a phrase, refusing the thought that our moral "talk is all"; line 112); and refusing the demented pretense that a child's death has nothing on us (refusing the illusion that leads us to say we do not know "how to speak" about it at all; line 46). Far and away the best critical treatments of this poem are those by Randall Jarrell and Joseph Brodsky; but the former represents the overwhelming majority of critics who seem to believe that their talk *is* all (that is, they work under the pretension that we can or need to *explain* Amy's plight), while the latter stands virtually alone in holding that, when all is said and done, no one—characters *or* critics—will have spoken appropriately ("language, in the final analysis, is alien to the sentiments it articulates").[8] Neither critical approach works—each seriously breaks down—because each violates the other's boundaries: either (inadvertently) reducing talk to blowing hot air or directly placing oneself beyond the circle of talk entirely. (Not coincidentally, this twofold trespass is the very subject the poem itself investigates.) A successful criticism must articulate more adequate language to acknowledge the powers, as well as the limits, of talk.

For it happens in this poem that Frost no less than Wittgenstein scrupulously attends to talk, to "what we say when," to "how we speak" about, for example, pain or grief or its simulation—what Wittgenstein and Cavell term the "grammatical criteria" by which we identify (for example) grief in terms of certain behaviors in certain circumstances.[9] Criteria constitute the standard against which philosophical claims of the sort that Amy and her husband presuppose may be tested: the lived understanding, the ordinary language we all possess as members of a community or culture: "Criteria, then, are the things by which we tell whether or not something is the case, which give us occasion to say that something is so, which justify us in what we say."[10] This appeal to what we "can" and "can not," "do" and "do not" say in order to mean what we mean, and even to mean what we sometimes "must" mean, as Cavell has argued, when we say what we say, redirects us away from inner consciousness as the mediator of meaning and toward the outer scene of the natural language we already know and share—our language-games and their uses that contextualize both what we know about the world and what there is about the world still to be said. It is a "linguistic Kantianism" in which language and world are mutually constitutive.[11] Cavell writes:

> But now imagine that you are in your armchair reading a book of reminis-
> cences and you come across the word "umiak." You reach for your dictionary
> and look it up. Now what did you do? Find out what "umiak" means, or find
> out what an umiak is? But how could we have discovered something about
> the world by hunting in the dictionary? If this seems surprising, perhaps it
> is because we forget that we learn language and learn the world *together,* that
> they become elaborated and distorted together, and in the same places. We
> may also be forgetting how elaborate a process the learning is. We tend to
> take what a native speaker does when he looks up a noun in a dictionary as
> the characteristic process of learning a language. . . . But it is merely the end
> point in the process of learning the word.[12]

Among other things, then, speaking and listening are matters of what is thought to be worth remarking, dependent upon what is valued (what will count) in practice and use. And learning to speak therefore entails a long and patient apprenticeship, a training by example and imitation in the practices in which a given word appears, whose possibilities and limits sometimes get flagged by modal auxiliary verbs ("must," "can," "cannot," "do not," and the like). It follows that the social nexus—our involvement in institutions, conventions, activities, and so on—comprises the background habits of our real linguistic skill. Together such habits and skill are better conceived as a "knowing-how" than a "knowing-that," to use Gilbert Ryle's useful (if subsequently overdichotomized) distinction—more the ability to do things with words than to theorize about our doings.[13] Wittgenstein would have us bring our language, hence ourselves, back "home" to our world—that is, recognize our metaphysical uses of words, those that impose a priori requirements and "theories" on the world, as illusions (*PI,* §116)—by bringing us back home to the multiform language-games we regularly engage in. Only in practice can we actually *test* what might be errors or new discoveries against more stable activities and concepts.[14]

In my view only Stanley Cavell, in his juxtapositions of Emerson and Thoreau with Wittgenstein and Heidegger, has thus far given a sufficiently complex *kind* of reading of what I take to be the rhetorical-philosophical themes and activities also to be found in Robert Frost. Cavell points us toward one version of what it would mean to to go on with Richard Poirier's definitive insight that Frost, who inherits the Emersonian legacy, is fascinated with the philosophic and literary problems of understanding and interpretation prevalent in our own time.[15] I propose that we can go further in this direction by situating this and other Frost poems within the philosophical purview of a Cavellian grammatical analysis and within the range of an appropriately expanded rhetorical criticism. In this essay my purpose is to link grammatical (philosophical) analysis—for example, *what* it is to say something of something, what properly constitutes the saying—with a rhetorical sensitivity to what it is to say it, in the language of rhetoricians, "appropriately."[16]

1. How to Speak

1.1

Of course learning, and being taught or trained, how to speak are the very matters that open *Philosophical Investigations*, with the figure of Augustine, as a boy, listening to his elders name objects, correlate words with the things that are their meanings, and then going and doing likewise (*PI*, §1). In "Home Burial," similarly, the husband speculates that he might be taught by his wife how to speak: "I don't know how to speak of anything / So as to please you. But I might be taught. . . . / We could have some arrangement / By which I'd bind myself to keep hands off / Anything special you're a-mind to name" (lines 46–47, 50–51). In this passage Amy's husband acts as though he feels himself to be a boy, no doubt a very bad boy. He speaks almost as though he were unconsciously seeking to replace the lost infant son about whom, a moment earlier, his wife chastised him for speaking (lines 29–30, 36), their own child who will now never learn to speak, tell a joke, befriend a dog, or pretend, say, to be someone else—in short, to be someone else. Previous readers have missed this philosophical preoccupation of the characters, of Frost, with speaking—with its conditions and requirements and its joys and sorrows as one grows into speech among others. To understand and accept these conditions, as Amy's husband appears half-willing to do, is contrasted with Amy's refusal to enter (or remain in) a world whose limits are the possibilities of the language she and her husband have known, the conventions which they can actually handle (*TLP*, 5.6) and which she labors to overthrow or exchange. In her pain Amy ambiguously struggles to raze, and possibly even to remake, the linguistic boundaries of their world, concluding suspensefully, "How can I make you——" (line 113)—presumably make her husband understand, presumably by means of words.

We know further that for Wittgenstein Augustine's picture model of language proves inadequate, since learning most words is not a matter of accumulating in one's mind "logical pictures" of objects or of external or internal states of affairs but rather embraces untold different interactive "games" involving myriad forms and functions—making jokes, asking questions, guessing riddles, playacting and simulating (*PI*, §23), and innumerable others. To understand such games requires a patient reflection on their details (their "moves") and only afterward cautious extrapolating of linguistic rules and testing for a "truth" appropriate to the kind of game each one is. In these tasks so-called ordinary language philosophy resembles the reading of legal hard cases. As in law, the aim is not to extract fixed and determinate rules purported to be lurking behind the lines but to formulate and apply more rhetorically sensitive rules as "signposts" (*PI*, §85) suggesting (not dictating) how to "go on" (*PI*, §§151, 210) with the case at bar, the game in play, or the poem before us. Now attention gets directed to interpersonal grammatical and rhetorical structures and occasions of our talk rather than to any genealogy of (for example) the wife's psychological motives. For Wittgenstein no less than the ancient grammarians and rhetoricians, and again for Frost, language cannot be prized apart from the *circumstantiae* (Gr. *peristaseis;* Ger. *Umständen*) of its use (*PI*, §§154, 164), the contextual practices and forms of life we share with others, including the griefs we suffer, resist, or avoid.

What has effectively effaced these complex philosophical-rhetorical activities in "Home Burial" for so long is the fact that Frost's investigation of them is not obvious. Or rather it is so obvious that previous critics have not noticed them. They were not in a position to notice them because, with this poem as with others, they have been trying so hard to look at the "inner" workings of the characters rather than the "outer" behavior and scene of their speaking, as though straining to penetrate the characters' words to grasp the mental anguish within. Such a model of knowing similarly tempts the characters to try to bypass words in favor of sight: only seeing is believing, and only unmediated first person presence counts as seeing. "We feel as if we had to *penetrate* phenomena" (*PI*, §90), Wittgenstein observes; "'But *this* is how it is————' I say to myself over and over again. I feel as though, if only I could fix my gaze absolutely sharply on this face, get it in focus, I must grasp the essence of the matter" (*PI*, §113)—as if "The essence is hidden from us" (*PI*, §92) and words are in the way.[17] It is true of course that persons can conceal their thoughts and feelings by not speaking or by baiting their own words as traps for others. Frost records as much in his earlier "Revelation" (*A Boy's Will*, 1913), whose opening lines also point to pretense:

> We make ourselves a place apart
>   Behind light words that tease and flout,
> But oh, the agitated heart
>   Till someone really find us out.
>   (lines 1–4)

But such dissimulation does not entail that others must, much less that they can, somehow get beyond or "behind" another's words altogether, as though "to know a person" required our being able to see, or somehow to get, inside her head. It indicates rather that a different or new set of words or gestures may be needed to spring the trap, or call the bluff, of another set.

Like the husband in the poem, critics have never noticed what everyone has grown accustomed to ("The wonder is I didn't see at once. / I never noticed it from here before. / I must be wonted to it . . ." [lines 20–21]), that variations on the act of sight, expressed in ordinary words like "look" and "see," occur a remarkable twelve times in just the first twenty-one lines of the poem and four or five times after that.[18] The stress—here, both the emphasis and the anxiety of the characters—is unmistakable: "He saw her at the bottom of the stairs / Before she saw him" (lines 1–2), Frost begins the poem, subtly linking, as the poem proceeds, physically seeing someone or something with knowing and having power over him or her or it: "'What is it you see / From up there always?—for I want to know.' . . . He said to gain time: 'What is it you see?'" (lines 6–7, 10). "She let him look, sure that he wouldn't see, / Blind creature; and awhile he didn't see" (lines 15–16). "'The wonder is I didn't see at once. / I never noticed it from here before'" (lines 20–21). And later: "'But I went near to see with my own eyes'" (line 83) and "'You had stood the spade up against the wall / Outside there in the entry, for I saw it'" (lines 89–90).

Again like the husband in the poem, readers and critics have also understandably wanted to see and thereby know not merely what the woman sees outside but (more to the point) what she feels inside, which is to say her pain and suffering, her grief. The general attitude is that her outer words are either a front or a substitute for the real inner pain. So Amy's husband would find her out the easy way by emptying her words of whatever meaning they have, reducing them to artificial valves for heartfelt feelings, hoping that he might solve the matter, end her pain (and his) by having those feelings *vented*: "There, you have said it all and you feel better" (line 108). It is, again, as though words here were themselves earthen vessels, conveyers of toxic materials. (If he is not flatly wrong in this, he is not just right, either.) Even a critic so sensitive to language as Randall Jarrell executes an almost predictable volte-face when he abandons the husband's surface "rhetoric" (his term) to look for the inner pain and suffering of the wife. As if eyeing a way in (and out) for himself, Jarrell proceeds as though inspired, in the presence of the woman's pain, not to respond to her actual words but to lobotomize them, to extract her deep-seated psychological mysteries and motives, her secrets and self-deceptions. Relying on an expertise he expects "we all understand" (220), and impatient (naturally) with what the woman is saying (221), Jarrell determines that Amy suffers, as some grieving mothers will suffer, from a displaced guilt complex, a diagnosis he offers strictly along Freudian lines (as he casually observes, "An old doctor says . . ."): "To her, *underneath*, the child's death must have seemed a punishment" (222; emphasis added).[19] But what can "underneath" refer to here if not to the woman's actions and words? And what could it mean to get underneath her actions and words, "behind" situated language-in-use (or, said another way, what force does his "must" have)?

Whether Jarrell could be right or wrong about what Amy "must" be feeling—his suggestion amounts to our viewing the death of the child as the mother's wish fulfillment, toward which she feels unconscious responsibility and guilt—his proposals collapse in view of the fact that, here, we cannot possibly have any way of knowing. (Or shall we summarily *decree* repression, guilt, and punishment as the primary "lesson" of this poem?) After all, if even the husband lacks, as he does lack, the sort of knowledge he would need to determine the matter, how much less in a position are we to determine it. Worse, Amy's husband beats Jarrell to the punch when he tactlessly asks aloud (asks himself more than his wife):

> What was it brought you up to think it the thing
> To take your mother-loss of a first child
> So inconsolably . . . ?
>
> (lines 63–65)

The moral here is not that a clinical anatomy of mourning "*must*" prove tangential to Frost's effort, but rather that it is not self-evident that (much less how) it might be relevant.[20] The critics' collective impatience has only brought upon themselves a serious bout of "aspect-blindness" to what stands patently before all of us ("blind creature" [line 16]), namely, that what the woman says has never before been parsed, dwelled in, followed out for its sense, or nonsense (or both):

> "We see emotion."—As opposed to what?—We do not see facial contortions and make the inference [she] is feeling joy, grief, boredom. . . . Grief, one would like to say, is personified in the face. This is essential to what we call "emotion." (*PP*2, 570)

In effect the critics abstractly theorize, overlooking the characters' manifest suffering in ways that are comic almost to the point of tears.

Meanwhile the temptation felt by the characters and critics to toggle back and forth between outside and inside continues to pull at us readers with a potent attraction: "[T]he difficulty is to remove the prejudice" that tempts us to want, or to think that we need, to guess what is inner (feelings of pain, grief) rather than to listen to what is outer (their manifestations). "It is not a *stupid* prejudice" (*PI*, §340) that continues to tempt us to do so; but it is also nothing more than the attractive, and familiar, apple of the modern epistemologist's eye. The model for such knowing has been given an empirical (Enlightenment) and a symbolic (Romantic) turn, but either way it is ultimately Cartesian ("A *picture* held us captive" [*PI*, §115]). Following Descartes's optical model of knowing, we suppose that we are to seek either some determinate account of inner mental life of another person constructed on analogy with our own thoughts and feelings, or a felt unity somehow beyond temporal categories and linguistic structures altogether. Either way words are felt to be, like the human body, encumbrances to their bearer, or obstacles, traps, or fronts to others. As Marjorie Perloff has put it, "even today, mainstream poetry often seems trapped in an oppressive circle of self-presence, the 'cry of the heart' designed to convey some sort of unique personal essence."[21] Failing to rush or maintain these defenses (as we must fail), we soon find ourselves entertaining a distant skepticism about people (or taking poems as celebrations of skepticism). We not only fear that we can never really "know," for example, another person, but we wonder whether that person is even human at all:

> As observers, we feel frustrated because instead of reaching the pain itself, we are restricted to observing merely indirect signs and superficial symptoms. In being conventional . . . these signs can seem arbitrary: what we hear as a groan might be . . . a song or a signal to a pet and not necessarily a sign of pain.[22]

As we have begun to see, the duplicity of these matters requires careful steps, which are laid out as follows. After completing our circumspection of the poem in subsections 1.2 and 1.3 following, the discussion divides into three subsequent sections. The next section contemplates all that it means for the husband not to know "how to speak." The following section unpacks the elaborate sustained claims of the wife, culminating in her charges of "pretense" and "evil." And the final section weighs the philosophic and cultural relevance of Frost's poem to some of the literary pretensions of our own time.

1.2

When we stop and look, we notice that the events of "Home Burial" occur on a stairway and at the threshold of a door. These are literally and figuratively pivotal places that provide scenes of instruction for characters in "The Death of the Hired Man" and "The Black Cottage," as well as (less distinctly) for "The Generations of Men," "A Hundred Collars," "The Housekeeper," and "The Fear"—in sum, nearly half of the poems in *North of Boston*. These and other images common in Frost signal moments of transition and change.[23] As Bakhtin has noted of the "chronotope of the threshold," it "can be combined with the motif of the encounter, but its most fundamental instance is the chronotope of *crisis* and *break* in a life. . . ."[24] When we apply this notion to the investigation in "Home Burial" of the self speaking to others, "self," "speaking," and "other" come to be understood as pivot concepts functioning more as sites of action and crisis (symbolized by stairs and threshold) than as determinate entities or containers, as Frost himself makes clear in the concluding stanza of the poem quoted earlier:

> But so with all, from babes that play
>   At hide-and-seek to God afar,
> So all who hide too well away
>   Must speak and tell us where they are.
>   ("Revelation," lines 9–12)

What proves unexpectedly important here is, once more, that little modal auxiliary "must," for it identifies not a priori transcendental conditions but pragmatic ontological conditions for the possibility of being known at all: to be known (by oneself as by others) requires coming (to use one of Frost's Heidegger-sounding phrases) "into the clearing" delimited by the conventions of a shared language.

Wittgenstein effectively catches the drift of Frost's "Revelation" in his celebrated dictum "Nothing is hidden" (*PI*, §445), a paradoxical claim which arguably stands to his thought in the way that Derrida's "Il n'y a pas de hors-texte" stands to his. Just as Derrida does not intend to deny the existence of the external world, so Wittgenstein does not wish to deny the inner reality that partly informs intending, being in pain, expecting, grieving, and so on.[25] Both pronouncements were designed to jolt us into realizing the linguisticality and physicality—there, on the surface—of what others inwardly know, feel, imagine, think. As Frost puts it: "Just the surface of it. That's the main thing, isn't it? The physical surface of it."[26] In "The Constant Symbol" (1946), a famous late essay written one year after the appearance in German of the *Investigations*, Frost offers his own strong version of Wittgenstein's "Nothing is hidden":

> How can the world know anything so intimate as what we were intending to do? The answer is the world presumes to know. The ruling passion in man is not as Viennese as is claimed. It is rather a gregarious instinct to keep together by minding each other's business. Grex rather than sex. . . . No more invisible means of support, no more invisible motives, no more invisible anything. (*SP,* 24)

In addition to subordinating the libidinal drive to the rhetorical motive in people to talk, Frost's more telling point, I take it, is that action, and more particularly speech, in its everyday forms such as gossip as well as its poetic forms such as dramatic dialogues, are the means by which "an outsider may see what we were up to sooner and better than we ourselves." "The bard has said in effect, Unto these forms did I commend the spirit" (*SP,* 24).

1.3

Previous readings of "Home Burial" form a tight circle around the belief that Frost's poem is centered on the woman's inner "grief." John Kemp and William Pritchard refer uncritically to "expressions of grief" and "the grieving wife." Reginald Cook announces that "grief is the key to the situation."[27] This "situation" is assumed to be as obvious, as "pathetic" and "tragic,"[28] as the omnipresent and "inconsolable" grief,[29] and we are brought to conclude that the poem expresses the tragic portrait of a grieving wife. Moreover, grief is thought by all the critics to be something inner, not only for the good reason that the wife is said to conceal her feelings even from herself (her husband says "Let me *into* your grief" [line 59; emphasis added]; and Cook: "Amy . . . wants to hug her grief"),[30] but because it is assumed that "grief" is equivalent to feelings at best only analogically inferable from words and physical movements, and in itself irreparably sealed away from others (as if we need to look into ourselves in order to see what others might be feeling—as if we must finally *guess*). As though to compensate for their supposed estrangement from these feelings, accordingly, nearly all critics either express what I take to be pretentious sympathy for the woman's "tragedy," or self-righteously upbraid and even condemn Amy for her self-imposed plight or flight.[31]

All of this is further aggravated by the fact that "grief" is not only the critics' term but Frost's own chosen word for what he is attempting to express in "sad" (*SP,* 67) poems like "Home Burial." We can lessen this aggravation, fortunately, by noting how distinctively Frost uses the term. In his well-known introduction to Robinson's *King Jasper,* Frost distinguishes "griefs" from "grievances" (*SP,* 61). Griefs are "immedicable woes—woes that nothing can be done for—woes flat and final" (*SP,* 67); they furnish the material for what Frost considers the most genuine poetry. Grievances by contrast grow out of the stuff of local urgency, more or less passing (Frost was thinking of political) complaints, which he rejects as poetry's point: "I don't like grievances. I find I gently let them alone whenever published. What I like is griefs. . . ."[32] And most tellingly: "Grievances are a form of impatience. Griefs are a form of patience" (*SP,* 62). In other words, grievances are temporary and symptomatic; griefs are permanent and ontological. Grievances spring from removable dissatisfactions; griefs constitute indispensable limitations and finalities (boundaries) of some part of the world. Presuming for now that Frost succeeds in his stated aim in "Home Burial," we can conclude from our previous arguments that the specific "grief" it expresses must be: (1) "immedicable," ontological; but also, as we learned earlier, (2) visible, manifesting Frost's own (only putatively inner) "intending" in ways that the world normally does, as a matter of fact, presume to be able to know.

Thus we arrive at the problem we have been circumambulating for some time. The "grief" which the wife is widely said to suffer—"grief-over-a-death"—

is a grief that is also said by the critics to be *concealed*, not visible; and it is a grief that Amy wants to dissociate from others, whose boundaries she wants to *change*, if she can ("I won't have grief so / If I can change it" [lines 106–7])—which latter option would, needless to say, render it something other than ontological, other than "immedicable." Precisely what it is about grief that Amy would change and how she might change it we can leave for later. The thrust of the matter here is that, throughout the poem and especially in lines 91–107, the wife undertakes so impassioned a "protest"[33] of some kind that one comes to suspect we ought to liken it more to Frost's impatient "grievances" than to patient, forbearing "grief." Thus Richard Poirier observes: "The catalogue of her complaints is a symptom of how for her they have become a way of deadening a deeper grief too painful to be borne. Her list of grievances is no adequate metaphor, that is, for the grief she feels."[34]

If it is a deep *grievance against* "grief-over-a-death" that the wife airs to protect herself, as it were a means of self-medication, what then is *Frost* doing in the poem as a whole—I mean on his stated instruction that poems such as this one manifest "immedicable woes"—which is to say, grief. I propose that it will not do to say, as Cook and others say, that the aim of "Home Burial" is to give us a "tragic portrait of a grieving wife." What Frost invites us to attend to resides elsewhere, neither mostly concealed "in" the wife (her "grief-over-a-death") nor in ourselves (our sympathy with or judgment of the characters) but concealed in the clearing between us. What can bridge (not close) the gap between us and the characters, between one character and another, and between a character and itself, are just those easy, ordinary words, those junk bonds that Amy accuses her husband of putting too much stock in. Thus her "'You—oh, you think the talk is all'" (line 112). Of course Amy is right as far as it goes—talk is not all. But Amy is right for the wrong reasons: "you think the talk is all" means (to her) that her husband neglects feelings, which is also true enough but not because those feelings are "inner," as she all along implies. In fact what she no less than her husband misses between them is the rhetorical-philosophical effects of their own palpable words. Talk is not all, not because it leaves out inner feelings but because it manifests the inner *in* the outer—in the daily practices, circumstances, and purposes, in interlocutors and audiences and agendas, with which words comport and which speakers and audiences must engage. Together inner/outer embodied in speech and action in a physical world is all that we humans have.

What, then, is Frost's grief and how might it be understood to organize and comprise this poem? Hypothesizing this grief other than Amy's, imagining that it rests its case on the characters' actions and words, I suggest that the critics' directing us "inside" is not wrong absolutely but rather so inadequate as to be misleading, inviting us to overlook the grief *there*, in front of us. And I propose that the pained grievances of the wife are naturally, secretly, against *that* grief, whatever it is. In which case, what Frost said of Edward Arlington Robinson ought to be applied to Frost himself: "Not for me to search his sadness to its source. He knew how to forbid encroachment" (*SP,* 67).

2. The Grammar of Grief

2.1

If the place at which we have arrived is entangled, the way out is arduous and steep, for our working through must go "by the long road of the interpretation of signs,"[35] there being no shortcut to any essence, to some metaphysical "grief itself." The phenomenon facing us in "Home Burial" is not grief as an inner event behind the behavior and talk but the characters' own approaches to and avoidances of that grief, and their own (and the critics') misunderstanding of its expression as a logical picture or (failed) "representation" of the inner—in short, the grammar of grief and the rhetoric of its refusal. When Wittgenstein writes, " 'Grief' describes a pattern which recurs, with different variations, in the weave of our life" (*PI,* p. 174), he provides us with resources to begin to discern that the pattern in the weave of this poem has been overshadowed by fold upon fold of psychological speculation and mythology. Rather than adding to these speculations, we would do better to ask: What is the pattern in the textual weave of "Home Burial"?[36] That is, what do we understand these words "as"? Equally important: How do we recognize variation and norm in grief? What are our *own* lives such that grief may be said to be constitutive of them, part of their textual weave, rather than something else (say a discrete, extraordinary event)?

I said that previous readers have evinced impatience with this language-game and missed the complex pattern when they failed to see or remark Frost's insistence on "sight" in lines 1 to 21 and following, and when they failed to consider the couple's obsession with speaking and not knowing how to speak, culminating at the end of the poem in the wife's "*You*—oh, you think the talk is all" (line 112), and "How can I make you——" (line 113). As we turn to focus our attention on how the couple does succeed and fail in talk, we overtake another critical oversight regarding the pattern in the weave, for no one to my knowledge has mentioned the unprecedented occurrence in a Frost poem of such a large number of modal auxiliary verbs.[37] I count 78 instances of such verbs, in 116 lines totaling 1,023 words, or one such verb every line and a half and the amazing ratio of 7.7 percent overall. "Don't" tops the list with 18 occurrences, roughly half issuing from the wife. Numbers alone reveal little, of course, since they tell us nothing about the different language-games in which the verbs are employed. Not surprisingly these verbs exhibit varying meanings, purposes, and effects. "Don't," for example, is sometimes used descriptively, sometimes prescriptively, sometimes conjecturally, and sometimes with moral, with psychological, or with other consequences and causes.[38] When we recall that modal auxiliary verbs have the power of marking off boundaries, limits, and possibilities of speech and action in someone's world, as in the wife's summary "You *can't* because you *don't* know how to speak" (line 71; emphases added), we can begin to see that at least some uses of such verbs can be "transcendental" in the pragmatic sense of linguistically indicating the conditions for the possibility of something. What possibilities of which phenomena (*PI*, §90), then, do these neglected auxiliaries signify?

In addition to matters of seeing, previous readers have also failed to remark that Amy sustains, across the intense moments that constitute this poem, an elaborate argument—or rather several different arguments, in fact different kinds of argument—first regarding her husband's apparent lack of feelings of grief, then the "pretense" of friends at such feelings, and finally the "evil[ness]" of the world. More than any other aspect, this escalating outward of her claims tips us off to the human (grammatical, rhetorical-philosophical) investments at stake for all of us.

2.2

What, then, is Amy so upset about throughout the poem? If we take it as sufficient explanation that her child has died, then what is she so angry about? But then (it will be insisted) how is this not equally obvious? Her anger, even if we finally call it "irrational," even if others label it "hysterical," at least plausibly constitutes, as we have allowed, a normal part of nonpathological grief. Hence we might be tempted to agree with those critics who assert that *whatever* she is angry about—or whatever she *says* she's angry about—should be held as insignificant in comparison to her husband's willingness or ability to respond to her appropriately. Inasmuch as he fails at this, as he obviously does, he arguably deserves her dismay and ire.

Yet this line of response condescends to the woman and convicts the husband without due process. It misdirects the question, "What is she angry about?" away from what the woman *has to say*—as if her words "cannot" count, so irrational are we to assume her anger to be—and refuses to discriminate her husband's failures from his lack of success, his failures from his mistakes, and his failures and mistakes from hers. For, though what she says she is angry about is precisely his failure to respond *appropriately* to "what was in the darkened parlor" (line 96) and to her as a person, we cannot simply assume that we know what she means or wants here ("One cannot guess what a word means. One has to look at its use and learn from that" [*PI*, §340].) Specifically we know up front that she rebuffs him in anger because he hasn't seen what she thinks he ought to see outside (line 19); that he doesn't "know how to ask" questions (line 43); and that he "can't" speak (line 36) because he doesn't "know how to speak of anything / So as to please" her (lines 46–47). On reflection, however, these grievances bespeak a complexity beyond the many obviously wrong things that the husband does say and do, and beyond the things that he does and says obviously wrongly. Auxiliary verbs like "can't" and "don't" can signal many possibilities, so we need to try to untangle their meanings. What precisely is her husband's mistake, or failure, here?

The question is made more pointed by the profound ambiguity of attitude that we just mentioned: whereas Amy's anger drives her past the ordinary boundaries of speech and its normal proprieties onto barren land (How, she implies, can one possibly speak about death and grief? How is one's grief possibly to be understood by anyone else?), it remains unclear whether Amy wants to keep her husband and others permanently outside her sphere of suffering or to invite or somehow make them breach its outer limits. Perhaps she herself, in her pain, does not know what she wants (certainly her husband does not know). Most likely she wants both at different times or even simultaneously. In any case the threefold argument she conducts throughout the poem centers on the claim that her husband does not know how to speak and that others merely pretend to do so. What does *this* mean?

In the dramatic context of the poem, the husband's "not knowing how to speak" is shorthand for several related failures of communication, verbal and otherwise: not only his (1) speaking when he should not, (2) in a manner and (3) about what he should not (cannot, must not) speak; and not only, in addition, (4) his *acting* when and (5) how he should not (digging the grave, mending the fence, standing the spade in the hall, wearing his muddy shoes inside—all of which "speak" or "say something" to her); but (6) his insisting that his wife speak when, plainly, she will not (lines 12–13); (7) that she listen when she turns away to leave (lines 39, 116); and even, in effect (8), that she shut up ("Amy!") when "There's someone coming down the road!" (line 111).

This is a considerable ensemble of grievances. Even when Amy's husband responds to her direct request to tell her what he thinks she sees outside (line 18), he fails to get things right, not because his answer is factually wrong but because it *is* right and to her intolerable, and because he appears intent on not merely identifying what she sees outside but, first of all, prefacing his belated astuteness with ostensibly idle remarks and, worse, gearing up to say *more*, to elaborate on "the child's mound——" (line 30), provoking her to interrupt: "Don't, don't, don't, don't . . ." (line 30)—don't, that is, *go on* about this intolerable reality that he should not have mentioned in the first place (her own request for it notwithstanding). The offense here seems to be his lack of comprehension of her situation, manifested in both his improprieties of speech and action and his emotional failure (fault? inability?) even to recognize impropriety, to recognize that the boundaries between them are now shifting and different.[39] In a different context Gerald Bruns speaks to this last point: "As Wittgenstein says, to know the meaning of a word"—a word like "graveyard" (line 23) or "child's mound" (line 30) or even "child" (line 35)—

"is to know how to use it—and also *when* to use it, and, above all, when *not* to use it. Rules of usage are not simply rules of grammar or semiosis but also rules of suitability and decorum."[40] Thus Amy's husband unwittingly plays the Augustinian semiotician: Words for him get exhausted by reference, not degraded (or renewed) in abstinence or use.

For Amy these particular violations against suitability or decorum (propriety), however, seem to pale when compared to what she takes to be her husband's mortal fault or failure (or both) responsible for them, a fatal lack which (for her) explains those otherwise venial infractions—namely, his absence of feelings of grief:

> If you had any feelings, you that dug
> With your own hand—how *could* you?—his little grave;
> I *saw* you. . . .
>
> (lines 72–74; emphasis added)

Now if we pause at this point in the investigation to ask *how* Amy knows what her husband feels or does not feel, we come into certain advantages in our task of understanding what Frost is up to. First, asking this question gives us enough distance from Amy's terrible pain to allow us to reflect that we may not already understand that pain *or* her situation, just because the seeming transparency of his or her ordinary words is belied by the extraordinary context and the multiple uses to which the words are being put. Further, it enables us to wonder *what*, exactly, it is that Amy does see when she sees her husband do the things he does and hears him say what he says with his "rumbling voice / Out in the kitchen" (lines 81–82).[41] That is, what does she see them "*as*"? We are not challenging Amy's faulting her husband's lack of feelings—to her that lack, in general, is his shame. But, specifically, *how* does she know that he lacks feelings, much less what that putative lack involves and what is responsible for it? (It is as though she, like her husband, sees his movements and hears his voice as physical, even mechanical, events rather than as human actions.) The answer is crucial if we want to understand what her argument (hence what much of the poem) means. Obviously Amy is furious about this alleged lack, implying from the outset that it is not merely a factual absence of some kind—a failing for which her husband might, or might not, be responsible—but a fault for which, by definition, he bears some (presumably moral) responsibility. Hence part of the difficulty of answering this question—What is she angry about? What is she accusing him of?—arises from that ambiguous "you *couldn't* care" (line 97) and previous similar charges—that is, from the ambiguous modal auxiliaries, to which we now need to turn.

The explanatory sequence that she implies seems to me to go like this: (1) he "can't" speak because he doesn't "know how to speak" (line 71); (2) he doesn't know how to speak because he "couldn't" feel what he ought to be feeling (line

97); and (3) he "couldn't" feel either because (a) he's morally or otherwise unable (for whatever unexplored causes or reasons, excluding his own moral agency); or (b) he's somehow wrongly rendered himself morally or psychologically unable to feel such feelings. Another possibility is that (4) "couldn't care" (feel) is used merely to indicate *that* there are signs that in fact he "doesn't" care (who knows why?). Against the likelihood that these distinctions ring hollow even to the patient reader ("Who *cares* about what she is going on about? What counts is her *pain*"), we may note that the wife might have responded entirely differently—with a stupefied silence, or inarticulate screams, or patently incoherent rambling on about her child. For us *not* to struggle to understand this particular reaction, *these* angry words of hers, would be tantamount to dismissing them, excusing ourselves from responding to her (and thus to the poem). Yet how would we support such presumption to dismiss them and to excuse ourselves, short of subsuming her situation (which we would need to claim we already understand) under some "theory" of grief we had tucked away for the purpose from the start? Lacking such theory myself, I must come back to the contexts in which to listen to her.

2.3

For present purposes these contexts begin with her husband's talk and the sequence just mentioned, that is, with what his words may plausibly suggest and, therefore, how decorous they and he may or may not be. "He said twice over before he knew himself: / '*Can't* a man speak of his own child he's lost?'" (lines 35–36; emphasis added). Amy's husband suggests here that he *can't* speak because his wife will not *allow* him to speak (vid. her "Don't, don't, don't, don't"), *not* that he considers himself rhetorically or grammatically *unable*—not, that is, because he cannot find or does not know the right words, as his wife believes and he himself later allows (line 46). Here the "can't" is normative and prescriptive, not empirical. And he implies that he *doesn't* "know how" to speak for reasons most likely related to what he takes to be *her* arbitrariness, the unreasonableness of her sanctions upon him, and not, again, at least at this point, his own limitations, failings, or faults. Moreover, his asking this painful question ("Can't a man speak of his own child he's lost?") *twice,* "before he knew himself," is therefore multiply suggestive: before he realized that he was talking (hence oblivious to situation and audience); before he realized the implications of what he was saying (hence not in control of his words); before he himself realized it (hence, perhaps, lagging behind his wife's grasp of things); before he knew the answer himself (hence as if stumped by his own rhetorical question); and also, perhaps, before he could reorient himself as to who he was *as speaker* (husband, male, grieving father) posing such a question.

The ambiguity of these verbs matters because it betokens the same lack of control or decorum to which the husband later confesses, the limits or status of which is unclear: are they a social blunder, or a lapse in memory, hence *limits* to his world? Thus, by "can't" here *he* may, as we said, mean that he is not being *allowed* to speak of his child, but he betrays in his complaint that very lack of sensibility, of decorum, that his wife soon accuses him of. Similarly, it matters that the particular language-game he is rhetorically playing (and losing) here and throughout is the one we would call "lodging a complaint" rather than (say) merely asking a rhetorical question, or whining, or inquiring. These latter would turn his words in quite different directions. As a complaint they suggest that, in spite of his own lack of control, Amy's husband hopes the situation, whatever it is, can be rectified (as, perhaps, does Amy). After all, the speaker is willing to try to *change* himself, whoever or whatever he is, including even curtailing his sphere of male influence, so to speak, if that is necessary: "But I might be taught [how to speak], / I should suppose. I can't say I see how. / A man must partly give up being a man / With womenfolk" (lines 47–49).

Now what is of interest here is twofold. First, the husband's uses of "can't" and "don't" in lines 35 and 46 ("Can't a man speak of his own child he's lost?") differ from Amy's uses in line 71 ("You can't because you don't know how"), for her verbs include but reach beyond mere description or prescription and gesture toward an explanation (that is, he "can't" even if he wants to; he is constitutively unable because of some particular *cause*). Thus we are in the presence of an argument of hers about the moral and psychological limits of her husband, of his world. Second, and more important, her later, philosophical uses of these and similar verbs— "can't" and "can" and so on (lines 71ff.)—will differ from, and even ultimately contradict, her own empirical, moral, and other uses here—bringing us into the region of limits on the world *as such*: a metaphysical argument. But first, how does Amy know? Or better, what is Amy presuming in order to know what her husband is or is not feeling? And is she correct in her surmise?

2.4

Clearly Amy has to have what all of us tacitly have—a notion of what grief is. For Wittgenstein, we have indicated, any such notion must identify the "criteria" that must be met for her (for anyone) properly to say that it is "grief" that is present, or absent, in her husband's demeanor. But identification of grief may also include what Wittgenstein calls "symptoms" (what classical rhetoricians call *semeia*, certain or probable signs) that are only sometimes present, indicating that some more complex condition (here, grief) does or does not obtain. Thus, for most human beings two necessary (but nevertheless situated and varying) criteria of "grief" are that one has suffered some grave loss and that one's zest for life is thereby curtailed; whereas possible (not only varying but not necessary) symptoms of grief are, for instance, tears, a circumspect countenance, a certain automaticity of speech or movement (e.g., "Making the gravel leap and leap in air, / Leap up, like that, like that," lines 75–76), and so on. [42] Of course Amy's grievance from the start has been that *all* of the symptoms suggest (to her) that her husband is not grieving at all—in effect, that he "couldn't" be grieving when he talks, acts, and looks as he does:

> If you had any feelings, you that dug
> With your own hand—how *could* you?—his little grave.
> (lines 72–73; emphasis added)

Thus Amy seems to have taken her husband's automaticity of movements not "as" signs of grief but as symptoms of lack of feeling altogether, as it were an inhuman mechanics. And naturally enough, Amy has not specified criteria for grief, only relied on them—although her talk implies that the pertinent criteria (whatever they are) are simply incongruent with "everyday concerns" (line 86), that they remain unfulfilled in her husband's demeanor, and that the other signs (symptoms) that are present further indicate a culpable lack of grief feelings, hence an absence of grief. Ultimately, whether this moral-psychological argument is a good one or not must involve our own notions of grief and the range of its normal expressions (its pattern or weave in life).

We can gain some perspective on Amy's position when we notice that she has no sooner made this first argument than she abruptly shifts gears and picks up a very different *type* of argument, one she had only broached moments earlier, virtually to herself, when she speculated, "I don't know rightly whether any man *can* [speak of his dead child]" (line 38; emphasis added). Not only are this particular husband and wife playing different language-games, but Amy hints ambiguously here ("I don't know rightly whether any man *can*"; emphasis added) at a "grammatical" inability of men *as such* to speak forth, to represent—precisely because they *cannot* feel grief properly, and a fortiori a mother's—grief at the loss of a child. [43] This is the second claim that Amy then extends when she alludes to a similar inability in others:

> The nearest friends *can* go
> With anyone to death, comes so far short
> They may as well not try to go at all.
> (lines 97–99; emphasis added)

Obviously this is a claim of a kind different from the empirical and normative psychological explanations and judgments made by her (and her husband), and we would do well to ask what reasons she gives for it—whether, for example, this claim also rests, like her first, on an inference from physical symptoms, and even whether it has any basis at all (for she had admitted, "I don't know *rightly* . . ." [emphasis added], where the squinting modifier points ambiguously to herself as much as to others). The scope and implications of this second claim are, again, profound, for its modal verbs implicate not only her husband or even all men but all "friends" and, in the end, the world itself. For this reason it is a grammatical (philosophical) claim concerned with ultimate limits and boundaries of our knowledge of each other.

The drift of Amy's arguments seems to be this: (1) where her husband culpably *failed* to feel, (2) men as such *cannot* feel sufficiently or really. And not only men but—here she gets vague—(3) all "friends," indeed *all* others "cannot" (as she puts it) "go / With anyone to death" (lines 97–98). In lieu of real grief, "Friends make pretense of following to the grave" (line 102). Of course on reflection it is not clear whether "following to the grave" and "going to death" are the near equivalents they seem to be, much less what it is that they mean (exactly what does she want?). Nor, again, is it clear *how* Amy knows that others cannot do these things. Once more she has not specified but only relied on the criteria necessary for us to identify these feats. Do they involve the same criteria as those for "grieving," as they seem to do? To keep from falling into the black hole drawing us from the depths of "Home Burial," then, we need to inquire into the grammar of "going to death" and "following to the grave." Are they even roughly that of the grammar of grief? What is it, to go and to follow, precisely? Why is the world "evil"? What scheme of rhetorical-grammatical propriety governs this world that Amy declines to inhabit?

3. "Myself as one his own pretense deceives . . ." ("A Boundless Moment")

3.1

We have said that in order to know that her husband is not grieving, Amy needed both a conception (criteria) of what grief is and a basis upon which to argue that, in fact, *he* is not feeling grief. That basis was found in outward symptoms (digging the grave, going about his ordinary work) inconsistent with *her* criteria, from which she then inferred, by analogy from her own feelings, an inner lack. How then does Amy proceed to speculate that "all men" "can't" grieve, or to argue that "friends" are (only) *pretending* to grieve—making a "pretense" of "following to the grave" (line 103)? Again, she needs to know what a pretense of this would look like and needs to have reasons to believe that their behavior is in fact a pretense.

If we consider pretending in general, we are likely to think of outward signs that someone is not really doing what he or she appears to be doing. We may say that someone is "pretending" to be punching someone else when a closer look reveals that those punches are not hitting home, or that a person is pretending to be Winston Churchill when he talks, scowls, and chomps a cigar like Churchill.[44] In his provocative essay "Pretending," J. L. Austin shows us a further, often overlooked way we use the word, as when we realize or say that someone is pretending to wash the windows when he is really casing the joint.[45] In such an instance the person in question does, in fact, wash the windows—*does fully do* what is said is being pretended—yet he is still said to be pretending because the action is otherwise known to be part of something else, some larger circle of affairs that leads us in the particular case to account differently for what is usually meant by "washing the windows." Here we know about the pretense not from outward signs—someone on close inspection not performing some set of actions or performing them in-adequately (punches not connecting, the window washer not really soaping the windows)—but rather from other sources, say from a tip to the police putting them on the lookout for a cat burglar pretending to be a handyman who says he will "do windows." This is an a priori knowledge about some greater scheme of things to which the activity in question is known to be subordinated. So again the question: How does Amy *know* that others ("friends") are "making a pretense of" going to death, following to the grave?

I want to say: not as she concluded that her husband wasn't feeling grief, not, that is, by inference from outward signs (symptoms). We can say this not because her claim that "The nearest friends can go / With anyone to death, comes so far short . . ." (lines 97–98) *could* not meaningfully be construed as something one can infer from outward signs but because this is not in fact how Amy infers it. If it were, we could enumerate here the ways those ersatz mourners betrayed their false "going to death" and "following to the grave." Reading those phrases literally, for example, we would say that "going to death" is already, obviously falsified—not because the mourners do not physically die but because none of them pretends to. Such a literalist reading would be impossible to credit, in other words, in part because this is not what anyone *means* when one talks of "going to the funeral" or "comforting the mother"—phrases rhetorically similar, I take it, to Amy's "going to death" and "following to the grave." If it is insisted that, ordinary language notwithstanding, physical dying is precisely what Amy means, then it may be noted that *Amy* doesn't physically die any more than the others do, in which case her accusation of pretense doubles back on herself, rendering her complaint against others all the more difficult to understand as anything more than a long moan of pain. Though this is a logically possible line of interpretation, and though emotionally Amy probably does wish literally to die (*is* moaning in pain), still it's a stretch to see how she could conclude that those unnamed "friends" are actually pretending "to die" (taken literally). What then does she mean? Nothing at all?

The conventional and most plausible tack is to take her as saying that those who "follow to the grave" only *pretend* to mourn, that is, pretend to be sad, to be in pain, to feel loss—that they do not really *mean* what they say and do, not only do not mean it the way that *Amy* means it but in any way at all that could be said to constitute "grief." But again, how does Amy know this? We might say by the signs (symptoms). Perhaps she saw the mourners alternate their haggard looks with funny faces to amuse each other. Or they sent look-alike substitutes to the funeral and their ruse exploded during an intimate moment of hand-holding. Or they invited Amy's husband to play first base in their softball game later in the day. The problem with these suggestions, of course, is that we never get any indication that Amy in her suffering has pinpointed any such signs of betrayal, of pretense. Just the opposite, in fact. Because nothing indicates the contrary, we may assume that these friends *do* in fact do what friends would normally be expected to do, what we would expect *ourselves* to do, in the face of another's loss: say kind words, show sad faces, wear black, remove our hats, tread heavily to the grave site, perhaps join the prayers. (As far as that goes, even if these friends *had* made faces or did play ball or dine out later, we may, but we also may not, want to call their previous behavior pretending. If we try to save the conventional reading by saying that Amy simply means that the others do not, as a simple matter of fact, feel as *she* feels, then we fail to do justice to how harshly she judges them and how she seems willing to act as a result (i.e., to shut out the world). Where then is the pretense?

If what I have suggested holds together, it implies that Amy must infer this pretense from some source other than physical signs—in short, that she possesses an a priori knowledge (or what she takes to be knowledge) about a larger scheme of things within which friends' *actual* following to the grave is understood to be belied. Our question, then, becomes: What is this a priori information and how does she use it?

3.2

What Amy implicitly relies on here—perhaps has long held in secret even from herself, or perhaps has newly arrived at in spite of herself, as the desolate issue of her loss (it doesn't matter which)—what her actions and words perceptibly betray when held against the light of more adequate criteria of grief, is her unspoken assumption that no one *can* ever really "know" what another is feeling or thinking, just because one is irreparably cut off from others, a lone body rent asunder from other bodies and left high and dry. One sees a person from across the room, *stares* at him; but one cannot be said really to "know" anything since one cannot see what is "inside," which is hidden. So Amy stares and stares at things, at a spade, at shoes, at her husband—and eventually comes to confess: "I thought, Who is that man? I didn't know you" (line 78)—quite as though the world were already well lost. And she explicitly concludes: "One is alone, and he dies more alone" (line 101). This hard nugget of common sense is immediately flattened into the golden hook and thread to stitch up her grief wound (so she thinks) with the unbreakable binding of Human Fate. In this way her body, rather than her embodied words, becomes the limit of her world, and she is snagged in the nets of skepticism:

> "In hiding something from me, [she] can hide it in such a way that not only will I never find it, but finding it will be completely *inconceivable.*" This would be a metaphysical hiding. (*PP2*, 586; emphasis added)

Of course it is true that our ties of bondage, the bonds of our alleged metaphysical separateness from each other, promptly *seem* to relax, for Amy further observes, "From the time when one is sick to death, / One is alone . . ." (lines 100–1). It is as though she is conceding here that human solitude begins only with sickness, that it is strictly another's *physical* pain that we cannot know (and so one "dies more alone")—this being our manumission, as it were, from total anonymity. But then this gloss will not cover everything Amy claims. The pain that she implies her husband, all men, "friends," and finally the world do not or *can* not feel is not her child's physical pain or death but her own soul anguish. To her no other *can* touch this pain because, from their beginning to their end, human beings can only stand and stare. To Amy in her plight we are each as it were island-bound people unsure of our neighbors on the horizon. One suspects the other of being human, but the glass through which we peer is spotted and weak. In the end, after all, the most that can be said for that phrase of Amy's, "From the moment one is sick to death," is that it is ambiguous, despite its seeming to pinpoint a specific time at which our failure to know others begins. In its familiar sense, of course, "sick to death" means being fed up with something, being alienated—perhaps from life itself. But that alienation can transpire at any time, *can* even always be present and may (for all we know) have always been present to Amy. It follows that human solitude can be ontological and even itself the cause of life sickness-unto-death. This claim to knowledge of our human subjugation to isolation is what Amy implicitly has a choke hold on—what has a choke hold on her—as she looks up at her husband on the stairs. Because he does not speak and act precisely as she does, he is said not to be feeling anything; because men cannot know what women feel, a fortiori they "cannot" know what a *mother* feels; because others (friends, the world) act as though they know what they *cannot* know (what another feels), they are, they "must" be, pretending.

3.3

This a priori, transcendental assumption, that we humans stand alone, an imported claim dissimulated by Amy ("without calling it a lie"; *PP2*, 586) to *look* like a conclusion soberly drawn from experience, shows its true colors when we turn back momentarily to Amy's earlier psychological argument about her husband's lack of feeling and ask: Is *that* argument any good? Does her view of his behavior support the claim that an absence of feelings accounts for his inability to speak and act appropriately? Furthermore, does it support her larger claim about the "evil" of the world, evil because, though each of us is alone and cannot know what others feel, in fact others insist on pretending to do so? In truth how distorted her inference about her husband is (perhaps how stunned by the burden of loss Amy is) can be gathered from the fact that her husband *does* (obviously!) suffer. Then why has Amy not seen this?

No doubt we can agree with Amy that her husband avoids and resists feeling more than he does. But his rambling self-absorption about the dead and how weather will rot a birch fence manifest in context both grief for his lost son and anxiety that he may be losing his stricken wife. No doubt he goes about things ineptly and inappropriately, but he goes about them. If at first we miss the fact that more adequate grief criteria are fulfilled here, it is because we see and hear him chiefly through Amy's distorting scope. After all, the husband importunes his wife, he declares himself "in the face of love" (line 65), he is willing to try to change himself, he coaxes her (unhappily he bullies her) to express her grief, he somatically displaces his own mental pain through his digging,[46] he dwells on the ravages of time, he distracts himself momentarily by remembering his own "people." This is not what we call pretense and certainly not apathy, for the signs and criteria are, if not unambiguous, at least available on the surface of things: He is in anguish on his own. For all her looking, her staring, her obsessive spying—"I crept down the stairs and up the stairs / To look again" (lines 79–80)—Amy is sadly aspect-blind to her husband's behavior, unable in her all-consuming grief to see it "as" grief behavior, even as *human* behavior (in Stanley Cavell's words, one aspect blinds her to another). What Amy takes as evidence of her husband's mechanical coldness is merely the well-known variability of human behavior in the face of breakdown and loss. As a result, moreover, Amy gathers from her observations *no evidence at all* for her larger argument about the pretense of others, because, again, that argument is a priori and not based on evidence at all; it is, instead, itself a pretense of argument (!), of which she may be said to be both perpetrator and victim.

How do we understand Amy's blindness here? After all, she is not physically or psychologically mad (neurotic, hysterical, and so on). Or rather, if she is, Frost has discreetly denied us any superior position from which to speculate about it, not because we lack medical knowledge (in the way that the husband earlier lacked information about her psychological etiology) but because such psychologizing has all along been irrelevant to our leading question, namely: How can she have missed what was right before her eyes? How can she have argued in the way that she has? The questions are philosophically important to us, for the fact is that we, too, suffer periodically from Amy's condition, in our own moments as "mad" as she (hence the critics' systematic overlooking of this philosophic problem staring at us), mad in the way that Wittgenstein uses the term: "Madness need not be regarded as an illness. Why shouldn't it be seen as a sudden—more or *less* sudden— change of character?" (*CV*, 54e). It is merely the extremity of the variation of Amy's madness from our own ordinary madness that renders hers and her husband's fate so fateful for us, for we see ourselves as in a mirror darkly, and we are turned around.

We can say, then, that Amy radically misconstrues (not mistakes) the phenomena of her world and their possibilities due to a more or less sudden and more or less lasting change of character brought on by crushing loss. And it is a change that culminates in her skepticism toward others, that is, her skepticism about the power of words, of talk, to know others as human and as individuals. This skepticism may be read as her positive approach toward reintegration, or as a flight from and avoidance of loss, or, most interestingly, as both (Frost shrewdly makes each reading plausible). What is central is that Amy's high argument about human solitude places in grammatical and rhetorical relief what *we* ourselves mean when we say that human beings, separate from each other, nevertheless can and do come to know each other. It flushes out our own temptation to *avoid* facing our true separateness from Amy and her husband, either by going silent (Brodsky) or by playing doctor (Jarrell)—in short, by not speaking at all or by not speaking appropriately. In this way we are likely to miss the chance for our own change of character by overlooking our loss of autonomy, the fantasy of ours and of the characters' of having no limits or boundaries.

The observation I want to make, then, is that Amy *imposes* unreal criteria of "grief"—"going to death," "following to the grave"—onto others, criteria that could not possibly be fulfilled by anyone, for two reasons. First, the criteria require that someone (husband, friends, others) feel someone *else's* (namely her) pain, and second, the criteria occlude how variously, in fact, people grieve, suffer, heal in the world—how we human beings do these things—demanding that this allegedly pretentious variation be reduced to its essence (herself). Separated from her child, Amy craves the total *oneness* that each of us is tempted to fantasize as the only surety of knowledge or love. Employed unwittingly, it may be, to protect herself from the grief she cannot (yet? ever?) face, her criteria derive strictly from the closed circle of her desire, a tightly spun fantasy of ideal unity of self and other within which (*per impossibile*) no boundaries *can* exist. From this circle she excludes husband, friends, and world, all of which are, perforce, always already other than herself. Thus they stand as reminders of the one separation she fights to forget. What Amy hugs unspoken is her unreal desire to erase all boundaries, belie every body, deny all separateness. In this desire she will fail, as she must, for her speech in lines 71 and following is grammatically nonsensical (though it may be, rhetorically, efficacious, either as a hand raised in self-defense or as a hand held out in hope to her husband). In fact this abnormal separation of grammar (the sense of linguistic possibilities) and rhetoric (sensibility to grammatical appropriateness) is, I think, itself a symptom of her avoidance of the world, her blindness to their inseparability.

Meanwhile, as a proleptic consequence of her avoidance, Amy treats words and bodies as barricades and borders, though she may also come to use them as bridges. Nor is she alone in her desire (far from it), for her husband similarly complains against "things 'twixt those that love" (line 53; emphasis added)—the very things (limits, boundaries) that she cannot abide and harshly projects, on herself and others, by default if not by fault. This desire for symbiosis with another is of the sort that only a mother might be said actually to enjoy with an unborn child, although a moment's thought reminds us that, by definition, such symbiosis involves two beings and that, in any case, the deceptive desire for unity belongs to us all. This fantasy of immediate knowing wills the common legacy of our struggle with skepticism in the face of others. So, at the end of the *Tractatus*, Wittgenstein observes, "Scepticism is *not* irrefutable." But he adds, "but obviously nonsensical, when it tries to raise doubts where no questions can be asked" (*TLP*, 6.51). In "Home Burial" the separation caused by death prompts Amy to raise these doubts to the furthermost degree, while her husband and the rest of the world, sensibly (though not always appropriately) acting on the unreality of the questions, necessarily appear to Amy as "evil."

Thus the skepticism that leads to the couple's obsessive staring also logically accounts for remarks of theirs entirely ignored by critics: I mean their half-suspecting that the other may not even be *human*. Amy's husband wants her to "Tell me about [what she feels] *if it's something human*" (line 58; emphasis added)— as though not just her anguish but she herself may not be human at all! This is entirely in keeping with his distrust of what humans do—in particular, talk—for perhaps this talk is alien imposture, a plague of pestilential gas to be expelled. How, after all, can one *know*? He continues: "I'm not so much / Unlike other folks as your standing there / Would make me out" (lines 59–61), sensing that she too skeptically fears *his* own possible inhumanness. Just behind their anxiety resides a mad fantasy on a level with *Invasion of the Body-Snatchers*. Both seek to prove and explain in the way that philosophers obsess about reasoning, justifying, explaining, proving: "The difficulty here is: to stop" (Z, 314). Thus, "how *could* you [dig his grave]?" can be heard to be spoken as if the act were something a human being whose child had died "could not," that is, could not *humanly*, do. This is no longer a matter of one's needing "criteria" to determine humanity, for, as Wittgenstein and Cavell point out, there are no criteria by which we know the "humanity" of human beings: "Criteria come to an end" (CR, 412). We do not "know" such a thing as another's humanity, thereby defeating skepticism. In fact, no hard and fast criteria are available to us that another has a human soul, a psychic life, human feelings, a mind. We can only "acknowledge" that another is human by relying on our "mutual attunements" in a form of life—or we can fail, or refuse, or avoid doing so.[47] Thus says Cavell:

> The truth here is that we *are* separate, but not necessarily *separated* (by something); that we are, each of us, bodies, i.e., embodied; each is this one and not that, each here and not there, each now and not then. If something separates us, comes between us, that can only be a particular aspect or stance of the mind itself, a particular *way* in which we relate . . . to one another. . . . (CR, 369)

"The *nearest* friends can go with anyone to death, comes so far short" (lines 97–98; emphasis added), Amy says dismissively. But how near is near?

In his celebrated essay "Experience," Emerson says of his own son's death, "I *cannot* get it *nearer* to me."[48] Sharon Cameron reads the comment as an avowal of personal failure to mourn on the part of the author, but Cavell reads it as the opposite: Emerson can't get grief nearer because it's already as close as he can possibly get it. In contrast, Amy's similar words are spoken not of herself but of her friends, declaring their failure and inability: Even though they are Calvinistically preordained to pretense and failure, they are no less culpable for that. But Amy excludes herself from this alleged human plight of pretending to mourn, an obvious contradiction unless we want to suggest she is not human.

In the end, of course, this is precisely what Amy has simulated, what she pretends is true: that she is not human, bounded, embodied, and subject to loss—therefore that she is not constrained to speak to be known (hence her contempt: "you think the talk is all"). This unfathomable fact of her humanity she avoids, perhaps wisely, for to face such facts would mean not merely facing a fantasy but facing away, finally, from the burial mound of her child who *is* separated from her by death and becoming a new person again. Instead she imposes onto others criteria so strict that it looks for all the world like *their* failure, their pretense at grief, and by contrast like her own discovery and practical wisdom:

> It is as though we try to get the world to provide answers in a way which is independent of our responsibility for *claiming* something to be so . . . and we fix the world so that we can do this. . . . [then] we take what we have fixed or constructed to be *discoveries* about the world, and take this fixation to be the human condition rather than our escape or denial of this condition through the rejection of the human conditions of knowledge and action and the substitution of fantasy. (CR, 216)

4. Schemes of Propriety

> Of course, if water boils in a pot, steam comes out of the pot and also pictured steam comes out of the pictured pot. But what if one insisted on saying that there must also be something boiling in the pictured pot? (*PI*, §297)

In *The Claim of Reason* Stanley Cavell explains Wittgenstein's parable of the boiling pot as exposing "false views of the inner and outer," "between the soul and its society" (*CR*, 329). More than a cautionary tale, it invites us to reconsider the (ineradicably) human temptation to skepticism in view of another person's pain, or grief, and ultimately in view of another person's humanity or "soul." Perhaps only later, in the philosopher's study, long after we have seen and heard the "steam" (e.g., tears, a cry of pain) escape from someone else—after a dog, say, has drawn blood from somebody's leg—does it occur to us to ask: *How* do we know there's pain "inside the pot," an *inner* pain to go along with those *outer*, possibly faked, tears and cries? Do we really "know" that those "others" around us have an inner life as we do—that they are human? The drift of Wittgenstein's parable is to tease out not only the insolubility of universal skeptical doubt but equally the (unavoidable) impertinence of asking what's boiling in the pictured pot—the normal unreality of the question: " 'Yes, but there is something there all the same accompanying my cry of pain. And it is on account of that I utter it. And this something is what is important—and frightful.'—Only whom are we informing of this? And on what occasion?" (*PI*, §296).

The problem with such talk about something in the pictured pot, some pain "accompanying" some cry, is not that there is *no* occasion on which such a statement can make sense. One can imagine insisting on one's own pain to a late arrival who had missed the dog's bite and overlooked the flow of blood and who laughed, thinking the commotion was all in fun. (One can imagine Amy's crying, "I *hurt*," just because her husband avoids acknowledging this fact.) The problem resides rather in just the wanting to "insist" on "something accompanying my cry of pain" in any and *all* circumstances, that is, apart from some specific language-game altogether, as if one could finally defeat the skeptic's universal threat, to the effect that the parable of the pot rightly pictures the facts involved in another's failing to know our grief or pain. Wittgenstein, we remember, does not want to deny that there are (inner) feelings but rather to subvert our additional "insisting" on it to others in order to—as if one needed to—"enforce the *connection* between something inner and something outer" (*CR*, 338). The "pain itself" *is* part of the account but "not as a picture" (*PI*, §300), not as a representation. That insistence is just a barking up the wrong tree, working from the wrong model of what it is to "know" that another is suffering physical pain (or grieving, or pretending). It is a positing of two discrete things, the behavior we see and that which (we suppose) is left out ("the pain itself"), leading us to think that we need to find a way to bridge the two (Amy's "How can I make you . . . ?") when in fact they are already existentially one, albeit unacknowledged. Human tears and cries, in sum, are not a "representation" of inner anguish but its manifestations. And others appropriately *hear* them "as" pain or grief in context and act accordingly, or do not. Of course they (we) can be wrong about another's pain at any time; even when the criteria for pain are fulfilled, that fact does not guarantee the presence of the phenomenon we are supposing. But then Wittgenstein holds that there are no such guarantees, even when there are criteria, and that in any event guarantees are beside the point, which is the human need for human acknowledgment. When rightly positioned, and equipped (trained), we just "see" that someone is hurt; our seeing is a "seeing-as" or better, a "continuous seeing-as" rather than a "seeing-through" or "into" some opaque object (what was in the darkened parlor, a husband, a grave), and we act accordingly, appropriately, or we refuse or fail to.

For his part, Amy's husband helps bring language to grief by mistaking the ordinary for the cheap, oblivious to the value of contexts, audiences, timing— in a word, decorum. Instead his words whirl like exhaust fans, blowing hot and cold. And when he concedes to Amy that "We might have some arrangement / By which I'd bind myself to keep hands off / Anything special you're a-mind to name" (lines 50–52), he transforms a delicate "know-how" into a blunt "knowing-that," covertly hearkening to the decorum of the disengaged expert: "One thinks that learning a language consists in giving names to objects" (*PI*, §26) or witholding names when the objects offend, as if some determinate list of forbidden words can exhaust the multiple situations of future offense. In other words, Amy's husband reduces infinitely ramified skills in the grammar and rhetoric of a form of life, a propriety needing constant adaptation and sensitivity to the "stage-setting" that stands behind any naming (*PI*, §257), to the itemizing of objects and activities. Indeed, he would if he could reduce words beyond recognition of their uses, either by going silent like his wife ("Don't!") or by indulging her and himself in empty talk: "[A]ll [you] can do is to groan, to weep, to laugh, to rage, to talk, to talk, to talk!" (*CR*, 382).

Notes

1. Ludwig Wittgenstein, *Philosophical Investigations*, trans. G. E. M. Anscombe (New York: Macmillan and Co., 1968), §250; hereafter cited as *PI*, with Wittgenstein's numbered paragraphs, or "remarks," indicated by the symbol § and page numbers by "p." Reference will also be made parenthetically to Wittgenstein's

Tractatus Logico-Philosophicus (London: Routledge and Kegan Paul, 1961); hereafter cited as *TLP.*

2. This problematic can be quite differently presented, with stress on community and shared conventions or on autonomy and the shattering of conventions. For the first, in addition to Cavell's own works, see the excellent studies by Stephen Mulhall, *Stanley Cavell: Philosophy's Recounting of the Ordinary* (Oxford: Clarendon Press, 1994), and Michael Fischer, *Stanley Cavell and Literary Skepticism* (Chicago: University of Chicago Press, 1989); and for the second, see Henry Staten, *Wittgenstein and Derrida* (Lincoln: University of Nebraska Press, 1984). On the concept of the ordinary as both odd and not odd ("even"), see Stanley Cavell, *In Quest of the Ordinary: Lines of Skepticism and Romanticism* (Chicago: University of Chicago Press, 1988), especially "The Uncanniness of the Ordinary" (164ff.) and "Being Odd, Getting Even," 105–30.

3. Robert Frost, *Letters to Louis Untermeyer* (New York: Holt, Rinehart and Winston, 1963), 223.

4. Quoted in William H. Pritchard, *Frost: A Literary Life Reconsidered* (New York: Oxford University Press, 1984), 100.

5. Robert Langbaum, *The Poetry of Experience: The Dramatic Monologue in Modern Literary Tradition* (New York: W. W. Norton, 1957), 83.

6. Ludwig Wittgenstein, *Remarks on the Philosophy of Psychology*, 2 vols., ed. G. E. M. Anscombe and H. H. von Wright (Chicago: University of Chicago Press, 1980), vol. 2, sec. 72; hereafter cited as *PP2.*

7. See P. M. S. Hacker, *Wittgenstein: Meaning and Mind; Part I: Essays* (Oxford: Blackwell, 1990), 134. Of course it is also true that we speak as though dogs pretend when we say that they "play dead." We mean that they simulate not pain but the lack of any pain or feeling whatever. If we challenge ourselves on this point, however, we will find ourselves saying that, after all, dogs don't "really" play dead but rather that *we* play that they play dead, and that, to enhance our play, we *say* that dogs play dead, for the most part unaware that we do not fully mean what we say—that is, that we playfully mean something else.

8. Joseph Brodsky, "On Grief and Reason," *New Yorker,* 26 September 1994, 84, 82; Randall Jarrell, "Home Burial," in *The Third Book of Criticism* (New York: Farrar, Straus and Giroux, 1969), 191–231. Pritchard (*Frost,* 103) says that, for Frost, "the talk *is* all"; but this overlooks Frost's lively sense of the boundaries and limits of language.

9. Cf. Ludwig Wittgenstein, *The Blue and Brown Books* (New York: Harper and Row, 1965); and Stanley Cavell, *The Claim of Reason* (Oxford: Oxford University Press, 1979); hereafter cited as *CR.*

10. Hanna Fenichel Pitkin, *Wittgenstein and Justice* (Berkeley: University of California Press, 1972), 126.

11. Ibid., 120.

12. Stanley Cavell, "Must We Mean What We Say?" in *Must We Mean What We Say? A Book of Essays* (Cambridge: Cambridge University Press, 1969), 19.

13. Gilbert Ryle, "Knowing How and Knowing That," in *The Concept of Mind* (Chicago: University of Chicago Press, 1949), 25–61.

14. See especially Stanley Cavell, *The Senses of Walden*, expanded ed. (Chicago: University of Chicago Press, 1981); *This New Yet Unapproachable America* (Albuquerque, N.M.: Living Batch Press, 1989), hereafter cited as *NYUA; Conditions Handsome and Unhandsome: The Constitution of Emersonian Perfectionism* (Chicago: University of Chicago Press, 1990). To my knowledge, only John Hollander has recognized Cavell's specifically rhetorical abilities; see *Melodious Guile: Fictive Pattern in Poetic Language* (New Haven, Conn.: Yale University Press, 1988), 220. Also excellent is Herbert Marks, "The Counter-Intelligence of Robert Frost," *Yale Review* (1982): 554–78, and of course Richard Poirier, *Robert Frost: The Work of Knowing* (Stanford: Stanford University Press, 1990).

15. Stanley Cavell, "The Thought of Movies," in *Themes Out of School: Effects and Causes* (Chicago: University of Chicago Press, 1984 [hereafter cited as *T*]), 18: " . . . conceive the following possibility: that Emerson and Thoreau are the central founding thinkers of American culture but that this knowledge, though possessed by shifting bands of individuals, is not culturally possessed. It would be an expression of this possibility that no profession is responsible for them as thinkers. Mostly they do not exist for the American profession of philosophy; and the literary professions are mostly not in a position to preserve them in these terms." Cf. Richard Poirier, *Poetry and Pragmatism* (Cambridge: Cambridge University Press, 1992); *Robert Frost: The Work of Knowing;* and James M. Cox, "Robert Frost and the End of the New England Line," in Jac L. Tharpe, ed., *Frost: Centennial Essays* (Jackson: University Press of Mississippi, 1974), 545–61.

16. Cavell himself works toward complicating the distinction between "grammar" and "rhetoric" in his essay "Must We Mean What We Say?" 32, viewing semantic and pragmatic aspects of meaning interlocked with each other, just as Austin sees constative and performative aspects of language use; for an even stronger recognition of the continuity between grammar (hermeneutics) and rhetoric, see the introduction to the essay "Existentialism and Analytical Philosophy" and "The Politics of Interpretation (Politics as Opposed to What?)," in *T*, 197, 41–44. On the relations between hermeneutics and rhetoric, see Walter Jost and Michael J. Hyde, eds., *Rhetoric and Hermeneutics in Our Time* (New Haven, Conn.: Yale University Press, 1997).

17. On sight in Frost, see Reginald L. Cook, *Robert Frost: A Living Voice* (Amherst: University of Massachusetts Press, 1974), 115.

18. Actually Brodsky is observant about the word "see," though he misses its larger ramifications.

19. For more pertinent psychological speculations about *Frost's* motives, see Pritchard, *Frost*, 54: "The move to the farm at Derry may have been given further impetus by the sudden death from cholera of the Frosts' three-year-old first child, Elliott. Frost blamed himself for the tragedy, since he had neglected to call the family doctor, mistakenly relying instead on the advice of his mother's doctor who misdiagnosed the disease. The guilt, anger, sadness, and recriminations ensuing from Elliott's death are felt most painfully in 'Home Burial'. . . ."; also Fischer, *Cavell and Skepticism*, 38.

20. Margery Sabin makes this point when she writes that "[Jarrell's] essay in *Poetry and the Age* remains the most subtle and discriminating appreciation of Frost that we have, but Jarrell does not construct a way of thinking about speakers and speech" ("The Fate of the Frost Speaker," *Raritan* 2 [1982]: 129).

21. Marjorie Perloff, *Wittgenstein's Ladder: Poetic Language and the Strangeness of the Ordinary* (Chicago: University of Chicago Press, 1996), 183.

22. Fischer, *Cavell and Skepticism*, 62. It is generally understood that the Augustinian-Cartesian model of mind, knowledge, language, and self accords in important ways with the essentialism—call it the "metaphysics of presence"—upon which Wittgenstein's earlier *Tractatus Logico-Philosophicus* (1922) was raised. In that work Wittgenstein aligns a logical semanticism with a Cartesian "disengaged reason" to construct a rational method for achieving a neutral, certain, procedural, and ultimately extralinguistic knowledge of self and world as determinate entities. (The phrase "disengaged reason" is from Charles Taylor, *Sources of the Self: The Making of the Modern Identity* [Cambridge: Harvard University Press, 1989].) The problem with which Wittgenstein begins is this: ostensive definition (as the model for learning language) runs aground on the fact that mere *pointing* to an object, as the way to teach what a word means, fails to discriminate what is being pointed *at*—is it the color, shape, number, movement (see *PI*, §§1–5 *passim*)? Contrary to the impression that Wittgenstein gives here (for he was citing only *The Confessions*), Augustine shows in *De Magistro* ("The Teacher," in *Augustine: Earlier Writings*, vol. 6 of *The Library of Christian Classics*, trans. John H. S. Burleigh [Philadelphia: Westminster Press, 1953]) that he, too, is aware of this problem, though his solution (divine investment of meaning in the mind) could not be more opposed to the later Wittgenstein. (For a useful account of Augustine's essay, see Ann K. Clark, "Unity and Method in Augustine's *De Magistro*," *Augustinian Studies* 8 [1977]: 1–10; on Augustine and Descartes on these matters, see Taylor, *Sources of the Self*, 143–58; and for an account of Wittgenstein's method, Staten, *Wittgenstein and Derrida*, especially 99–108, and Newton Garver and Seung-Chong Lee, *Derrida and Wittgenstein* [Philadelphia: Temple University Press, 1994].) As is also known, this labeling account of language then furnished the model against which the *Philosophical Investigations* set itself (*PI*, preface, p. vi). Rather than replacing the former work with another

"theory," the later *Investigations* exemplifies a "method" or practice of thinking, fully instantiated only in creative application to new cases.

23. Frost consistently places the reader imagistically and thematically en route, usually at a turning point on the way, at some boundary or limit of one's world: at the point where two paths diverge in a wood ("The Road Not Taken"), at the edge of an ocean, or wood, or well curb ("Devotion," "Once By the Pacific," "A Dream Pang," "Stopping by Woods on a Snowy Evening," "For Once, Then, Something"), between heaven and earth ("Birches"), between consciousness and sleep ("An Old Man's Winter Night," "After Apple-Picking"), at midnight ("Snow," "The Need of Being Versed in Country Things") or noon ("The Vantage Point"), along a boundary or border or wall ("Blueberries," "Mending Wall," "A Time to Talk," "Two Look at Two"), at a window ("In the Home Stretch"), at the point of decision to continue or return ("The Telephone," "The Wood-Pile," "The Bearer of Evil Tidings"), at the surface or horizon ("Neither Out Far Nor In Deep"), between seasons ("The Oven Bird," "Two Tramps in Mud Time," "A Hillside Thaw," "A Boundless Moment" [*sic!*]), and many others.

24. Mikhail Bakhtin, *The Dialogic Imagination* (Austin: University of Texas Press, 1981), 248.

25. See *PI*, §308: "And now it looks as if we had denied mental processes. And naturally we don't want to deny them"; also Jacques Derrida, "Deconstruction and the Other," in Richard Kearney, *Dialogues with Contemporary Continental Thinkers: The Phenomenological Heritage* (Manchester: Manchester University Press, 1984), 123.

26. Robert Frost, "For Glory and For Use," *Gettysburg Review* 7 (1994): 96.

27. Pritchard, *Frost*, 146; John C. Kemp, *Robert Frost and New England: The Poet as Regionalist* (Princeton: Princeton University Press, 1979), 118; Reginald L. Cook, *The Dimensions of Robert Frost* (New York: Rinehart and Co., 1958), 130, 129. Also Philip L. Gerber, *Robert Frost* (Boston: Twayne Publishers, 1966), 120, 121: "She clutches her grief"; "She can only hate. . . ." So Eben Bass ("Frost's Poetry of Fear," in *On Frost: The Best from "American Literature,"* ed. Edwin H. Cady and Louis J. Budd [Durham, N.C.: Duke University Press, 1991], 78), argues that "[s]everal [Frost] poems show the man as outer by instinct, but tied to the 'inner' wife by love," and that in "Home Burial" the husband is "outer and does not see. . . ." Also Poirier, *Work of Knowing*, 130; Mordecai Marcus, *The Poems of Robert Frost: An Explication* (Boston: G. K. Hall and Co., 1991), 47; Jeffrey Meyers, *Robert Frost: A Biography* (Boston: Houghton Mifflin, 1996).

28. Pritchard, *Frost*, 100; Cook, *Dimensions*, 128.

29. Cook, *Dimensions*, 130.

30. Ibid.

31. The wife in the poem, for example, has regularly been charged by some critics with being "neurotic" or "possibly neurotic" (Cook, *Dimensions*, 130; Poirier,

Work of Knowing, 22) and "masochistic" (Frank Lentricchia, *Robert Frost: Modern Poetics and the Landscapes of the Self* [Durham: Duke University Press, 1975], 64), or (alternately) defended as being in an early stage of grief. The basis of such claims seems to be a body of either psychological studies or at least lore (the first variant), or of epiphanies and intuitions (often kept discreetly in the background) regarding inner reasons and motives properly divined (the second variant).

32. Writing this in the 1930s, Frost was reacting to the new, roughly Marxist interest in political poems and criticism; but the attitude persists: see *PP2*, 449.

33. Pritchard, *Frost*, 153; Poirier, *Work of Knowing*, 132.

34. Poirier, *Work of Knowing*, 132.

35. Paul Ricoeur, *The Conflict of Interpretations* (Evanston, Ill.: Northwestern University Press, 1974), 170.

36. See Ludwig Wittgenstein, *Lectures and Conversations on Aesthetics, Psychology and Religious Belief*, comp. from notes taken by Yorick Smythies, Rush Rhees, and James Taylor, ed. Cyril Bennet (Berkeley: University of California Press, n.d.), 41: "I [Rush Rhees] spoke of the harm it does to writing when an author tries to bring psychoanalysis into the story. 'Of course,' he [Wittgenstein] said, 'There's nothing worse.'"

37. Entangled in the texture—heard, as it were, but never seen or registered—are the following (in order of occurrence, excluding copulative forms of "to be"): "was," "will," "must" (line 12), "wouldn't," "didn't," "don't," "didn't" (line 20), "must," "don't" ("don't, don't, don't") (line 30), "can't," "don't," "must," "must," "don't," "don't," "won't" (line 40), "don't," "don't," "might," "should," "can't," "must," "could" (line 50), "[woul]'d," "don't," "don't," "can't," "do," "can't," "don't," "don't," "don't," "[a]'m," "would" (line 61), "do," "[woul]'d," "might," "[a]'m," "[a]'m," "[ha]'s," "can't" (line 70), "can't," "don't," "had," "could," "didn't," "don't" (line 82), "could," "had," "shall," "[a]'m," "don't," "[a]'m," (line 90), "can," "were," "will," "can," "had," "*couldn't*," "can," "might" (line 99), "won't," "can," "won't," "won't," "have," "won't," "[a]'re," "[ha]'s" (line 110), "must," "can," "was," "do," "[wi]'ll,"—and the last word of the poem—"*will*" (line 116).

38. Thus Jarrell, "Home Burial," notes the husband's use of "must" in line 12—"I will find out now—you must tell me, dear"—and calls this "the 'must' of rational necessity" (198). But he never explains, or justifies, what he means, and he never links this occurrence with the larger patterns indicated here. To me the appeal seems to be one of moral prescription, or perhaps like a cry of pain, help, or despair—or all three and something more.

39. Poirier (*Work of Knowing*, 134–35) shrewdly refers to "violations of decorum" but underestimates how the rules of decorum are being redrawn.

40. Bruns, *Inventions*, 117.

41. Ludwig Wittgenstein, *Zettel*, ed. G. E. M. Anscombe and G. H. von Wright (Berkeley: University of California Press, 1970) [hereafter cited as Z],

§225: " 'We *see* emotion.'—As opposed to what?—We do not see facial contortions and make inferences from them (like a doctor framing a diagnosis) to joy, grief, boredom. We describe a face immediately as sad, radiant, bored, even when we are unable to give any other descriptions of the features.—Grief, one would like to say, is personified in the face."

42. For *p* to be a "symptom" of *q*, one presupposes an independent means of identification of *q*. Thus, for a fever to be a "symptom" of infection, one needs some independent way of determining that there is, in fact, an infection. This is empirical. But criteria are normative: "To say that q is a criterion for W [e.g., grief] is to give a partial explanation of the meaning of W, and in that sense to give a rule for its correct use" (Hacker, *Wittgenstein*, 250). The presence of criteria and symptoms cannot logically guarantee the objective presence of their condition; but then, for Wittgenstein, the search for, and failure to achieve, such logical certainty and presence constitute part of the epistemological illusion of conceiving grief or pain as "inner." Instead, when it is thought of in terms of criteria and symptoms, pain or grief is to be simply "acknowledged" in the absence of any reasons not to.

43. Brodsky ("On Grief and Reason," 83) shares this claim—"Thus you've got a clash not just of two sensibilities but of two languages"—but he also argues that the poem is not "a tragedy of incommunicability" but "a tragedy of communication, for communication's logical end is the violation of your interlocutor's mental imperative" (82). Brodsky is no doubt right to urge the gap between, for example, the wife's emotion and the inadequacy of language; but here he insists on favoring the wife's perspective over the husband's to explain the poem as a whole. Frost explores *both* perspectives (and thus both the failure and potential of language), avoiding Brodsky's disjunction of what is at stake—a move that Brodsky allows in the back door later as a "fusion" of reason and grief (85).

44. Earlier we discovered the pitfalls awaiting us when we say that dogs pretend to be in pain or to play dead; but pretending in general is more involved than even these examples suggest. As a rule, not just one sign alone will suffice to alert us to pretending. On Halloween we are more likely to say of a friend that he is "dressed up like Winston Churchill" than that he is actually "pretending" to be Churchill, since pretending involves an effort to dissimulate one's own identity in ways that Halloween does not require. Of course, at the costume party the fellow dressed up like Churchill might take it upon himself to do an imitation, and we might later say that he was very good when he "pretended to be Churchill." For our purposes here, however, which fall well short of the full complexity of pretending, I want to examine one aspect that will prove especially pertinent to "Home Burial."

45. J. L. Austin, "Pretending," in *Philosophical Papers*, 3d ed. (Oxford: Oxford University Press, 1961), 259ff.

46. Cavell might call this somatisizing a "hysterical conversion," which, being associated (for both Cavell and Freud) with women more than men—although,

to be sure, Amy has her own symptoms (e.g., obsessive staring)—significantly conflates gender here, as Frost often does elsewhere. As Stephen Mulhall notes (introduction to *The Cavell Reader* [Oxford: Blackwell, 1996], 12ff.), such conversions may be thought positive phenomena in context inasmuch as they function much as recounting criteria do, that is, as affirmations of bodily reality over disembodied skepticism. See Stanley Cavell, "Psychoanalysis and Cinema: The Melodrama of the Unknown Woman," in *Images in Our Souls: Cavell, Psychoanalysis, and Cinema*, ed. Joseph H. Smith and Williams Kerrigan (Baltimore: Johns Hopkins University Press, 1987).

47. Fischer, *Cavell and Skepticism*, 73.

48. Ralph Waldo Emerson, "Experience," in *The Portable Emerson*, ed. Carl Bode (New York: Penguin, 1946), 266–90; emphasis added.

Reading, Writing, Re-Membering: What Cavell and Heidegger Call Thinking

Stephen Mulhall

Stanley Cavell's interest in Martin Heidegger's writings, both early and late, has lately become a more open secret; but the specific causes and effects of that investment, the ways in which the two thinkers repeatedly arrive at and depart from a seemingly endless sequence of common tropes and themes, largely remain an open question. My aim in this essay is to follow out a small number of these intellectual transactions in more detail, in the hope that this might prepare the ground for a more penetrating assessment of the fundamental terms of trade in this particular philosophical economy. Cavell's *The Claim of Reason*[1] and Heidegger's *What Is Called Thinking?*[2] will provide the textual focus; the essay will first lay out an aspect of their common thematic content and then turn to an aspect of their form or method—with the ultimate aim of demonstrating that this way of distinguishing those aspects is legitimate only as a means of securing its own supersession. Readers familiar with my introduction to *The Cavell Reader*[3] and my article "On Refusing to Begin"[4] will recognize certain stretches of the readings to follow. Without the context that their reiteration here works to provide, the ways in which I now feel able to go on from them into Heidegger's text would lack any justification.

1. Skepticism and Finitude: Cavell's Wittgenstein and Heidegger's Nietzsche

As its notorious opening sentence makes clear, *The Claim of Reason* is above all a reading of Wittgenstein; more particularly, it is a reading of Wittgenstein's notion of a criterion in relation to the problem of skepticism. On Cavell's account, Wittgensteinian criteria are the linguistic specifications in terms of which competent speakers judge the applicability of a particular concept. In this way they link human beings with one another and align them with the world; they tell us "what counts," in a dual sense of that phrase. First, criteria are criteria of individuation: In determining what counts as a chair or a table, they determine what differentiates a chair from a table. Second, criteria make manifest what counts for human beings: By determining how human beings individuate things, they trace the distinctions and connections which matter to them—the ones which count. Criteria are thus an expression of human interests, of those aspects of the world we deem significant enough to get a grip on; and our agreement in criteria is an expression of the ways in which our interests in and reactions to the things of the world are attuned. To agree in criteria means that we share routes of interest and feeling, modes of response, a sense of similarity, significance, outrageousness, and so on—that we share in what Wittgenstein calls forms of life.

On this account, criteria specify what must be the case if something is to count as an instance of a given kind, but they do not themselves claim that any given thing *is* of that kind; they articulate the grammar of the words we employ in judging the world and so are made manifest in those judgments, but they are not themselves judgments. It follows that criteria do not and cannot make the existence of any particular thing certain; thus their invocation cannot directly rebut skeptical doubts about the existence or reality of the external world (or of the existence or reality of human beings within it). To think otherwise would be to think that the expressibility of pain in behavior is something we believe to be the case or that the existence of material objects is something that we know to be the case—simple matters of fact. Skeptics are right to reject such views—this is one aspect of what Cavell calls the truth in skepticism; but they are wrong to combat those views by denying what their opponents attempt to assert, for that merely continues their misguided assumption that our relationship to the world is most fundamentally a matter of knowledge and judgment (merely reversing the signs from positive to negative). If the criteria for pain fix what is to count as pain, then they also fix what will count as evidence for or against someone's being in pain; and that means that no evidence can conceivably count either for or against the criteria themselves.

In other words, unhesitating belief in the truth of criteria as well as skeptical doubts about it are equally misplaced. Nevertheless, a skeptical repudiation of our agreement in criteria remains a standing human possibility, for anything essentially dependent upon consent must be vulnerable to its withdrawal. What then becomes critical in the philosophical response to skepticism is to measure the true cost of that repudiation. For if criteria govern the use, and so the meaning, of our words, to refuse them is to deprive oneself of the power of coherent speech. In short, the skeptics' predicament is that they find themselves compelled to say something other than what they meant, or to say nothing meaningful at all.

In part 4 of *The Claim of Reason*, Cavell explores the legitimacy of this diagnosis in the specific case of skepticism about other minds. The roots of this exploration lie in Wittgenstein's response to the skeptical claim that others can "learn of my sensations *only* from my behaviour" (*PI*, §246).[5] He points out that the remark's apparently unremarkable use of the word "only" implies the existence of another, superior route to the relevant knowledge—in this case, one utilized by the person whose sensation it is. But this in turn implies that a person in pain typically learns that she or he is in pain—thus picturing that person as distanced from her or his own sensations in just the way that the original skeptical claim was meant to deny (effectively eliminating the very difference between first and third person perspectives of which the skeptic originally took herself or himself to be reminding us). Cavell adds that this misuse of "only" seems expressive of the speaker's disappointment with behavior—not with some particularly ambiguous twitch or wince but with behavior as such, as if the speaker sees her or his body as standing in the way of other people's knowledge of her or his mind. But picturing one's body as an impenetrable integument places one's mind beyond reach in a way that satisfies a number of all-too-human desires:

> A fantasy of necessary inexpressiveness would . . . relieve me of the respon-sibility for making myself known to others—as though if I were expressive that would mean continuously betraying my experiences, incessantly giving myself away; it would suggest that my responsibility for self-knowledge takes care of itself—as though the fact that others cannot know my (inner) life means that I cannot fail to. It would reassure my fears of being known, though it may not prevent my being under suspicion; it would reassure my fears of not being known, though it may not prevent my being under indictment.—The wish underlying this fantasy covers a wish that underlies skepticism, a wish for the connection between my claims of knowledge and the objects upon which the claims are to fall to occur without my interven-tion, apart from my agreements. As the wish stands, it is unappeasable. (CR, 351–52)

Here, Cavell ends by suggesting that the skeptic repudiates criteria because she or he can—or, more precisely, because of what the fact that criteria are open to repudiation shows about them, namely, that they are ours, merely human, expressive of the differentiations and desires that count for human beings. The skeptical repudiation of criteria is thus an attempt to repudiate any merely human accounting of the world. Cavell elaborates the motivation and the consequences of such a repudiation toward the end of part 1 of *The Claim of Reason.*

First, the consequences. If criteria always both determine kinds of object and attribute value or interest to those kinds, then any philosopher who repudiates them loses the capacity to discriminate between and to respond to the phenom-ena of the world. By aiming to speak outside our language-games, philosophers annihilate the differences between the things of the world and deny that those things matter to them—they withdraw their investment of interest in it, are driven past caring for it. By stripping it of its variegated specificity and value, the world goes dead for them and recedes from their grasp; skeptics accomplish the death of the world and of their interest in it (which amounts to the death of a part of themselves).

Second, the motivation. Criteria constitute the limits or conditions of the human capacity to know, think, or speak about the world, but it is fatally easy to interpret limits as limitations, to experience conditions as constraints. This, as we have seen, is the skeptic's underlying assumption: Skeptics repudiate what we ordinarily count as knowledge because it appears anthropocentric, partial, and mediated. But it would make sense to think of the conditions of human knowledge as limitations only if we could conceive of another cognitive perspective upon the world that did not require them; and philosophers from Kant onward have variously striven to show that there is no such perspective—that the absence of the concepts in terms of which we individuate objects would not clear the way for unmediated knowledge of the world, but would rather remove the possibility of anything that might count as knowledge.

> [W]e want to know the world as we imagine God knows it. And that will be as easy to rid us of as it is to rid us of the prideful craving to be God—I mean to rid us of it, not to replace it with a despair at our finitude. (CR, 236–37)

In other words, what the skeptic understands as a process of disillusionment in the name of true knowledge, Cavell interprets as a despairing inability or refusal to acknowledge the fact that human knowledge—the knowledge available to finite creatures, subjective agents in an objective world—is necessarily conditioned. But then, as Cavell finds himself having to remind us, nothing is more human than the desire to deny the human, to interpret limits as limitations and to repudiate the human condition of conditionedness or finitude in the name of the unconditioned, the transcendent, the inhuman. Philosophical skepticism, flourishing in a culture conditioned by the death of God and the rise of the new science, thus appears as a modern inflection of the perennial human desire to deny one's own humanity.

The first part (at the very least) of Heidegger's *What is Called Thinking?* is largely devoted to a reading of Nietzsche and in particular to developing a Nietzschean interpretation of the spirit motivating our culture's devastating inclination to picture thinking as reflection, as a matter of forming ideas or representations of the world. This interpretation links that inclination to skepticism. Heidegger retrospectively makes these links explicit with a series of rhetorical questions:

> Could it be that this manner of forming ideas at bottom sets upon everything it sets before itself, in order to depose and decompose it? What manner

of thinking is it that sets all things up in such a way that fundamentally it pursues and sets upon them? (*WCT,* 84)

But the key ideas of deposition and decomposition are first set to work in his earlier, extraordinary discussion of the blossoming tree.

There Heidegger takes it that those of us who understand thinking to be a process of forming ideas will also take the sciences of psychology and neurophysiology to be the best way of investigating the nature of this process. Accordingly, when, for example, we perceive a tree in bloom, we will be inclined to investigate the nature of our experience by exploring whatever events are then taking place in our minds or brains.

> But—while science records the brain currents, what becomes of the tree in bloom? What becomes of the man—not of the brain but of the man, who may die under our hands tomorrow and be lost to us, and who at one time came to our encounter? What becomes of the face-to-face, the meeting, the seeing, the forming of the idea, in which the tree presents itself and man comes to stand face-to-face with the tree? (*WCT,* 42)

In Heidegger's view, what becomes of the tree is that it is declared to be unreal. It is transformed into "a void, thinly sprinkled with electric charges here and there that race hither and yon at enormous speeds" (*WCT,* 43), a sprinkling that becomes what we think of as a tree only in our consciousness; the earth on which it spreads its branches exists only in our head, its meadow only in our soul. In short, the representational theory of thinking "drops the blooming tree"; it "never lets the tree stand where it stands" (*WCT,* 44). Such theories both depose and decompose the tree. They decompose it into hypothesized constituents (electrons or psychic atoms) which the human subject must reconstitute in order to form the thing itself, and this amounts to the deposition of the tree from its proper place in the perceptual relation. The tree loses its authority as an independent being whose existence makes possible and whose nature governs our perception of it. Instead, the tree becomes an inner construct, whose existence and nature depend upon the subject's determining constitutive activity.

Heidegger cites Schopenhauer as exemplary of the philosophizing that underlies this movement of thought:

> [H]owever immeasurable and massive the world may be, yet its existence hangs by one single thin thread: and that is the given individual consciousness in which it is constituted. (*WCT,* 40)

If "the world is my ideal," then the very existence of that world and everything in it is subject to the threat of skepticism. But this threat is not a discovery about the way things are really set up between human beings and their world; it is rather created by a particular conceptualization of that relationship. We set up the world and its objects in such a way that we set upon them. Skeptical doubts assail us because we have assailed the independent reality of things by decomposing and thereby deposing them.

Heidegger takes Nietzsche to have seen what fuels this assault, when (in *Thus Spake Zarathustra*) he says:

> The spirit of revenge, my friends, has so far been the subject of man's best reflection; and wherever there was suffering, there punishment was also wanted. (quoted in *WCT,* 85)

Heidegger's reading is that skepticism about the external world is a punishment we impose on reality in revenge for some species of suffering that we take it to have inflicted on us. And since vengeance exacts an eye for an eye, he further implies that our decomposition and deposition of the world aims to inflict upon reality the kind of suffering that we take reality to have inflicted on us. We aim to avenge what we experience as its attack upon our independence and reality, its attempts to decompose and depose us. We do not allow the tree to stand where it stands because we take ourselves to have suffered from the tree's refusal to let us stand where we stand.

Heidegger further takes Nietzsche to indicate how and why we might have come to think such thoughts, when he defines the spirit of revenge as follows:

> This, yes, this alone is revenge itself, the will's revulsion against time and its "It was." (quoted in *WCT,* 93)

To begin with, the blossoming tree exemplifies the worldliness of our existence, the fact that we are environed and so always already standing outside ourselves before the reality of other existent beings. It forces us to attend to the fact that our experience is given to us, that it is something we suffer rather than dictate— that it is the experience of a finite creature. It tells us that the earth does not exist in our heads but that we exist on earth, and so it points to the earth's existence beyond us, to the fact that it will continue to exist beyond our deaths, that it will survive our own going whereas we could not survive its extinction. Second, the tree's blossom indicates its thralldom to the seasons and to processes of growth and decline. It thereby exemplifies the connection between time and alteration, forcing us to attend to the transitionality or becoming of existence.

By stressing that our being is both being-in-the-world and becoming, the blossoming tree doubly decomposes our sense of ourselves. Rather than underwriting any fantasies of absolute self-sufficiency or unconditionedness, it underlines a double articulation in human being, between the human being and her or his world, and between the human being as she or he was and as she or he can be. It is Heidegger's Nietzschean intuition that, rather than accept such a disarticulation, rather than acknowledge that we must suffer the world's otherness to us and our otherness to ourselves, human beings have disarticulated the world. They have preserved their own sense of independence by assailing that of the world, making its reality conditional upon our supposedly constitutive consciousness.

In this domain, however, motivation becomes consequence. For just as revenge understands itself to inflict that which it has suffered, so Heidegger understands revenge to suffer that which it inflicts.

> The revulsion of revenge remains chained to this "It was"; just as there lies concealed in all hatred the abysmal dependence upon that from which hatred at bottom always desires to make itself independent—but never can, and can all the less the more it hates. (*WCT,* 103–4)

Since human existence can never not be being-in-the-world and becoming, so the punishment the will inflicts on reality is necessarily a species of self-punishment. And since the punishment was decomposition, another passage from Nietzsche's *Zarathustra* (not quoted by Heidegger, but recently examined by Cavell)[6] can be taken to offer us a glimpse of its reflexive consequences:

> I see and have seen . . . things . . . so monstrous that I should not wish to speak of all of them; but of some of them I should not wish to be silent; and they are, men who lack everything except one thing, of which they have too much—men who are no more than a great eye or a great mouth or a great belly or something else great—I call such men inverse cripples. . . . Truly my friends, I walk among men as among the fragments and limbs of men! The terrible thing to my eye is to find men shattered in pieces and scattered as if over a battlefield of slaughter.[7]

These thoughtless men who hide within them the wasteland that Heidegger and Nietzsche perceive we have made of our culture are both monstrous and fragmented, at once reduced to a single part and to a scattering of many parts; and this is because, underneath it all, they cannot overcome their dependence on that upon which they wish to avenge themselves. As essentially worldly beings, their decomposition of the world must effect a self-decomposition, a disarticulation of the internal relation between human being and world; their revenge on the world fragments them. And as essentially transitional beings, their denial of worldly transience effects a denial of their own transience, their otherness to themselves. The articulation between themselves as they are and as they might become is recomposed as a single, fixated state, one in which they have turned away from self-transformation in favor of the single state they presently occupy. Their revenge on time deforms them into a single, monstrous part or fragment of themselves.

2. Fragment and Parataxis: The Lyric Drama of Modernist (De)Composition

Just as both Cavell and Heidegger aim to link skepticism with the denial of human finitude, so both perceive a connection between the goal of overcoming the skeptical impulse and the distinctive form of their writing—a connection hinging on two ideas: that dismemberment or decomposition can be overcome only by a mode of composition that is a form of remembering and that genuine thinking, like any genuinely human mode of existence, is a matter of knowing how to go on, of managing transitions, of maintaining an openness to becoming.

In Cavell's case, this connection emerges very early in *The Claim of Reason* through his sensitivity to the form of Wittgenstein's philosophical work. As he puts it, "while Wittgenstein's philosophizing is more completely attentive to the human voice than any other I think of, it strikes me that its teaching is essentially something written, that some things essential to its teaching cannot be spoken" (*CR*, 5). Cavell devotes the fourth (entirely parenthetical) paragraph of his opening to an elaboration of this impression.

(If one asks: When must a work, or task, be written, or permanently marked?, one may start thinking what makes a work, or task, memorable. . . . It seems to me that a thought I once expressed concerning the development of music relates to this. I said ["Music Discomposed," 200, 201] that at some point in Beethoven's work you can no longer relate what you hear to a process of improvisation. Here I should like to add the thought that at that point music, such music, must be written. If one may speculate that at such a stage a musical work of art requires parts that are unpredictable from one another [though after the fact, upon analysis, you may say how one is derivable from the other], then one may speculate further that Beethoven's sketches were necessary both because not all ideas are ready for use upon their appearance [because not ever ready in any but their right company], and also because not all are usable in their initial appearance, but must first, as it were, grow outside the womb. What must be sketched must be written. If what is in a sketch book is jotted just for saving, just to await its company, you may say the juxtaposition, or composition, is that of the lyric. If it is sketched knowing that it must be, and gets in time, transformed in order to take its place, you may say that its juxtaposition, or composition, is essentially stratified and partitioned; that of the drama; the drama of the metaphysical, or of the sonata. Here are different tasks for criticism, or tasks for different criticisms.) (*CR,* 5–6)

The general terms in which this elaboration is couched, taken together with the implicitly reflexive inflection of the opening of *The Claim of Reason* (which begins with a discussion of how to begin reading Wittgenstein), suggest to me that Cavell intends these words to contain guidance for reading not only Wittgenstein but the reading of Wittgenstein which it at once interrupts and introduces. Taken this way, what guidance does it offer? One reason for thinking that a certain teaching must be written is the idea that it would otherwise be impermanent; if it were not written, it would be forgotten. Presumably, then, it is written in the name of a past or future human circle, of a kind that our present (philosophical) culture cannot recall or create (remember or re-member). But why this inability to preserve this teaching? Cavell advances his present insight by recalling a claim from his earlier writing, as if that insight amounted to a rereading of his earlier self, a way of going on from it. It will help to have those past words, in which he describes Beethoven's earlier work, before us now.

One can hear, in the music in question, how the composition is related to, or could grow in familiar ways from, a process of improvisation; as though the parts meted out by the composer were re-enactments, or dramatizations, of successes his improvisations had discovered—given the finish and permanence the occasion deserves and the public demands, but containing essentially only such discoveries. . . . Somewhere in the development of Beethoven, this ceases to be imaginable.

Why might such a phenomenon occur? . . . The context in which we can hear music as improvisatory is one in which the language it employs, its conventions, are familiar or obvious enough (whether because simple or because they permit of a total mastery or perspicuity) that at no point are we or the performer in doubt about our location or goal; there are solutions to every problem, permitting the exercise of familiar forms of resourcefulness; a mistake is clearly recognizable as such, and may even present a chance to be seized; and just as the general range of chances is circumscribed, so there is a preparation for every chance, and if not an inspired one, then a formula for one. But in the late experience of Beethoven, it is as if our freedom to act no longer depends on the possibility of spontaneity; improvising to fit a given lack or need is no longer enough. The entire enterprise of action and of communication has become problematic. The problem is no longer how to do what you want, but to know what would satisfy you. We could also say: Convention as a whole is now looked upon not as a firm inheritance from the past, but as a continuing improvisation in the face of problems we no longer understand. Nothing we now have to say, no personal utterance, has its meaning conveyed in the conventions and formulas we now share. . . . Our choices seem to be those of silence, or nihilism (the denial of the value of shared meaning altogether), or statements so personal as to form the possibility of communication without the support of convention—perhaps to become the source of new convention. . . . Such, at any rate, are the choices which the modern works of art I know seem to me to have made. [8]

Add to this, as Cavell immediately does in his citation of it, the thought that at such a point, such music must be written, and the work of the *Investigations* and *The Claim of Reason* appears as essentially modernist. Their teaching is triply devoid of memorability. Its parts or elements can no longer be read as reenactments or memorials of insights originally discovered by improvisation, because neither writer nor readers possess a common fund of conventions which they might call upon to control their sense of what a philosophical problem is, what might count as its solution, what resources might be used to discover those solutions, and what might count as a mistaken resolution; and the absence of such familiar landmarks puts the direction of any exercise of philosophical thinking, and so the task of predicting or recalling its progress in the absence of a permanent record of it, essentially beyond us. In these conditions, philosophical teaching must be written, and written in face of the thought that the entire enterprise of creative thinking has become problematic, that thinkers in the present circumstances of human culture lack any grasp of what they want of thinking, let alone how to achieve it. In short, there are no given philosophical conventions; the present philosophical task is continuously to improvise them, and to do so through the writing of texts that offer statements so personal as to permit communication without convention, or the origination of new conventions.

Heidegger could hardly avoid seeing in this account a version of his own analysis of the devastation of modern culture and the disorientation of what is presently called thinking, and of his own account of himself as attempting to turn away from such thoughtlessness by turning toward what can genuinely satisfy our desire to attend to the essence of things. But this account is also an apt description of the sentences of *The Claim of Reason*, and Cavell's incorporation of his earlier writing within these later sentences enacts that description's sense that the directions opened up for a modernist philosopher even by his own earlier sentences are essentially unpredictable—that the orientation they provide will unfold in ways beyond any contemporaneous grasping (although not beyond any retrospective accounting), when they attain a certain kind of otherness to, a relative autonomy from, their own author. In addition, however, this parenthetical paragraph also contains an account of certain modes of composition toward which writing in the condition of modernism naturally gravitates (those of the lyric and the drama) that offer insight into the structure of *The Claim of Reason* as a whole, as a book or text.

The text is thematically articulated into four parts, involving (according to the book's subtitle) a reading of Wittgenstein, an exploration of skepticism, a set of forays into moral philosophy, and an examination of relations between skepticism about other minds and tragedy. But the book's foreword suggests that it might be decomposed otherwise, along a biographical or autobiographical axis linking the form of the text to the intellectual trajectory of its author, for it was originally supposed to be a revision of Cavell's 1961 dissertation. And although we are told that "it is no more properly speaking a revision than its predecessor was properly speaking a dissertation" (CR, xi), we are also told that it could not have appeared had Cavell not decided that the central two-thirds of that dissertation, with its original structure and ideas and prose broadly intact, could be included within it (CR, xv); so the concept of "revision" must be understood as being itself revised rather than jettisoned. In these terms, the book consists of the following parts: the concluding, more or less heavily edited, two-thirds of the dissertation (parts 2 and 3); original dissertation material interspersed with more recent passages (part 1); and thirty pages of 1960s lecture notes introducing writing more recent than anything Cavell had published in 1979 (part 4).

Given this, would we want to say that *The Claim of Reason* is a lyric or a dramatic composition? Were its elements fully formed on their first appearance and written down only to await their right company; or were they preserved so that they might grow outside the womb, to allow the transformations through which they might find their proper place? On the one hand, parts 2 and 3 appear as reduced but otherwise unaltered from their original dissertation appearance. Their pairing is intended to facilitate comparisons and contrasts between epistemological and moral debates (CR, 250) and so amounts to juxtaposing independently establishable sketches of two modes of claim assessment; and the reader's sense of shock in making the transition from part 3 to part 4, thereby encountering prose possessed of a very different range, complexity, and intensity, indicates that parts 3 and 4 appear to be at best related by juxtaposition—with neither adapting to or accommodating the specificities of the other's style and substance. On the other hand, Cavell's description of the dramatic mode of composition as "essentially stratified and partitioned" seems an apt characterization of *The Claim of Reason* as a whole: It is partitioned into four portions and multiply stratified by its shifting periods of composition and its alterations of textual telos. Moreover, part 1 has been heavily revised, parts 2 and 3 have at least been edited in order to take their place in this company, and part 4 is itself composed of passages that appear to progress by constant self-revision or evolution.

If the question of this book's composition concerns both its structural integrity as a whole and the nature of its parts or elements, then our answer to it depends upon whether we read those parts as prefabricated units or as organically premature—as building blocks or body parts. The fact that the textual indications point to two different answers shows, I believe, not that we can read the book either as a lyric or a dramatic composition but rather that we must read it as both. This is the book's theory of itself—as composed of fragments, as essentially fragmentary. As Schlegel's aphorism has it: "Many works of the ancients have become fragments. Many works of the moderns are fragments right from their beginning."[9] This confirms and further specifies *The Claim of Reason*'s sense of itself as a modernist work. Taken dramatically, the book's fragments will appear as both embryos and members—each is capable of further growth (even if outside the womb), but each thereby grows toward taking its place as a member of, to re-member, a larger organic whole. But there remains the undeniable sense that this book does not quite achieve such wholeness, that it remains somehow fragmentary, its members never shaking off the aura or memory of dismemberment, perhaps because they aren't meant to do so. We might then ask why this air of the embryonic is internal to the book's work; and if we now take its fragmentariness in lyric terms—in terms of building blocks rather than body parts—we may start thinking of the book as an edifice arising from ruins, and of its material as stones, slabs, pillars, and blocks strewn along the ground.

Such an image recalls the work of the builders at the opening of the *Investigations*. It also recalls Wittgenstein's sense that philosophy as he practices it destroys everything that is important, "[as] it were all the buildings, leaving behind only bits of stone and rubble" (*PI*, §118), against which Wittgenstein claims that he is only "clearing up the ground of language" on which structures of air, philosophical houses of cards, once stood. So is a modernist philosophical text engaged in destruction or reconstruction, or both, or neither? Is destroying structures of air true destruction? Is clearing up the ground of language on which they stood a form of construction, or reconstruction, or a preparation for (re)construction? What are the materials for such a project, and what does it aim to build? From what we have learned so far, we might say: The birth or rebirth of a new human circle, which means a new dispensation of culture, one which dispenses with the present illusion of cultivation in the name of a possibility of genuinely creative thought, of a form of life in which thinkers (which means language users, which means all human beings) can discover genuine satisfaction, in which the fragments of past communities of meaningful thought and value can be used in the reconstruction of new but personally authorized conventions. In such a circle, what Wittgenstein and Cavell hope to teach can indeed be usefully said. But since the texts they now write are composed in the name of that future possibility and in the shadow of the present actuality, on a ground where construction is possible but only with the ruins of the past and amid the ruination of the present, they must take on a form that is both dismembered and embryonic, a half-built edifice whose form acknowledges both its origin in ruins and the completion it foreshadows.

The words of *What Is Called Thinking?* confront their readers from the outset with the distinction between oral and scriptural modes of the human voice that framed Cavell's perception of Wittgenstein's and his own reliance upon the memorability of their writing. For, of course, Heidegger's words are presented as transcriptions of lectures—and thus at once as mere representations of the original oral performance—and yet also as the indispensable supplement or fulfillment of the intentions of that prior drama (for if Heidegger thought of the original lectures as having essentially done their work, or if he thought that their work was essentially dependent upon their oral delivery, then the idea of publishing written versions of them would have appeared either superfluous or self-subverting). The implication would appear to be that the work of the lectures depends upon composing words in such a way as to retain the marks of speech, but speech that essentially looks forward to its remarking in writing.

The most obvious fact about the form of the written text is that it is divided into lectures which are divided from each other by passages entitled "Summary and Transition." The overt point of these passages is that they allow the lecturer to go over the key points of the preceding presentation and prepare the ground for the next, an acknowledgment of the difficulty of attaining a perspicuous overview of thoughts delivered to the ear rather than the eye. But then, of course, they would have absolutely no place in a written record of the lectures. And yet Heidegger preserves them there, as if inviting us to listen to his text as well as look at it. Moreover, the content of these passages uniformly exceeds the purposes acknowledged in their common title. In reiterating and presaging material from the lectures, Heidegger takes steps that are nowhere else taken and that are as absolutely indispensable to his progress as anything in the lectures proper. In this sense, the lectures could as easily be read as transitional between the passages of summary and transition; more precisely, each portion of the text is essentially transitional, because the text as a whole is essentially transitional—it enacts Heidegger's Nietzschean picture of the genuine thinker, like the genuine human being, as essentially in transition.

> Man, unless he stops with the type of man as he is, is a passage, a transition; he is a bridge; he is, "a rope strung between the animal and the superman." (*WCT,* 60)

To be human is to point beyond oneself and thus to represent the standard of genuine humanity to others, to show that they too must become transitional, that humanity is achieved and maintained precisely not by achieving and maintaining some particular self-understanding but by achieving and maintaining transitionality, by seeing any particular self-understanding as essentially self-overcoming, as a shell from which another, more authentic self-understanding can and must emerge.

For any thinker, then, progress on the way of thought will be a matter of reading oneself, of deriving guidance for the future from one's best past self-understanding. Heidegger composes such readings in a number of ways in these lectures, two examples of which must suffice to illustrate his general approach. The first relates to his early claim that thinking is a handicraft, a claim he develops as follows:

> "Craft" literally means the strength and skill in our hands. The hand is a peculiar thing. In the common view, the hand is part of our bodily organism. But the hand's essence can never be determined, or explained, by its being an organ which can grasp. Apes, too, have organs that can grasp, but they do not have hands. The hand is infinitely different from all grasping organs—paws, claws or fangs—different by an abyss of essence. Only a being who can speak, that is, think, can have hands and can be handy in achieving works of handicraft. The hand does not only grasp and catch, or push and pull. The hand reaches and extends, receives and welcomes—and not just things: the hand extends itself, and receives its own welcome in the hands of others. The hand holds. The hand carries. The hand designs and signs, presumably because man is a sign. Two hands fold into one, a gesture meant to carry man into the great oneness. The hand is all this, and this is the true handicraft. (*WCT,* 16)

There is far more in this passage than can be drawn out in these pages. But those of its readers aware that the concept of the hand was utterly central to the first division of Heidegger's early work *Being and Time* cannot avoid understanding the passage as a meditation upon the strengths and weaknesses of its influence in that work, a revision of that famous, originating division between readiness-to-hand and presence-at-hand.

In one way, the reminder acts as a rebuttal to those who would condemn the Heidegger of *Being and Time* for passing over the fact of human embodiment in his fundamental ontology of Dasein. Since Heidegger's uncovering of the worldliness of Dasein turns precisely upon the ontological structures that reveal themselves when the handiness of equipment is disrupted, it would be more correct to say that his account insists upon the internal relation between human embodiment and our inhabitation of a world. We could then read Heidegger's strangely unsuspicious opening acceptance of the traditional definition of human beings as rational animals (*WCT,* 3) to continue the line of this thought, by signaling his intention to reincarnate the essentially disembodied conceptions of the human capacity to think that dominate that tradition (and its readings of its own definition).

At the same time, however, Heidegger's revised account of the hand is undeniably self-critical. In particular, the famous early example of the handy hammer fits far too easily into a picture of the hand as grasping, pushing, and pulling. The talk of handicraft in this passage is precisely designed to shift our attention from the active, imposing, clutching connotations of the hand (and thus implicitly from the hammering hammer and its picture of human worldliness as primarily a matter of occupying an arena in which to transform objects in the service of human goals and purposes) to its more receptive implications to the idea that one most properly attains the essence of beings by allowing oneself to be struck or impressed by them, by allowing their essence to come to realization through our actions, thoughts, and words. Heidegger's point is not that mere possession of a hand (as opposed to paws, claws, or fangs) will guarantee such receptivity in thinking and in existing but rather that unless our thought handles things in a receptive, welcoming way, it will grasp or catch at them in a way that makes the human relation to things indistinguishable from that effected by paws, claws, and fangs. As we saw earlier with Schopenhauer, prevailing human ideas of thinking have pictured this handicraft as a way of clutching or setting upon its objects— the very idea of a concept (*Begriff*) contains the idea of grasping (*greifen*)—and have helped thereby to generate the wasteland of thoughtlessness of which Nietzsche speaks.

What Is Called Thinking? works through such implicit criticisms of Heidegger's earlier thought in a number of places, but its author's capacity to treat his own words as transitional is even more radical than that. For Heidegger relates himself to the thought which initiates the whole sequence of lectures—"Most thought-provoking in our thought-provoking time is that we are still not thinking" (*WCT*, 6)—in a peculiarly distanced and impersonal way. He italicizes the sentence, as if quoting from another source; he makes interpretative starts which turn out to be false; he asks us to weigh the relevant words carefully and separately and justifies inferences about the implications of the thought solely by reference to the precise form and content of its linguistic expression. Heidegger's refusal to short-circuit his explorations simply by declaring his intentions in so formulating his thought and the obtrusiveness with which he avoids utilizing the authority over a speech act's meaning which we typically attribute to the person who is engaged in it suggest that in his view the best way to learn from one's own thoughts is to treat them as one would the thoughts of another—as if they can best bear fruit for the future if one takes them as an expression of a self-conception, and so an aspect of oneself, from which one has already departed or become distanced. The procedure enacts Heidegger's conviction that genuinely to take thought is to become other to oneself, unendingly to use oneself (even one's most recent self) to go beyond oneself, relating to one's actual understanding of the realm of thought as that from which one's more authentic, unattained but attainable understanding of that realm can and must be born.

Heidegger later characterizes his receptive, nongrasping or clutching, manner of reading—both his own thought and the thoughts of others—by means of a number of figures or images. The first relates to a seasonal image of the harvest:

> We normally understand by reading only this, that we grasp and follow a script and written matter. But that is done by gathering the letters. Without this gathering, without a gleaning in the sense in which wheat or grapes are gleaned, we should never be able to read a single word, however keenly we observe the written signs. (*WCT,* 208)

We gather that Heidegger wishes to think of reading as food and drink for the thinker, and of words as the sacraments of a secular communion, a way in which human handicraft reaches out, extends, and welcomes. But the picture is complicated by his earlier acknowledgment of a connection between language and gaming:

> We are here venturing into the gambling game of language, where our nature is at stake. (*WCT,* 128)

Reading words is akin to a gambling game: the stake is our nature as thinking beings, the wager is that the hand of words (the cards or the lot) that we draw will give us the resources we need to draw again when the round is over, to continue in the game of allowing our words to determine our destiny as thinkers. Heidegger further claims that words must be understood not as buckets but as wells.

> Words are not terms, and thus are not like buckets and kegs from which we scoop a content that is there. Words are wellsprings that are found and dug up in the telling, wellsprings that must be found and dug up again and again, that easily cave in, but that at times also well up when least expected. (*WCT,* 130)

To think of words as conventional, as marks that human beings fill with or empty of sense, is to think of them as vessels from which meaning can be scooped, as if by a paw or claw; it is to set up words to set upon them, to handle them unthinkingly. To think of them as wellsprings is to think of their meaningfulness as theirs to preserve and dispense, as always already laid out in the landscape of language. We may have to uncover the wellspring, but the water that pumps out does so under its own pressure—it gives itself to those who can divine its subterranean presence. And for

Heidegger, such divination must be sensitive to the strata of the past beneath the ground of the present; it involves a responsiveness to words as historical entities, a receptivity to the etymological traces they continue to preserve of past significance and of the losing and winning gambles of their translation from one language or culture into another.

Heidegger finally allows Hölderlin to draw together his images of harvest and history by connecting well shafts with plowed fields:

> "It is useful for the rock to have shafts / And for the earth, furrows. . . ." Shafts are no more necessary to the rock than furrows to the earth. But it belongs to the essence of welcome and being at home that it include the welling of water and the fruits of the field. "It is useful" says here: there is an essential community between rock and shaft, between furrow and earth, within that realm of being which opens up when the earth becomes a habitation. (*WCT*, 190–91)

Thus, thoughtful reading is associated with establishing a dwelling place in the wasteland; and it does so by associating words as wellsprings with words as furrows—reminding us that lines of words on a page are raked or plowed in parallel straight lines and so can (if properly irrigated from the wellsprings of their history) bloom and bear fruit for the gleaning.

It is toward such gleaning that Heidegger's climactic reading of Parmenides is devoted. He begins by inserting three colons into the received text "to give a sharper articulation to its word structure" (*WCT*, 182); he thus dismembers the traditional translation into four parts (so that it reads "Needful: the saying also thinking too: being: to be"), and retranslates each of the four elements thereby differentiated. Talking specifically about the first two of these elements, he calls this procedure paratactic as opposed to syntactic reading.

> In our saying, the words follow upon each other without connection. They are lined up side by side. . . . The word order of our saying is paratactic and not, as the usual translation represents it: "One should both say and think that." By this "both" and "that" the words are put in a specific order. The connection co-ordinates them, puts them together in an order . . . by inserting connecting words. In regard to its word order, the translation is syntactic. (*WCT*, 183)

Syntactic translation imports connections into Parmenides' thought that are not there in the original language; the autonomous reality of his words is denied, an order originating in the reader being imposed upon them in order to make them conform with given notions of completeness or sophistication in thought and expression. For Heidegger, this is simply one more example of the way in-authentic thinking is grasping or coercive. Syntactic reading, like thinking on the Kantian model of synthesis, imposes an alien order on its objects because it presupposes that the elements of which that object appears to be made are fragments or precursors of a more sophisticated integrity or wholeness. Just as the first moment of the Kantian transcendental synthesis (that of the apprehension of the given as a manifold) involves grasping the given in terms of elements suitable for the reintegrating functions of the understanding, so syntactic readings of a text must begin by imposing a suitable fragmentation if they are later to impose a reintegration.

By contrast, Heidegger's paratactic reading minimizes the order it imposes on Parmenides' words by restricting itself at the outset to acknowledging their spatial order, the line or furrow of juxtaposed marks they trace out on the page. Any further connections it elaborates are driven purely by an intensive gleaning of the historical wellspring represented by each individual word; in effect, the connections that it posits well up from the words themselves, from the neigh-borliness or nearness to one another that their meanings establish. And in fact, each word turns out to support and be supported by its neighbors. Just as the separate words in the second, third, and fourth phrases ("letting-lie-before-us," "taking-to-heart," and "the presence of what is present," according to Heidegger's revised translation) are interwoven with their fellow words, so the three phrases are internally related to one another and to the phrase that precedes them ("It is useful"). All four hang together by pointing us toward other links in the lexical chain set up by the ideas of the hand, memory, and thanking. What results from a paratactic approach is thus the kind of remembering which recounts an existing neighborliness in language, an endless chain of translation that is the linguistic equivalent of the transitionality of human existence, rather than one which must obliterate any preexisting connectedness by means of a disarticulation along lines that will facilitate the kind of reintegration it always already wanted to impose.

3. Conclusion: Further Steps

The next links in the chain of intellectual exchanges that this essay has attempted to recount would aim to justify at least the following intuitions: that Cavell's talk of dramatic and lyric modes of composition might usefully characterize Heidegger's governing notion of paratactic reading and writing; that Cavell would recognize in Heidegger's imagery of reading as gleaning and gambling, and words as wells and furrows, an instance of what he calls a "mythological" register of utterance (CR, 364), a register which he employs throughout the fourth part of The Claim of Reason; and that Heidegger's moves along chains of neighboring words (for example, his opening lecture's modulations from animality to want to desire to interest to inclination) might usefully be thought of as responsive to what Cavell calls the aesthetics and economics of speech (to the ways in which given orderings of words might sustain or subvert authentically human desires and genuinely human interests [CR 94–95]). But no philosophical economy of any significance can cease to generate new exchanges; so no genuinely receptive reading of it can hope to find an end that is not also a beginning.

Notes

1. Stanley Cavell, *The Claim of Reason: Wittgenstein, Skepticism, Morality, and Tragedy* (Oxford: Oxford University Press, 1979); hereafter cited as *CR*.

2. Martin Heidegger, *What Is Called Thinking?* trans. J. Glenn Gray (New York: Harper and Row, 1968); hereafter cited as *WCT*.

3. Stephen Mulhall, *The Cavell Reader* (Oxford: Blackwell, 1996).

4. Stephen Mulhall, "On Refusing to Begin," *Common Knowledge* 5 (1996): 25–41.

5. Ludwig Wittgenstein, *Philosophical Investigations*, trans. G. E. M. Anscombe (New York: Macmillan, 1953); hereafter cited as *PI*, with Wittgenstein's numbered paragraphs, or "remarks," indicated by the symbol §.

6. In Stanley Cavell, *A Pitch of Philosophy* (Cambridge: Harvard University Press, 1994), 46.

7. Friedrich Nietzsche, *Thus Spake Zarathustra*, trans. R. J. Hollingdale (London: Penguin, 1961), 160.

8. Stanley Cavell, *Must We Mean What We Say? A Book of Essays* (Cambridge: Cambridge University Press, 1969), 200–2.

9. August Schlegel, "The 24th Athenaeum Fragment," in *Lucinde and the Fragments*, trans. P. Firchow (Minneapolis: University of Minnesota Press, 1971).

The Grammar of Telling:
The Example of Don Quixote

Anthony J. Cascardi

1

At one point in the *Philosophical Investigations*, Ludwig Wittgenstein makes some remarks about *telling*; they would not, on the surface of it, seem the most auspicious place to begin an essay on the grammar of telling, but there are reasons for taking up Wittgenstein which will, I think, become clear over the course of what follows: "'But when I imagine something, something certainly *happens!'* Well, something happens—and then I make a noise. What for? Presumably in order to tell what happens.—But how is *telling* done? When are we said to *tell* anything?—What is the language-game of telling? I should like to say you regard it much too much as a matter of course that one can tell anything to anyone."[1] You cannot, of course, tell *just* anything to anyone; telling has its occasions like any other human practice.[2] You cannot, for instance, just tell me your name—unless I ask or unless you propose thereby to accomplish some other action (for example, to introduce yourself). Yet notwithstanding such constraints of occasion, Wittgenstein's remark is likely to seem either excessively cautionary or simply superfluous in light of the ordinary kinds of telling we do: I can tell you a secret, tell you the (awful, whole, and so on) truth, tell you my love, tell you a story, or even tell you off, in which cases I apparently *do* tell something to someone. And I can also tell time, tell if it looks like rain, tell a forgery, and tell when I've had enough, in which case there is no temptation to say that I tell anything to *anyone* at all.

In order to make sense of Wittgenstein's remark, we need to look more closely at the grammar of telling. Here, I shall limit my considerations to some of the most salient features of telling, broadly understood, drawing on Cervantes's *Don Quixote* for my specific examples; the *Quixote*, it seems to me, marks the distinctions among certain kinds of telling with great clarity, while at the same time revealing common features among them that we can describe as part of a single grammar or "language-game." The first distinction I shall make cuts across the classes of telling described previously. The one is telling in an *epistemological* sense, telling as discerning or distinguishing (for example, "to tell twins apart"), in which case the telling is patently a kind of knowing; the other is telling in a narrative sense, as in telling a story or a tale. Beyond this distinction, however, I want to propose that epistemological telling is grounded in the narrative mode and that both are alike in that they grant certain privileges to the teller. The teller's "privilege" is his or her special relationship to the telling itself: in the case of epistemological telling, his or her right to a claim of knowledge, and in the case of narrative telling, his or her (implicit or explicit) right to the tale.[3] As I shall say, none of this requires us to think that in either kind of telling there is something behind or beyond the telling itself which is told, and seeing how this is so should help explain the sense of Wittgenstein's remarks. Besides doing that, however, this will show what it is about the narrative function of telling that might allow us to grant tellers a privilege on the basis of the narrative grounds of their telling—namely, the *rational* nature of narrative itself.

I shall begin with epistemological telling and with various bases of appeal which may be sought for the claims of knowledge which such tellings express. My purpose is to show, for the case of *Don Quixote*, at least (a case that is in turn paradigmatic of the question raised by the existence of fiction, which I shall say is the question of skepticism), that these bases are not sufficient to certify the truth value of epistemological claims (tellings) in the face of the kinds of radical doubts or gross discrepancies that occur between things said by Don Quixote and by the other characters in the novel. The actions of the *Quixote* turn on such problems of epistemological telling, that is, the contrasting identification of specific objects made by Don Quixote on the one hand and by Sancho Panza and the townspeople of La Mancha on the other. As the novel proceeds, this pattern is disrupted in the spirit of practical joking, but it is enough to start with the more familiar and orthodox incidents: Don Quixote identifies a castle where the innkeeper identifies an inn; he takes as giants what Sancho tells him are windmills and as an advancing army what the Squire assures him is a flock of sheep; where the barber identifies a barber's basin, Don Quixote identifies Mambrino's fabled helmet. When we find that epistemological procedures fail to provide a basis for the identification of objects such as these, our knowledge (identification) of them may be found in a narrative mode of telling, whose appropriate mark is not truth but rationality.

There are two ways by which one might begin to establish the identity of such things, hence two classes of what one would recognize as "bases" for saying that something is so: either by reference to the *object* and its attendant circumstances or by reference to the acumen, ability, or competence of the *person* making the claim. These are the two lines of epistemological inquiry which J. L. Austin, to take a representative case, sets forth in his essay "Other Minds."[4] But it can be shown that Austin's epistemology is unable to deal with the problems raised by *Don Quixote* or by the problem of fiction as such; and it is here, I would suggest, that Wittgenstein's procedures, rather than Austin's, are of greater avail.

The innkeeper in *Don Quixote* might point out some feature of the building in question or, more completely, make a list of the features that Don Quixote has mistaken or failed to notice. (Austin: "I indicate, or to some extent set out with some degree of precision, those features of the situation which enable me to recognize it as one to be described in the way I did describe it" ["OM," 83].) But the procedure of pointing out features will present a problem when dealing with someone like Don Quixote, whose telling differs so vastly from ours. Certainly we cannot say that Don Quixote has simply failed to notice a certain set of traits when misidentifying the inn. One is tempted to say instead, in this case, not that there is *some* difference between two objects but that there is *every* difference between them. One might as well start a list of the significant features anywhere as nowhere, because there is everything to describe and no sufficient description to be had (that is, none that would prove, to the satisfaction of the epistemologist, that this is an inn). If someone can so much as imagine something—which is of course exactly what the novelist must do—then it might always be something else. Perhaps that is why, rather than attempt to provide Don Quixote with a list of the distinguishing traits of the inn, the innkeeper demurs, deciding instead to humor him.

Similarly, all account of the claimer's right to the claim on the basis of appeal to his special experience, learning, or training is no more insurance against skeptical threats than is any list of an object's features. In Don Quixote's encounter with the innkeeper, as throughout most of the early adventures of the novel, what come under scrutiny are common and ordinary objects, not specialized things— objects whose identification should be perfectly obvious to anyone at all. This is in sharp contrast to Austin's model of the epistemological investigation, where we are customarily asked to consider "specialized" examples. To see this difference is to see that Austin's procedures are meant to model problems of knowledge on cases which can be resolved by epistemological means and so to avert rather than to answer skepticism, whereas the problem of "telling" in the *Quixote*, as in Wittgenstein's *Philosophical Investigations*, courts skepticism at every step. The failure to tell a gold*finch* from a gold*crest* (an Austinian example) may be explained by someone's deficient training, but there is no special training which will seem very pertinent in the face of someone's failure to identify such ordinary objects as inns, windmills, or barbers' basins. Similarly, that is why Wittgenstein, at the beginning of *On Certainty*, takes up G. E. Moore's case that "here is one hand"; if that much could be proved then, as Wittgenstein went on to say, "we'll grant you all the rest."[5] There is no reply to someone who offers, as grounds for his knowledge that *this is a hand*, that he has "very good credentials" for knowing it. There is no special training which might be offered as grounds for such knowledge, not because of an extraordinary feature of the training required but rather because of what knowledge in such ordinary cases is. On Wittgenstein's account, it is not a matter of epistemology but depends rather on what he calls a "form of life."

The discrepancies we see in the *Quixote* characteristically center on individual objects, yet they raise the more pervasive, general doubt that we may be unable to be certain in our knowledge of the world. Perhaps that is why these discrepancies cannot be explained in terms of epistemology alone. What separates Don Quixote from the others in the book is something closer to the differences in forms of life that Wittgenstein imagines among different groups of people; in *The Blue and Brown Books*, he refers to these groups as different "tribes." Such discrepancies fall within the range of cases covered only by the objection to an Austinian epistemological account that says "But that's not enough. . . . What you say doesn't prove it," the suggestion being that a given object might in fact be *anything*—anything I can so much as imagine. This objection, and the discrepancies in *Don Quixote* that resemble it, suggest also that all that is necessary for skepticism is the ability to imagine the world, to form and use concepts—which is to say the ability to imagine a language, at least insofar as Wittgenstein says that "to imagine a language means to imagine a form of life" (*PI*, §19). (Following Wittgenstein's approach, it could thus be said that fiction differs from nonfiction not in essence but in kind.)

In the skeptical objection registered earlier, "enough" is not meant to cover questions about the reality of objects but rather means "enough to show that (within reason and for present intents and purposes) it 'can't' be anything else, [that] there is no room for an alternative, competing description of it" ("OM," 84). In the *Quixote*, however, as in any world, one does not immediately know what "enough" would be. For every feature of an object in question, Don Quixote may give an "alternative, competing description" of it, so that one does not so much as know where to start working toward "enough." "Enough" would have to mean telling everything about an object, a telling which might be endless. Endless telling would provide the exhaustive description of objects or a world, but we know in advance that no description may ever be complete. Indeed, we customarily do arrive at a point where we are willing to say that "enough is enough." However, it is important to know that, were we challenged further, we could continue our account in a consistent and coherent fashion. Then our ability to go on will be the sign not necessarily that we have gotten the object or the world right but of our rationality in saying what we say and in doing what we do. In that case, a competing description of an object will no longer look like a claim entered from outside the bounds of reason; rather, it will be seen as within the bounds of reason, that is, for (someone's) present intents and purposes.

To be able to tell what a giant, a castle, a helmet, and so forth are is to be able to sustain a (consistent and coherent) form of life with such objects. When the one who is doing the telling can sustain such a form of life, then we do not, or ought not, question further; his telling is privileged not by what he "knows" nor by what he says but by what he does, by his ability to "go on." That does not mean that he has any greater or closer access to information than we do; indeed, if that were the case, then we should ask him to publicize the information and judge what he tells us on that basis. Instead, we appraise his telling in the ways we would appraise a narrative account. In suggesting that the nature of narrative is a model for the rationality of our "forms of life," I am thinking for instance of the children Wittgenstein describes in the *Brown Book* in connection with the most primitive forms of narration. In one example, a child has learned the name of a dozen or so toys and has played with three of them, a ball, a stick, and a rattle. A grown-up takes the toys away and on one occasion says "He's had a ball, a stick, and a rattle"; on a second occasion, the grown-up does the same but leaves the list of toys incomplete and induces the child to finish it, and so on, until he prompts the child only with the words "He's had," and finally only with his facial expression of expectancy.[6] When the child is able to go on—on his own—with the story of these objects, then we will have to grant him certain privileges in relation to certain things, namely his form of life with these objects. He will have established himself, and his right to his telling, as deeply as reason may require.

2

Having said that we do not privilege a teller (as a knower) on the basis of any information which he or she alone has but instead judge his or her telling as we would judge narrative accounts, I may immediately encounter the objection that there is a large class of narrative tellings over which we would want to privilege the teller precisely because of his or her special access to some information or knowledge. I am thinking of accounts of personal experiences such as are told in dreams or personal diaries. There are several such "personal" narratives in *Quixote*, and they are submitted to complex and often stringent evaluations. (I shall take as representative instances Don Quixote's account of his dream in the Cave of Montesinos and the replies of Sancho and the Humanist Cousin in chapters 22 through 24 of part 2.) We are initially tempted to say that in such cases the teller is privileged because he is intimately familiar with the experience he relates; his position as a knower would seem little short of unimpeachable. Indeed, we might say that a teller of personal experiences has a right over his or her tale not so much on the basis of his or her privileged experience of it as on the basis of his or her privileged access to the information. I shall argue, however, that this is not so, and in so doing I shall suggest that we may privilege the telling of personal experiences on the same basis that we privilege "epistemological" tellings—which is to say, in just the ways appropriate to narrative accounts.

It will not be difficult to see that the epistemological procedures used to identify objects cannot be extended to cases of personal experience with any great success, although the reasons for this may not at first be clear. When Don

Quixote tells of his vision of the legendary Montesinos, Durandarte, and Belerma (and it is important to keep in mind that the dream is presented only in Don Quixote's [re]telling of it), Sancho and the Humanist Cousin interrupt with a series of questions and observations about the underworld figures Don Quixote claims to have seen: Do these spirits eat? Do they sleep? Do they bother with the usual bodily functions? In a lengthy reply, the Humanist Cousin says that he will include some of what Don Quixote has told him in the two books he is currently writing, a *Spanish Ovid* and a supplement to *Virgilius Polydorus on the Invention of Antiquities;* the latter title is characteristically pedantic, but then the information in the book itself is a mixture of learned trivia and inane inference (the mythological transformations of the Guadiana River and of the Lakes of Ruidera, and a note on the history of playing cards).

Clearly something has gone awry here, and it is due as much to the epistemological commentary surrounding Don Quixote's dream as to the dream itself. Sancho and the Humanist Cousin are not initially in error, since they were the ones who led Don Quixote to the Cave where he fell asleep. A confusion of dream and reality is nonetheless implicit in their questions and comments on the dream, and this confusion follows from the way in which they appraise what Don Quixote tells them. All that is necessary for the type of epistemological inquiry they pursue is the ability to compare the features of an object with what that object is called, so there is nothing ostensibly wrong with the details of what they do. Yet all such an analysis of dreams might show is whether a given dream image has in fact been correctly named; it will not reveal whether a given experience is *dreaming* and will in fact have to silence that potentially skeptical worry if the detailed investigation is to proceed. The case of dreams is rather like that of fiction, where epistemology is only of avail once we are "inside" a given world. In both cases, those procedures assume we somehow have a given world, in the way that Frege said that *every* assertion contains an assumption. Wittgenstein, commenting on Frege's idea, found nothing wrong with it but thought it unrevealing and perhaps potentially misleading, giving us to think that there might be something more than an assumption (a "given") behind every assertion (every world) (*PI,* §22).

What of the possibility of justifying claims of personal knowledge by appeal to one's position for making the claim? The Humanist Cousin is especially concerned about such things, and he makes it quite plain that his newfound information is authoritative, and implicitly true, because it bears Don Quixote's imprint. He and Sancho presume that Don Quixote is the privileged authority over what he tells because of his special access to his dream. If all that is necessary for this branch of the epistemological investigation is that there be an authority and that there be something over which to claim it, then there ought not to be anything wrong with what the Humanist Cousin does. But all that this might show for dreams—if indeed it would show anything at all—is that everyone is the highest authority over his or her own dreams. In order to extend that authority beyond the dream, which is to say beyond the legitimate bounds of the narrative of which it consists, one would have to make the mistake Sancho and the Humanist Cousin implicitly make— confusing dreams and reality—when they take Don Quixote as an authority on the behavior of underworld spirits and the identity of mythologically transformed lakes and rivers. In Wittgensteinian parlance, one would have to confuse two language-games.

What these foiled attempts at epistemological analysis suggest is that our relationship to "personal experience" (for example, dreams, emotions of anger, feelings of pain, and so on) still remains to be understood. We assume, for instance, that the teller of personal experience in fact knows the experience of which he or she tells; but what if we thought of him or her as so close to it that he or she could be said only to *experience* it? In the *Philosophical Investigations*, Wittgenstein makes the following quip (I take it as an illustration of the hidden absurdity involved in claiming that anyone's relationship to his or her private experience is that of *knowing*): "Imagine someone saying: 'But I know how tall I am!' and laying his hand on top of his head to prove it" (*PI*, §279). What we should then say is not that the dreamer is privileged over his or her dream because he or she is especially close to something he or she knows (the content of the dream), but that he or she gives a privileged—because perhaps the only—expression of it. This means that whatever is expressed in telling personal experiences, it is not an inner state over which the teller has privileged *knowledge*—merely a privilege in telling. It could be said that this is because his or her knowing *is* the telling, the account which he or she gives.

When Wittgenstein says, then, that we regard it too much as a matter of course that one can tell anything to anyone, he means that there is nothing there behind the telling which we can inspect, nothing beyond the words in which the telling is done. The case is like that of the picture he describes in paragraph 523: "I should like to say 'What the picture tells me is itself.' That is, its telling me something consists in its own structure, in *its* own lines and colours." Here too he proceeds to remind us not to take it as a matter of course, "but as a remarkable fact, that pictures and fictitious narratives give us pleasure, occupy our minds" (*PI*, §524). Another example he adduces is that of telling time by a clock: "'The clock tells us the time. *What* time is, is not yet settled'" (*PI*, §363); rather, the clock tells us what time "it" is. And whatever "time" is, it is not the inner state of the clock as we find it on certain occasions; looking inside the clock will not tell you the time unless you also invent some way to "read" that state—for instance, by giving the clock hands and a face. As with the picture, what the clock tells "consists in its own structure," in its hands being in certain positions. To know how to tell time is to know that *these* hands in *that* position tell us it is *this* time.

Such propositions about telling, however easy to overlook, are not terribly difficult to accept for the case of material objects or even for such intangibles as time; but they are likely to meet with resistance when the telling of personal experiences is at issue. There, we are reluctant to give up the idea that there is something behind or beyond the telling which is communicated in it. When Austin, following Wittgenstein, objects that we move too hastily to talk about knowing the experiences of others—their feelings or their thoughts, or even their dreams—as an extension of the way we talk about material objects, he means first to give credit to the sense of such claims as "I know your feelings" where we would not find any sense in parallel first person claims. As Wittgenstein said in the *Philosophical Investigations,* "It can't be said of me at all (except perhaps as a joke) that I know I am in pain" (*PI,* §246); to say so was, he said, the equivalent of nonsense, at least as barbarous as saying that the man who ostensibly measures his height "knows" his height better than anyone else (*PI,* §279). The claim to "know someone's feelings" makes sense, to be sure, but only if we read the grammar of that claim as parallel to the grammar of claims to "know someone's tastes" (for example, "I know your feelings [views] on the matter"). What it means to "know someone's tastes," if it means anything at all, is to know what someone would do in a given situation, the choices he or she would make, how he or she would go on. It does not mean "knowing what he tastes" in the sense of knowing (tasting) the sense-data themselves.

In a related context, Stanley Cavell said something about what might be the possible motives behind our reluctance to settle for this parallelism: We want our knowledge of the experience of others to reach all the way to the experience *itself,* and our knowledge of others to reach all the way to *them,* so that knowing what someone feels would be *having* his or her feelings, sharing them with him or her.[7] If we could imagine such a thing, then we could imagine ourselves as *inside* others and thus avoid the facts of our outsideness to them and our inability to penetrate their lives—facts which we avoid as much because we fear our inability to make *ourselves* known as because we fear our inability to know others' lives. Thus one could say that our reluctance to settle for the parallelism of claims to know feelings and claims to know tastes is motivated by the fear of losing *connection* between our experiences and our words. We might instead take Wittgenstein's suggestion (*PI,* §656) and look on personal experiences—the dream, the pain, the anger— as interpretations of the telling, rather than vice versa. Anger is what the telling is *of* as a wince is of pain, a frown of disappointment. The experience becomes the interpretation of the telling, in the sense that it is the context which must be granted or imagined in order for the telling to mean anything at all.

Wittgenstein's account of our knowledge of the private experience of others can be seen as providing ways to overcome our fears of senselessness and unintelligibility. Of course there is the risk of losing the idea of anything like an "inner life" of personal experiences available to be known or told, but this can be minimized if we ascribe sufficient weight and consequence to the telling of the experience itself.

Consider the following points. In response to the objection that "I ought not to say I know Tom is angry, because I don't introspect his feelings," one may reply, with Austin, that (1) *"of course I don't* introspect Tom's feelings," and (2) *"of course I do* sometimes know Tom is angry" ("OM," 115). These may be taken together to say that (3) "to suppose that the question 'How do I know that Tom is angry?' is meant to mean 'How do I introspect Tom's feelings?' . . . is simply barking up the wrong gum tree" ("OM," 116). But that still leaves us with the question: How do I know that, or when, Tom is angry? I want to suggest, following Wittgenstein, that the only way to know is by what Tom tells, by the signs he gives—physical, verbal, or otherwise; beyond this, there is no other—certainly no *better*—way to know. For if what I have been saying is correct, then we will not say there is anything like a firsthand *knowledge* of the man's experience to be considered "best," only a firsthand or first person telling of it. This means that Tom is indeed in a privileged position over his personal experiences, but that the privilege is located in his *telling* of the experience, not his *knowledge* of it.

Of course, there is no way to guard against the possibility that someone might be lying about his or her personal experiences, bent on deceiving us, but I think it can be shown that those will only amount to local worries, not general ones. To say that we cannot ever know the personal experiences of others because someone might always be deceiving us is like inferring, when identifying a bird, that it might be stuffed or made of plastic. For all we know, Austin's goldfinch might be stuffed, and the man who tells us he is angry might be lying. But then the question becomes one of knowing why we are *ever* justified in believing what someone says. Austin would say that there is no such justification to be had, which is true; but there is some further explanation of it which lies no farther afield than the fact that language exists at all. When Austin imagines the case of a man who, having in his lifetime given the appearance of holding a certain belief, is found to have written a diary in which he confesses that he never did believe it, and when Austin says that in response "we probably should not know what to say" ("OM," 114), it is difficult to know what this silence means. For it seems that we might very well know what to say: that the man was schizophrenic, lived a divided existence, was intent on fooling the world, was in the end only fooling himself, and so on. One suspects that Austin's silence is his reaction to an incompletely imagined case of the more radical "private language" argument that Wittgenstein takes up in the *Philosophical Investigations*. If language were rigorously private, there would be no hope of discovering "what the man really felt" or whether he "meant" what he said, or wrote, or both, because one imagines the case of a diary written in signs of private sense alone. *Because* language is by nature shared and public and cannot be wholly private, because in order to imagine a language one has also to imagine a form of life (a world), there is no real question of making a "correct" discovery about the man's personal experiences at all; hence there is no room for deep disappointment of the skeptical kind should our discoveries prove mistaken. Our "discoveries" will go no deeper than one or the other telling of personal experience, and the worry that we might always be deceived is no longer meaningful and no longer carries the force necessary for skepticism to take hold.

The Wittgensteinian line of approach I have been proposing is meant to allow for the possibility that, in any particular case, we might be deceived, but also to show that claims made about personal experiences may be supported just as tellings are. We will make our appraisals of such accounts, as I have already suggested, in the ways appropriate to narrative tellings. All one can ask of accounts of personal experience, and all that would be needed to meet the requirements of rationality when so asked, is that the account be consistent, coherent, and capable of being carried on. When these requirements have been met, which is to say when I tell of my personal experiences what can be fashioned into a narrative account, then I have told all I can of myself; then your knowledge of me will in the end depend not on anything so personal as your trust in me but rather on your inability as a rational being to refuse such an account. You may of course refuse and continue in your doubts, but that will not mean anything about the truth of what I tell, only something about your ability to participate in this rational form of life.

3

I have argued earlier in this essay that there is a common basis by which we may privilege epistemological tellings and the tellings of personal experiences, and I have characterized that basis roughly in terms of consistency, coherence, and, with Wittgenstein, the ability to "go on." I have said that these features, in addition to being marks of rationality, are marks of narrative, so that one can judge the rationality of a telling, if not its truth value, by asking whether or not it might conceivably be a narrative. If this is so, then what I have called the "privilege" we grant to various kinds of tellers is justified not by the truth of what they tell but by the rationality of their telling. But I have said little about how it is we judge narratives, or exactly what it means for them to be consistent, coherent, and capable of being carried on. In this final section, I shall argue that if narratives are appropriately judged rational (or not) rather than truthful, then they can best be considered as *accounts*. This characterization already hints at the similarity of narration and counting, or recounting, for which an older word is also "telling."

In part 1 of *Don Quixote*, chapter 20, Sancho tells a story in which Cervantes hits off the relationship between telling and counting especially well. It is the story of the love and jealousy of Lope Ruiz, a goatherd, and the shepherdess Torralba. At one point, as Torralba is in pursuit of him, the goatherd comes upon a river which he and his flock must cross; Sancho relates that:

"As he was looking about, he saw a fisherman alongside a boat so small that it would hardly hold one person and a goat, but, nevertheless, he spoke to the man, who agreed to take the goatherd and his flock of three hundred to the opposite bank. The fisherman would climb into the boat and row one of the animals across and then return for another, and he kept this up, rowing across with a goat and coming back, rowing across and coming back—Your Grace must be sure to keep count [*Tenga vuestra merced cuenta*] of the goats that the fisherman rowed across the stream, for if a single one of them escapes your memory, the story is ended and it will not be possible to tell another word of it [*contar mas palabras del*].

"I will go on, then, and tell you that the landing place on the other side was full of mud and slippery, and it took the fisherman a good while to make the trip each time; but in spite of that, he came back for another goat, and another, and another."

"Just say that he rowed them all across," said Don Quixote; "you need not be coming and going in that manner, or it will take you a year to get them all on the other side."

"How many have you got across up to now?" Sancho demanded.

"How the devil should I know?" replied Don Quixote.

"There, what did I tell you? You should have kept good count [*que tuviese buena cuenta*]. Well, then, by God, the story's ended, for there is no going on with it."[8]

The telling and the counting are perhaps too literally linked in Sancho's mind, but nonetheless the content of his story, as well as the wordplays on *contar*, bring out the special importance of being able to go on, as one goes on counting, or as one continues an ordered series of numbers. Indeed, Cervantes here adds another, equally important perspective to the idea of "going on" which is so crucial to narratives: that ordinarily we do *not* go on, not ad infinitum. To be able to go on is, I have said, a mark of rationality, but it is also one of the marks of rationality *not* to have to offer endless evidence of being rational; one must also have the sense of an ending and recognize when to stop. For the requirement of rationality, as for narrativity, it is sufficient that you be *able* to go on, not that you actually do so.

What then is one to say to Sancho, who from the start insists that "in my country . . . they tell fables just the way I am telling this one, and cannot tell it in another way, nor is it right for your Grace to ask me to adopt new customs" (*DQ*, 152–53)? I imagine Sancho here as a member of one of those "tribes" Wittgenstein so often invents in order to expose the depth in which we are bound by certain customs and practices, in some cases a depth that rivals the depth in which language binds us. Seen as a form of counting, narration is itself one of those deep practices that Wittgenstein calls "forms of life." At one point in the *Remarks on the Foundations of Mathematics,* he says that "what we call 'counting' [*zahlen*] is an important part of our life's activities. Counting and accounting are not—e.g.—simply a pastime."[9]

We might ask, in response to Sancho's caveat, what one should say of those people whom Wittgenstein imagines in the *Remarks on the Foundations of Mathematics* (*RFM,* §§142–49) counting piles of wood according to the surface area covered by the piles rather than by what we would call the "volume":

> How could I shew them that—as I should say—you don't really buy more wood if you buy a pile covering a bigger area?—I should, for instance, take a pile which was small by their ideas and, by laying the logs around, change it into a "big" one. This *might* convince them—but perhaps they would say: "Yes, now it's a *lot* of wood and costs more"—and that would be the end of the matter.—We should presumably say in this case: they simply do not mean the same by "a lot of wood" and "a little wood" as we do; and they have quite a different system of payment from us. (*RFM,* §149)

We will say that we would have no use for their idea of counting in our affairs, where wood is valued, and paid for, in certain ways, for certain uses. (Compare: "The *truth* is that counting has proved to pay [*bewährt hat*].—'Then do you want to say that "being true" means: Being usable (or useful)?'—No, not that; but that it can't be said of the series of natural numbers—any more than of our language— that it is true, but: that it is usable, and, above all, *it is used*" [*RFM,* §4].) Could one imagine a (human) "tribe" which had *no* idea of counting—and hence no idea of narration—*at all,* a culture completely lacking these forms of life?

There are a variety of reasons to think that this would not be possible, only some of which I can discuss here. There is, for instance, the idea that counting and narrative both involve iteration and hence depend on the ability to perceive the "same." (Could we think of a human culture that had no idea of the "same"?) This is in fact part of the more embracing concept of "following a rule," the rule for sameness being something like repetition (compare: "The use of the word 'rule' and the use of the word 'same' are interwoven" [*PI,* §225]).[10] Throughout his later writings, Wittgenstein consistently offers counting and such related practices as continuing ordered series of numbers as examples of what it means to follow a rule (so then the question would be whether we could imagine a culture that lacked the idea of a rule or was unable to "go on" or follow a rule). Wittgenstein will imagine, for instance, a teacher copying out the natural numbers in decimal notation for a student; then the student will try to do so independently but will make some mistake, copying only every other number in one case. The teacher will try to wean him from the mistake until he can write the series 0 to 9 to the teacher's satisfaction; at some later point he will be able to go on well above 9, say to 100 or so. At some point, which is not well defined, we will say something significantly more than "now he knows the natural numbers in decimal notation from 0 to 9 (or to 100)." We will say that he understands a system, that he knows how to follow this rule.

In more complex cases, with a series such as 1, 5, 11, 19, 29, we may be tempted to say that the rule of a series is a formula (an algebraic formula would be $a_n = n^2 + n - 1$), but Wittgensteinian rules are not necessarily formulas. We may teach someone to count and to follow the rule of the natural numbers in decimal notation without ever telling him or her anything about algebra (children learn to count this way) and without their intuiting any algebraic formula: "B does not think of formulae. He watches A writing his numbers down with a certain feeling of tension, and all sorts of thoughts go through his head. Finally he asks himself: 'What is the series of differences?' He finds the series 4, 6, 8, 10 and says: Now I can go on. Or he watches and says 'Yes, I know *that* series'—and continues it just as he would have done if A had written down the series 1, 3, 5, 7, 9.—Or he says nothing at all and simply continues the series. Perhaps he had what may be called the sensation 'that's easy!'" (*PI*, § 151). The conclusion to be drawn from the fact that Wittgensteinian rules are not formulas is that knowing something is not the same as knowing the formula for producing it. If telling, or narrating, is at all like counting, then there must be something of importance about it other than the fact that narratives can always be *described* by structural formulas.

What is important for my purposes about the idea of following a rule as exemplified by counting is that ordered series exhibit coherence, consistency, and the possibility of being carried on. Of course, this is just to say that they are *ordered series*, but it is also to say that they are examples of what it means to follow a rule— that is, that there is some rationality to them. All that is required for something to be ordered, or for a rule to be followed, is that the practice be universalizable among the members of some (human) culture, that there be some "tribe" capable of sustaining the practice (for instance, able to "go on"). Such formulations leave the notion of culture purposefully vague and the concept of rationality open-ended, for no one will want to say what forms of culture or rationality we, as a species, may develop over time. It is perhaps enough to say, with Wittgenstein, that we as a culture have developed the practices called "counting" and "telling" and that these are among our current forms of life. If, as I suggested at the outset, there is a meaningful connection between "telling" as knowing and "telling" as narrating, then one may further say that the nature of human knowledge is that of a deeply rational form of life. This is so in part because narrating, as I have explained, may be seen as a form of counting, that is, as a central example of what Wittgenstein means by our ability to "follow a rule" or to "go on."[11]

Notes

1. Ludwig Wittgenstein, *Philosophical Investigations,* 3d ed., trans. G. E. M. Anscombe (New York: Macmillan, 1958), §363; hereafter cited in text as *PI,* with Wittgenstein's numbered paragraphs, or "remarks," indicated by the symbol §.

2. Barbara Herrnstein Smith also makes this point; see *On the Margins of Discourse* (Chicago: University of Chicago Press, 1978), 16–17: "It is worth noting that the existence of an object or event or even, as we say, an 'idea,' is never a sufficient reason for responding to it verbally. In other words, the fact that something is true is never a sufficient reason for saying it."

3. The idea of "privilege" is used by J. F. M. Hunter in his *Essays After Wittgenstein* (Toronto: University of Toronto Press, 1973), 91–114, in a chapter entitled "Telling."

4. J. L. Austin, "Other Minds," in *Philosophical Papers,* 2d ed., ed. J. O. Urmson and G. J. Warnock (Oxford: Clarendon Press, 1970), 76–116; hereafter cited as "OM" in text.

5. Ludwig Wittgenstein, *On Certainty,* ed. G. E. M. Anscombe and G. H. von Wright, trans. Denis Paul and G. E. M. Anscombe (New York: Harper, 1972), §1.

6. Ludwig Wittgenstein, *The Blue and Brown Books: Preliminary Studies for the "Philosophical Investigations"* (New York: Harper, 1953), 104–5.

7. See the final section, entitled "Between Acknowledgment and Avoidance," of Stanley Cavell, *The Claim of Reason* (Oxford: Clarendon Press, 1979).

8. Miguel de Cervantes, *Don Quixote.* See, for example, trans. J. M. Cohen (Harmondsworth: Penguin, 1950), 152–53; hereafter cited as *DQ.*

9. Ludwig Wittgenstein, *Remarks on the Foundations of Mathematics,* ed. G. H. von Wright, R. Rhees, and G. E. M. Anscombe, trans. G. E. M. Anscombe (Cambridge: M.I.T. Press, 1967), part 1, §4; hereafter cited in text as *RFM,* with numbered paragraphs or remarks indicated by the symbol §.

10. On Wittgensteinian rules in connection with the "same," there are some helpful remarks in Saul Kripke, *Wittgenstein on Rules and Private Language* (Cambridge: Harvard University Press, 1982).

11. See also Anthony J. Cascardi, *The Bounds of Reason: Cervantes, Dostoevsky, Flaubert* (New York: Columbia University Press, 1986), for a development of the Wittgensteinian approach.

The Shadow of a Magnitude: Quotation as Canonicity in Proust and Beckett

William Flesch

Although literary criticism is often descriptive, in arguments about "the canon" not much analysis is devoted to the internal experience of canonicity (as opposed to what might be called its external use, that is, its function or putative value in shaping other experiences); the best such analysis might be Walter Benjamin's account of the aura of the work of art before the age of mechanical reproduction,[1] but there he is talking about unique artworks and not about reproducible texts, and it is these of which the canon is comprised. The experience of canonicity does loom very large in Harold Bloom's account of poetic influence,[2] but what is it?

A first approach to the experience of canonicity might be attempted through an account of the experience of quotation. By this latter experience I mean the experience that both reader and writer, speaker and auditor, have of a third presence, that of the material quoted. Of course there are countless reasons for quoting; a partial catalog would include appealing to authority, calling on commitments, jeering at judgments, picturing postures taken, retailing the role played by the person or text quoted in some incident being narrated, and so on. But we come closer to the internal experience of canonicity in those quotations that are cited simply for their own sake, those quotations that in some sense work best because they are quotations out of context. "Next to the originator of a good sentence is the first quoter of it," says Emerson. "Many will read the book before one thinks of quoting a passage. As soon as he has done this, that line will be quoted east and west."[3] To quote something for its own sake is to make a gesture analogous to, if more attenuated than, that of literary creation, and at the same time to take a stance analogous to, but more active than, that of literary reception. It is more active than reception because it shares with creation the aspiration to assert the canonicity of the set of words it proffers, even if such a proffer is necessarily an attenuated version of originality. Quotation for its own sake models literary experience, both of reading and writing, especially that aspect of literary experience which comports with a sense of the canonicity of the literary object.

The bifurcation of the experience of quotation—attenuated writing, intensi-fied reading—stands for the ambiguous status of the passage quoted: It is mine and other than mine. To quote something for its own sake is to quote it out of context; it is to divorce it from the role it might perform within its original situation and therefore to grant it a canonicity its utterer may not have originally asserted for it but which it is now made to assert for itself. The out-of-context quotation then is simultaneously appropriated by the quoter, to whom it now belongs (Emerson on the first quoter again), and disengaged from belonging to anyone at all (any empirical being at all), since it is entirely self-standing.

These two facets of quotation are not strictly speaking dissoluble from each other, as my foregoing formulations should make clear. In quoting, I ascribe canon-icity to the passage quoted by displaying it as self-evidently canonical, by dis-playing its canonicity as self-ascribing. Canonical quotation (as one might call quotation for its own sake) depends on its resistance to a context, and thus it dialectically requires at least the idea of a context, which might then be resisted. I utter or display the quotation and so display its canonical independence from the occasion of its utterance, either in its original context or in the context which consists in my display of it. I produce a token; the canonical words are a type, and their canonicity consists in the difference from the token nevertheless required to instantiate or index that canonicity.

Why do I display the quotation? Because in producing the token I become the impresario of the type. I aspire to its prestige. That very prestige depends on its independence from my utterance. Attenuated writing, intensified reading coincide in the gesture by which my utterance contributes to the quotation's canonical independence and then coincide again in the way that I seek to share its canonical independence. Krapp's attenuated agency with regard to the tapes he plays back captures the way the gesture of quotation takes place on the frontier between uttering and receiving.[4] By uttering the quotation I attempt to make it mine, the better to have it appropriate me.

I will use Marcel Proust and Samuel Beckett to exemplify these two aspects or moments of quotation. Very roughly speaking, Proust can help convey the first moment, in which the eerie independence of the canonical quotation comes to prominence, and Beckett the second moment, in which the quoter seeks to share in the prestige of that canonicity. That second moment can also help shed light on the nature of literary inspiration, which will in turn redound upon the first moment, since inspiration is another word for the serenely independent authority that might divinize the canonical work.

The nature of quotation helps illuminate the converse relation between can-onicity and inspiration as well. The experience of inspiration is an experience of a relation between being and receiving, between an impossible-to-imagine self-sufficiency (the divinity of the muse or canonical work as precursor) and a more or less needy receptivity to the gifts of this self-sufficient muse. Canonicity is to inspiration as the written is to reading (to the act of reading). This is because, as Harold Bloom has tirelessly argued, inspiration is a trope for the experience of influence, especially of the influence of the works that inspire in the latecomer a sense of literary vocation. (This is Longinus's description of the experience of the sublime.) You read works which are canonical, and it is only after taking the precursor as muse that you yourself wish to compose.

Let me stress again that by "canonical" here I don't want to mean the sort of thing that has been the subject of so much spilled ink lately: the list or syllabus or closed corpus of works with the supposedly objective imprimatur of greatness. I am suggesting that canons in that universality-claiming sense are derivative of a prior subjective literary experience, of the sort that Kant describes in the Third Critique. That prior subjective experience, as Kant claimed, works like this: A person will regard a work as canonical which seems to that person to have a power or force that everyone ought to recognize. Now to feel that way about a work is to feel that the work itself is beyond what can be imagined in the mode of identification, since identification enables the give-and-take that constitutes the community, our sense of the "everyone," who ought to recognize the work's greatness. But the canonical work is beyond this community of reciprocal identification and understanding, like the charismatic figure whose charisma entails refractoriness to identification. Kant says that you can't imagine what it would be like to be God, since you would necessarily wonder whence you received your power: "We cannot put aside, and yet also cannot endure the thought, that a being, which we represent to ourselves as supreme amongst all possible beings, should, as it were, say to itself: 'I am from eternity to eternity, and outside me there is nothing save what is through my will, but whence then am I?'" This is why "Unconditioned necessity . . . is for human reason the veritable abyss."[5] Yet the hallmark of (what I am calling) the canonical is just this unconditioned necessity. I argue elsewhere that this is the way people (for example Keats) see both Shakespeare and his strongest characters, as charismatic figures who are able to say of themselves that there is nothing save what is through their wills and yet who are not tormented by the question of where they received this power.[6] Canonical literature is literature whose source seems to be beyond any human capacity to plumb; the ascription to it of quasi-divine status signals its fundamental opacity to identification. And, as I say, this is where quotation comes in: The canonical work is the quoted work, language quoted rather than language meant. Not only a source of quotation, it has itself the unalterable status of the verbatim, and we treat it as the verbatim object, and not simply as a vehicle of meaning. It has become unalterable. The song tells us, Ashbery says, of an old way of living, of life in former times—and so not of our life. We quote from the song, but the song itself has become nothing but a quotation. (Indeed, the practice of indenting quotations comes from the indentation of choral songs in the manuscripts of Greek plays.)[7] The canonical work is a work that has become pure quotation, quotation without a speaker, the work whose speaker (as an empirical being) has become irrelevant to the work itself. The canonical work is (in Maurice Blanchot's sense) anonymous. Hence the "alienated majesty" that Emerson and thence Bloom locate in the canonical.

The phenomenon of literary quotation helps bring out the intrinsic importance of the experience of canonicity to literary experience. It raises and relates a host of central questions about the status of literary language and helps show their internal connections. Quotation raises first of all the vexed question about the relation of inside to outside in a text, since the quoted material is by its nature external and imported into the quoting discourse. Quotation raises as well the question of the relation of form to content, since it can make vivid the usually elided difference between the two. The material quoted is a content that comes, as I say, from elsewhere; but it is either assimilated to or resists assimilation to the form of the work that is doing the quoting. This becomes particularly obvious in poems which quote bits of texts originally from a different prosodic background.[8] The form of the quoting poem either imposes itself upon the matter that it quotes or founders upon that matter. The phenomenon of quotation raises questions about the relation of repetition (and difference) to content and positive terms and, more generally, diachronic questions about priority and the contestation of meaning and synchronic questions about the relation of self to other. (Psychoanalysis has shown the connections between these questions.) Now all of these questions also turn out to be related (the phenomenon of quotation relates them) to the questions of inspiration and canonicity that I've already raised. This is because, very broadly, the act of quotation may be said to mark some (perhaps originally extraliterary) content as literary—to canonize—and to mark the quoter as receptive to this canonized literary string of words.

The history of the marks of quotation can help indicate this. Quotations used to be signaled through the use of italics (themselves supposed to be an imitation, a kind of quotation, of Petrarch's handwriting); but italics were used for all extraneous material, including proper names, as though they too are canonized—rendered unalterable—through a sort of primal baptism. Inverted commas have a different origin and only came into widespread use as the frame for quotations around the beginning of the eighteenth century. They originated as diples, pointers used in medieval manuscripts to alert a reader to a text drawn from Scripture, so in its origin our quotation mark is a signal of the canonical form of canonicity. The diple is a kind of arrowhead; it originally looked a bit like the greater-than sign (>), or like one of the angles in a closing guillemet. It was used in antiquity by readers to signal noteworthy elements of texts, as M. B. Parkes points out;[9] a diple *peri stichon* (with a dot inside it) was used in texts of the *Odyssey* particularly to signal Olympus as the name of the material mountain and not simply the (more figurative) home of the gods. [10] Thus in its origin the inverted comma already signals the unalterable—the mountain itself—and thence the unalterable words of God and, further, of any recognized authority, in particular the patristic writers.

From such sources our contemporary use of the quotation mark develops. That development, as the move from the Bible to Homer already indicates, is one in the direction of secularization, and the modern idea of quotation combines the practice of citation from authoritative (canonical) texts with the practice of reporting direct speech, as in dialogue. (Indeed, because the diple was sometimes used in Hellenistic times as a sort of paragraph marker or indicator of breaks in the text, it was used to indicate new episodes and new speakers in a first- or second-century copy of the *Iliad*. [11] Thus quoting verbatim makes a claim to an accuracy in what it quotes that fixes the quotation, and this fixity is the first step (of many) in the process of canonization. I'll hope to exemplify some of these hastily sketched features of quotation subsequently, but first I want to stress the more ontological questions about the status of canonicity through a reading of a few passages from Beckett and Proust. I choose these writers because I think that Beckett is obsessed with the idea of quotation, including the quotation of his precursors in Joyce and Proust; and because Proust in his turn is fascinated with the quotational question of the origin and persistence of meaning despite the successive deaths of the successive *moi* which mark the passage of time: In his memories of Balbec, it is at once dead and immemorial.

This is the process of canonization, and a good example of it occurs in a famous passage in Combray. The narrator has surprised his mother on the stairs after he is supposed to have gone to bed, and for this he expects terrific punishment. But, against all hope, his father relents and tells his mother to spend the night with him as he desires: "Va avec le petit." This sentence becomes for him canonical, although not exactly what he's reported his father as saying:

> For an instant he looked at me, seeming surprised and irritated, then when mama had explained with a few embarrassed words what had happened, he said to her: "But go with him [*Mais va donc avec lui*], since you yourself said you didn't want to sleep, stay in his room a while, I don't need anything." [12]

After this the narrator compares the scene to one from an engraving of Gozzoli that Swann had given him of Abraham insisting that Sarah must depart from Isaac's side: an antithetical and oddly apt allusion. And he continues, in one of the only present-tense moments in all of *A la recherche*:

> It has been many years since then. The wall of the stairway where I saw the reflection of his lamp rising up hasn't existed for a long time. In me too many things have been destroyed that I thought would last forever and new

things have been built giving birth to new pains and joys which I couldn't
have then foreseen, just as the old have become difficult to understand. It has
been a very long time too since my father ceased being able to say to mama,
"Go with the little one [*Va avec le petit*]." The possibility of such hours will
never be reborn for me. But for the last little while, I have begun to perceive
very clearly, if I lend an ear, the sobs that I had the strength to contain in
my father's presence, and which only burst out when I was alone again with
mama. In reality, they never ceased, and it is only because life is now more
silent around me that I hear them again. . . . (*RTP*, 37)

The narrator quotes his father once more, farther down the page, and alters the
phrase again: "[O]nce he had comprehended that I was grief-stricken, he had said
to my mother: "Go then and console him [*Va donc le consoler*]" (*RTP*, 37–38).

I quote this passage at length for several reasons. First, it seems to me a perfect
example of the canonical moment in Proust, in which the general formula—"*Va
avec le petit*"—is the canonized essence cited from the speech actually reported (and
then later summarized). This is the formula that his father will never be able to
say again; this is the sentence that is beyond the reach, the intention, the living
meaning of its speaker. The sentence endures as a quotation without an original,
just as the narrator's cries continue to endure, even after the narrator's dizzy pains
and joys from those years are no more. I quote it also because this is one of the
moments in Proust that clearly obsessed Beckett, whose story "First Love" ends
with its narrator's attempt to escape the sounds of a mother's ceaseless cries placed
into elegiac juxtaposition with the memory of his own dead father. His wife has
gone into labor, and from this disaster of undesired paternity he seeks to escape,
making a terrible racket as he goes:

Precautions would have been superfluous, there was no competing with
those cries. It must have been her first. They pursued me down the stairs
and out into the street. I stopped before the house door and listened. I could
still hear them. If I had not known there was crying in the house I might not
have heard them. But knowing it I did. I was not sure where I was. I looked
among the stars and constellations for the Wains, but could not find them.
And yet they must have been there. My father was the first to show them
to me. He had shown me others, but alone, without him beside me, I could
never find any but the Wains. I began playing with the cries, a little in the
same way as I had played with the song, on, back, on, back, if that may be
called playing. [He had heard her singing as she sat on his bench during the
time of their "courtship": I'll quote the relevant passage in a little while.] As
long as I kept walking I didn't hear them, because of the footsteps. But as
soon as I halted I heard them again, a little fainter each time, admittedly, but

what does it matter, faint or loud, cry is cry, all that matters is that it should cease. For years I thought they would cease. Now I don't think so any more. I could have done with other loves perhaps. But there it is, either you love or you don't. [13]

The persistence of these cries, as well as their comparison with the song he had before heard her sing, raises in a stronger form the question already prompted by Proust's variations on the father's relenting words, the question of what it is that counts as quotation. Do quotations have to have content, or can cries have their canonical status? In describing that earlier song, he says, "At first I heard nothing, then the voice again, but only just, so faintly did it carry. First I didn't hear it, then I did, I must therefore have begun hearing it, at a certain point, but no, there was no beginning, the sound emerged so softly from the silence and so resembled it" (*JS*, 26). What is the relation of quotation to voice, since quotation is about the repetition in one voice of something said by another one? The narrator in Proust remembers both the father's words, or a canonical abstract and purification of them, and his own muted and inarticulate cries. It is those cries that Beckett's narrator hears as well—not the cries of the narrator of *A la recherche*—not the cries as moored to their utterer, but the cries as unmoored, out of the range of intention, interaction, performance, until (to quote Stevens) at last the cry concerns no one at all: "Cry is cry," so that Proust's narrator's and the cries in "First Love" are the same. (Beckett, who couldn't bear to have his book on Proust translated into the language of the original, adds this clause to the English translation of *Premier Amour*.) [14] Blanchot dramatizes this question of the relation of voice to presence in *L'attente l'oubli*, where the two figures who give voice to that book come together in a contiguity of voices outside of their presence. [15] But it's dramatized in Proust as well, in the scene when the narrator talks to his grandmother on the telephone and suddenly hears only her voice in all its fragility, denuded of her reassuring presence. Albertine's two letters to him, delivered after her death, might be called a written version of this denuded voice. And what about a different sort of quotation in Proust, one that is the pure articulation of voice (rather than its inarticulation in the cry) although (or rather because of this) we never hear it: *la petite phrase* of Vinteuil? Clearly these questions are related to the status of memory and the precariousness of the quotation when removed from all context.

Another passage from Proust, this time from *Jean Santeuil*—a book of fragments—can help make this point. His fairly new friend Servois, soon to leave for the army, has just told Jean that they had actually seen each other once before, long ago, on a train. Jean had forgotten the whole scene, which now comes flooding back as an involuntary memory; he recalls vividly his fascination with a young cyclist who rode outside on the platform with his bicycle, while his two female companions rode with Jean in the railway car. In his memory, he's transported back to the car:

> But once in the car of that small railroad of Pont-Labbé, forever vanished from his memory and which he'd never have thought of again in his life without [Servois's] chance utterance and which no one else would ever have thought of again afterwards since no one else had seen it, but which now rolled slowly into the sunset before his eyes, what most struck him wasn't who the two ladies turned out to be, but that the cyclist [i.e., Servois] whom he thought he'd never see again, who was part of the landscape just like the railbed, like the trees, like all that was before his eyes then without his imagining any will there that he knew, was his friend of today. And that, both times, like a mirror-apparition in a fairy play whose image had flickered before his eyes, nature had only acted as in those fairy plays where first a character appears thus as a reflection, but soon afterwards a real actor takes its place and says a few words, to disappear himself as well, it is true, like the reflection—and wasn't that what Servois was going to do in a few days? It would finally always be the case that Jean had seen him only between two trains. [16]

What looks like a grounding of an otherwise untethered moment reverses so that the ground itself becomes untethered. Interestingly, the cyclist comes back in *A la recherche* as one of the people who make up the staffage of the narrator's first encounter with Albertine, finally herself a fairy-tale part of his life between two metaphorical trains.

In *Jean Santeuil* the Proustian theme of the relation of present to past, of the fact of repetition—of quotation—and not the content of what's quoted, sometimes gets raised explicitly as a matter of quotation, as when Jean's memory is awakened, in what is now familiar Proustian fashion, by an inadvertent phenomenon of quotation:

> The name of Saint-Géran came up. "Oh! him," said Vésale, "there's a friend, there's a rare spirit, in whom I'd confide any secret, who will only say good things about me." Many years later, going home from the house of a dancer with whom he was infatuated, with the director of the Châtelet theatre where she was engaged, because the director mentioned the admiration that Mlle Zita had for Jean and because they were speaking with a friendlier gravity, Jean asked him what he thought of an actor who had come to Zita's house for a minute the same evening and whom she had introduced to him. "Oh!" the director said, "he is an exquisite person whose like I've never known; and he knows that he can count on me just as I count entirely upon

him." These words immediately reminded Jean, as an identical harmony reawakens a forgotten air, of that already distant return home with Vésale whom he never saw anymore now. (*JS*, 767)

I quote these passages both for their own sake and to show one canonical writer's intense analysis of the treatment of the quotational canonicity he aspires to. I've always been fascinated by the anonymity of the narrator of *A la recherche*, whose name we never find out for certain, the very narrator who explicitly denies referential status to the book, "where everything has been invented according to the needs of my demonstration"(*RTP*, 3:846), who explicitly denies referential status even to his own first person pronouns.[17] There's a strong sense in which *A la recherche* is itself pure untethered quotation, since the book couldn't have been written by its dying, indeed its posthumous, hero at the stage at which he arrives when the narrative ends. The book's claim to canonicity is partly a claim to the radical and anonymous opacity of pure quotation.

As I've already suggested, contiguous but antithetical to Proustian quotation are the phenomena of quotation in Beckett, where these themes find a perhaps more explicit treatment. Thus the appendix to *Watt* of the *disjecta membra*, the unincorporated fragments, makes for something like a catalog of pure quotations, as though their existence *out of context* could be said to precede any contextualization.[18] *Krapp's Last Tape* presents something like the rebuke of the canonical (a rebuke similar to that which Rilke hears from the archaic bust of Apollo, the fragment of the god of poetry: "you must change your life," or like its echo quotation in James Wright: "I have wasted my life"). The fragmentary passages on the tape are for the old Krapp more and more occasions for despair, as their literal repetition, their playback, becomes more and more the index of their distance and not the permanence of the experience they describe. They become estranged as they become, for Krapp and for us, pure quotations and so simultaneously pure lyric.

Not that quotations in Beckett are always occasions for despair: *Happy Days* suggests the opposite, when Winnie remembers if not actual lines at least the shadows of their magnitudes: "Oh well, what does it matter, that is what I always say, so long as one . . . you know . . . what is that wonderful line . . . laughing wild . . . something something laughing wild amid severest woe."[19] (The actual line,[20] from Gray's "Ode on a Distant Prospect of Eton College," is: "And *moody Madness* laughing wild / Amid severest woe" [*HD*, 79–80], so that Winnie's forgetfulness can transmute horror to optimism.)[21] At least three of her half-remembered quotations are about the word "woe" (from Gray, from *Hamlet*, from *Paradise Lost*), but in each case it is the wonder of the quotation, or the ghost of a quotation which saves her from the quotation's woeful content, at least as long as the quotation continues to echo:

"The sadness after song. (*Pause*) Have you run across that, Willie? (*Pause*) In the course of your experience. (*Pause*) No? (*Pause*) Sadness after intimate sexual intercourse one is familiar with of course. (*Pause*) You would concur with Aristotle there, Willie, I fancy. (*Pause*) But after song. . . . (*Pause*) It does not last of course. (*Pause*) That is what I find so wonderful. (*Pause*) It wears away. (*Pause*) What are those exquisite lines? (*Pause*) Go forget me why should something o'er that something shadow fling . . . go forget me . . . why should sorrow . . . brightly smile . . . go forget me . . . never hear me . . . sweetly smile . . . brightly sing. . . . (*Pause. With a sigh*) One loses one's classics. (*Pause*) Oh not all. (*Pause*) A part. (*Pause*) A part remains. (*Pause*) That is what I find so wonderful, a part remains, of one's classics, to help one through the day." (*HD*, 57–58)

What remains from one's classics—from the canon of quotations—are fragments and rhythms, so that the double trochee "something something" stands for "moody madness" in the Gray quotation, and the second quotation, "why should something o'er that something shadow fling," is rhythmically (though not grammatically) equivalent to its source in Charles Wolfe: "Why should sorrow o'er that brow a shadow fling?"[22]

It is as though in *Happy Days* we've returned to an argument that Millman Parry made about the origin of rhythm as the residue of oral epithet: The Homeric epithets don't fit the rhythm, the rhythm is determined by the prior epithet.[23] But quotations can be even more attenuated than their rhythms, as is clear from the fragments that Winnie is reduced to at the end: "brightly smile . . . go forget me . . . never hear me . . . sweetly smile . . . brightly sing. . . ." These are fragments of rhythms and stand in the same relation to the rhythmed line as that line stands in relation to its full articulation. Quotation here can become a ghostly phenomenon indeed, but I think that what finally makes it so unnervingly eerie—what paradoxically lends it its canonicity—is the fact that it is the ghost of a phenomenon or that it renders phenomenal events—such as the original utterances—ghostly.

It does so both in the canonical mode of memory and conservation, as I've been suggesting, and also in the related mode of inspiration. Winnie's example in *Happy Days* can show how inspiration is related to the canonical as a kind of faithfulness to the ghost of the verbatim, to a verbal scrupulosity that is at the same time occulted and clouded. I want to call this faithfulness to thought or to thinking. It's this faithfulness to the ghostly or occult that makes writing so surprisingly difficult, surprising since the doctrine of inspiration—of the infusion of the thought—might give rise to the idea of writing as the easy reproduction of mental contents (the claim Milton makes in *Paradise Lost*). In this question of faithfulness to thought, and to the extent that thought may sometimes be regarded as synonymous with judgment, the question of truth arises, and so I am also interested in the relation of truth to quotation.

One way to approach the relation of quotation to thought is to consider the psychological phenomenon of suggestion. In its simplest form, the suggestion of a word or an idea can affect a person, so that she or he will now internalize that word or idea, as though what is in fact an outer prompt came from inside. Under suggestion the subject neglects or forgets the external origin of the idea and acts as though on his or her own initiative. What seems to have happened is that the suggestion has breached a generally pretty opaque boundary between inside and outside (something there is that doesn't love a wall), or between self and other. What is the nature of that boundary?

I think that you could call that boundary something like a mark of quotation. When you hear someone speak, you generally don't mistake the heard words for your own (the merit of noticing the phenomenon of suggestion is to show that such a mistake could be possible; the psychotic hearing of voices would be a converse mental miscue). This fact, though obvious, nevertheless deserves some notice, since it shows something about ideas and how they can get communicated. What it shows is that "having an idea" and "getting an idea" are different things— that it's possible to share the contents of an idea with someone else (when you understand what that person is saying), without sharing the idea. You can dis- agree. Frege invented what he called an "assertion sign" ($\vdash$) to show when a person actually holds an idea, as opposed to simply understanding its content. In Frege's terminology, the addition of the assertion sign shows that a proposition is being asserted rather than simply being considered.[24] (This is essentially the argument for the important distinction between meaning and reference, *Sinn* and *Bedeutung*.) Now the assertion sign might in actuality be regarded as the converse of the quotation mark. A Fregean sentence without an assertion sign would be something like a natural-language sentence surrounded by quotation marks: We are considering something (perhaps its meaning) about the concatenation of the words thus mentioned rather than using them to say something about the world outside of this concatenation of words.

The idea of disquotation makes this clear. The "disquotational account of truth" is Quine's name for Tarskis' idea that a particular sentence *p* is true if and only if p. That is, "snow is white" is true if and only if snow is white. Quine summarizes: "Ascription of truth just cancels the quotation marks. Truth is disquotation."[25] To say of a quoted sentence that it's true is the same thing as to say the sentence without its framing quotation marks. The truth predicate and the quotation marks cancel each other out. As Donald Davidson points out, this yields a remarkable fact about the definition of truth thus conceived. In general, a satisfactory definition is one that can replace the term to be defined. But, Davidson writes, "What is striking, of course, is not that the phrase 'is true' can be replaced, for that can be the point of definition; what is striking is that it is not replaced by anything else, semantic or otherwise."[26] Rather, it's nullified out by the simultaneous disappearance of the quotation marks. The truth predicate says that a certain named sentence is true, and disquotation asserts the same thing.

Thus the assertion sign is something like the predication of truth. I assert something to be true by using the assertion sign. Or I can assert something to be true by just saying it, without quotation marks. (Indeed, Wittgenstein will appeal to the perfect naturalness of this procedure in his critique of Frege as not saying anything real.)[27] Just to say a sentence—as a sentence—is to say something you want regarded as true. So the quotation mark and the assertion sign are converses of each other, and you'd only need the assertion sign if all sentences otherwise came with quotation marks; then it would cancel out the quotation marks.

When someone says something to me, she or he is asserting it (in most cases), which means she or he is saying it without quotation marks. But my reception of what this person says doesn't mean my automatic agreement. Rather, in most cases, I will entertain the idea before I judge its truth or falsity, before I decide whether the predicate "is true" ought to follow the sentence I've just heard; or whether "is false" would be better; or whether some hedging predicate would be best. In entertaining the idea, I consider whether I would want to assent to it, espouse it, approve it, Milton would say, add my own internal assertion sign to it, or, equivalently, remove the psychic quotation marks that frame it as the idea of another and make it my own idea as well. The difference between what I hear and what I think is a difference that the idea of the quotation mark brings out. It is for this reason that I'm not liable for the verbal content of thoughts that might echo in my mind: even if the words are there, they're not *my* thoughts if I don't approve them: "Evil into the mind of God or Man / May come and go, so unapproved, and leave / No spot or blame behind" (*Paradise Lost*, 5.117).

Now this question of the origin and espousal of thought has to do with questions of literary origination, questions often ranged under the category of inspiration, and questions of the communication of literary affect, which also might be ranged under the category of inspiration (as at the end of Shelley's *Defence of Poetry*, where it is the poets who inspire). All of this has something to do with our relation not only with the words but with the thoughts of others: not merely their words but their words as espoused. Wittgenstein says, "I can know what you are thinking, but I cannot know what I am thinking"(*PI*, p. 211), and one way to understand that is as an aphorism on the nature of thought, rather than according to the more usual Austinian interpretation, which makes it a comment on the nature of knowledge. Knowing and thinking in some sense seem incompatible, because if you know, you're not thinking, and if you're actually thinking, you're not in the position of knowing. This raises ancient questions about the origin of thought. Here I just want to cite some psychoanalytic formulations, from Freud and the Kleinian Wilfred Bion (Beckett's psychoanalyst!), that seem to me relevant. Freud argues that the act of judgment originates in the practice of determining whether to ingest something or not, that is, whether to bring what is outside across the boundary between self and other and to incorporate it.[28] Any act of judgment becomes thus a decision whether to remove the quotation marks from a proposition and to admit it as a thought one espouses and holds as true. Bion similarly treats thoughts as having a sort of referential value, as being something distinct from thinking itself. Like Freud, he regards thinking as the mind's temporizing before its judgment whether to admit something as a thought. Rather than equating thinking and thought, Bion argues that we should "regard thinking as dependent on the successful outcome of two main mental developments. The first is the development of thoughts. They require an apparatus to cope with them. The second development, therefore, is of this apparatus that I shall provisionally call thinking. I repeat—thinking has to be called into existence to cope with thoughts. It will be noted that this differs from any theory of thought as a product of thinking, in that thinking is a development forced on the psyche by the pressure of thoughts and not the other way round."[29]

Thoughts then come to us, you could say, as quotations, and thinking, according to Bion's argument, will consist in taking these alien quotations as ever or never so well expressing the self's own desire. These quotations more or less meet needs whose primary or fantasized objects have been frustrated. I think that this gives a good first approximation of literary experience: words from without which sustain our faltering interiority.

Now thoughts as quotations seem to have something of the character of mental contents, any theory of which it was Wittgenstein's concern to debunk. Yet I think that the psychoanalytic and the Wittgensteinian insight can be brought into harmony by emphasizing Wittgenstein's differentiation between thinking and knowing, which parallels Bion's distinction between thinking and thoughts. What you know are mental contents—what other people are thinking—but the very idea of a mental content is an idea of alterity, an idea of something that belongs to others and not to yourself. The notion that thoughts come to us as quotations, and that our thinking and judging takes the form of a decision whether to remove the quotation marks (or append the assertion sign), shows the alterity of any content and shows that thinking consists in a sort of Kantian limit, that provided by the framing of the quotation marker and not the content thus framed.

Indeed, Kant himself gives some weight to the kind of argument for the simplicity of the soul based on precisely this distinction. That argument, as he paraphrases it, runs this way: "[S]uppose it to be the composite that thinks: then every part of it would be a part of the thought, and only all of them taken together would contain the whole thought. But this cannot be consistently maintained. For representations (for example the single words of a verse), distinguished among different beings, never make up a whole thought (a verse), and it is therefore impossible that a thought should inhere in what is essentially composite. It is therefore possible only in a simple substance, which, not being an aggregate of many, is absolutely simple" (*CPR*, A352, p. 335).[30] Kant doesn't accept this as proving the simplicity of the soul (as James will make a similar argument for the simplicity of mental states within the stream of consciousness), but he does see this as one way of getting at what he calls the absolute unity of the subject of thought in the form of apperception. This unity is not a mental content, then, since it is "not itself an experience, but the form of apperception which belongs to and precedes every experience" (*CPR*, A354, pp. 336–37). The subject as limit, then, is the subject as focus of quotation; the subject itself becomes the instantiation of quotation, not as a content but as a one-sided marker or boundary or asymptote at which the words of the verse are unified. This is why they can be unified even if, as with Winnie, they're entirely forgotten. Thinking and subjectivity are limit phenomena, and they occur at and in the gesture or mark of quotation, not as signs or objects, whether quoted or "internalized."

Consider *Krapp's Last Tape* again. Krapp's listening, thinking, brooding subjectivity is attenuated to the simple act of pushing *forward, rewind, play,* and *stop*. His tape recorder is a kind of Augustinian machine whereby the texts that he rehearses are always mapped, for good or for ill, into the present point on the unspooling tape. Krapp's thinking, his apparatus for dealing with the thoughts that the tape revives in him, is reduced to the tape recorder's control of the activity of quotation: start, end, repeat, skip. These are boundary phenomena, setting boundaries on the words they display, so that Krapp through his machine becomes the marker of the quotations he recites—a marker in both senses in that he actively determines where to start and to stop but passively suffers the fact that this is what he is reduced to: the boundary perception of a fullness of thought that has now become estranged from him.

On this argument, then, it's not the case that inner and outer are two equivalent regions separated by the boundaries between data and the espousal of data, boundaries that I've been relating to the idea of quotation. Rather, the inner is itself the boundary, the moment of quotation or of the framing of the content that comes from outside. Elizabeth Bott Spillius usefully relates Esther Bick's arguments about the formation of the notion of skin to the origin of infantile thinking: Skin is a two-dimensional membrane that marks the boundary between self and other, but the self is two-dimensional, simply the membrane that marks the limit of the three-dimensional world, which is the origin of thoughts and their dangerous impingements.[31] Here you could also think of Zizek's Lacanian account of the sublime as materiality in Hegel, or of Derrida on the trace, especially in "Freud and the Scene of Writing." But Derrida's argument is fundamentally skeptical, and what it's primarily skeptical of is the notion of any content whatever, which is different from

Wittgenstein's dissolution of the notion of mental contents that would correspond to or picture the outside world. Against Derrida's skepticism I want to make an argument for the preservation of some relation of outer content to the quotational self, because I want to say that it is in this relation that literary experience consists. (Here, I think, I am ultimately following Derrida's great precursor Blanchot.)

I'll do so by returning to the issue of the sublime. Longinus, as Neil Hertz has shown, relates the experience of the sublime to the phenomenon of quotation.[32] In that experience, Longinus writes, "the soul takes a proud flight, as though she herself has written what she has only heard or read." This describes precisely the moment of espousal of what originally comes to the self as quotation, and it shows how such a moment of espousal may also be a moment of exaltation. Harold Bloom's idea of the sublime as quotation framed by an "all-but-primal repression"[33] of the context that the quotational boundary replaces shows again how the antithetical moments of espousal and of quotation may be—far from opposed—telescoped. In the experience of the sublime, the acts of quotation and of disquotation become one. This is also, I think, the classic way of describing the phenomenon of inspiration: The poet or writer finds herself or himself inspired to write what will inspire others as well.

Such inspiration is not the inspiration of mental contents but rather of something we could again call the experience of quotation itself. I want to consider one more example from Beckett's *Molloy*, which may help make this clear. Molloy has been describing how he has tried to arrive at a method of sucking his sixteen sucking stones one after another, without repeating any, despite the fact that he has only four pockets. This passage may be said to describe something like the origin of literary vocation:

> And while I gazed thus at my stones, revolving interminable martingales all equally defective, and crushing handfuls of sand, so that the sand ran through my fingers and fell back on the strand, yes, while thus I lulled my mind and part of my body, one day suddenly it dawned on the former, dimly, that I might perhaps achieve my purpose without increasing the number of my pockets, or reducing the number of my stones, but simply by sacrificing the principle of trim. The meaning of this illumination, which suddenly began to sing within me, like a verse of Isaiah, or of Jeremiah, I did not penetrate at once, and notably the word trim, which I had never met with, in this sense, long remained obscure. Finally I seemed to grasp that this word trim could not mean here anything else, anything better, than the distribution of the sixteen stones in four groups of four, one group in each pocket, and that it was my refusal to consider any distribution other than this that had vitiated my calculations until then and rendered the problem literally insoluble.[34]

Probably most readers have never met with the word "trim" used in this sense (something like its nautical sense of the distribution of ballast: in French it's *arrimage*).[35] But the word doesn't remain obscure; like so much in Beckett, the lyric suggestiveness of this passage conveys the meaning without the necessity of decipherment. What else *could* "trim" mean here? And it must be in this sense that the word was also, at some point, suggested to Molloy, so that its lyricism can now "sing within me, like a verse of Isaiah, or of Jeremiah." The word, or the illumination whose light it provides, is like a meaningful archaism, a sense that we have of meanings in language older than *our* meanings. The pleasure in defamiliarization that we can take in coming across an archaism, while still finding that we can penetrate its obscurity, is like the pleasure of a quotation out of context, the pleasure of an epigraph. Archaisms—as Spenser knew—place estrangement within reach of our understanding and give us a sense of the decontextualized, since they alone provide their own context. This is what the word "trim" does here. Its lyricism, singing within Molloy, occurs within a scene describing partial internalization, as Molloy puts the stones in his mouth and sucks on them, to relieve his hunger and thirst. This is a nice parable on Freud's insight into judgment's relation to ingestion, whereby the mind judges whether to incorporate a thought on the model of deciding whether something is nutritious or noxious. For it is not only the stones that Molloy revolves, it is also the martingales or systems by which he might make the revolution of the stones work out (in the French he "ruminates" them, which makes the same connection). The word "martingale" has probably also never been met with, quite in this sense; it's again part of Beckett's lyric suggestiveness that its meaning should be clear and that it should seem to echo our own internal vocabulary rather than add to it. The sucking stones and the martingales are partially incorporated things, not entirely satisfactory, still midway between outside and inside, that is to say still outside, even if "outside within the periphery" (to quote Ashbery). Yet even the real solution, when he discovers it, remains outside: there *are* no internal contents. True, it begins to "sing within" him. But even then it takes a while to "penetrate" its meaning, that is, to penetrate through the quotational boundary, even then there's a difference between the solution as quoted and the solution as penetrated. The solution is within him, but still partially outside, since he has not yet penetrated the solution and effaced the boundaries between it and his understanding. And when he does penetrate it, this is something quite different from the assimilation that ingestion would figure, since you penetrate something outside of you, and go inside it, rather than vice versa.

The theme thus sung within him, the illumination that dawns on him, nevertheless remain obscure for a time, so that the inspiration is still a kind of externality. On the other hand, what it is compared to is something actually external—the verses of Isaiah or of Jeremiah; yet it is these verses that sing within him. But they do not sing within him as completed thoughts, or completed meanings or texts; wonderful indeed in this passage is the word "or" in that phrase: "like a verse of Isaiah, *or* of Jeremiah." Molloy isn't thinking of any particular verse (though the word "trim" does appear in Jeremiah and is used by the King James translators as an intentionally opaque word to cover over an obscurity in their understanding of the text), [36] nor indeed of any particular book in the Bible that the verse might come from. Beckett is no doubt thinking of prophets in the wilderness, and of jeremiads, which is of course part of the point in the allusion. But as for Molloy, he finds it possible to characterize a certain kind of lyric exaltation without needing the specific text as an example. This is another version of Winnie, with her repeated overture to failed quotation: "What are those marvellous words?" She never can remember the quotation, but she always remembers how she felt, even if *what* she felt she remembers not, and the ghost of the quotation, not the quotation itself, is sufficient to make her marvel. (Here again, William James has described this experience with great pertinence, when he describes the phenomenon of having a word on the tip of your tongue. [37] Neary in *Murphy* has this experience looking for the right word to describe Murphy: "There seemed for once to be a right word.") [38] The ghost of the quotation is what inspires her, just as Molloy is inspired by a general memory of the way the verses of Isaiah or Jeremiah sing, rather than by the actual singing of any particular verse. And we as readers feel a similarly general memory for the lyricism of the major prophets, without ourselves hearing the actual singing of their verses as we read this passage. (I think the origin of this is Hamlet, trying to remember the speech he loves so well from Aeneas's tale to Dido, and misremembering it at first.)

The ghost of the quotation from the Bible Molloy compares to an actual sentence, with very specific words: "I might perhaps achieve my purpose without increasing the number of my pockets, or reducing the number of my stones, but simply by sacrificing the principle of trim." (We know that these are the words that sing within him because he says that what gave him notable trouble in this illumination is "the word trim.") So the difference between actual words and the ghost of a memory of words, as a phenomenon of mental life and particularly of inspiration, doesn't come down to very much. Illuminations can sing without being very meaningful; indeed, verses can sing without our being able to refer to them specifically at all or even to the biblical book they come from. Our experience of poetry, like our most passionate but most attenuated memories of poetry, is an example of what Paul de Man calls allegory: There is no internal object which founds this experience, but only a sense of quotation without origin, of the canonical form of the verbatim without its verbatim contents, the difference between magnitude and shadow come undone.

Notes

1. Walter Benjamin, "The Work of Art in the Age of Mechanical Reproduction," in *Illuminations*, trans. Harry Zohn (New York: Schocken, 1969), 217–51.

2. See, inter alia, Harold Bloom, *The Anxiety of Influence* (New York: Oxford, 1973), and *The Western Canon* (New York: Harcourt, 1994).

3. Ralph Waldo Emerson, "Quotation and Originality," in *Letters and Social Aims*, in *The Complete Works of Ralph Waldo Emerson* (Cambridge: Riverside, 1904), 8, 175–204, 191.

4. See Samuel Beckett, *Krapp's Last Tape: With a Revised Text*, ed. and with an introduction and notes by James Knowlson (London: Faber, 1992).

5. Immanuel Kant, *The Critique of Pure Reason*, trans. Norman Kemp Smith (New York: St. Martin's, 1965), B641, p. 513; hereafter cited in text as *CPR*.

6. See my essay "The Ambivalence of Generosity: Keats Reading Shakespeare," *ELH* 62 (1995): 149–69.

7. See Patrick McGurk, "Citation Marks in Early Latin Manuscripts," *Scriptorium* 15 (1961): 3–13.

8. See two other articles of mine: "Quoting Poetry," *Critical Inquiry* 18 (1991): 42–63, and "The Poetics of Speech Tags," in *Renaissance Literature and Its Formal Engagements*, ed. Mark Denis Rasmussen (New York: Palgrave, 2002), 159–84.

9. M. B. Parkes, *Pause and Effect: An Introduction to the History of Punctuation in the West* (Berkeley: University of California Press, 1993), 57–58.

10. Isidore of Seville, *Etymologiarum*, ed. W. M. Lindsay (Oxford: Oxford University Press, 1911), 1.21.14, who following an ancient source attributes this rule to Leogaras of Syracuse.

11. McGurk, "Citation Marks," 4.

12. Marcel Proust, *A la recherche du temps perdu*, 8 vols. (Paris: Gallimard, 1954), 1:36; hereafter cited in text as *RTP*. All translations from Proust's French are my own.

13. Samuel Beckett, "First Love," in *First Love and Other Shorts* (New York: Grove, 1974), 35–36.

14. See Samuel Beckett, *Premier Amour* (Paris: Minuit, 1970), 56.

15. Maurice Blanchot, *L'attente l'oubli* (Paris: Gallimard, 1962).

16. Marcel Proust, *Jean Santeuil* (Paris: Gallimard, 1971), 701; hereafter cited in text as *JS*.

17. See my article "Anonymity and Unhappiness in Proust and Wittgenstein," *Criticism* 29 (1987): 459–76.

18. Samuel Beckett, *Watt* (New York: Grove Press, 1959), 247–54.

19. Samuel Beckett, *Happy Days* (New York: Grove Press, 1970), 31.

20. Beckett identified all the obvious quotations, and some less obvious allusions, several times; his identifications may be consulted most easily in James

Knowlson, ed., *Happy Days: The Production Notebook of Samuel Beckett* (London: Faber and Faber, 1985), 54–61. See also Knowlson's notes to these pages, 143–49.

21. There's a further complication to this moment. As usual, Beckett is thinking of Joyce, here of the end of the "Proteus" chapter in *Ulysses*. Stephen is thinking of the coming of the solstice: "By the way next when is it Tuesday will be the longest day. Of all the glad new year, mother, the rum tum tiddledy tum. Lawn Tennyson, gentleman poet" (James Joyce, *Ulysses: The Corrected Text*, prepared by Hans Walter Gabler with Wolfhard Steppe and Claus Melchior [New York: Random House, 1986], pt. 3, pp. 490–92). This preserves the meter, just as "something something" does in Winnie's speech, of Tennyson's "The May Queen": "Tomorrow'll be the happiest time of all the glad New-Year; / Of all the glad New-year, mother, the maddest merriest day" (2–3 and 42–43). Thus Winnie's elision is a sort of quotation of Stephen's elision—they both elide the idea of madness ("moody madness" and "maddest merriest"). And of course Beckett's allusion to the lines remembered by Stephen is an allusion also to lines that suggest the title of his play—"the happiest time . . . the merriest day."

22. These substitutive "somethings" are used to effect by other writers interested in the phenomena of forgotten quotation. Thus Praed, in a comic poem, refers to the banal fate of his once etherealized beloved as to have become "Mrs. Something-Rogers." Nabokov will have Humbert Humbert trying to piece together the words of

a song hit in ful—to the best of my recollection at least—I don't think I ever got it right. Here goes:

O my Carmen, my little Carmen!
Something, something those something nights,
And the stars, and the cars, and the bars, and the barmen—
And, O my charmin', our dreadful fights.
And the something town where so gaily, arm in
Arm, we went, and our final row,
And the gun I killed you with, O my Carmen,
The gun I am holding now.

(Vladimir Nabokov, *Lolita* [New York: Berkeley, 1977], 58–59)

Alvin Feinman begins his poem "Pilgrim Heights" with a sense of loss reduced to a fiercely rhythmical elemental residue: "Something something the heart here misses" (Alvin Feinman, *Preambles and Other Poems* [New York: Oxford University Press, 1964], 11), a line that Jay Wright, in his more soothing answer, "Indian

Pond," quotes simply as "Something the heart here misses" (Jay Wright, *Transfigu-rations: Collected Poems* [Baton Rouge: Louisiana State University Press, 2000], 553). Joyce makes Leopold Bloom, trying to remember an off-color limerick, display his far less rhythmical memory when he adds superabundant somethings as place holders for single syllables he can't remember: "Who ate or something the some-things of the Reverend Mr MacTrigger" (James Joyce, *Ulysses: The Corrected Text*, ed. Hans Walter Gabler [New York: Random House, 1986], 8.748). As I'll suggest below, Shakespeare was interested as well in forgotten quotations, and in forgotten thoughts more generally. Compare Cleopatra's farewell to Antony:

> Courteous lord, one word.
> Sir, you and I must part; but that's not it.
> Sir, you and I have loved; but there's not it;
> That you know well. Something it is I would—
> O, my oblivion is a very Antony,
> And I am all forgotten.
> (William Shakespeare, *Antony and Cleopatra* 1.4.87–92)

In all these cases, *something* flits and oscillates between use and mention, cipher and source.

Elsewhere I hope to discuss forgotten and elided quotations at greater length (e.g., dashes, et ceteras, hiatuses): consider the way Bishop represents her Crusoe as forgetting the word "Solitude" on his island when he (anachronistically) tries to quote Wordsworth to himself; Georges Perec, in *Je me souviens*, forgets the word "bliss" in the same passage from "I wandered lonely as a cloud." I wish to note here the relevance of another punctuation mark that Isidore of Seville explains: the asterisk, as sign of elision "that through this sign may dawn what things are omitted. For in Greek star is called *aster*, whence asterisk is derived" (1.21.2, my translation).

23. Or at least they are dialectically mutually determining. See Millman Parry, *The Making of Homeric Verse* (Oxford: Clarendon, 1971). Similarly, in English, iambic meter is dictated by the fact that most English bisyllables are trochees (consider: "English," "meter," "trochee," "moody," "madness," "something"); intro-duced and followed by particles or other common one-syllable words, they will fall into iambic patterns. This means, as well, that in English iambic meter, word and phrase boundaries mostly don't correspond to foot boundaries, a fact we've already seen exemplified in overlaying "o'er that brow a shadow fling" over "something something shadow fling."

24. See his *Begriffsschrift und andere Aufsätze*, 2d ed. (Darmstadt: Wissenschaft-liche Buchgesellschaft, 1964).

25. W. V. Quine, *The Pursuit of Truth* (Cambridge: Harvard University Press, 1992), 81, 80. See Alfred Tarski, "The Concept of Truth in Formalized Languages" (1936), in his *Logic, Semantics, Metamathematics,* trans. J. H. Woodger (Oxford: Clarendon, 1956), 152–278, where he gives a particularly rigorous account of the relation of expressions surrounded by quotation marks (or "functors") to names, and "The Semantic Conception of Truth," in *Philosophy and Phenomenological Research* 4 (1944): 341–76.

26. Donald Davidson, *Inquiries into Truth and Interpretation* (New York: Oxford, 1984), 285.

27. Ludwig Wittgenstein, *Philosophical Investigations,* trans. G. E. M. Anscombe (New York: Macmillan, 1958), §22; hereafter cited as *PI.* As is traditional, citations from part 1 are by aphorism number (indicated by the symbol §); part 2 is cited by page number (indicated with "p.").

28. See Sigmund Freud, "Negation," in *The Standard Edition of the Complete Psychological Works of Sigmund Freud,* trans. James Strachey (London: Hogarth, 1981), 19, 235–39.

29. Wilfred Bion, "A Theory of Thinking," in *Melanie Klein Today,* vol. 1, ed. Elizabeth Bott Spillius (London: Routledge, 1988), 179.

30. This argument may derive from Augustine:

> . . . without voice or lips we can go through poems and verses and speeches in our minds, and we can allow for the time it takes for their movement, one part in relation to another, exactly as if we were reciting them aloud. If a man decides to utter a longish sound and settles in his mind how long the sound is to be, he goes through that space of time in silence, entrusts it to his memory, then begins to utter the sound, and it sounds until it reaches the length he had fixed for it. . . .
>
> Suppose that I am about to recite a psalm that I know. Before I begin, my expectation is directed to the whole of it; but when I have begun, so much of it as I pluck off and drop away into the past becomes matter for my memory; and [the] whole energy of the action is divided between my memory, in regard to what I have said, and my expectation, in regard to what I am still to say. But there is a present act of attention, by which what was future passes on its way to becoming past. The further I go in my recitation, the more my expectation is diminished and my memory lengthened, until the whole of my expectation is used up when the action is completed and has passed wholly into memory. (Augustine, *Confessions,* trans. F. J. Sheed [Indianapolis: Hackett, 1993], 228–29 [chap. 11, pp. 27–28]).

31. See Elizabeth Bott Spillius, *Melanie Klein Today,* vol. 1 (London: Routledge, 1988), 158, and Esther Bick, "The Experience of the Skin in Early Object-

Relations," in *Melanie Klein Today*, vol. 1, ed. Elizabeth Bott Spillius (London: Routledge, 1988), 187–91.

32. Neil Hertz, "A Reading of Longinus," in *The End of the Line* (New York: Columbia University Press, 1985), 1–20.

33. See Harold Bloom, "The Sublime Crossing and the Death of Love," in *Agon: Towards a Theory of Revisionism* (New York: Oxford University Press, 1982), 241.

34. Samuel Beckett, *Molloy, Malone Dies and the Unnamable* (New York: Grove, 1959), 71.

35. Samuel Beckett, *Molloy* (Paris: Minuit, 1951), 108.

36. "Why trimmest thou thy way to seeke loue? therefore hast thou also taught the wicked ones thy wayes" (Jer 2:33 AV).

37. See William James, *The Principles of Psychology*, vol. 1 (New York: Dover, 1950), 251–52:

> Suppose we try to recall a forgotten name. The state of our consciousness is peculiar. There is a gap therein; but no mere gap. It is a gap that is intensely active. A sort of wraith of the name is in it, beckoning us in a given direction, making us at moments tingle with the sense of our closeness, and then letting us sink back without the longed-for term. If wrong names are proposed to us, this singularly definite gap acts immediately so as to negate them. They do not fit into its mould. And the gap of one word does not feel like the gap of another, all empty of content as both might seem necessarily to be when described as gaps. When I vainly try to recall the name of Spalding, my consciousness is far removed from what it is when I vainly try to recall the name of Bowles. There are innumerable consciousnesses of want, no one of which taken in itself has a name, but all different from each other. Such feeling of want is tota coelo other than a want of feeling: it is an intense feeling. The rhythm of a lost word may be there without a sound to clothe it; or the evanescent sense of something which is the initial vowel or consonant may mock us fitfully, without growing more distinct. Every one must know the tantalizing effect of the blank rhythm of some forgotten verse, restlessly dancing in one's mind, striving to be filled out with words.

38. Samuel Beckett, *Murphy* (New York: Grove Press, 1957).

The Self, Reflected: Wittgenstein, Cavell, and the Autobiographical Situation

Garry L. Hagberg

It is widely understood, first of all, that Ludwig Wittgenstein's multifarious writings on language hold deep significance for the philosophy of mind, to an extent that, because of his writings as well as what has followed in their wake, many are now reluctant to even go so far as to draw a distinction between the philosophies of mind and of language. To achieve a fuller comprehension of language, to gain an overview of what Wittgenstein called in the preface to *Philosophical Investigations* the "landscapes," the sketching of which required his traversing "a wide field of thought," precisely is to gain an overview of many various and interrelated facets of the mind in its multifarious deployments.[1] Second, it is widely understood as well that Wittgenstein was fundamentally opposed to what he revealed to be a particularly pernicious conceptual model, or "picture," of linguistic meaning, the dualistic picture separating the inner from the outer. Third, it is equally widely understood that Wittgenstein's opposition to—or rather undercutting of—the inner/outer distinction is directed with as much force to its employment in the philosophy of mind—in our conceptual modeling of the human subject—as it is to its employment in the philosophy of language; thus this third point serves as one of the many supporting reasons for the first.

But there is, in this line of thought, a curious and at least seemingly strange inability to progress to a fourth point. One would like to be able to add to this list that the general overview of language, along with a developed appreciation of the significance of this work for our understanding of the mind, has brought us to a point of clarity concerning Wittgenstein's conception of the self. But this subject seems veiled; there is an air of mystery surrounding the conception of the self that lingers after we work through Wittgenstein's related yet separate discussions. Indeed, if there should be a widespread understanding here, or, given what we have to work with from the writings Wittgenstein has left us on this topic, then is the topic—indisputably among the most significant and, one imagines, deep questions not only of the philosophy of mind but rather of all philosophy—permanently veiled? Has Wittgenstein simply failed to provide an account anywhere near as full as his accounts of the related but different issues? Why, given the profundity of his work elsewhere in the philosophy of mind, would he leave the matter where he did?

The answer to this question requires our looking into not only where he left the matter but where he started it, as well as into those surrounding issues closely related to the question of the nature of the self. These would include his remarks on philosophical seclusion and his intertwined critique of introspection; his stout rejection—and here perhaps not always so widely understood a rejection—of behaviorism; his equally forceful rejection of Cartesianism; his employment of the concept of avowal (supplanting our conception of the verbal *description* of an inner state with the verbal *expression* of an inner state—where the phrase "inner state" is thus differently understood); his penetrating remarks on consciousness; and his positive or nondualistic conception, unfortunately more intimated than argued and explicated, of genuine introspection. And all of these, taken together, would lead to a position from which the epistemological value of those forms of literature in a sense closest to human beings, that is, autobiography, and full literary depictions of mental life—in short, the literature of the self or, as it is now called, life-writing—can perhaps be perspicuously understood.

1. Observing Consciousness

It cannot be plausibly argued that Wittgenstein simply did not care about the philosophical problem concerning the nature of the human subject. First, it was certainly implicit, if not explicit, in the philosophical positions to which his work responded or reacted: it is clearly at the center of rationalism, most obviously in the Cartesian conception of the thinking thing, the inner point of consciousness that constitutes the self; it is in empiricism in the various forms of Locke's personal identity problem, Berkeley's idealism, and notably Hume's "bundle theory" of the self; it is in Kant's transcendental unity of apperception; it is in Schopenhauer's conception of the Will; it is in James's introspectionist self in his psychology; it is in Russell's work on the analysis of mind; and—perhaps most significantly for Wittgenstein—it is in Frege's revised employment of the traditional ontological distinction between the mental and the physical in his "first realm" of ideas, which are private to the mind of the thinker, and the "second realm" of outward material objects. Second, the fact that this concern is in truth deeply important to Wittgenstein and was so from an early stage is clear from a memorable entry from 1916 in the *Notebooks*: "The I, the I is what is deeply mysterious!"[2] But of course it is within the context of his working on the *Tractatus Logico-Philosophicus* that the question fully comes to the surface, and it is treated in a way suggesting that this may be one of the very few areas in which Wittgenstein's thought remains fairly consistent throughout his life, at any rate in terms of the conclusion—even if the manner of reaching that conclusion differs in method and substance considerably. He writes, fairly amazingly, at 5.631, "there is no such thing as the subject that thinks or entertains ideas." But it is important to realize that he has already said at 4.003— and here too is another rare line of continuity in his thought from the earliest to the latest—"most of the propositions and questions of philosophy arise from our failure to understand the logic of our language." There is indeed something— in fact a number of different things[3]—that lead us to misconstrue the logic of our language of the human subject, the self, the I; it is thus, even at this very early stage, a distinctively *philosophical* myth he is opposing. As we shall see, the foregoing claim is not really so amazing—it is not, for one thing, self-refuting, in that it is written by a thinking, idea-entertaining subject and communicated to another thinking subject, the reader, who is implicitly expected to entertain its central idea. There is, in short, not a kind of cogito argument readily available against this claim. Wittgenstein is not self-contradictorily writing that a thinking writer is not now writing but rather that a particular—and particularly pernicious—philosophical picture of the self, the subject, is what is false, what does not exist. He later writes, in the *Blue Book,* that it is only through the tricks that language plays on us, it is only through the bewitchment of our intelligence by means of language, as he would go on to express the matter in *Philosophical Investigations,* that we come to believe in the myth that the first person pronoun refers to "something bodiless, which, however, has its seat in our bodies." "In fact," he says, "*this* seems to be the real ego, the one of which it was said, '*Cogito, ergo sum.*'"[4] One way to more accurately identify the mythical picture of the self to which he is opposed is to examine a number of his remarks on introspection and the picture,[5] the conceptual model, of inward psychological seclusion that it enforces.

It is apparent from virtually any inquiry into anything whatsoever that one needs an *object* upon which to focus one's attention, if we are to employ the concept of *inspecting.* But to go this far—which is seemingly not very far at all—is already to allow language to lead us astray, to establish a fundamental analogy—in truth a misleading analogy—between the mental and the physical or, as Wittgenstein warns us, to lay the foundation for conceptually modeling the mental on the physical. To inspect, we think, we need an object; to introspect, we consequently think, we need an object of another kind. And that object, if we are puzzled about or indeed mystified by the nature of the self, will be separated from the physical or the material, and the sense of mystery will be heightened as the separation proceeds. In *Philosophical Investigations,* §412, Wittgenstein opens by referring to the "feeling of an unbridgeable gulf between consciousness and brain process" but then just as quickly establishes the other pole, the pole of ordinary experience: "[H]ow does it come about that this does not come into the considerations of our ordinary life?" Back to the philosophical pole, he goes on by identifying a feeling that accompanies the thought: "This idea of a difference in kind is accompanied by a slight giddiness," and now moving again, but this time to a new position, one in which, grounded in ordinary experience, we are aware of philosophical artifice: "—which occurs when we are performing a piece of logical sleight of hand." "When," he now asks, "does this feeling occur in the present case?" The answer to this question, along with his subsequent reaction to the answer, reveals the conceptual model of introspection that he finds unacceptable. "It is when I, for example, turn my attention in a particular way onto my own consciousness, and, astonished, say to myself: THIS is supposed to be produced by a process in the brain!—as it were clutching my forehead.—" And this depiction of introspection is just as quickly met with a return back to the other pole: "But what can it mean to speak of 'turning my attention on to my own consciousness?' This is surely the queerest thing there could be!"

It is thus not a Humean point Wittgenstein is here making; he is not asserting that when we introspect, when we focus our inward gaze on the self, we find not a self but one of a larger number of particular experiences of sensation or reflection, impression or idea, so that we can never really arrive at anything but the bundle of impressions and ideas. He is rather pointing to the very *strangeness* of this way of describing an attempted mental act (and this phrase "attempted mental act," too, as is naturally the case, is in turn a strange way of describing the strangeness). It is the very idea of an "inward gaze" that is fundamentally problematic, and Wittgenstein's following words can be read as an implicit criticism of that familiar philosophical notion; in what follows he does *not* use the word "gaze" metaphorically: "It was a particular act of gazing that I called doing this. I stared fixedly in front of me— but *not* at any particular point or object. My eyes were wide open, the brows not contracted (as they mostly are when I am interested in a particular object). No such interest preceded this gazing." And his glance, he adds, "was vacant," and underscoring the word *"like"* precisely because the glance only resembled, it did not equal, as there was no object upon which visual scrutiny rested, adds "or again *like* that of someone admiring the illumination of the sky and drinking in the light." Wittgenstein closes this section by observing that the proposition he found paradoxical in a philosophical voice ("THIS is produced by a brain process!") in another, ordinary voice has nothing at all paradoxical about it; it might have been said in a neurophysiological experiment in which the effect of light is produced in a subject by stimulating a part of the brain. He adds two important final thoughts in this section, one concerning the social context of the utterance, the other concerning the psychological state of the imagined speaker, neither of which involves any inner occult process for its comprehension: "But I did not utter the sentence in the surroundings in which it would have had an everyday and unparadoxical sense. And my attention was not such as would have accorded with making an experiment. (If it had been, my look would have been intent, not vacant)." We thus have the grounds upon which Wittgenstein says, opening §413, "Here we have a case of introspection," and he further suggests that it is from a similar case that William James derived his conception of the self.

Seeing a direct connection here to the philosophy of language, he notes that "James's introspection shewed, not the meaning of the word 'self' (so far as it means something like 'person,' 'human being,' 'he himself,' 'I myself'), nor any analysis of such a thing." This is a telling remark in relation to our fundamental questions concerning Wittgenstein's conception of the self and the conception(s) of the self to which he is opposed. First, it clearly indicates an antireferential position with regard to the self; introspection does *not* show the meaning of the word "self," supported by the twin claims that (1) more specifically, the introspective act only *pretends* to focus on an object that would serve as an inward referent of the word "self," and (2) more generally, we should free ourselves from the illusion (also generated by the misleading analogies language readily offers us, specifically that all words function like names, which goes back to the opening of *Philosophical Investigations*)[6] that words get their meanings exclusively from the objects to which they refer. Second, it moves, again, between the poles of the philosophical voice and the ordinary voice, and speaking in the latter, Wittgenstein reminds us, if only in brief, of the contextualized employments of terms or phrases such as "persons," "human beings," and "he himself." The grammatically misled philosophical conception of the introspective self is utterly remote from our *uses* of such phrases; again, Wittgenstein is implicitly relying on the sense of strangeness as an indicator of conceptual confusion[7] or, in this particular case, of the presence of a philosophical myth. Third, Wittgenstein adds, significantly if briefly, that James's introspective project did not provide an *analysis of* the concept of the self; it does not in truth go behind or beneath the allegedly superficial appearance of language in anything like the style of his own earlier and Russell's atomistic works.[8] The stance taken here is thus antianalytical (in this restricted sense of atomistic analysis only; it certainly is not against conceptual *clarification*) as well as antireferential. Both of these, Wittgenstein is indicating, would lead us astray—the referential leading us into inward reification, the analytical leading us to look *beneath* precisely what it is we need to look at *directly*, that is, the language-games in which self-terms operate.[9]

Indeed, what James's introspective project shows is rather "the state of a philosopher's attention when he says the word 'self' to himself and starts to analyze its meaning." Wittgenstein adds parenthetically that a good deal could be learned from this, which, given its clear relation to the belief with which Wittgenstein is concerned throughout his late philosophy, namely, that the meaning of a word is its referent, seems true enough. But at present it is important to see one of the things that Wittgenstein is *not* saying in this passage. He is not arguing that introspection, as a method for achieving self-knowledge, is fallible and therefore of dubious epistemological value. This is in fact the position James himself develops, [10] and thus on this point James differs substantially from the Cartesian position, which holds that introspection, because of its unmediated nature, is infallible. Wittgenstein's point is *very* different; it is, again, not only that the very idea of introspection as construed within this philosophical voice is mythological and that the self upon which we place our introspective gaze is a part of conceptual mythology as well but also that we do not in truth *perceive* or *observe* our own consciousness. [11] One way briefly to recall to mind this element of Wittgenstein's philosophy as it pertains to the question of the self is to try to find an intelligible context in which we can give a ready answer to the question "How do we know we are in pain?" This linguistic exercise suggests that *knowledge* is an ill-suited concept for this kind of context, because there is not an epistemic divide between there being a pain and our knowing of it. There is such a divide, by contrast, with external objects; there can be a book on my desk without my knowing that it is there. Thus here the grammar of the external world leads us astray when the internal world is modeled upon it. An insufficient intricacy in these matters, as Wittgenstein repeatedly shows, is an ever present danger: to speak of the "internal world" in contrast to the external is to incline our subsequent thinking in turn toward the idea of an inner mental world populated by mental objects or, as Ryle put it, a private stage, [12] and this is precisely the "picture" of the mind Wittgenstein is combating in his multifront war with grammatically induced misconceptions. The fundamental point, possessing the greatest power to undercut the very idea of Cartesian or Jamesian introspection, is thus again, contrary to our preconceptions that exert their power only so long as we remain under the influence of misleading analogies, that we do not perceive or observe consciousness. [13]

In *Philosophical Investigations* (§416), Wittgenstein writes, again in the interlocutor's philosophical voice: "'Human beings agree in saying that they see, hear, feel, and so on (even though some are blind and some are deaf). So they are their own witnesses that they have consciousness.'" The intuitively plausible introspectionist idea being put forward is clear enough, and Wittgenstein again responds to it immediately with a return to the ordinary voice, again employing the criterion of strangeness: "—But how strange this is! Whom do I really inform, if I say 'I have consciousness'? What is the purpose of saying this to myself and how can another person understand me?" And, once again, returning philosophical language to its ordinary employment, Wittgenstein observes that we *do* say such things in medical contexts, contexts of repeated fainting ("I am conscious again"), and so forth. The challenge, indeed the assault, contained within this remark is powerful and profound. Can we get so far as to even *understand* the claim that would seem absolutely necessary to the articulation of the Cartesian conception of the self? Or are we relying, at the most fundamental level in the articulation of this model of the self, on a form of expression, on a phrase allegedly self-defining (in both senses, in that it would deliver its own first person meaning intrinsically as well as give definition to the word "self") that in truth delivers sense only if we take it away from its philosophical and remove it back to its ordinary voice—in which case it means something (as in the medical contexts) but (and here is the potency of the observation) not what it alleges or pretends to in its philosophical position. Disguised nonsense was the particular variety of nonsense that interested Wittgenstein the most in his later works, and one of the reasons for this is perhaps that the disguises can present appearances not only of seemingly obvious irrefutability ("I know I am conscious because I observe it, I perceive it") but also appearances of capturing the essence of the mysterious "I."

The argument gains clarity in the next section. In §417, Wittgenstein asks, "Do I observe myself, then, and perceive that I am seeing or conscious?" This question is answered, indirectly, with a question asking why we should talk about *observation* at all; indeed, why not simply say that we *perceive* we are conscious, since the act of observation seems clearly otiose if we already perceive our consciousness? But again—and Wittgenstein is moving through intermediate steps from the philosophical to the ordinary voice—we can ask, in an equally direct manner, why should we say *perceive*? Why not just say "I am conscious," since the act of *perceiving* now seems equally otiose? There is, I believe, at this point a missing step that needs to be inserted, or made explicit if it is implicit, in order to show the force of Wittgenstein's position; it is also at the point of this missing step that the argument becomes significantly more intricate. If indeed we remove *observation* from the claim of first person consciousness, then the very concept of introspection is losing its content: what would it mean to say that introspection is the inviolable source of knowledge of the self if the very act of in(or inward)spection, that is, the experiential substance of the word "introspection," is absent?

We might then say, moving to a position closer to the Cartesian than to the Jamesian, that we still know it because we *perceive* it immediately, without the mediating mental act of in(tro)spection, but this retort in the philosophical voice has a two-pronged answer, here only one of which Wittgenstein has provided explicitly. The first prong, as we have seen, is to remove the mental act of perceiving just as we did observing, thus severing consciousness from the perception of it. The second prong is to make clear that this strands the philosophical voice, leaving it isolated from the *knowledge* of consciousness, from independently assessing the fact of consciousness (as, for example, we might imagine an animal being conscious without simultaneously "knowing" of its consciousness). And without the capacity to independently assess the fact of consciousness, without the autonomy of the knowing subject who declares himself conscious, the content of the "I" seems irremediably unclear in the first person claim of knowledge of consciousness.

Another way to put this is to say that the second "I" in the judgment "I perceive I am conscious" is not isolable from the consciousness, and thus to note that it possesses this property seems at the very least otiose, if not unintelligible. And the initial phrase "I perceive," where the object of perception is the consciousness of the I," seems, to put it another way, reflexively claustrophobic: the "I" can never get away from the consciousness it (allegedly independently) attributes to itself or judges itself to possess. But to simplify, if, having removed observation and perception, we say now only "I am conscious," we might well understand this—if only in the ordinary voice—but then it does not in any clear (or other) way rest on a foundation of introspection; indeed, it appears impossible to wedge introspection into this context. Wittgenstein's next explicit step, again with growing intricacy, is to remark "—But don't the words 'I perceive' here shew that I am attending to my consciousness?—which is ordinarily not the case." If this is true, he then observes, the sentence "I perceive I am conscious" does not perform the job of saying that we are conscious, but rather the job—a very different one, and one that again brings the philosophical back to the ordinary voice—of saying that our attention is disposed in a particular way. And again he closes this section by asking his question that continually reaffirms the necessity of context for intelligibility: "In what situations do we say it?"

2. The Picture of Metaphysical Seclusion

Despite the qualms one may have, after following Wittgenstein's discussion, about the very possibility of getting so far as to comprehend the concept of introspection, much less to determine its precise character both as a mental act and as a fundamental source of knowledge of the self, one may still feel assured in positing the ultimate seclusion of each individual mind, each private self.[14] Wittgenstein also argues against this picture of the self or, more precisely, against this conception of the circumstances in which the "I" finds, indeed, itself. In *Philosophical Investigations*, part 2, section xi, we find the errant interlocutor, or the philosophical voice, again speaking a language bewitched by the tricks of grammar and misleading analogies. He makes this assertion: "'A man's thinking goes on within his consciousness in a seclusion in comparison with which any physical seclusion is an exhibition to public view'" (*PI*, p. 222). This gives very clear and forceful articulation to the view that many find philosophically obvious as the first brute fact of life.

Wittgenstein's initial step in unsettling this conception, this picture of the self's most fundamental predicament, is to respond in the interrogatory: Would people who were somehow able to "read" the "silent internal discourse" of other people—and here he adds, significantly (in that his remark suggests a *physical* rather than ghostly or immaterial mode of access, or mind reading, to that inward discourse), that they accomplished this remarkable feat by closely observing the larynx—be inclined to employ this picture of complete seclusion, the picture of ultimately inviolable isolation that in turn motivates and nourishes other-minds skepticism and, at the logical extreme, solipsism? His implication is clearly that they would not. Yet, for a number of interrelated, and as it were conspiring, reasons—here including a misconception of language in dualistic terms of physical, outward signs and internal, mental meanings (thus lodging the permanent possibility of skepticism within language itself), along with a corresponding misconception of the possibility, indeed the naturalness, of a private language that only the speaker can understand (because the inner referents of this language are private experiences)—we are, or can easily be, strongly inclined to say that they (and we in that imagined condition of inward-discourse readability) indeed *would* embrace the picture of the metaphysically secluded self. It seems that the inner world is, in this distinct, ontological sense (in that the self is not and could not be the *kind* of thing open to public view), *hidden*. Wittgenstein immediately takes this term "hidden" back to the ordinary voice, beyond the grasp of this particular manifestation of skepticism, by simply observing, "If I were to talk to myself out loud in a language not understood by those present my thoughts would be hidden from them." This bracing observation performs two services simultaneously, in that it contextualizes the concept "hidden," showing us where we readily understand it—where we use it—and thus how remote this usage is from its philosophical guise, and it reminds us that the comprehension of "hidden" in this sentence does not necessitate—and in this case in fact excludes—any metaphysical conception of an inner, private, ghostly realm wherein thoughts are hidden.

Wittgenstein continues to develop his argument in this vein, observing, in the imaginary case of a person who always guessed right what we were saying to ourselves in our thoughts, that the criterion for his guessing right is that we are truthful and confess that he has guessed right. And, severing the picture of secluded inner thought from the understanding of "right," he observes that the criteria for truth of such a confession of thought are not coequal with the criteria for the description of a process; moreover, the importance of the true confession of thought "does not reside in its being a correct and certain report of a process." Thus, against the predictions cast by the picture of inner seclusion, when we look to the actual details of lived experience, we find—to greatly abbreviate[15]— that what it means to understand a person is not equivalent to what it means to understand the descriptions of the inner processes of that person's private mind. And again, what will strike us as important about a confession of inward thought is not that the report of such an inner process is certain but rather—and here too we see an extreme abbreviation—that it is given "in the special consequences" of the confession, whose truth is guaranteed not by its correspondence to an inner process but by "the special criteria of *truthfulness*."[16]

There is a further example Wittgenstein gives in this discussion that serves to reorient us away from the conception of psychological interiority. He mentions a game of guessing thoughts with variants: A speaks a language B does not, and B is supposed to guess what A meant; or A writes down a sentence unseen by B and B has to guess its sense, or A is putting a jigsaw puzzle together and, although B cannot see A, periodically guesses A's thoughts, saying things like "Now where is this bit?" "The sky is always the hardest part," and so forth (*PI*, p. 223). In each case, what is hidden is not *metaphysically* hidden; the meaning of the unknown language, the hidden words—these contextualize the word "hidden" in ways that fail, instructively, to correspond to the picture of the self's complete seclusion. But does the puzzle case really do this, exactly? Here we may insist, under the influence of the picture, that the *thoughts* are themselves hidden. But Wittgenstein's point operates at a more subtle level: If B is right on occasion, his rightness does not depend on a correspondence between his sentences and the silent or out-loud utterances of A; indeed, Wittgenstein adds, "but I need not be talking to myself either out loud or silently at the time." What this discussion points to is: (1) the language in which we express our convictions concerning first-person privacy may be language that we in truth do not understand; (2) the picture of seclusion is motivated in part by, ironically, a misunderstanding of what it actually is to understand people; and (3) the picture of seclusion is nourished, again, not only by a large-scale misconception of linguistic meaning but more narrowly by an erroneous conception of the meaning determinants, that is, inner referents, of emotion terms.

Each of these topics will resurface in what follows, but, to complete the reconsideration of this part of Wittgenstein's discussion as it pertains to the nature of selfhood, he now claims explicitly what he implied earlier, that thoughts are no more hidden than "unperceived physical proceedings." He suggests a new analogy for hiddenness. In reply to the interlocutor's philosophical voice restating with renewed emphasis (despite all these various conceptual desiderata) that "what is *internal* is hidden from us," Wittgenstein says that the future is hidden from us but that an astronomer is not thinking this way when he predicts an eclipse of the sun. He reminds us that when we see a person writhing in pain with clear cause, we do not think that nevertheless his feelings are in truth hidden from us. He reminds us that we can in circumstantial fact be as *"certain* of someone else's sensations as of any fact," then adding, against the philosophical impulse to assimilate diversity into a simple uniformity, that this does not make reports on people's moods, mathematical calculations, and self-descriptions of the "I am x years old" kind, "similar instruments," but rather that the certainty in each case is determined by the language-game in which it operates. There is an *appearance* of a psychological difference between the claims "He is much depressed," "25 times 25 equals 625," and "I am sixty years old," but the difference is rather logical, which at this point in his philosophy means that the language-games are different. We are not less certain that a person is in pain than that twice two equals four; our inclination to believe this is yet another symptom of the widening influence of the picture of the metaphysically secluded self.[17]

The fairly uniform clothing of language can make very diverse language-games appear alike, and in response to the philosophical voice insisting " 'While you can have complete certainty about someone else's state of mind, still it is always merely subjective, not objective, certainty,' " Wittgenstein flatly replies, "These two words betoken a difference between language-games" (*PI*, p. 225). Again, a logical difference is misconstrued as a psychological one; the very word "subjective" shows its danger[18] in calling us back to the philosophical voice, and the influence of our own language over us (in making us want to say what fits the metaphysical picture) is approximating a condition of autoventriloquism. But we should, Wittgenstein suggests, at this stage of these considerations, show strong resistance if not outright rejection. If the doubt concerning our capacity to know the mind of another because of its inviolable privacy reenters through this (or any similarly metaphysically freighted) word, we should—having remembered the facts of our "form of life"[19] that are otherwise open to view—reject *artificial* doubt: The interlocutor says, " 'But, if you are *certain*, isn't it that you are shutting your eyes in face of doubt?' " and the reply comes, "—They are shut."[20]

As one progresses through Wittgenstein's examinations of the concept of introspection and the picture of first person seclusion, it becomes increasingly clear that (1) the developed idea of the subject as an interior point upon which introspection can focus, (2) the very conception of introspection itself, and (3) the forms of speech that a distinctively philosophical voice generates along with its fundamental concept of the metaphysically hidden, are all expressions of a single self-concept, and this concept—against the initial appearances when coming to the subject laden with the presuppositions and conceptual preoccupations of traditional philosophy—is not only not given in experience but is a self-concept that is in truth incompatible with what is so given. And it is precisely the argumentative strategy of moving ever back and forth between the two opposed poles, the philosophical versus the ordinary voice, that gradually erodes, and perhaps ultimately breaks down, that false sense of givenness, the illusory sense of the experientially given obviousness of the metaphysical predicament of self-isolation.

3. The Stage of Speech

It is in the writings of Stanley Cavell that we find an Austinian sensitivity to the multiform distinctions between the utterances of the philosophical and of the ordinary voice. And it is in these writings, ranging across a number of years and volumes, that we also find a deeply sustained investigation into the logic of the very thinking that would—if unanalyzed, if unchecked—lead us into the previously described belief in the experientially given obviousness of the self's most fundamental predicament of metaphysical isolation. Let us glance at a few of the episodes of this sustained investigation, drawn from various stages along that investigation's way.

In his early essay "Knowing and Acknowledging," Cavell situates what is, for him, the problem of privacy and private experience.[21] Of the much-discussed issue of the knowing of the pain of another (the Wittgensteinian example that has grown into the modern discussion of the classic problem of other minds), Cavell insists, against strong protestations, that the very phrase "being unable to feel another's sensations" is inherently confused, is in urgent need of conceptual elucidation and clarification:[22] "But there *is* someone who knows, there is a position which is totally different from mine in the matter of knowing whether he is in pain." Insisting here on the fundamental metaphysical asymmetry between the third and first person cases, he adds "different not only in being better (as if certain factors in my position were increased in accuracy or range) but in being decisive, making the best position I can be in seem secondhand," and then, underscoring the metaphysical asymmetry, finishes the thought: "namely, *his* position." And Cavell at this early stage finds the authority of the other's mind—the distinctively privileged position of the feeler of pain—itself deeply plausible from one's own first person perspective that "phenomenologically, as a datum, it seems to me undeniable." After this claim—or rather, after this philosophical picture of the self in its most fundamental metaphysical position as it is given in experience, he adds, "I think everyone recognizes the experience which goes with it, that it is some terrible or fortunate fact, at once contingent and necessary, that *I* am not in that position," and, emphasizing that this thought propels other-minds skepticism, further adds that "the skeptic merely comes to concentrate upon it" ("KA," 259).

It is notable that Cavell, again at this relatively early point, did not find John Cook's analysis (itself a model of ordinary language philosophical method as inspired by Wittgenstein's philosophy) sufficient, or sufficiently conceptually satisfying for him to (as Wittgenstein puts it) stop doing philosophy on this topic, that is, to achieve a condition of conceptual equipoise. Against Cook's compelling linguistic analysis, in which he argues that the difference between the first and third person utterances regarding sensations like pain cannot be intelligibly, or if minimally intelligibly than only wholly misleadingly, captured in the language of *circumstance* (as Cook says, like the circumstance of "being unable to see my neighbor's crocuses") and that the difference lies in the language-game (and hence that identifying the circumstance as "being unable to feel another's sensations" is pernicious and linguistically misled confusion), Cavell persisted. "Why is 'being unable to feel another's sensation' not a circumstance?" While acknowledging that the force of Cook's point derives from the notion that first/third person asymmetry is not a circumstance because it cannot be imagined within the bounds of coherence to be other than it is, that the asymmetry does "not describe an *inability* of ours," Cavell still asks, "But why can't a general fact of nature be thought of, accurately, as a circumstance, a permanent circumstance?" And then giving a somewhat startling sense to his notion of a permanent circumstance, indeed a sense that I think transgresses the bounds of Austinian ordinary language,[23] adds, "The circumstance is, I feel like saying"—this latter phrase does distance Cavell from the claim and betokens an awareness of the philosophical voice's impulsion to speak, an awareness of the possibly "autoventriloquistic" aspect of this utterance, as discussed earlier—"*him.*" One sees here that, again, Cavell is not stopped from doing philosophy on this fundamental topic at the level of language; despite the linguistic problems, he finds the more important residue at the level of experience:[24] "The problem . . . may be that the formulation 'inability to feel' tries but fails to capture my experience of separation from others," adding a still stronger doubt concerning what he here finds to be the limited reach of linguistic analysis with the words: "This does not make it inherently confused, but, one might say, much too weak—as though words are in themselves too weak to record this fact" ("KA," 260).

Given the sizable and conceptually rich body of work to follow on countless aspects of this topic, one might speculate that Cavell here defended the skeptic (against whom Cook's Wittgensteinian linguistic analysis was arguing) in this bat-tle in order to go to war with him later. Cavell sees—or finds given in experience as an undeniable phenomenological datum—what he calls "the truth to which he [the skeptic] is responding," despite, or beneath (as we might say, having introduced talk of the differing levels of language and experience), the very real difficulty of coherently articulating this metaphysical asymmetry. Cavell's position at this stage is thus expressed in this remarkable way:

I take the philosophical problem of privacy, therefore, not to be one of finding (or denying) a "sense" of "same" in which two persons can (or cannot) have the same experience, but one of learning why it is that something which from one point of view looks like a common occurrence (that we frequently have the same experiences—say looking together at a view of the mountains, or diving into the same cold lake, or hearing a car horn struck; and that we frequently do not have the same experiences—say at a meeting, or learning the results of an election, or hearing your child cry) from another point of view looks impossible, almost inexpressible (that I have your experience, that I *be* you). What is it I cannot do? Since I have suggested that this question is a real one (i.e., that the sense of "cannot" here is real), and since nevertheless I have suggested that the question has no answer (on the ground that the words "cannot have his feeling" are "too weak" for the experience they wish to convey), I would need, in accounting for these facts, to provide a characterization of this sense of incapacity and provide the reason for our insistence upon putting it into words. I find that, at the start of this experience, I do not want to give voice to it (or do not see what voice to give it) but only to point (to others, or rather to the fact, of the being, of others) and to gesture towards my self. Only what is there to point to or gesture towards, since everything I know you know? It shows; everything in our world shows it. But I'm filled with this feeling—of our separateness, let us say—and I want you to have it too. So I give voice to it. And then my powerlessness presents itself as ignorance—a metaphysical finitude as an intellectual lack. (Reverse Faust, I take the bargain of supernatural ignorance.) ("KA," 262–63)

Within our language-games, within the bounds of sense, we know we can have the same experiences—we say so. Yet, although I can walk a mile in your shoes and vice versa, I am not you, nor will I be, and you are not me, nor will you be. A philosophically sensitized Austinian ear will not want to attempt to give voice to the metaphysical truth thought to lurk beneath this empirical fact, yet one feels an impulsion to do just that—a philosophical impulsion which manifests itself in pointing first at the other, then to the self. Then the futility dawns on us, and we are left with the (seemingly preverbal) feeling of human separateness and the very human desire for company—for accompanied solitude, for being alone together—that then refuels the drive of the voice. And thus, with an awareness of the limits of philosophical language, we nevertheless speak—but in ways that seem to either fall far short of the true nature of this metaphysical human separateness or transgress the boundaries of the coherently sayable. This description of the self's state of affairs, I would suggest, defines Cavell's position toward the beginning of his investigation; it acknowledges the human need to voice the circumstances (if we can use that word) in which the self finds itself; it simultaneously acknowledges the imperatives of Wittgensteinian and Austinian linguistic sensitivity, or indeed the claims of ordinary language philosophy; and—I want to insist—it begins to show why literature of the self and of the self's metaphysical predicament is necessary. It shows what cannot be said.[25] There is, it will be obvious, far more to say about this.[26] But the present task is to consider at least a few more episodes in Cavell's work as they pertain to the topic at hand.

In the course of providing context for his suggestion that religious life and expression in language might profitably be construed as a Wittgensteinian form of life[27] in his essay "Kierkegaard's *On Authority and Revelation*," Cavell quotes Wittgenstein's remark from *Philosophical Investigations* that "One human being can be a complete enigma to another." And he continues the quotation, in which Wittgenstein shows where we can intelligibly speak, in an ordinary voice, of matters of an incapacity or inability to understand a human being: "We learn this when we come into a strange country with entirely strange traditions; and what is more, even given a mastery of the country's language. We do not *understand* the people. (And not because of not knowing what they are saying to themselves.) We cannot find our feet with them."[28] In this example, it is clear that in one sense we understand their words, yet in another, less shallow sense, we do not understand them at all.[29] Understanding is not reducible to one unitary phenomenon, and it is certainly not reducible to what we would call, perhaps in the context of learning a foreign language, knowing the meanings of each of the words in their sentences; Wittgenstein's example shows this. Similarly, misunderstanding is not reducible to a unitary essence, or one isolable mental experience. Cavell, however, does not at this point draw out the content of Wittgenstein's words; he instead juxtaposes a passage from Kierkegaard, which begins with the unforgettable line, "Most men live in relation to their own self as if they were constantly out, never at home. . . ." The significance—or one line of significance—is clear.

Full engagement with the problem, with the nature of (as well as the articulation of) the metaphysical predicament or condition of the self that runs throughout Cavell's work, demands the recognition of a deep problem doubled: the asymmetry between the first and third person can be mirrored in an internalized version of this problem, such that the self does not understand, does not know, itself. This, one might say, is the internal psychological doubling of an external social problem, or the single-mind version of the other-minds problem, or to express it still another way, perhaps the solipsistic turning of skepticism on itself. And this, as in Wittgenstein's work, greatly disturbs the philosophical picture of the mind's introspective access to itself as the transparently accessible, epistemically privileged, circumstance of self-knowledge, or self-understanding. Thus Cavell writes, following both Kierkegaard and Wittgenstein, "One may want to say: A human being can be a complete enigma to himself; he cannot find his feet with himself." And emphasizing the difference in understanding that Wittgenstein's example shows, he adds that "he understands his words, but he is foreign to his life." These passages of Cavell's not only continue the unearthing and removal of the misleading picture of the given nature of introspective self-knowledge as parsed by Wittgenstein, they also, in showing the complexity of the problem of other minds, of other-understanding, through their implications reveal part of the human complexity of any biographical—and as we now also begin to see, autobiographical—undertaking.

Given its foundational nature, it is not surprising to see resonances of this doubled problem throughout Cavell's work. In "Moral Perfectionism" (in *Conditions Handsome and Unhandsome*), in the context of writing on Emerson and Thoreau, and particularly in relation to Emerson's notion of the "unattained but attainable self"— itself an internal doubling—Cavell discusses Thoreau's remark, "with thinking we may be beside ourselves in a sane sense."[30] The self, beside itself, is *precisely* the internalization of the structure of the problem of other minds. Cavell observes that Thoreau's remark characterizes thinking as "a kind of ecstasy," but I believe one might also see in it the characterization of thinking as a kind of autobiographical reckoning, a kind of perpetual self-estimation. Indeed, elsewhere (in *The Claim of Reason*) Cavell offers his own characterization, if not of thinking per se, then of philosophical work. Following Wittgenstein's deservedly much-discussed motto, "To imagine a language means to imagine a form of life" (*PI*, §19), Cavell writes:

> In philosophizing, I have to bring my own language and life into imagination. What I require is a convening of my culture's criteria, in order to confront them and my words and life as I pursue them and as I may imagine them; and at the same time to confront my words and life as I pursue them with the life my culture's words may imagine for me: to confront the culture with itself, along the lines in which it meets in me. This seems to me a task that warrants the name of philosophy. [31]

The culture's—perhaps in Wittgenstein's sense, the form of life's—criteria are brought into creative self-confrontation, but in a way that is ineluctably auto-biographical as well; thinking, as Wittgenstein has shown us with the private-language argument, with his remarks on introspection and consciousness, and with his remarks on thinking itself, is inescapably social, and yet, at the same time, conducted within the first person in a way that would impel the voice of private experience, of human separateness. For Cavell, it seems that philosophy itself is one kind of reenactment of these doubled problems: the self against the other (the culture's criteria); the impulsion to give voice to metaphysical autonomy against the criteria of Austinian ordinary language; and the self against, indeed, itself. Philosophical thinking is, for Cavell, in one distinct aspect, autobiographical; and although it may not follow necessarily, nevertheless it would not be surprising to find plausibility in the claim that autobiography is, in one distinct aspect, philosophical in turn. And as to Cavell's phrase, "In philosophizing, I have to bring my own language and life into imagination," in particular, one could hardly find a more succinct description of much literature and perhaps all autobiography; in Cavell's voice, although he may not state this explicitly, speaking for and of philosophy can be tantamount to speaking for and of (varieties of) literature.

The position of the self in self-reflection, the idea of the self inwardly dou-bled, the suggestion of Thoreau—in which Cavell rightly sees so much—that with thinking we may be beside ourselves, are intertwined ideas that can illuminate and deepen. They can also, if taken in other ways, severely mislead us in our efforts to more fully understand the nature of the self in its literary depictions, in its artistic self-presentations. It is not difficult to see that these ideas could strengthen the Cartesian or metaphysically dualistic misconception of the self against (or beneath) which Wittgenstein has argued, and in doing so strengthen the misconception of the self as it functions in the creation of an autobiography or any other self-revelatory literary undertaking. In short, they can, if we are not both cautious and patient in ways that Wittgenstein, Austin, and Cavell all encourage, powerfully work against the achievement of what Wittgenstein would call a "perspicuous representation" of the facts, our practices, concerning the nature of the self.[32] Here I want to move to still another episode in Cavell's engagement with the ever evolving threat of other-minds skepticism, but in this case I would like more to apply Cavell's observations to the just-mentioned danger of misconstrual rather than to describe the encounters.

In the essay "The Avoidance of Love: A Reading of *King Lear*," Cavell at one point investigates the logic of the position of the narrator in a novel, in contrast to the absence of a narrator in drama. This can, I believe, reveal a good deal about our pre-Wittgensteinian intuitions concerning what we may too easily misconstrue as the *ideal*, not only of the nature of the autobiographical self, but more particularly of autobiographical truth.

Cavell emphasizes that "no character in a play could (is, logically, in a position from which to) narrate its events."[33] Cavell finds three principal reasons for this, and each I believe holds considerable significance for our understanding of the autobiographical situation. First, no character can or could possess the credibility of a narrator, not because this character's honesty may be in question but for the far more metaphysically significant fact that the character, as *actor*, "is part of what is happening; he is fixed in the present." The *actor* cannot "insert a break in [the present]," and "if he narrates, then *that* is what he is doing," that is, narration is now the action being depicted on the stage. Cavell contrasts this—a striking contrast—to that of the narrator, who *cannot* act in the dramatic present, who *cannot* "make anything happen," and this is one source of the narrator's privileged epistemic position vis-à-vis the reader's credulity. I want to suggest that this contrast provides an intuition-shaping conceptual model—potentially a very misleading one—for our pre-Wittgensteinian thinking of the autobiographer, or for that matter any self that is engaged in truthful self-revelation. The autobiographical position, we too easily think, is that of the narrator; the past actions of that prenarrating self (now recollected and reported), are the actions of the "actor." And this divide between the acting and narrating self naturally nourishes Cartesian conceptions of self-knowledge and introspective access: Only the autobiographical narrator has privileged access to the intentions and motivations of the actor. Truthful self-reportage would be, for a narrator on this model (assuming an unimpaired memory), transparently easy, and the ideal of first person truthfulness would simply be the active and full (both of which would be, on this model, unproblematic) disclosure—here a distinctively metaphysical disclosure—of the mind and action of the prenarrating past actor. However, the matter of the logic of the autobiographical situation, along with the attendant issue of first person truth, is vastly more complex, as Wittgenstein's and Cavell's writings show. But this model can easily lead us to stop far short of such post-Wittgensteinian complexities. And, indeed, an autobiographer, like any first person sensation reporter (a rather unordinary phrase itself), *is* engaged in the *action* of self-narration; there is no "perch" above life's analogy to the dramatic stage upon which to sit (and from there, as Cavell has rightly observed, we could do nothing anyway). It is perhaps worth noting that this runs perfectly parallel to the claim that the ordinary language philosopher makes to the metaphysician: Intelligible uses of language will be, for reasons Wittgenstein and Austin show at length, (verbal) acts *in contexts*, that is, on, not above, the stage of speech.

Second, Cavell, taking note of the two narrations that do occur in *King Lear*, observes that those narrations are actions and that they take place "within the same continuity of causation and freedom and responsibility as every other act of the play." This, as I am suggesting, is the truer position of the autobiographer. The narration is an action within the ongoing continuity of causation, freedom, and responsibility of the autobiographer, and thus it houses the complexities of meaning and of interpretation that are resident in any other verbal or written first person report; the model of the omniscient narrator is a false ideal. It is notable that Cavell points out that in the play "Edgar's choice to narrate then and there is as significant as the content of his narration," and this is precisely what should be said from the vantage point of ordinary language philosophy, for as Cavell puts it: "Philosophy which proceeds from ordinary language is proceeding from the fact *that* a thing is said; that it is (or can be) said (in certain circumstances) is as significant as *what* it says; its being said then and there is as determinative of what it says as the meanings of its individual words are." It may be true that this way of expressing this point about ordinary language philosophy itself gives rise to problems of ordinary language philosophy, that is, that it is a *fact* that a thing said is dependent on the details of context of utterance; what actually constitutes a "circumstance" of utterance will be similarly context-dependent; the very question of the *significance* of a phrase will arise, or not, in context; the issue of *determinants* of meaning will be occasioned by the use of "determinants"; the very notion of the meaning of individual words is—as Cavell is as aware as anyone—philosophically troublesome in the extreme (not only in that it invites meaning atomism rather than meaning holism, but then this distinction too would not fare well under the scrutiny of ordinary language analysis); and the notion of measuring and then finding equal in weight the meaning-determinative force of the "fact" of saying along with the atomistic word meanings is far from unproblematic.

But here again one experiences the kind of impulse to give voice to a thought in the face of ordinary language challenges—and in this case, the thought is in favor of, in support of the value of, ordinary-language analysis; one wants this general point made concerning the contribution (as we may feel forced to call it generally), the very fact (if we can give ourselves license to call it that), that the narrative is uttered at all makes to the meaning (as we dangerously call it) of that utterance (as we generally categorize the self-revelatory narration). If this, incidentally, seems overly hampered by qualifications and doubts, I will only say that, by the standards of post-Austinian ordinary language philosophy, it is reckless; one can use a more fine-tooth comb.[34] But the fundamental point I want to make, or try to make, is in truth a comparison: that the autobiographer, as a special case of the first person narrator, is inevitably *in* the position of Edgar; that the fact that the autobiographer is narrating is part of, and not above, beyond, or outside, the life—the causal and contextual continuum—of that writer or teller. And this means, as Cavell points out next in his discussion of the logic of the fictional narrator, most significantly, that "a 'first-person narrative' is not a narrative." The position of the first person narrator indeed *cannot* be, or become equivalent to, the position of the narrator in fiction: The fictional narrator does not enter into the causal and contextual continuum, and not only does he or she not, he or she metaphysically *cannot*, precisely because he or she does not have a causal foothold in that world, thus precluding the very capacity to act.

The contrast between the first person and the fictional narrator is in truth even more striking, precisely in that the fictional (or perhaps third person) narrator cannot conceal, cannot willfully mislead as a causal intervention in the action, cannot be duplicitous, cannot employ self-protective descriptions of events, because he or she does not possess a self (in the requisite sense of the first person narrator) to conceal, to protect, to hide behind dissimulation. Cavell expresses the point this way: "The third-person narrator, being deprived of self-reference, cannot conceal himself, that is to say, he has no self, and therefore nothing, to conceal." Yet, despite the metaphysical impossibility of converging with that of the (imaginary) fictional narrator, it is nevertheless far too easy to hold up this latter position as the conceptual model for the autobiographical position—a model or picture of the self and its position that shapes our intuition and buttresses, if not directly causes, the philosophical misconstruals of the self Wittgenstein is combating, often by employing the methodological practice of returning words used in the philosophy of the self to their uses in the ordinary voice.

Third, Cavell observes that there is conceptual room for the activity of a reporter who is giving a report simultaneous with the event the report is describing (and it is thus written or said in the present tense), because the reporter is there at the event, while we are not. In a theater, Cavell notes, there is no such position, no such conceptual room, because, quite indisputably, "[w]e are present at what is happening." Here once again, although perhaps well beyond what Cavell intended, this observation is significant for our understanding of the self-narrator, and in a way somewhat less evident than the previous two observations. Our already strong inclination toward Cartesian self-misconstrual can be further strengthened by the misapplication of this "reporter-from-elsewhere" model to the case of the first person narrator. Directly stated—with this model lodged in the intuitive subterranean—it becomes easy to conceive of the first person narrator as a reporter of an occurrence from which we are absent—the private, mental occurrence, we think, from which we must always, as a metaphysical necessity, be absent, and to which there can and will forever be only one "reporter," the mind present at and to its own inward occurrences. But again, this simple dualistic dichotomy separating the self-mind from the other mind cannot withstand the scrutiny of linguistic analysis: the usages of the ordinary voice on these matters both refuse to acknowledge and are far too nuanced for this simple Cartesian dichotomy, and it is again literature that shows the philosophically most significant facts in contexts of linguistic usage, in human language-games. In truth, we can be present at, or absent from, countless lived experiences that we may well call "mental," just as we may call some of them "private" (and others not); the particular way in which we are present or absent or, in some cases, both, will depend on *particular circumstances* and not on what can be taken to be a grand metaphysical truth of the self's metaphysically enforced solitary confinement, as given as the first brute fact of human experience. But the conceptual undertow dragging us back to this conception, this picture, of the self and its predicament is powerful, and, again, it is only strengthened by the misleading analogy of the narrator in fiction. The autobiographer and, much more broadly, the first person narrator or teller is a very different kind of creature.

Again, Cavell's sustained investigation of the logic of other-minds skepticism thoroughly acknowledges the force of what I'm calling this conceptual undertow, and in the essay "Being Odd, Getting Even," Cavell offers memorable examples of the motivating utterances of the metaphysical voice, what he here calls "the move to the metaphysical."

> This move to the metaphysical is like saying that since it makes sense to suppose that I might lack any or all of my limbs I might lack a body altogether, or that since I never see all of any object and hence may not know that a given object exists I may not know that the external world as such exists. Ordinary language philosophy, most notably in the teaching of Austin and of Wittgenstein, has discredited such a move to the metaphysical, as a way of discrediting the conclusions of skepticism. [35]

Such metaphysical utterances, such skeptical claims, are indeed examples of what Wittgenstein called "language gone on holiday," the transgressions of the bounds of our language-games. But Cavell is here, too, as in his previous commentary on Cook's Wittgensteinian linguistic analysis, unwilling to give up the seriousness, perhaps the human profundity, of the insight, born of the inward phenomenological feeling of human separateness or isolation, that in part motivates these conceptual-linguistic transgressions. Thus Cavell adds next: "But in my interpretation of Wittgenstein, what is discredited is not the appeal or the threat of skepticism as such, but only skepticism's own pictures of its accomplishments." The appeal and the threat, consistent both with Wittgenstein's vision of the organic growth and ever changing evolution of our language (games) and his insight into the myriad tricks that language plays on its users and the ever evolving "bewitchment of our intelligence by means of language," present themselves in ever new guises. To employ the language of Wittgenstein's therapeutic analogy for ordinary language philosophical work, to diagnose one case is not to cure all cases—just as it is not necessarily to *cure* the case diagnosed.

In his essay "Ending the Waiting Game," Cavell offers an encapsulation of the view of the self we have been considering in its relation to autobiographical revelation and, more fundamentally, autobiographical knowledge. Drawing out the comparison of a number of skeptical philosophical views to forms of madness, Cavell, listing such positions as believing the world is only illusion, or doubting the external world, or claiming that our world is composed out of isolated bits of experience, includes the belief that "each thing and each person is a metaphysical enclosure, and no two ever communicate directly, or so much as perceive one another."[36] He shortly turns to Wittgenstein's analogy between philosophical work and therapy, noting that "his late methods (he compared them to therapies) were to bring philosophy peace at last" and then quotes Wittgenstein's famous dictum from the *Remarks on the Foundations of Mathematics:* "The philosopher is the man who has to cure himself of many sicknesses of the understanding before he can arrive at the notions of the sound human understanding."[37] And that sound understanding is the possession of a perspicuous grasp of a field of our practices, a clear view not gained from ascending theoretical heights but of what lies before us on the level of praxis. It is the understanding achieved by the ordinary voice,[38] having, as T. S. Eliot has it, "returned once again to the place it started but knowing it for the first time."[39] Moving between the poles we saw Wittgenstein initially identify, it has returned from—having felt, expressed, grappled with, and come to terms with—the impulsions of the metaphysical voice.

It has been possible only to sketch a few of the remarks, observations, and arguments Wittgenstein has made on language and mind as they pertain to the achievement of a clear—indeed philosophically peaceful—understanding of the autobiographical subject, the first person narrating self. And it has similarly been possible to review only a few sites of investigation of Cavell's larger philosophical undertaking as they pertain to this subject. But this may be sufficient to at least suggest a number of the ways in which misleading conceptual models, or philosophical pictures, as Wittgenstein and Cavell after him used the phrase, can prevent a clear view. Much of the language of the self—the *ordinary* language of the self, for all its philosophical significance—is found, of course, in autobiography, in a different sense in biography, and in still different senses in various literary depictions of the mind and mental activity. It would take lengthy and separate studies to consider the multifarious ways in which Augustine's *Confessions*, Nabokov's *Speak, Memory*, Mill's *Autobiography*, Stein's *The Autobiography of Alice B. Toklas*, Rousseau's *Confessions*, *The Autobiography of Bertrand Russell*, autobiographical works by de Beauvoir, Nietzsche, Sartre, Voltaire, Kierkegaard, Vico, Henry James, Thoreau, and countless other pieces of life-writing—including Cavell's *A Pitch of Philosophy: Autobiographical Exercises*[40]—are all significant for the achievement of what Wittgenstein called a perspicuous presentation, a "sound understanding." But it is clear that the "deeply mysterious I" *has* been investigated at length in literary contexts with great philosophical resonance, and if Wittgenstein left something of a Tractarian silence directly on the nature of the autobiographical self, he certainly provided the conceptual tools with which to philosophically clear our view so that we can see the multiform literary and linguistic practices that lie before us. Perspicacity presumes conceptual clarity, and given the analogies, the models, the pictures—the undertow—we have considered, it is far too easy for the self—devoid of the stabilizing and grounding influences of ordinary language and literary investigations—to view its image in a reflecting but darkening glass.

Notes

1. Ludwig Wittgenstein, *Philosophical Investigations*, 3d ed., trans. G. E. M. Anscombe (New York: Macmillan, 1953), p. v; hereafter cited as *PI*, with Wittgenstein's numbered sections or paragraphs, which he called "remarks," in part 1 indicated by the symbol § and page numbers in part 2 by "p."

2. Ludwig Wittgenstein, *Notebooks, 1914–1916*, ed. and trans. G. E. M. Anscombe (Oxford: Blackwell, 1961), entry on 5 August 1916. It is significant to the context of this entry that Wittgenstein was working at the time (1916 through 1917) on the mystical themes in his *Tractatus Logico-Philosophicus*, trans. D. F. Pears and B. F. McGuinness (London: Routledge and Kegan Paul, 1961); hereafter cited as *TLP*.

3. And indeed very many of these things are linguistic in nature, thus reconfirming the close, in fact indissoluble, link between the philosophies of language and of mind in Wittgenstein's work. One unambiguous symptom that language has misled us, that is, that an unwitting presumption about language has generated illusory conceptual difficulty, is the intuitively deep belief that, first given the (erroneous) presumption that all words get their meaning through direct reference (a belief that Wittgenstein subjects to the closest scrutiny in very many different

contexts of inquiry, throughout his conceptual "landscape"), the first person pronoun must also thus get its meaning through direct reference to, if not an outward, then an inward, substantive thing. Our understanding of the self, the "I," is thus related to language in a way that certainly does not reduce to what is taken in some quarters to be mere semantics. Linguistic usage—and our close investigation of it—is metaphysically (and not merely semantically) significant.

4. Ludwig Wittgenstein, *The Blue and Brown Books* (Oxford: Blackwell, 1958), 69.

5. For some of Wittgenstein's uses of the term "picture," meaning, roughly, a conceptual model of which we may be unaware or, if we are aware of it, one that we erroneously take as unproblematically given (often when this is the result of misleading grammatical appearance) and that shapes or determines our subsequent thought on any philosophical matter pertaining to the picture, see *PI*, §§ 422–27 and p. 223.

6. For two interwoven sets of remarks on the opening passages of *Philosophical Investigations* written from different points in time, see Stanley Cavell, "Notes and Afterthoughts on the Opening of Wittgenstein's *Investigations*," in *Philosophical Passages: Wittgenstein, Emerson, Austin, Derrida* (Oxford: Blackwell, 1995), 125–86.

7. The instructive and enlightening employment of this criterion of strangeness (along with a highly nuanced sensitivity to it) was given one of its best expressions in the work of J. L.Austin; see in this connection the extraordinarily close study of the philosophical voice's claims and pronouncements on perception in his *Sense and Sensibilia*, ed. G. J. Warnock (Oxford: Oxford University Press, 1962).

8. For an excellent overview of the position of Wittgenstein's late philosophy in relation to both earlier and later analytical work in the philosophy of language, see P. M. S. Hacker, *Wittgenstein's Place in Twentieth-Century Analytical Philosophy* (Oxford: Blackwell, 1996).

9. There are two particularly helpful sets of metaphors on the matter of the distinction between (1) satisfying the philosophical impulse to attempt to look *beneath* the cultural phenomena in question versus (2) remembering the value of looking *directly at* those phenomena; see Hans-Johann Glock's distinction between "logical geology" and "logical geography" in *A Wittgenstein Dictionary* (Oxford: Blackwell, 1996), 278–83, and Stanley Cavell's distinction between the "horizontal" and the "vertical" conceptions of the difficult Wittgensteinian phrase "forms of life" in his "Epilogue: The *Investigations'* Everyday Aesthetics of Itself," in *The Cavell Reader*, ed. Stephen Mulhall (Oxford: Blackwell, 1996), 369–89.

10. Centrally, in *The Principles of Psychology*, 3 vols., ed. Frederick Burkhardt (Cambridge: Harvard University Press, 1981), although James's full development of his concept of the mind runs throughout his many writings.

11. For closely related remarks outside of *Philosophical Investigations*, see

Ludwig Wittgenstein, "Wittgenstein's Notes for Lectures on 'Private Experience' and 'Sense Data,'" ed. Rush Rhees, *Philosophical Review* 77 (1968), 275–320; see especially 278–80. See also Rush Rhees, "The Language of Sense Data and Private Experience—Notes taken by R. Rhees of Wittgenstein's lectures, 1936," *Philosophical Investigations* 7 (1984): 1–45, 101–40; see especially 111–12.

12. See Gilbert Ryle, *The Concept of Mind* (New York: Barnes and Noble, 1949); in connection with present issues, see especially his classic chapter "Self-Knowledge," 154–98.

13. Indeed one might think, given that we speak of consciousness, that there must be a kind of "second-order" consciousness from which we observe first-order consciousness (in order—and here again we are misled by the presumption concerning meaning-as-naming—to use the word "consciousness" meaningfully, i.e., to attach the name to the thing). Against this picture-induced confusion, compare Wittgenstein's remark about philosophy itself in *PI*, §121: "One might think: if philosophy speaks of the use of the word 'philosophy' there must be a second-order philosophy. But it is not so: it is, rather, like the case of orthography, which deals with the word 'orthography' among others without then being second-order."

14. For a discussion and particularly helpful set of references throughout Wittgenstein's writings on this topic (and from which my section title is borrowed with emendation), see Garth Hallett, *A Companion to Wittgenstein's "Philosophical Investigations"* (Ithaca, N.Y.: Cornell University Press, 1977), chapter 38, "The Picture of Complete Seclusion," 714–42.

15. One might characterize one of the contrasts between philosophy and literature in precisely these terms; the latter does not in philosophy's sense abbreviate, and thus itself constitutes both a corrective and an invaluable resource for philosophical understanding. The diagnosis of the *impulse* to abbreviate in this sense is still another matter, about which Wittgenstein has said a good deal in his various remarks on philosophical method and, broadly speaking, his wisely cautious analogies between his later philosophical style and psychoanalysis.

16. Even the phrase "the special criteria of truthfulness" is too abbreviated and thus misleading, suggesting both uniformity among them and that they travel, as a coherent and invariant set, from context to context. Such criteria are best *shown* in literature and perhaps best examined in the philosophical criticism of literature. (To show them *in detail* is the only way to render them visible.) In this connection it is perhaps worth noting that the many episodes in Wittgenstein's life as they pertain to truthfulness (as discussed in Ray Monk's very fine biography or, e.g., in Fania Pascal's memoir) display philosophical significance. See Ray Monk, *Ludwig Wittgenstein: the Duty of Genius* (New York: Free Press, 1990), especially the chapter "Confessions," 361–84, particularly the observation that "it is no coincidence that Wittgenstein wrote the set of remarks with which he remained most satisfied at a

time when he was most ruthlessly honest about himself" (367); and Fania Pascal, "Wittgenstein: A Personal Memoir," in *Recollections of Wittgenstein*, ed. Rush Rhees (Oxford: Oxford University Press, 1984), 12–49. Or to put the matter in Gilbert Ryle's terms, there will not be one single overriding criterion of autobiographical truthfulness that follows from "Privileged Access" to "facts of a special [inner] status." He writes, "The fact that retrospection is autobiographical does not imply that it gives us a Privileged Access to facts of a special status. But of course it does give us a mass of data contributory to our appreciations of our own conduct and qualities of mind. A diary is not a chronicle of ghostly episodes, but it is a valuable source of information about the diarist's character, wits and career" (*Concept of Mind*, 167). The criterion is not, in short, fidelity to *ghostly* episodes.

17. The inclination to so believe is not *exclusively* a symptom of this picture of the self: Plato's divided line separating the sensory from the intellective, Descartes's fundamental epistemological dichotomy between sense and pure reason, and Kant's distinction between the a priori and a posteriori all strengthen the plausibility of the picture of the metaphysically secluded self at issue here.

18. The danger of the very word "subjective" can be seen as one manifestation of a kind of linguistic danger well examined in the work of Wittgenstein's student, Maurice Drury, in his *The Danger of Words* (London: Routledge, 1976), reissued in *The Danger of Words and Writings on Wittgenstein* (Brighton: Thoemmes Press, 1996).

19. Although this phrase is used only six times in all of Wittgenstein's published writings, it has generated a great deal of interpretive secondary writings. See *PI*, §§7, 19, and 23, and p. 226, for what are perhaps the central sources; see also the entry "Form of Life (*Lebensform*)" in Glock, *Wittgenstein Dictionary*, 124–29, for a helpful brief review of the matter, and Stanley Cavell, *Conditions Handsome and Unhandsome: The Constitution of Emersonian Perfectionism* (Chicago: University of Chicago Press, 1990); hereafter cited as *CH*.

20. The rejection of artificial doubt (and the correlated belief that doubt is or can be volitional) constitutes one of the affinities relating Wittgenstein's later work to American pragmatism. See, for example, C. S. Peirce, "Some Consequences of Four Incapacities," reprinted in *Classical American Philosophy*, ed. J. Stuhr (New York: Oxford, University Press, 1987), 32–33.

21. Stanley Cavell, "Knowing and Acknowledging," in *Must We Mean What We Say? A Book of Essays* (Cambridge: Cambridge University Press, 1969), 238–66; hereafter, references to this essay are cited as "KA" and to the entire book as *MW*.

22. Cavell at this juncture is writing in response to John Cook's deservedly classic essay, "Wittgenstein on Privacy," in *The Philosophical Review* 74 (1965): 281–314, reprinted in G. Pitcher, ed., *Wittgenstein: The Philosophical Investigations* (New York: Doubleday, 1966).

23. For the reason that—to encapsulate a lengthier linguistic investigation into the range of uses of the word "circumstance"—a *person* is not, as Cook rightly

sees, a *circumstance*; the person may be *in* a circumstance, and probably only temporarily so. The ability to intelligibly use the word in description of the person's condition does not outlive the context within which we say this of the person, after which we of course speak of the circumstance (however we might describe it, which itself is internally related to the intelligibility of the particular use of the word "circumstance") in the past tense.

24. My purpose here is to capture Cavell's position at this point in his fluid thinking; I in fact find the distinction between the level of language and the level of experience problematic: The problem is that the distinction is both too general and too quick. Following Austin, we could find cases in which we speak of the level of language apart from, or in contradistinction to, the level of experience (and vice versa), but I would not, on Austinian-Cavellian grounds, expect this distinction as made in a particular case to prove generalizable; an investigation of our various uses of the term "levels" would, I expect, show that the contextually circumscribed meanings are not in truth transferable out of context.

25. The saying/showing distinction derives from Wittgenstein's early work in the *Tractatus Logico-Philosophicus*; see especially the preface and 6.41–6.522, in which the relative insignificance of the sayable is emphasized. In the preface he writes, "Thus the aim of this book is to draw a limit to thought, or rather—not to thought, but to the expression of thoughts: for in order to be able to draw a limit to thought, we should have to find both sides of the limit thinkable (i.e. we should have to be able to think what cannot be thought)." But in a widely influential passage in a letter to von Ficker—"Letters to Ludwig von Ficker," ed. Allan Janik, trans. B. Gillette, in *Wittgenstein: Sources and Perspectives*, ed. C. G. Luckhardt (Ithaca: Cornell University Press, 1979), 94–95—he writes that "my work consists of two parts: of the one which is here, and of everything which I have *not* written. And precisely this second part is the important one. For the Ethical is delimited from within, as it were, by my book . . ." and goes on to refer to that which he has defined by remaining silent about it, warning von Ficker that although the book may "have much to say which you want to say yourself," he (von Ficker) may well—owing to the *Tractarian* silence—not "notice that it is said in it." Wittgenstein's conception of the very nature of philosophy is changing because of this issue. Because the logical form of propositions cannot be stated (contra his Russellian background), philosophical work must instead yield *clarification*, signifying "what cannot be said, by presenting clearly what can be said" (*TLP*, 4.115). And clarification—perspicuous presentation—is the aim of the later philosophy, where clarification is achieved not through, but in the *absence* of, substantive (traditional) philosophical assertions. For a fine brief essay on the saying/showing distinction, see Glock, *Wittgenstein Dictionary*, 330–36. This distinction has been applied to aesthetics in various ways (suggesting, broadly, that the arts show distinctive varieties of meaning that cannot be said): see Susanne Langer, *Feeling and Form* (London: Routledge and Kegan Paul,

1953), and *Philosophy in a New Key* (Cambridge: Harvard University Press, 1978), especially 79, where she makes the reliance on Wittgenstein's early philosophical distinction explicit, and B. R. Tilghman's thoughtful *Wittgenstein, Ethics, and Aesthetics: The View from Eternity* (London: Macmillan, 1991). Tilghman closes his searching study with a *Tractarian* sentence: "Art does indeed, Wittgenstein would say, provide an experience not to be obtained by any other kind of activity: it shows the meaning of life" (178). I offer an analysis of Langer's position in *Art as Language: Wittgenstein, Meaning, and Aesthetic Theory* (Ithaca, N.Y.: Cornell University Press, 1995), chapter 1, "Art and the Unsayable," 8–30.

26. A small part of which will follow in this essay. I explore some closely related themes in "The Self, Thinking: Wittgenstein, Augustine, and the Autobiographical Situation," in *Wittgenstein, Philosophy, and the Arts*, ed. Peter Lewis (London: Ashgate, forthcoming), and in "The Self, Speaking: Wittgenstein and the (Mis)Construal of Introspective Utterances" in *Revue Internationale de Philosophie* 2, no. 219 (2001), a special issue on Wittgenstein edited by Jean-Pierre Commetti.

27. I consider the meaning of Wittgenstein's phrase "form of life," and its significance for an understanding of the arts, in *Meaning and Interpretation: Wittgenstein, Henry James, and Literary Knowledge* (Ithaca, N.Y.: Cornell University Press, 1994), chapter 2, "Forms of Life and Artistic Practices," 45–83.

28. This and the following passages appear in Cavell, *MW*, 172–73.

29. In relation to this contrast between the shallower and deeper understandings of words, see Cavell's helpful remarks on (what I take to be) a parallel contrast in understanding the meaning of Wittgenstein's phrase "form of life," in *This New Yet Unapproachable America: Lectures after Emerson after Wittgenstein* (Albuquerque, N.M.: Living Batch Press, 1989), 41: "A conventionalized sense of form of life will support a conventionalized, or contractual, sense of agreement. But there is another sense of form of life that contests this. Call the former the ethnological sense, or horizontal sense. Contesting that there is the biological or vertical sense." Those who misconstrue Wittgenstein as a sociological relativist seem to greatly emphasize the horizontal sense of his foundational phrase while de-emphasizing—or missing—the vertical.

30. Cavell, *CH*, 8.

31. Stanley Cavell, *The Claim of Reason: Wittgenstein, Skepticism, Morality, and Tragedy* (Oxford: Oxford University Press, 1979), 45.

32. See Cavell's discussion of this fundamental Wittgensteinian notion in "Epilogue," 369–89, especially 380–81.

33. Stanley Cavell, "The Avoidance of Love," in *MW*, 335, also collected along with other writings in Shakespearean interpretation in *Disowning Knowledge in Six Plays of Shakespeare* (Cambridge: Cambridge University Press, 1987). Passages subsequently quoted are from "Avoidance of Love," 335–37. This position, that the character, as actor, is inextricably part of, and not separable from, the proceedings,

and thus metaphysically cannot rise above the situation upon which we might ask or expect him to pass Olympian judgment, is comparable to Nietzsche's pithy observation that the value of life cannot be estimated by any living human, precisely "because he is a party to the dispute, indeed its object, and not the judge of it." Friedrich Nietzsche, *Twilight of the Idols*, trans. R. S. Hollingdale (Harmondsworth: Penguin, 1968), 30. (Nietzsche adds that the judgment cannot be provided by any dead person either—"for another reason.")

34. See, for example, among the highest achievements of ordinary language philosophical work, both O. K. Bouwsma, *Philosophical Essays* (Lincoln: University of Nebraska Press, 1965), and (here also for the most sustained writing in the field) Frank B. Ebersole, *Things We Know: Fourteen Essays in Problems of Knowledge* (Eugene: University of Oregon Press, 1967), *Meaning and Saying: Essays in the Philosophy of Language* (Washington, D.C.: University Press of America, 1979), and *Language and Perception: Essays in the Philosophy of Language* (Washington, D.C.: University Press of America, 1979).

35. Stanley Cavell, "Being Odd, Getting Even (Descartes, Emerson, Poe)," in *In Quest of the Ordinary: Lines of Skepticism and Romanticism* (Chicago: University of Chicago Press, 1988), 110–11.

36. Stanley Cavell, "Ending the Waiting Game: A Reading of Beckett's *Endgame*," in *MW*, 126; this and the following brief quotations.

37. Ludwig Wittgenstein, *Remarks on the Foundations of Mathematics*, ed. G. H. von Wright, R. Rhees, and G. E. M. Anscombe, trans. G. E. M. Anscombe (Oxford: Blackwell, 1967), 157.

38. Against the uncomprehending view that a reliance on ordinary language is tantamount to antiintellectualism, see Cavell's discussion in "The Ordinary as the Uneventful (A Note on the *Annales* Historians)," in *Themes Out of School: Effects and Causes* (Chicago: University of Chicago Press, 1984), 184–94; see especially 192–93.

39. T. S. Eliot, "Little Gidding," in *Four Quartets* (San Diego: Harcourt, Brace, Jovanovich, 1943), 59 (sec. 5, lines 240–43).

40. Stanley Cavell, *A Pitch of Philosophy: Autobiographical Exercises* (Cambridge: Harvard University Press, 1994). Given the large-scale trajectory of Cavell's intellectual project, the move into autobiography—the long-term occupancy of the autobiographical situation and its exploration from the inside (without reintroducing Cartesian conceptions of selfhood)—seems not only philosophically motivated but in fact necessitated.

Cavell's Imperfect Perfectionism

Charles Altieri

The man who has the word "I" at his disposal has the quickest device for concealing himself.

—Stanley Cavell, "The Avoidance of Love"[1]

Can philosophy become melodramatic and still be philosophy?

—Charles Altieri

1

Stanley Cavell has taught us that one plausible ideal for writing is to seek representativeness by insisting upon and intensifying what seems most compelling in one's own experience, especially in one's experience of reading. Here I find myself in the ironic situation of wanting to heed his advice for negative reasons: When I read Cavell's recent work, my most compelling experience is a sense of profound disappointment. So that is what I hope to make representative in this essay, partially because I think this enterprise will also help clarify by contrast other ways of carrying out Cavell's very important basic projects. Disappointment is my primary reaction because, like many of my generation, I had invested so much hope in Cavell's earlier work. He freed then young literary critics to bring philosophical thematics to the work of close reading, and he developed a compelling account of the limitations of all disciplines that ground themselves on their capacity to overcome a skepticism invented largely for the purpose of that display of mastery. Cavell was the first and is still probably the most powerful thinker to turn Wittgenstein's suspicions about philosophical authority into a full-fledged analysis of the psychological and dispositional problems that follow from insisting that disciplines such as philosophy must rely on establishing and satisfying firm epistemic conditions for testing the propositional value of sentences. And his early work still provides one of the few, still vital exemplars for criticism that concentrates more on the distinctive qualities of particular working intelligences than subsuming those intelligences within social allegories that analyze the roles such works play in the social dispositions of power.

And then Cavell discovered Emerson. In many ways this discovery brought Cavell even closer to the arts. It forced him to more elaborate thinking on the various aspects of expression, and it allowed him even bolder efforts at treating philosophy as also a modernist art thriving on experiment and resistance to convention. Emerson stimulated Cavell to the risky work of exploring how philosophy might turn against its ascetic heritage, feeding instead on those aspects of personal performance and emotional intensity which philosophy had suppressed in order to secure what it could defend against the skeptic. As Cavell put it, in the work of American philosophers like Emerson, "in their stubborn, accurate superficiality, perhaps for the first time in recognizable philosophy, this threat of world-consuming doubt is interpreted in all its uncanny homeliness" (Mul., 319). To deal with this "uncanny homeliness," Cavell had to pay much more attention to depth psychology and to his own subjective readerly states than had been called for by his earlier masters, Austin and Wittgenstein. So Emerson and his heirs offer Cavell the prospect of merging his commitment to ordinary language thinking with his love of the melodramas of self-formation projected in romantic writing.

However, this merger seems to me to create a philosophical corporation badly in need of downsizing, because its various enterprises prove almost impossible to correlate. Cavell wants both the elemental perspicuity sought by ordinary language philosophy and the dazzling aphoristic personal intensities and self-exposures that make Emerson so exciting a writer. But then everything in his early work that stressed the ordinary and the communal has to be recast to fit into the values provided by the concept of the uncanny. Only in the discourses then brought to bear can one treat recovering the ordinary as a feature of Emersonian perfectionism, with its insistence on the construction of subjectivity through expressive acts that struggle to overcome the shame of conformity. So it seems to me important to attempt explaining why this more ambitious Cavellian enterprise seems doomed to failure or, more accurately, why I hope I am representative in the intensity of my disappointment in what these ambitions have produced.

Much of this frustration stems from my sense that Cavell's recent work sacrifices much of its Wittgensteinian subtlety in its efforts to correlate a Wittgensteinian minimalism he can defend and an Emersonian theatricality he wants to explore and identify with. For Cavell there are deep affinities between Wittgenstein's struggle with his interlocutor and Emerson's and Freud's accounts of the struggle of active spirit to express what otherwise would remain passive and hence unacknowledged in one's own existence. But I think that if we patiently examine some of the oppositions that become part of that case, we can see how ill-matched the two traditions are. Thematically Cavell is forced to what I will show are problematic claims about subjective agency, and stylistically he feels justified in writerly indulgences that in my view simply negate what is most important in Wittgenstein's ascetic ways. For as demands of the personal pull against the containing structures of the ordinary, it becomes extremely difficult even to isolate Cavell's ideas as objects of criticism without having to take them all tout court as aspects of the person they enable or the readings they produce. I have no problem with this turn to the personal as such. Indeed, I think it part of a revolution in philosophy of which Cavell is in the forefront. But I have severe problems with the qualities of character that his Emersonian mode of philosophizing encourages. Therefore, I want here to force on him a more intense confrontation with the contradictions and limitations his thinking embodies, and I want ultimately to contrast his version of the personal in philosophy to the more severe and challenging model of the personal one finds in Nietzsche.

A second source of frustration will require my attempting to develop an elaborate framework for the specific criticisms I will be elaborating. For if Cavell fails, he does so in a most noble enterprise that we have to understand if we are to appreciate what is at stake in working out particular criticisms. His ultimate ambition is to develop a path by which Western culture can work itself free of problems inherent in its fundamental philosophical commitments, commitments that bind it to the epistemic programs most dramatically articulated by Descartes. Not content to criticize specific Cartesian concepts, Cavell wants us to recognize what is severely limited in the overall edifice of values, models of judgment, and understandings of social relations kept in place by the demand that we trust as knowledge only what we can demonstrate by objective or method-governed means is the indubitable case. This epistemic orientation imposes an impersonality, an inflexibility to contextual shifts, and an insensitivity to the intricacies of psychological life that forces philosophy into formalism or metacritique or pure identification with science. But the more eager one becomes to have a feasible alternative that does encourage philosophy to engage the complexities and uncertainties fundamental to most of the values making life worth living, the more Cavell's turn to perfectionist discourse and to psychoanalysis seems a disappointing follow-up to his groundbreaking *Claim of Reason* and related essays. Therefore it will not suffice to deal only with the specific conceptual problems that fealty to Emerson produces for Cavell.[2] I want simultaneously to insist on the limitations of this work and to show how awareness of these limitations sharpens our appreciation of lines of thinking that offer more promising alternatives to the dominant epistemic models, especially when they are extended into discourse about values. In order to satisfy both interests, I will follow my efforts to characterize the antiepistemic project by an analysis of what seems problematic in four fundamental oppositions that seem the inevitable groundwork for his dazzling readings and for his therapeutic ambitions.

Many other contemporary philosophers have similar views of the Cartesian legacy. But Cavell's work is the obvious place to begin intensive analysis of what this antiepistemic line of thinking can accomplish, because he provides a powerful account of its underlying emotional structures. He shows that the ideal of overcoming the skeptic is not simply a philosophical device for achieving certainty. Those invoking that ideal and those seeking to overthrow it buy into intense and problematic emotional investments. To defeat skepticism, philosophy has to establish absolutely secure ways of showing how representations link to what they refer to as the real. And that linking requires "method," with its demands for the impersonal and the unequivocal. But while method may expel affect as an element of judgment, it cannot dispel the affects that pervade the attitudes that it brings to bear. The very dream of conquering doubt preserves a sense of possible power and control for philosophy that may be no more than an illusion, an illusion inviting the skeptical critiques it then gets to continue attempting to defeat. Perhaps overcoming the skeptic is an inhuman fantasy, or fantasy of an inhumanity enabling us to project a stance impervious to our various limitations and even enabling us to take revenge on those very limitations when we reveal them.

Cavell proposes an alternative philosophical stance based on two concepts that have no place within the entire framework of discourse projected by the demand to defeat skepticism. The first can be formulated from within skepticism but not pursued there: "[S]ince we cannot know the world exists, its presentness to us cannot be a function of knowing."[3] All knowledge must presuppose the world's existence, so that the condition of our responsiveness to objects simply drops out of those discourses which are governed by method and its criteria. Moreover, if we pursue the issue, we realize then that there must be two quite different kinds of presentness: "The presentness achieved by certainty of the senses cannot compensate for the presentness which had been elaborated through our old absorption in the world" ("DK," 94). Certainty of the senses "is not enough" (Mul., 64) because that certainty at best appeals only to an impersonal mind and confers only specific, depersonalized, and decontextualized perceptual phenomena. Presentness experienced as the more fundamental experience of the world coming into some mode of existence will require very different attitudes if we are to be able to bring it and its implications to consciousness.

The second concept elaborates one of these possible different attitudes. Rather than base our philosophical reflection on questions involving how representations are anchored in the world, we can focus instead on how persons manage to operate under the constant possibility of skepticism. From this perspective the experience of presentness is less a matter of how things are than of how agents are disposed toward the worlds they encounter. Presentness is primarily an issue for psychology. And once psychology is put at the center of philosophical reflection, we have a powerful instrument for dwelling on actual practices and for clarifying what is at stake in the various investments these practices are asked to sustain. On the most general level, this psychological perspective enables us not only to register what is inhuman in Cartesian ideals but also to understand why that inhumanity appeals to philosophers. In effect, the epistemic model of philosophy promises both to overcome the limitations of our humanity and to enable our taking revenge on all those aspects of our lives which resist such overcoming.

Conversely, the best way to combat the skeptic position is not to fantasize over-throwing it but to treat skepticism as an inescapable temptation that follows from the necessarily incomplete and dependent nature of our efforts to secure our judgments as knowledge. Once we can so internalize the skeptic, we begin to focus on how agents come to negotiate a world they can mutually accept without anyone projecting a fantasized certainty ("DK," 95). And once these negotiations take center stage, the dreams of apodictic clarity give way to an emphasis on ordinary language. For the heritage of Wittgenstein and Austin now can be seen to sustain an ethics as well as a pragmatics because it keeps our attention focused on how we rely upon and need trust as a fundamental condition of exchange. Philosophy becomes inseparable from therapy by reminding us of how learning to acknowledge our limits is inseparable from making articulate what binds us to each other. Recognition of those ties, in turn, provides a basis for perfectionism because that allows each of us to call out in others what may help reveal to them their various ways of being embodied within webs of interactive possibilities.

To bring out what is most problematic in Cavell's recent Emersonian versions of these antiepistemic directions for philosophy, I will now place his thinking in relation to two other antiepistemic stances—a more socially oriented one devel-oped by Charles Taylor and a quite different psychological one developed most fully by Friedrich Nietzsche. This approach of Nietzsche is very different from Cavell's Emersonian construct but also present in psychologists such as Sylvan Tomkins and in contemporary philosophical work by thinkers such as Richard Moran, who stress conative values and orientations that do not depend on self-interpretation.[4] Taylor's essay "Overcoming Epistemology" makes this task much easier than it would otherwise be, because it elegantly lays out in more analytic terms than Cavell's what is most problematic within epistemic thinking.[5] Then I will use the problems I discuss in Cavell's treatment of these issues in order to show how a non-Emersonian Nietzsche affords a richer exemplar for spelling out how we might construct alternative models of judgment based not on how we constitute knowledge but rather on how we constitute selves, hence also on how individuals best recognize and take responsibility for their embedment in complex social organizations.[6]

Taylor is fundamental because a smug antiepistemic position has to explain why epistemically driven philosophy is so deeply problematic that it makes sense not to try alternative epistemic frameworks but to seek quite different fundamental principles. Cavell has his psychological critique of the fantasy that philosophy can overthrow skepticism, Nietzsche his psychological critique of the will to truth. But Taylor most directly engages the specific philosophical underpinnings of this epistemic tradition, and he carries out that engagement in ways whose own prob-lems also dramatize the need for bringing into play the psychological concerns shared by Cavell and by Nietzsche. Taylor can remain within something like traditional philosophical discourse because he finds in phenomenology a tradition that provides the core of a necessary critique. Phenomenologists like Husserl and Heidegger expose epistemic ideals of "method" as doomed efforts to shore up a problematic structure of representational principles. Once philosophy tries to define knowledge as "the correct representation of an independent reality," once it tries to reduce knowledge to a pictorial relation bracketing the specific conditions of apprehension that self-reflection might provide, the only way to secure a stable fit between "inner depiction" and "outer reality" is to establish workable objective criteria for assessing propositions ("OE," 466). If we focus on how easily what the mind represents distorts what an unbiased eye might see, we then have to distrust our immediate judgments and suspend all affective tinges that our position projects into those judgments. We need "method" as a prosthetic for failed natural capacities. And method by its very nature produces the impersonal and the mechanistic, since these qualities allow the repetition necessary if impartial observers are to assess the claims our representations make and if their judgments are to be trusted. Moreover, as we give this impersonal cast to knowledge, we also redefine what might constitute knowledge of ourselves. Hence Descartes proposes that knowledge of the self consists in developing a map of how our thoughts can be ordered, and he insists that we base our judgments about the self as real object in the world on the very same practices we use for establishing certainty about objects ("OE," 469).

Because these ideals of knowledge so clearly apply also to the self, Taylor can show why there has been an easy and powerfully attractive homology between what we bring to bear in our representations and how we make moral and political judgments. Certainty in the physical world has as its correlate in morality and psychology the dream of self-responsibility, a finding of purposes in oneself that can be stated in terms that allow universal approval because we align ourselves with reason. We can make the judgment that we are aligned with reason because we can deal with ourselves as if we had achieved transparent equations between what we will and what we know—each justifying the other. But it is precisely at this great triumph of the epistemic, this point where it asserts its authority over ethical practice, that the three basic problems emerge which incite antiepistemic theorists to develop alternative models of judgment:

> The first is the picture of the subject as ideally disengaged, that is, as free and rational to the extent that he has fully distinguished himself from his natural and social worlds, so that his identity is no longer to be defined in terms of what lies outside him in these worlds. The second . . . is a punctual view of the self, ideally ready qua free and rational to treat those worlds—and even some of the features of his own character—instrumentally, as subject to change and reordering in order the better to secure the welfare of himself

and like subjects. The third is the social consequence of the first two: an atomistic construal of society as constituted by, or ultimately to be explained in terms of, individual purposes. ("OE," 471–72)

Taylor thinks he can establish an adequate alternative by concentrating on the limitations of the epistemic model of representation that underlies all three problems. Rather than take the knower "for granted as 'subject' and examining what makes it possible for him to have knowledge" ("OE," 474), Taylor shares Cavell's view that we base our understanding of the world on our ways of dealing with it. Relying on Wittgenstein's critique of picture-based models of knowledge and Heidegger's of the unsituated subject, Taylor insists that what underlies our representations is not some independent state of affairs but "a certain grasp we have of the world as agents in it" ("OE," 477). And hence to understand knowing we cannot examine only independent sentences. We have to attend to the specific work speakers do with them: "We can draw a neat line between my *picture* of an object and that object but not between my *dealing* with the object and that object" ("OE," 477).

From this vantage point Taylor can propose plausible criticisms of each of the three negative consequences he attributed to thought dominated by epistemic concerns. Agents clearly cannot be disengaged from what counts as their knowing. Knowing must be considered an aspect of their activities. So their knowledge claims are also assertions of responsibility, since these attest to their basic modes of responding to and within their worlds. Analogously, the self cannot successfully separate itself into punctual moments without losing both the capacity to respond and the sense of belonging that these responsibilities can produce. Agents are embodied and are enmeshed in history, not as a series of moments but as a set of modifiers affecting and connecting their various actions. And they are never in control from any point not itself within that history, so the most they can do is account for their orientations; they cannot take what Thomas Nagel calls a "view from nowhere."[7] Finally one can show "the priority of society as the locus of the individual's identity" ("OE," 478)—both as the source of its commitments and as the structure that affords the recognitions by which those identities take on substance and force. Hence the antiepistemic stance generates as a minimal ethics a demand for "self-clarity about our nature as knowing agents" ("OE," 479), now not as some total self-reflexive clarity about the referential adequacy of our beliefs but as awareness of what constrains us and hence connects us to other human beings. The most important dimensions of our knowledge claims consist in how we take responsibility for particular perspectives and the filiations they entail.

All of this seems perfectly reasonable to me. Taylor relies on phenomeno-logical accounts of how knowledge is situated in order to sustain what we might call an expressivist ideal for ethical and political values that provides a powerful alternative to epistemic ways of engaging those issues. How we know is bound up with very specific social conditions defining our expectations and priorities, so ethics becomes a matter of taking responsibility for what is contingent in our lives, and politics becomes a matter of securing possibilities for the recognition of such self-definitions. What Taylor gains for ethics and politics, however, he loses in the domain of psychology. His expressive agents offer only their awareness of how they claim to know and their sense of responsibility for how their values are shaped by their links to specific communities. Taylor fails to provide a convincing or deep account of just what particular factors bind persons to society. Why must the most important contingencies be defined by specific developmental bonds to communities rather than by other aspects of a person's development, such as the pursuit of identifications with models for cultures that are quite distant in time or in space from the values initially forming the person's structures of concern? Consequently, it is never clear that the kinds of recognition political society can afford these agents will provide what they want or need as individuals. While Taylor can replace the epistemic with a strong sense of identity-based social negotiations, the psychology on which this model of recognition is based cannot address the range of difficulties his subjects face in their pursuit of much of the reward that they might gain from accepting such responsibilities. Even recognition comes dangerously close to being an empty concept unless we have some sense of the specific drives and tensions and contradictions that occur in its pursuit.[8]

Taylor's resistance to psychology is most striking, and most vulnerable, in the last section of the essay I have been following. Here Taylor invokes Nietzsche only to dismiss him because Nietzsche, like Foucault, rejects epistemic values in a way that also entails abandoning the very idea of "truth." For Taylor, one can reject epistemic models of truth and still preserve an ideal of truth based on "the tradition of self-critical reason" ("OE," 483). This tradition invites us to treat intentionality itself as something we can deal with as an object for critical analysis. Nietzsche of course is quite suspicious of such projected clarities, since, once we grant that intentions are situated, we have to see every intention as emerging out of complex and not quite recoverable originating conditions. But Taylor can ignore this aspect of Nietzsche by reducing him to a historicist concerned only with denying all forms of objectivity. Consequently Taylor's own antiepistemic expressivism does not allow for a strong or intricate model of those agents who do the expressing. Taylor's agents remain driven by imperatives to self-knowledge that are dangerously close to the epistemic ideal he anatomizes. This kind of expressive agent remains abstracted from the various aspects of need, power, and surprising social affiliations that I think circulate around and through intentionality.

Therefore we need Cavell: We need a historical account that attributes the dangers of the epistemic to specific psychological orientations, which include ideals of self-knowledge, and we need a much richer psychological theater for dramatizing what is at stake in the process of seeking and conferring recognitions. But we also need to be very wary of Cavell. His recent efforts to restore psychology seem inseparable from a return to Freudian ways of reading that I think simultaneously too relative in their emphasis on individual interpretative responses to the world and too substantialist in their having to explain those readings in terms of a deep dynamic self underlying appearances. Consequently the sense of personal interactions that Cavell hopes will replace epistemic models of judgment seems to me to flirt dangerously with the worst excesses of romantic subjectivity. And that model of agency cannot provide a sufficient basis for any politics, as Cavell's inadequate engagement with John Rawls makes apparent.[9] Yet criticizing Cavell is difficult business because of how brilliantly he puts into practice basic differences between philosophizing within epistemic traditions and philosophizing within models of judgment based on the kind of self-consciousness persons manage to sustain within certain orientations of thought. Cavell is less concerned with testing ideas against some independent world than with seeing how far they will carry his affective life, leaving to the reader the task of determining at what point quite useful insights drift over into the kind of excess that either will invite the Emersonian friend to intercede or provoke the curious academic to try other more congenial discourses.

More important, Cavell is difficult to criticize because his enterprise (post his discovery of Emerson) seems to be very delicately balanced, or perhaps just constantly equivocating, between a Wittgensteinian minimalism defining the person in terms of grammatical criteria and a dangerous idealism stressing processes of performative self-interpretation that are not congruent with Wittgenstein's best thinking on this topic.[10] This stress on self-interpretation entails transforming intimacy into a theatricality that ultimately entirely rejects the great Wittgensteinian enterprise of seeking an intimacy on the level of grammatical functions, where questions about "who I am" simply do not arise in that abstract form. And relying on "melodrama" as the self's basic expressive medium does not, indeed probably cannot, adequately handle the critiques of self-representation one finds so elegantly bruited in Lacan.

This essay might then be considered a challenge that Cavell show how his version of an antiepistemic stance can in fact reconcile what is most radical in Wittgenstein with the modes of discourse within the humanities that Cavell wants to have exemplify the necessary alternative processes of judgment. To formulate that challenge, I will argue that any use of Wittgenstein on subjectivity which remains responsive to his originality must be able to replace the question "who am I" with the question "where am I." Then we can shift from a need to interpret the self to needs to clarify how intensities and interests mark a person's engagement and ultimately how both require and sustain a person's positionings in relation to the social discourses competing for its allegiance.[11] In such clarifying, Cavell must face the further challenge of having to engage some basic aspects of Nietzsche the psychologist not subsumable under the role of either Foucauldian historicist or Emersonian perfectionist. Where Cavell locates the basic problem in epistemic stances in the specific psychology of skepticism, Nietzsche the psychologist concentrates on the more general dynamics of the epistemic's dependency on a will to truth: Unable to pursue power directly, philosophy cloaks individual perspective under the form of abstract argument and gives individual will the appearance of being warranted by universal imperatives. This broader sense of psychological dynamics takes us all the way back to Plato, providing a framework for treating the skeptic as only one version of philosophy's all too human inhumanity. And it is deeply suspicious of the therapeutic impulses so important to Cavell, because, for Nietzsche, the therapeutic is usually a covert means of wielding power over others. Claiming to act in their interest, it keeps them trapped in the forms of nihilism that are inevitable when agents let generalized wisdom constitute what they take to be their own basic subjective imperatives. While Cavell and Nietzsche share the idea of aversion to conformity, Nietzsche's thinking allows a thoroughgoing antiidealism with a very different vision from Cavell's of what constitutes satisfying subjective agency and, consequently, of what might best count as perfectionist possibilities for such subjects. Where Cavell's subject is irreducibly self-interpreting and hence melodramatic, Nietzsche's is irreducibly suspicious of interpretive theaters in the service of a more immediate commitment to what I will call (modifying Henry Staten's work) "conative autoaffection."[12] This conative subject will turn out to be much more compatible than Cavell's Emersonian one with Cavell's earlier commitments to a Wittgensteinian intimacy and to the intricate social textures sustained by ordinary language as phenomenon and as metaphor. And while for obvious reasons I do not think it feasible to find a politics in Nietzsche, I will argue that he offers a clearer case than Cavell does for what must be addressed if we are to reconcile liberal politics with a fully psychologized, antiepistemic expressivism.

2

Now I can no longer use the stating of large ambitions to defer the frustration of having to abstract arguments from Cavell's supple and intricate readings. So I will begin with Cavell's most abstract and programmatic treatment of the conative subject, his essay "Being Odd, Getting Even." Rather than simply criticize Descartes's construction of what becomes the subject of modernity, as Taylor does, Cavell here tries to go Descartes one better by working out a version of the cogito that can no longer be subsumed under ideals of method and of critical philosophy. Taking his departure from what he claims is an allusion Emerson makes to Descartes's "I think therefore I am," Cavell shows how Emerson's version of the cogito cannot be reduced to the processes of an impersonal thinking: "Descartes' discovery is that my existence requires, hence permits, proof (you might say authentification)—more particularly, requires that if I am to exist I must name my existence, acknowledge it" (Mul., 297).

In other words, Emerson extends what had been a common critique of Descartes—that his analysis shows only that "cogitans" exists and does not sanction any inference from the existence of thinking to the existence of an empirical subject who does the thinking. Cavell's Emerson tries to show how we can connect the life of cogitans to the stakes brought to bear by an empirical subject. The "cogito" takes on full substance when the "I" not only thinks its existence but locates itself within the work of making that existence articulate. Then the dynamics of expression require recasting the old body-spirit duality in the more dynamic terms of a self divided into a "thing . . . with two magnetic poles—say a positive and a negative or an active and a passive" (Mul., 297). For there has to be something that is the substance with which the cogito identifies, and there have to be crucial differences between passive and active versions of that identification. The cogito's basic activity then can be characterized as the process of facing and overcoming shame and conformity. Descartes himself realized that his purely punctual model of the self's activity required some kind of supplement, since he once remarked that "even if my existence is certain, how long do I exist and can I exist when I cease thinking" (Mul., 298). Emerson's perfectionism begins in his capacity to provide a "grammatical answer" to these questions: "I am a being who to exist must say I exist, or must acknowledge my existence—claim it, stake it, enact it" (Mul., 299). And with this realization, "our waiting for philosophy is at last no longer vain" because philosophy arrives at a point where it can be "fulfilled in the form of psychoanalysis" ("Psychoanalysis and Cinema," Mul., 235).

But it is precisely with this Emersonian version of Descartes that Cavell may create an unbridgeable distance from his Wittgensteinian heritage. For there are two quite different ways to understand these dangerously equivocal Emersonian claims, and Cavell in practice often seems to take the stronger and far more problematic alternative. A thin version of this grammatical answer to "who I am" would say only that we prove our existence by placing within our actions some measure of personal attention and personal investment. *How* we engage in our actions can suffice to constitute who we are. Or, more philosophically, what matters is the nature of a way of being there, regardless of whether or not the enacting is sustained by a claiming and an overt staking. As Heidegger put it, "Dasein's being is such that its being is an issue for it." But when Cavell cites this Heideggerian statement, he emphasizes not being but the performance by which this issuing becomes a mode of self-expression. The simple conative embodiment of caring must for Cavell take substance in the activity of interpretation. Thus we find Cavell insisting that if there is to be proof for such existence, it cannot exist simply in how we act but requires "authentification" in terms of a "human proof of my human existence" (Mul., 300). And full authentification seems possible only by taking quite literally the figure of authoring oneself. That indeed brings us to the core of Emersonian self-reliance.

On the most concrete level, the basic force blocking this self-creating self-reliance is our propensity to shame. Fear of shame drives us into conformity and hence to abnegating authorship and authentification. Conversely, our one way beyond shame is to become "ashamed of our shame"—that is the imperative to expression which shapes Emersonian ideals and which accounts for the constant risk of melodrama in Cavell's work. Refusing conformity and refusing decorum requires a self-authoring that attempts to capture in language the nuances of the person's sensibility. Anything less would be to yield to whatever imposes passivity upon us and hence to fail to declare those aspects as knowable by others and ultimately to not allow oneself to be a potential representative for those others precisely because of the modes of self-definition that such risks make available. "The theory, not surprisingly, is a theory of communication, hence of expression, hence of character—character conceived, as Emerson always conceives it, as naming at once, as faces of one another, the human individual and human language" (Mul., 306).

But how do we judge these performances as philosophy, or even as simply the presentation of a personal presence? More pertinently, how do those of us who do not like this approach to philosophy express judgments that they feel justified in thinking are based on something other than personal taste or the opportunity to author a self in allegiance or in opposition? And how do we do so without the shame of merely conforming to established philosophical ideals? I think we can offer argument-based judgments here by concentrating on the structure of concern that Cavell relies on in order to work out this Emersonian model of expressive agency. Even when specific claims are extraordinarily dense and subtle, the claims develop and rely on structures of oppositions or of aversions that establish possible grids for reflecting on experience. If particular grids or sets of grids force us into uncomfortable denials or awkward acceptances, then there are strong reasons to seek alternatives, and there are clear contrasts that might be used to show what is valuable about those alternatives. Therefore, I will map four of these structures of opposition in Cavell's work, each of which forces his thinking into very strained avenues.

Consider first the most obvious of these oppositions, Cavell's Emersonian insistence that the antithesis of self-ownership is conformity: "self-reliance is the aversion of conformity," and "'aversion' is Emerson's way of saying conversion" ("Declining Decline," Mul., 347–48). Cavell has three basic reasons for this claim. If shame is the force that drives us to passivity, then the pressure to conform is the social instrument by which we protect ourselves from shame without having to become ashamed of our shame. If we are to be open to the work of aversion-conversion, we have to deny the comforts of conformity so that we are aware at every moment of the "poverty" of philosophy that is the necessary corollary of its commitment to wakefulness (Mul., 348).

Clearly this aversion to conformity is a basic value for modern intellectuals. But I have strong doubts that, as Cavell uses it, this value manages to achieve the representativeness he seeks. Indeed, Cavell's efforts may reveal the difficulty inherent in all fundamentally romantic efforts to make the intensities of individual experience stand as representatives for actual shared values (rather than as projections of possible values that some may be persuaded to pursue). For I suspect it simply is not true that most people experience their fullest moments of sensing their own agency in those moments when they produce performances that display and author an aversion to conformity. The agent's experience of his or her own capacities *may* involve a feeling that the person has managed to maintain some kind of difference from the norm—in doing some special kindness or in finding a quick way to complete a task or a slow way of making love. But aversion to mediocracy in small domains of our lives need not be aversion to conformity. One of my richest senses of self occurs when I manage to feel I can do exactly what is expected of me in accord with some role. Even academically it seems to me strange to make the aversion of conformity as central as Cavell does, because that value seems to me crucial only in our actual writing, which institutionally depends on the promise to offer something original. In many other cases, however, aversion to conformity can seem quite silly, for example, if one refuses on that principle not to join others in reading Emerson as primarily a philosopher of intuition. Surely there are considerations that might make conforming a preferable position to the hopeless spinning out of casuistic efforts to avoid the obvious. Indeed, it is difficult to imagine how Cavell can maintain both the aversion to conformity and the desire to imagine philosophers as representative men.

The issue of representativeness leads to even more serious problems in Cavell's treatment of conformity. Simple logic makes one wonder if representativeness can ever be achieved without some important level of conformity. My graduate school roommate once told me that the difference between Mao Tse-tung's and my attitudes was that I talked about the people while he simply said "we." And, socially, Cavell's model cannot honor those who, in achieving conformity, manage to express the structures of concern most important to them. Imagine those who simply seek acceptance. Or imagine those wounded by the fear that just such desires make them woefully inadequate for a world governed by the romantic values that intellectuals have helped propagate. Ironically, Cavell's model of authorship serves to comfort intellectuals as they continue to ignore what I think is one of our most fundamental social problems: the differences among natural gifts and educational opportunities and sociopolitical histories which make it very difficult to embrace wholeheartedly social ideals based either on the old universals produced by reason or on the new conditions of expressive singularity generated by commitments to performative sublimity. If psychology is to carry social force, it will have to be more abstract than Cavell is on what matters about individuation as well as more open to a wide range of conative satisfactions without specifying their performative and self-reflective dimensions. All the liberal state can desire is that people be aided in realizing whatever forms of conative intensity they choose without putting those of others at risk: One person's perfectionism, even in the guise of the Emersonian friend, is likely to be tyranny to at least some others. Perfectionism must remain only a structure of ideals postulated for humanistic education, where teleology (and some measure of conformism) can be rationalized.

Cavell would not leave himself so vulnerable were there not a powerful under-lying cause. His way of formulating that cause, however, seems to me to depend on a second problematic opposition. I refer to the crucial contrast between passivity and activity, a contrast that we can obviously never entirely avoid, but that also is very difficult to make do any plausible work in our philosophical reflections. As Cavell recognizes, there is an enormous difference between practical and meta-physical uses of this distinction. Practically, being active can take many forms, and being passive need not be a bad thing. In fact, one can be actively passive, for example, by working hard to be attentive and responsive. Being active, then, is not any one specific model of behavior; rather, it is a relational term that describes how a person is involved in particular processes: an active spirit is our way of staying on track. Since the term "active" applies to any behavior, there cannot be any independent value to being either active or passive. Value must be attributed to the action, not to the degree of activity, except as a supplemental concern.

Given this indefiniteness, purely practical judgments about activity and pas-sivity will not help support any substantial philosophical position, especially not a perfectionist idealization of self-reliance as aversion to conformity. To sustain such philosophical values one needs more abstract hypotheses projecting general values for certain kinds or qualities of activity. Unfortunately, Cavell's only way of at-tributing such values is by developing the relation to meaning sustained by certain kinds of self-interpreting activities. Hence passivity becomes being subjected to meanings imposed by others, and activity becomes visible authorship developing specific stylistic, figurative, and conceptual resistances to such conformity. But while one can certainly claim that such activity is valuable, one cannot easily make that value as central as Cavell does. For it is by no means clear that the pursuit of meaning as invention is the fundamental or most appropriate means for establishing the sense of presentness to self or conative power enabling agents to overcome the nihilism of not caring about that self as self. It may be the case that this demand for authored meaning actually encourages nihilism. That demand makes it impossible simply to accept the structures of activity within which meaning is already established and within which agents distinguish themselves not by how they author meanings but by how they perform tasks and respond to what situations afford.

Perhaps the easiest way to draw out the consequences of Cavell on activity versus passivity is to invoke Lacan. For Lacan beautifully shows how the metaphysical promise of activity as the production of meaning for the self is often actually an invitation to passivity. This happens because such vague ideals seduce us into identifying with certain projections, ironically fixing us in images that in fact greatly narrow our freedom. Lacan reminds us that wherever there is self-staging or self-authoring, there is at least the likelihood of two basic problems. There will be a gap between the representation we produce and the dynamics generating the production. And there will be a slippage between the direction we attribute to our activity and the fantasized audience whom we want to desire what our signifiers produce. When we honor these productions simply as active self-authoring and measure them simply by their contrast to passivity, we lay ourselves open to identifying entirely with fantasy structures—whether these be specific role images or ideals of the philosopher's constant state of remaining awake while the others sleep. The philosopher's remaining awake all night may well stem from his desire to be recognized the next morning as different from the others because he is a philosopher. And even if that is not the case, those like Alcibiades who do recognize the significance of his staying awake substitute that accomplishment for the principles that the philosopher wants to communicate—perhaps not only because of their own venality.

Plato's rendering of Socrates' plight may be sufficiently ironic to reabsorb such potential slippage within his own reconfiguration of meanings. But most people seduced by Cavellian rhetoric to the self-regarding pleasures of thinking themselves "active" are not likely to extend irony so far. For them the appropriate genre is melodrama, precisely the medium in which projections of sincerity and need are presented as so actively filling the present that an audience will suspend the temptation to ironic distance. And then they grow blind to the worst kind of conformity—not to specific social codes but to the imaginary structures by which agents celebrate themselves for participating in this entire melodrama. For once activity becomes a metaphysical principle carrying distinctive values, then it becomes an end in itself determined only by how people represent themselves and separated from any concrete social practices within which one can judge just what the activity does and does not accomplish.

Cavell cannot be satisfied with any simpler, less interpretation-based version of self-consciousness as presentness because of a third opposition deeply embedded in his Emersonian framework, this one between the superficial and the deep in psychic life. I will grant Cavell his claim that he does not want to return to romantic interiority. But I cannot grant that he has freed himself from the idealizations of self-consciousness sustained by that romantic vision. Perhaps to demonstrate his entrapment, one need only turn to his insistence on the figure of the dark woman, the idealized possessor of what must remain on the other side of language. But it is important to note how the romantic pursuit of some "contrary depths of oneself" ("Declining Decline," Mul., 326) also pervades his social thinking and makes it possible for him to insist on psychoanalysis as a perspective that remains crucial to perfectionist models of public life. Activity in Cavell is ultimately the realization of what has remained hidden or unspoken in the self. Therefore, the richer account he can give of what tends to remain hidden, the richer the sense of social benefits his model of self-authorship can offer. And if he can show that what is repressed is potentially a best self, he can sustain an entire perfectionist program aimed at fostering a social structure that helps each of us engage this hiddenness and bring it into active expression.

However, the society so produced (or so fantasized) remains one consisting of interpreters whose basic activity consists in negotiations about meanings for the self rather than about the assessment of actions and the developing of obligations that might follow from such assessments. Consequently, this opposition between the hidden and the real provides Cavell a very quick and almost total distance from other philosophical ways of talking about ethical and social values. There is only the drama of coming to realize the self more fully in language. And that means ultimately there is for philosophy only an alliance with the therapeutic work proposed by psychoanalysis. Cavell claims that "the advent of psychoanalysis" provides "the place, perhaps the last place, in which the human psyche as such (the idea that there is a life of the mind, hence a death) receives its proof":

> And it receives proof of its existence in the only form in which the psyche can (any longer) believe it—namely as essentially unknown to itself, say as unconscious. . . . Freud's assertion declares that for the mind to lose the psychoanalytic intuition of itself as unconscious would be for it to lose the knowledge that it exists. ("Psychoanalysis and Cinema," Mul., 235–36)

To find the self, we first have to show how it is concealed. But every self we do find turns out to be a false self, a representation or a specter, whose falsity must be demonstrated in order to locate its truth in the very authoring that our constant realization of the negative requires. This then means that we are condemned to an anxiety that keeps us focused on the self. And because we are so narrowly focused, we need a psychoanalytic priesthood that can lead us to the truth about what we can only believe in on the condition that we do not find it.

In Cavell's most recent work this motif of the hidden does lead beyond psychoanalysis, if only to sponsor a reading of ordinary language philosophy as having the power to help us realize the force of the uncanny within the domestic realm.

Yet he can only do so by in effect making Wittgenstein the object of psychoanalytic care. Instead of Wittgenstein the philosophical grammarian who presided over Cavell's early work, we are given a melodramatic Wittgenstein constantly struggling to save himself from the repressions proposed by his interlocutor. And then what is perspicuous and representative in Wittgenstein is not the paths he carves for avoiding bewitchment by metaphysics but his capacity to resist the versions of a lesser self that the interlocutor offers. Yet Cavell's specific efforts to bring Wittgenstein within this melodrama reveal how much Cavell surrenders when he lets Emerson lead him away from his earlier Wittgensteinian thinking.

When Wittgenstein invokes a speaker insisting "that there must be something boiling in the picture of the pot," the Emersonian Cavell sees him "deliberately" inviting us "to ask whether this insistence—this excess, this little scene of melodrama—comes from him or from his interlocutor" ("Declining Decline," Mul., 326). Then Cavell makes one of his characteristic brilliant leaps to Descartes, who also felt the pressure of an internal other pushed almost to madness by the intellectual scrupulousness needed to confront "the threat or the temptation to skepticism." To resist that madness, Cavell sees the *Investigations* committed to a constant struggle against repression, "never claiming a final philosophical victory" but learning "to place and replace madness, to deny nothing, at every point" (Mul., 326). Wittgenstein joins the romantic struggle against skepticism by refusing to let any abstract imperatives empty out the agent's "contributions to words so that language itself, as if beyond me, exclusively takes over the responsibility for meaning" (Mul., 338). Therefore, it is crucial that we not focus simply on language-games. Wittgenstein offers what can become a shared therapeutic cultural ideal because he makes even philosophy a discipline displaying how the aversion to conformity can produce a wakefulness pervading persons' most elemental relations to language.

As he develops this case, however, Cavell makes a curious admission that Wittgenstein does *not* sound "the note of excess" that Cavell's talk about madness is playing. Cavell does not press why that is the case, why Wittgenstein may have been more averse to melodrama than he was to conformity. The most obvious answer would simply point to Wittgenstein's investment in a form of writing that would lose its concrete tensile strength were it to allow itself any mode of self-reflection not intimately woven into specific grammatical cases. However, it is at least equally important to recognize that Wittgenstein probably wants to prevent the interlocutor from taking on any traits of a specific character. For were he to become a character, the temptations he represents could be psychologized and perhaps attributed to something hidden, something not directly woven into the specific linguistic situations. But Wittgenstein is dedicated to keeping the temptations entirely within philosophy, within the quite specific voicings that emerge as one tries out particular disciplinary paths. So there is nothing at all hidden in this drama, at least nothing hidden that psychology can disclose. What matters is the force of philosophical questions to produce specific and pervasive problematic lines of thinking. Wittgenstein does not psychologize those temptations, because he wants us to see that anyone doing philosophy, whatever his or her character, is likely to hear the interlocutors' voices, so that his readers will also recognize the need for exploring very different attitudes toward that discipline.

It is even more important for Wittgenstein that we not melodramatize or psychologize the freedom that one comes to feel when one understands the temptations as temptations endemic to Western philosophical traditions.[13] For this freedom is not to be confused with humanistic, "positive" accounts of freedom that link it with various forms of self-realization or the recovery for consciousness of what had been hidden aspects of the self's potential. Wittgensteinian freedom in philosophy is not freedom to become a self but freedom from the personality traits and conceptual orientations which doing philosophy elicits. This freedom from philosophy then has liberating effects, but not in terms of any concepts about the self that derive from those philosophical traditions. Rather, the freedom is closer to Wallace Stevens's "the pleasures of merely circulating", since once one can slide out of philosophical demand structures, one may be able simply to participate within the immense variety of ways of going on that cultural grammars afford. Wittgensteinian wakefulness is an ideal of being able not to worry about performing the self so that one can pursue potentials within the range of ongoing practices that are blocked by worries about identity and about authenticity. Freedom is being able to enjoy what and where one is without having to produce any supplemental claims that promise some "significance" not immediately evident. Ultimately this freedom allows forms of enjoyment that do not need excess as a supplement: indeed at the core of such enjoyment is a feeling that one has finessed those cultural dispositions that depend on such excess.

Clearly this perspective on freedom demands that one resist all temptation to hold out something important but hidden that somehow can be realized if we find some better or richer way of staging the self for ourselves. Wittgenstein invites us to suspect that we create ideals of hiddenness precisely in order then to dwell on concerns about how the subject can become more expressive and more "authentic." To overcome that temptation, we have to recognize that discourse about the psyche is already too much present in most arenas of life. And then we might see that Wittgenstein's basic philosophical stance holds out as its reward the possibility that we can align our wills to the world without the detour provided by attention to the kinds of adventures that take the stage when the individual psyche becomes the focus of self-consciousness. His work seeks representativeness not by presenting someone whose unique performances compel us to admire and imitate them but by making visible a way of engaging in the world so that we simply find ourselves more interested in the mind as it thinks than we are in the self as it whines for attention. Where Wittgenstein makes tact a minimalist means of encountering a sublimity distinctive to the mind's analysis of its own embodiment, Cavell seems an Ancient Mariner condemned to have to win an interest in the world that is inseparable from his own endless self-interpretation.

Finally, Cavell's commitment to psychology leads him to want to explain some of the fundamental oppositions within his thinking by postulating firm oppositions between the genders that I find both implausible and deeply inconsistent with his perfectionist project. Of course Cavell gives those oppositions the most sophisticated form possible, insisting that they are not descriptions of actual gender psychologies but of principles one can associate with differences between masculine and feminine orientations toward experience. Yet I doubt that, at this historical juncture, we need such oppositions in any mode, since they are likely to blind us to how much both genders participate together in most of the forms of life that our grammar sustains.

Cavell needs this opposition between genders in part as a defense against those feminists (and the potential for shame that they inflict) who found intolerable the primacy he gives to the internalizing of skepticism. But rather than complicate his picture of the range of interests that might sustain philosophy and even generate interests in acknowledgment, Cavell simply divides the pie along unfortunately conformist lines. He thinks there are good grounds for granting that the female principle cannot be identified with skepticism, so long as one takes seriously psychoanalytic notions of character development. For women know who their children are ("Psychoanalysis and Cinema," Mul., 241) and also do not have to worry about males faking their sexual satisfaction (Mul., 243)—the two basic concrete sources of the temptation men experience to seek to defend the self by hiding within skeptical negations. But then once one has so divided the genders, what can one do with the feminine? In our intellectual culture one must idealize it, but there are few available idealizations that are not also modes of patronizing those one would idealize.

As I read him, Cavell cannot escape this trap. His male is forced to skepticism because he seems to have only philosophical values on which to rely to defend the self threatened by emptiness and castration. And his female is forced out of the economy of knowing and doubting into another version of the old immediacy in violent conflict with all public processes of doubting and arguing, since these still represent male demand (Mul., 242). Woman takes on the value of the capacity to understand embodied expressiveness (Mul., 246–47). Therefore she is attuned to the otherness of the world as other. Where the male principle is oriented toward self-defense, female attunement to that otherness brings with it a capacity to mourn without reserve. And that capacity makes it possible to accept the sense or transience that is the inescapable condition of valuing an expressiveness not suited to the economy of doubt and proof. For males bound to that economy, the feminine other takes the spectral form of the dark woman haunting their world of commerce and power as an unassimilable memorial to her untellable story.

Cavell apparently needs all this mythologizing in order to preserve a sense of mystery about dark unknowable dimensions of psychic life. But he pays a large price, for the basic structure on which he bases his model of sexual difference seems too severely and revealingly flawed. Cavell roots the basic differences between male skepticism and female attunement and mourning in the quite different investments each gender has in questions about identifying children and judging sexual satisfaction. Males cannot be sure that they can confidently answer questions such as "Is this my child?" or "Am I the cause of your sexual satisfaction?" And indeed there is some substance here for projecting differences, even though it does not take a Wittgenstein to demonstrate to men that, since there cannot be satisfying answers to such questions, it is probably wise to resist investing in any projection. Nor can women be so sanguine about being the "cause" of sexual satisfaction, since men are rather notorious for being insensitive to differences in what produces their satisfactions. More important, in order to stress his gender story, Cavell seems to me to ignore the most important question the self has to ask about its activities. For Nietzsche, for Lacan, and for Wittgenstein, the crucial question is not whether she is faking but whether I am faking. And neither gender has a monopoly on the asking or the answering of that question. So while this traditional question may not wake up the students in the back rows of our lectures, it may keep us awake to what binds people and genders and social units within the possibilities that our language gives us for making and enjoying sense.

3

Let me try to end on a positive note. Even when Cavell is problematic, the scope, subtlety, and intensity of his thinking provide a powerful interlocutor. And where Wittgenstein's interlocutor leads us away from philosophy toward a kind of immanence, Cavell as interlocutor requires us to come up with competing speculative models for large questions about why we might care about philosophy and how we might understand the roles excess and confession play as fundamental features in our senses of subjective agency. That is why even when he is wrong about Wittgenstein, he keeps the kind of pressure on Wittgenstein that reminds us of how deeply concerned Wittgenstein was with questions of value that lead far beyond technical philosophical issues. And his specific way of being wrong provides the contrast we need to appreciate why Wittgenstein remains so ascetic and so committed to an intimacy that has nothing to do with confession and asks for no aid from psychoanalysis. [14]

Cavell's ways of being wrong are even more suggestive when we turn to Nietzsche, the philosopher who I think provides a necessary complement to Wittgenstein. Where Wittgenstein is superb at working through what is problematic in the specific habits of mind fostered by epistemic culture, Nietzsche provides a full-scale assault on its underlying psychology and uses that assault to introduce a set of themes about the conative self that contemporary thinking will have to elaborate and refine if it is to provide adequate alternatives to the still dominant epistemic worldview.

Cavell's Emersonian Nietzsche is not interested in this version of subjectivity—he is only a perfectionist individualist, as bound to ideals of self-staking, self-interpretation, and the overcoming of shame as Emerson. Yet Cavell does remind us of the importance of paying attention to Nietzsche the psychologist, a Nietzsche ignored by Foucauldian historicism, sanitized by analytic philosophers like Bernard Williams,[15] and melodramatized by deconstruction's efforts to establish an antiepistemic philosophy that also refuses the seductions of psychology. So Cavell creates for us the task of reading against his versions of Nietzschean psychology. We need to develop a case that what Nietzsche offers is a complex antiepistemic model of judgments about value. From this angle it becomes possible to use Nietzsche the psychologist against versions of staking and owning the self that are based on confessional or psychoanalytically inclined processes of self-interpretation. Instead, he offers a radical antiidealism that requires locating the satisfactions of will in the concrete display of conative satisfactions and that establishes as its ultimate measure of value simply the quantity of "life" that an individual manages to gather within those satisfactions. While this concept of "life" will not immediately leap out as one to which contemporary philosophers can subscribe, I hope to show how its vagueness at least enables Nietzsche to preserve a version of subjective agency responsive to a range of forces that we distort if we think we have successfully interpreted them within our self-accountings. Finally, while almost no one would say that Nietzsche is free of excess, I hope to show how his best thinking provides a version of tragedy that employs this excess as a means of restoring attention to the most fundamental autoaffective relations we establish. This attention will certainly not make it possible to argue that Nietzsche provides a feasible politics, but using his analyses and his stark opposition to Cavell's therapeutic attitude toward the tragic reminds us of how much we lose when we allow ourselves to be seduced by the prospect of using philosophy to transform the inherent dynamics of subjectivity into the well-meaning subjections that generate political filiations.

Nietzsche's basic differences from Cavell's version of the subject are strikingly clear when he too turns to Descartes's "cogito":

A thought comes when "it" wishes, not when "I" wish, so that it is a falsification of the facts of the case to say that the subject "I" is the condition of the predicate "think." *It* thinks; but that this "it" is precisely the famous old ego is, to put it mildly, only a supposition, an assertion, and assuredly

not an "immediate certainty." . . . Even the "it" contains an *interpretation* of the
process, and does not belong to the process itself.[16]

This passage is easily melodramatized so that it becomes a denial that there is
such a thing as subjective agency. But that reading ignores the subtlety of Nietzsche's quotation marks. His ambition is not to deny the subject but to gain some
distance between what we display as agents and what the imagination proposes
as humanistic versions of the "ego." By insisting that this "it" inhabits the "I" at
the most elemental levels, and that even the "it" is a projection, Nietzsche wants
to show how difficult it is to employ value terms like "owning" or "expressing"
or even "staking" the self. Similarly, he shows that developing oppositions like
that between active and passive is likely to ignore the fact that what seems active,
the imagination, may be what is passively shaped by the working of the "it." As
Wittgenstein also realized, capturing what is intimate to the dynamics of consciousness may be incompatible with employing those languages of intimacy that
presuppose the ego, since those are interpretations of interpretations and have
to be regarded not as descriptions of the self but as manifestations of the stakes
one brings to bear in caring about the imaginary constructs on which our ideas of
identity are based.[17]

   This Nietzschean view of the will has two important consequences for drawing a sharp distinction between how persons assert value and what forms of justification are required for them to assert knowledge claims. First, it provides a
powerful challenge to any kind of idealism. Whatever subjective agency is, it is
not to be located by attempting interpretations of who we take ourselves to be
when we reflect on our actions. Such reflections may tell us a good deal about
the person, but primarily if they are read for their performative rather than their
referential functions. That is, we learn from self-interpretation when we observe
in action the complex interplay between the "it" and the "I" that Nietzsche calls
to our attention. But this very interplay also dramatizes factors that are far too
complex and immanent to be dramatized by our self-interpretations. The second
consequence follows immediately. If we cannot locate subjective agency in these
interpretations, and if our performances of ourselves put into play features that can
be recognized but not thematized, then we are led back to models of subjective
agency like Spinoza's. We need a concept like conatus in order to emphasize the
dynamics of the embodied strivings within which self-interpretation plays a variety
of roles. Imagining subjective desire as conative activity enables us to treat the will
as something entirely immanent in our actions, not separable from thinking but
also impossible to treat simply as an object thinking can reflect upon:

   Willing seems to me above all something *complicated*, something that is a unit
   only as a word. . . . So let us for once be more cautious, let as be "unphilo-

sophical": let us say that in all willing there is first, a plurality of sensations, namely the sensation of the state *"away from which,"* the sensation of the state *"towards which,"* the sensations of this *"from"* and *"towards"* themselves, and then also an accompanying muscular sensation. . . . Therefore, just as sensations . . . are to be recognized as ingredients of the will, so, secondly, should thinking also: in every act of the will there is a ruling thought . . . [inseparable from the willing]. Third, the will is not only a complex of sensation and thinking, but it is above all an *affect*, and specifically the affect of command. (*BGE*, sec. 1:18, p. 25)

Now we have to face the most difficult question in any attempt to bring Nietzsche into the present: How do we build anything like an ethics out of this psychology? Let me begin by addressing first the question of whether judgment can play any role once we treat will as so complexly embodied within the very texture of the agent's actions. I think we can still say that it matters to elicit the reasons that agents might give for their actions. Nietzsche is not interested in treating the reasons as if they provided arguments that somehow could be judged as arguments, that is, as appeals to some kind of realist or epistemic criteria. Instead, his primary concern is to recognize how the giving of reasons is itself a display of power, of a will to bring coherence to an action and to impose meaning on an auditor. Then we can judge not the reasons but the agent as agent, that is, as someone attempting to live in the world in a certain way. And we can recognize that our own judgments function in exactly the same way as the agent's reasons— that is, they define how our own conative energies try to make themselves felt within the world.

Clearly this model of value bars Nietzsche from using the languages of either truth or goodness as his framework for talking about what is at stake in the giving of reasons and the making of judgments. He has to resist all epistemic models of value. In their place he develops what in honor of Cavell we might call a perfectionism based simply on the idealization of "life" or vitality: "Hence a philosopher should claim the right to include willing as such within the sphere of morals—morals being understood as the doctrine of the relations of supremacy under which the phenomenon of life comes to be" (*BGE*, sec. 1:19, p. 27).

For our culture, this idealization of "life" seems both vague and anachronistic, a fantasy of the late nineteenth century necessary for opposing a dominant yet impotent gentry. Yet I think we can use the concept, if only as a guideline, because it does suggest how we can attribute value to states of will without relying on any epistemic criteria. There may be nonheroic and nonmelodramatic ways to put Nietzsche's idealization of life to contemporary uses if we are willing to equate life with the satisfactions of conative drives. At the very least, this enables us to suggest that we do not need fantasies of heroic self-interpretation in order to explain how values do not need sanctions by epistemic criteria.[18] And if we give "life" an ordinary language cast, we can use this conative model to define the values at stake in our coming to feel ourselves at home within the practices fundamental to our situations. Value resides in our realizations of the degree to which we can move purposively among various language-games without seeking sustenance from some image of what we are doing and hence without depending on some audience whose approval must supplement the immediate satisfactions within the practice.

I have to insist that I am not proposing that philosophy begin idealizing the concept of "life." I am suggesting that Nietzsche's use of the concept helps us project models of value that do not depend on epistemic criteria, because the values consist in manifest states of enablement and intensity that we attribute to the working of a will, not to interpretations about what is the case with the world.[19] And then even to make this suggestion useful I immediately have to add the admission that pure Nietzsche will not lead us to anything close to an adequate ethics. Insofar as there can be a discipline of ethics, it has to focus on the justification of actions (not of lives) in public terms. And vague concepts such as "life" will not help us establish these justifications. Those depend on our accepting a shared grammar of evaluative practices and our seeking as reward only the kinds of discursive identities that such grammars can afford.

But once one grants those limits, Nietzsche's concept of "life" can play several important roles. For example, Nietzschean concerns for the intensity of conative states remind us that the discursive identities which ethics affords within the public sphere are inevitably abstract and, because public constructs, not entirely satisfying, because they cannot be fully responsive to the specific qualities of the investments the agents maintain in the actions or to the conflicts that bring nobility and point to the investments. It is not easy to state the alternative to such public concerns without seeming inordinately individualistic. Yet the converse is also true: Nietzsche's work helps make us wary of the philosophical temptation to make ethical value the only substantial model of value worth thinking about. From a Nietzschean perspective, that orientation cannot honor what is vital or distinctive in individual wills, and it cannot bring to reflection the various modes of spontaneity or self-possession which are not justified by concepts but simply by the states that they make available. More important, Nietzsche forces us to realize that there may never be adequate syntheses of these two domains—the one offering determinate but thin public identities and the other somewhat chaotic and unjustifiable flows of local intensities.[20] For Nietzsche the inevitability of such conflict provides the grounds for treating a sense of tragedy as fundamental to philosophical reflection about values. And once one makes that admission, self-interpretation becomes inseparable from assessments of the scope and persistence of will. We measure individuals by something very close to the degree of life that they are capable of maintaining because they do not shrink from contradiction.

Nietzsche's inadequate public morality becomes a vehicle for dramatizing the necessary yet problematic interplay between the aesthetic quest for absorption in particular features of experience and the moral demand that we produce a shape for those experiences which can win the approval of idealized communities. If there is to be a perfectionism, it cannot rely on the comfortable faith that pursuing individual intensities will also deepen our sense of communal bonds.

"Life" as Nietzsche conceives it has three basic attributes which can help us formulate perspectives on value attuned to these conflicts, especially when read against Cavellian perfectionism. First, Nietzsche bases his model of value on a concept as abstract and general (and inhospitable to philosophy) as "life," because that very generality calls our attention to what constantly varies within the overall category of "value"—namely, the degree or intensity with which appearances emerge and activities are carried out. By thinking about life, we realize our own tendencies toward such variation, and we have an effective reminder of what makes us seem most attuned to those possible intensities. Second, those intensities clearly do not depend directly on our constructing concepts about them or on the reflected versions of selfhood that we gain from how other persons interpret us or respond to our self-interpretations. Life provides a figure for a fully conative view of satisfaction that does not depend on these interpretations and reflections but locates value in the specific ways that a person remains focused within particulars. The person's states can be treated as if they shared with works of art the mode of existence of one-place predicates enabling us to distinguish a Hamlet-picture from a picture of Hamlet. Values attach directly to appearances, as if they were inseparable from how and where the psyche focuses its energies.

In this respect life is not quite opposed to "meaning" but also not quite dependent upon it. For a dependency on meanings often leads us beyond what we can take as life to some projected desire or satisfaction, and the projection almost always generates an aura of dissatisfaction in the present, often requiring fantasies that negotiate our feelings of lack. Life, on the other hand, has only the series of present moments in which to manifest itself. Because of this, that concept provides a powerful incentive to adapt moral ideals of measuring the self emphasizing how one manages to participate in that flow of time—always now and hence always raising questions of whether we could bear its eternal recurrence.

Finally, this opening into eternal recurrence, this intersection of life with the imaginative frames that tragedy brings to bear, requires our including within our models of value concerns for how we come to terms with the fact that we cannot be the masters of what moves us. Life is always larger than the participants in it. And while that is the inescapable ground of tragedy, of our contingencies and vulnerabilities, awareness of that capaciousness is also the means by which we at once preserve a sense of our own limitations and find cause to celebrate the very conditions that so limit us. "Every true tragedy," Nietzsche tells us, shows "that life is at the bottom of things, despite all the changes of appearances, indestructibly powerful, and pleasurable." By identifying with the Dionysian reveler in this life, the tragic audience "sees itself as a satyr, *and as a satyr, in turn, he sees the god,* which means that in his metamorphosis he beholds another vision outside himself, as the Apollonian complement of his own state": "[S]haring his suffering, the chorus representing the audience as satyr also shares something of his wisdom and proclaims that truth from the heart of the world."[21]

Cavell on tragedy in "Disowning Knowledge" paints a very different picture. For him tragedy has its source in particular attitudes in which skepticism and associated fantasies of power and control override possibilities of belief and trust, leaving only forms of revenge as potentially satisfying conative states. On this foundation he develops marvelously intricate readings. But the readings are always informed by his therapeutic ambitions: Tragedy seems fundamentally a matter of mistaken attitudes toward understanding other people, so that the condition is correctable, for viewers if not for the protagonists. Hence Cavell tends to dwell on the opening acts of the tragedies, at the moments where things first go deeply wrong. For there the audience can see clearly what the characters do not see, and it can perhaps realize from how skepticism takes hold how it might avoid what in the plays comes to seem inevitable. Nietzsche on the other hand seeks out that inevitability, putting it at the core of tragic experience and consequently focusing on how the very *last* act (or the entire *Oedipus at Colonus* as one long last act) projects transfigurations of the characters and audience figures who bear the burden of consciousness that the play imposes. For Cavell we have to learn to avoid tragedy; for Nietzsche we have to seek out the test of spirit tragedy demands, and we have to appreciate the affirmative relation to life and to otherness and to limitation that it makes possible by requiring that we take on life at its most intense, where its necessities seem much stronger than the devices consciousness has at its disposal. Confronting such necessity demands a positive view of the "I am" involving more than aversion to conformity. Nietzsche's "I" must be measured by its refusal of the temptation to shrink from conflict by turning to therapeutic hopes that there is some specific idea of the self in which one can take comfort.

For practical emblems of what these contrasting stances involve, I think we need look only at the different attitudes to skepticism that get played out in these accounts of the tragic. In Nietzsche's thinking, internalizing the skeptic is not a matter of realizing the importance of trust and accepted criteria but of freeing oneself from the need to seek justification: "Strength, *freedom* which is born of the strength and overstrength of the spirit proves itself by skepticism." For managing to maintain skepticism allows freedom from the prisons that convictions produce, and it trains us to turn from seeking justification to tracking our actions in terms of what they surpass or how we can see what one has left behind. The skeptic then is a "spirit who wants great things" and who also recognizes that the means to them entails making oneself free to see clearly: "Great passion uses and uses up convictions, it does not succumb to them—it knows itself sovereign."[22]

This version of the skeptic is not without its excess. Yet by courting excess here, Nietzsche opens a dimension of skepticism not present in Cavell's version. Nietzsche sees that in the Renaissance, in the cultural imaginings whose dying gasps take philosophical form in Descartes, skepticism was not simply philosophical doubt but a truly practical means of gaining space for this "affect of command" by which individuals might establish for themselves a sense of sovereignty not beholden to rhetorics of justification (which are more devastating than simple pressures to conform). Skepticism was the vehicle by which philosophy reached beyond the dominance of epistemic criteria in order to test just how fully an intelligence could dwell within the contradictions of experience.

Cavell's perfectionism lacks both this sense of limitation and the corresponding imperative to a sense of command, if only over one's own temptations to shrink from these contradictions. Nietzsche exposes that. And at his best Nietzsche the psychologist can make us suspect that we cannot have an adequate antiepistemic philosophical stance unless we go even further than Cavell in analyzing just what dispositional traits the epistemic attitude sustained and protected. If we ask what contaminates Cavell's efforts to get free of those epistemic criteria, I think we have to locate those satisfactions in the ways that the promise of truth still projects onto his thinking an idealism about self-interpretation and its therapeutic consequences. Then it seems as no accident that Cavell refuses to distinguish between the utopian and the actual ("Moral Perfectionism," Mul., 360–61). For this enables him to bypass worrying about the possibility that the dream of consciousness-raising may provide good consciences for those intellectuals who can remain quite comfortable with things as they are. And then one can fully appreciate the irony involved in how well Nietzsche's analysis of Euripides so fully captures analogous problems in Cavell's domesticating of tragedy. For Nietzsche, Euripides was the first major artist we know who in his heart preferred melodrama to tragedy. Seduced by an *"aesthetic Socratism"* that was the avatar of our epistemic philosophical commitments, Euripides developed a position "whose supreme law reads roughly as follows: 'To be beautiful everything must be intelligible'" (*BT*, 83–84).

Cavell's version of that law might be "To be beautiful everything must be interpretable." And to interpret that I cannot improve on Nietzsche's characterization of Euripides:

Here we no longer remark anything of the epic absorption in mere appearance, or of the dispassionate coolness of the true actor, who precisely in his highest activity is wholly mere appearance and joy in mere appearance. Euripides is the actor whose heart beats, whose hair stands on end; as Socratic thinker he designs the plan, as passionate actor he executes it. . . . Thus the

Euripidean drama is a thing both cool and fiery, equally capable of freezing and burning. It is impossible for it to attain the Apollonian effect of the epos, while, on the other hand, it has alienated itself as much as possible from Dionysian elements. Now in order to be effective at all it requires new stimulants. . . . These stimulants are cool, paradoxical thoughts replacing Apollonian contemplation—and fiery affects, replacing Dionysian ecstasies. (BT, 83)

Notes

1. This statement is quoted from Stephen Mulhall, ed., *The Cavell Reader* (Cambridge, Mass.: Blackwell, 1996), 151. Because I think it convenient to cite as many passages as I can from one source, I will use this collection whenever I can and abbreviate the source in my main text as Mul.

2. Let me briefly describe what I consider the two most problematic aspects of this specifically Emersonian dimension of Cavell's recent work. In order to develop a perfectionist stance, Cavell needs to transform what had been in his ordinary language phase a fundamentally social understanding of the self's basic interests and satisfactions into expressivist ideals of owning by owning up; then he has to provide a social dynamics for perfectionist principles by showing how structures of shame establish the necessary motives to change. But when shame becomes so fully subsumed within personal psychology, it loses much of its force as an expression of social bonds. What had been a framework that clarified how mutual recognition might be possible and how a sense of impersonal obligation might prove part of our interests in living up to what language affords us now comes to rely almost entirely on specific psychological encounters, handled in terms of a rhetoric of the "deep self" and stressing the role of individual interpretations. And these prove difficult to analyze without at least partially adapting the rhetorics of hiddenness and inwardness from which Wittgenstein sought to escape. Second, fealty to Emerson reinforces Cavell's investment in the therapeutic dimension of psychoanalytic discourse, which I think makes it impossible to provide an account or an application of the modes of understanding fundamental to Shakespearean and to Greek tragedy. In my view these tragedies are incompatible with Emersonian perfectionism because they insist that whatever values survive their bleak sense of the real have to be anchored in a profound sense of limitations and of the need for mutual sympathies based on that awareness. Ironically, it may be only by heeding these limitations that persons can adapt to their environments and not yield to the unlimited ambitiousness out of which skepticism is sustained and which tragedy both consciously avoided and unconsciously produced. Yet for

the Emersonian Cavell, it seems as if simply finding ways to express limitations provides a means of overcoming them or displacing them. And as a reader this Cavell seems to me to succumb to the analogous temptation of constantly filling in and hence transforming the strategic silences or tactful refusals one finds in the texts one encounters. Yet there may be a richer interpretive stance and more compelling ethical value in our forcing ourselves to respect silences and to focus our readings on what the author might have valued in refusing to provide supplementary interpretive contexts. Giving John Marcher, in James's "Beast in the Jungle," specific psychoanalytic motives for his resistance to "life" (as Cavell does in his debate with Eve Sedgwick) seems to me to ignore the way that James wants his condition to be a total one, inexplicable by specific sources and unamenable to projected cures.

3. Stanley Cavell, "Disowning Knowledge," in *Six Plays of Shakespeare* (Cambridge, Mass.: Blackwell, 1996), 95; hereafter cited as "DK."

4. See especially Sylvan Tomkins, *Shame and Its Sisters: A Sylvan Tomkins Reader*, ed. Eve Kosofsky Sedgwick and Adam Frank (Durham, N.C.: Duke University Press, 1995), and Richard Moran, "The Expression of Feeling in Imagination," *Philosophical Review* 101 (1994): 74–106. I have attempted to use Moran's work to develop a version of this conative case in my *Subjective Agency* (Cambridge, Mass.: Blackwell, 1994), 37–43, where I spend considerable time criticizing Cavell's version of what I there call "expressivism." I should add that many of the positive assertions I make in this essay are argued far more elaborately in that book.

5. Charles Taylor, "Overcoming Epistemology," in *After Philosophy: End or Transformation*, ed. Kenneth Baynes, James Bohman, and Thomas McCarthy (Cambridge: MIT Press, 1987), 464–88; hereafter cited as "OE."

6. There are many other contemporary versions of resistance to the primacy of epistemic considerations that are based on religious faith or on the intricate wielding of skeptical instruments that sanctions Derrida's celebration of singularity and responsibility. But I ignore those here since they do not involve the expressivist values that Cavell helps us articulate. I will also exclude perspectives like those of Rorty and of Habermas that criticize the foundational grounding that epistemic thinking idealizes. For in my view both thinkers eventually subscribe to a looser version of the same basic criteria-based ideals of knowledge, differing only in the fact that these are grounded in some version of communal practices or idealization of everyday communication. They refuse the move into the psychology that I think Cavell shows is necessary if we are to escape Cartesian ideals.

7. Thomas Nagel, *The View from Nowhere* (New York: Oxford University Press, 1986).

8. I develop this critique of Taylor in my *Subjective Agency*, 104–10.

9. Here I will support this claim only by attaching myself to the criticisms of Stephen Mulhall, *Stanley Cavell: Philosophy's Recounting of the Ordinary* (Oxford:

Oxford University Press, 1994), 284ff. In my *Subjective Agency*, I criticize Cavell's claims about "good enough justice" (193–202). Carey Wolfe, "Alone with America: Cavell, Emerson, and the Politics of Individualism," *New Literary History* 25 (1994): 137–57, provides a useful general criticism of Cavell's relation to politics.

10. Cavell's most recent writing on Wittgenstein suggests an effort to refold Emersonian performative concerns within a more concrete and conatively focused interpretation of Wittgenstein's meditation on "the style is the man himself." Here both person and world manifest a presentness based not on performance but on the ways that a writing seeking "perspicuous representation" can produce a sense of surprise and connectedness that carries a metaphysical charge (cf. "Epilogue: Everyday Aesthetics," in Mul., 384–85). But Cavell has still to show that this way of understanding the self is compatible with his work on self-reliance as aversion to conformity, which I will try to show is very problematic.

11. I was not Nietzschean enough in *Subjective Agency*, so I am trying here to use the question "where am I" as a means of developing a better picture than my book provides of those aspects of subjective life that are not accessible to self-reflection.

12. Henry Staten, *Nietzsche's Voices* (Ithaca, N.Y.: Cornell University Press, 1990).

13. Cavell is very good on how the relation to the interlocutor has a metaphysical effect because we do feel the issues as philosophical and hence as consequential. But I think this metaphysical effect is itself something within philosophy and not material for claims about activity vs. passivity.

14. I am not unaware of Cavell's famous essay "The Availability of Wittgenstein's Later Philosophy," in *Must We Mean What We Say?* (New York: Scribner's, 1969), 44–72, attempting to show that Wittgenstein's use of Augustine invites us to read the *Investigations* in relation to the tradition of confessional literature. I agree with that, but only because once we try that reading we realize how thoroughly the same concerns that Augustine is obsessed with can be handled without overt autobiography or dramatic conversion.

15. Bernard Williams, *Ethics and the Limits of Philosophy* (Cambridge: Harvard University Press, 1985).

16. Friedrich Nietzsche, *Beyond Good and Evil: Prelude to a Philosophy of the Future*, trans. Walter Kaufmann (New York: Random House, 1966), sec. 1:17, p. 24; hereafter cited as *BGE*.

17. For historical and political analyses of problems basic to these languages of intimacy that presuppose the ego, see *Critical Inquiry* 24 (1998), a special issue entitled *Intimacy*, edited by Lauren Berlant.

18. Were I to allow myself identification with Nietzsche at his melodramatic best, I would be in a poor position to criticize Cavell for similar melodrama. But I would be able to use some remarkable passages that further clarify how different

the two thinkers are. Here, for example, is Nietzsche on the relation of active to passive as he elaborates tragedy's capacity to affirm that "life is at the bottom of things, despite all the changes of appearances, indestructibly powerful and pleasurable":

> In *Oedipus at Colonus* we encounter the same cheerfulness, but elevated into an infinite transgression. The old man, struck by an excess of misery, abandoned solely to suffer whatever befalls him, is confronted by the supraterrestrial cheerfulness that descends from the divine sphere and suggests to us that the hero attains his highest activity, extending far beyond his life, through his purely passive posture, while his conscious deeds and desires, earlier in his life, merely led him into passivity. (*The Birth of Tragedy*, trans. Walter Kaufmann, in *The Portable Nietzsche* [New York: Viking, 1954], 59, 68; hereafter cited as *BT*)

And I could bring to bear Yeats's great Nietzschean melodramatic statement on the need to avoid melodrama and accept entirely the limited conditions that comprise one's allotment in life:

> The one reason for putting our actual situation into our art is that the struggle for complete affirmation may be, often must be, that art's chief poignancy. I must, though the world shriek at me, admit no act beyond my power nor thing beyond my knowledge, yet because my divinity is far off I blanch and tremble.

Here we see the possibility of a perfectionism based entirely on learning to resist dreams of possibility. Yeats's "Journal" is quoted in Richard Ellman, *The Identity of Yeats* (London: Macmillan, 1954), 240.

19. From this perspective we can even show why truth might be so highly valued, since agents have clear interests in being able to invest strongly in their descriptions of the world. Truth matters because of the qualities of self-enjoyment that it affords and because of the strength it gives when one has to fight off those who want to destroy those satisfactions.

20. My *Subjective Agency* offers one way to reconcile the two, but it only works for those cases where the "I" takes it as part of its aesthetics of itself or its morality to win the kind of identities that ethical judgments offer.

21. Nietzsche, *BT*, 59, 64, 65.

22. All these quotations are from Nietzsche's *The Antichrist*, in *The Portable Nietzsche* (New York: Viking, 1954), 638.

The Poetics of Description: Wittgenstein on the Aesthetic

Marjorie Perloff

—We might blame Wittgenstein for beauty's fall. Influential to conceptual artists
in the sixties and seventies, he had little patience for questions like, What is beauty?
In the summer of 1938, Wittgenstein devoted a lecture at Cambridge to the word.
Meanings of words like beauty result from their use. Beauty, he pointed out, is
most often used as an interjection, similar to Wow! or rubbing one's stomach. When
aesthetic judgments are made, aesthetic adjectives such as beautiful or fine hardly
play any role at all. "The words you use are more akin to right and correct than to
beautiful and lovely."

> —Bill Beckley, introduction to Uncontrollable Beauty (1998)[1]

W ittgenstein's impatience with theories of art is well known. In the *Lectures on
Aesthetics*, which Bill Beckley cites above, Wittgenstein goes on to declare contemp-
tuously, "One might think Aesthetics is a science that tells us what's beautiful—it's
almost too ridiculous for words. I suppose this science would also be able to tell
us what sort of coffee tastes good."[2] And the notebook entries collected in *Culture
and Value* are given to statements like the following:

> If I say A has beautiful eyes someone may ask me: what do you find beautiful
> about his eyes, and perhaps I shall reply: the almond shape, long eyelashes,
> delicate lids. What do these eyes have in common with a Gothic church that
> I find beautiful too? Should I say they make a similar impression on me?

"The concept of the beautiful," says Wittgenstein, "has caused a lot of mis-
chief." And again, "Am I to make the inane statement, 'it [the musical theme] just
sounds more beautiful when it is repeated'? (There you can see by the way what a
silly role the word 'beautiful' plays in aesthetics.) And yet there is just no paradigm
other than the theme itself."[3]

Yet the very Wittgenstein who scoffed repeatedly—and famously—at aesthetic theory (as he scoffed, of course, at *theory* in general as any sort of explanatory
model),[4] was himself an aesthete, uncommonly sensitive to the nuances of verbal,
musical, and visual form, just as he was uncommonly allergic to what he took to be

"bad" art. Himself a committed modernist architect—witness the Kundmanngasse villa he designed for his sister Margarete[5]—his own "philosophical" writing—as I argue in *Wittgenstein's Ladder*—was conceived as a way of "doing" poetry and has influenced subsequent poets and artists at least as much as it has influenced contemporary epistemology or ordinary language philosophy.[6] Indeed, reluctant as he was to theorize about art, Wittgenstein was quite ready to pronounce on this or that work, to praise or dismiss a given symphony or poem or novel. The words *großartig* (brilliant, splendid, or magnificent) and *herrlich* (wonderful) appear again and again in his journals and letters, with reference, say, to a Mozart symphony, a Morike poem, Lessing's *Nathan the Wise*, or Dostoyevsky's *Brothers Karamazov*. Schubert's Quintet in C Sharp, op. 163 is *"von phantastischer Großartigkeit"* (exhibits fantastic brilliance), Mozart and Beethoven are called *"die wahren Gottersohne"* (the true sons of God), the second movement of Beethoven's *Eroica* is *"unglaublich"* (unbelievable, fabulous), Brahms's "Handelvariationen," is *"unheimlich"* (uncanny, sublime).[7]

Negative judgments are just as emphatic: Alfred Ehrenstein's poetry is *"ein Hundedreck"* (crap), Mahler's music is *"nichts wert"* (worthless), "the characters in the second part of 'Faust' *erregen unsere Teilnahme gar nicht"* (are ones with whom we can't identify at all).[8] The almost comic vehemence of Wittgenstein's judgments has everything to do with his conviction that there really is something at stake in claiming, as he does at one point, that Dostoyevsky's *Brothers Karamazov* is *"noch großartiger"* (even more wonderful) than *Crime and Punishment*, or that, as Franz Parak, a friend and fellow prisoner of war at the camp in Monte Cassino, recalls, the "false pathos" with which an officer (a former actor) recited some poems, so Wittgenstein held, was so unbearable that it was like "receiving an electric shock."[9] For the Wittgenstein of the *Tractatus* (and there is no reason to believe he ever changed his mind on this particular issue), "Ethics and aesthetics are one."[10] Hence the references to Tolstoy's *Gospel in Brief* (*"ein herrliches Werk"*) as a "talisman" that "saved" Wittgenstein's life on the Russian front (*GH*, 19) and to Georg Trakl's poems, which Ludwig von Ficker sent to Wittgenstein shortly after the poet's suicide, as "genial" works that "have done me good" (*GH*, 43). "Good" writing—for example, William James's *Varieties of Religious Experience*—does the reader "good"; "bad" art almost physically "hurts" and "causes pain."[11]

But if words like *herrlich, phantastisch*, and *unheimlich* have, as Wittgenstein was to insist, no essence, no fixed meaning, what and how do they signify? Since "the sense of the world must lie outside the world" (*TLP*, 6.41), "there can be no ethical propositions" (*TLP*, 6.42) and hence no aesthetic ones. Are aesthetic judgments, then, purely relative and subjective, the expressions of one's own private responses to a particular artwork? And, if so, what difference can one's own assessment make to anyone else? The Wittgenstein of the *Tractatus* did not speak to the issue, but by the mid-1930s, he was discovering new ways of formulating the problem. Not that he ever rejected the notion that there can be no ethical or aesthetic propositions, no aesthetic theory. But he now began to study the way people (himself included) actually *did* evaluate works of art and how their specific judgments might function in particular language-games.

"What is the justification for a feature in a work of art?" he asks in a 1932 lecture. "What reasons can one give for being satisfied?" And his own answer relates value to *knowledge*: "The reasons are further descriptions. Aesthetics is descriptive. What it does is to *draw one's attention* to certain features, to place things side by side so as to exhibit these features."[12] "Drawing one's attention" to this or that feature in a given poem or sonata involves *knowing* how it is put together. In the *Lectures on Aesthetics*, known primarily for their ironic comments on the futility of defining the "beautiful," Wittgenstein writes:

> When we make an aesthetic judgement about a thing, we do not just stare at it and say: "Oh! How marvelous!" We distinguish between a person who knows what he is talking about and a person who doesn't. If a person is to admire English poetry, he must know English. Suppose that a Russian who doesn't know a word of English claims to have a highly favorable impression of a sonnet generally considered to be a good one. We would say that he doesn't have a clue what it's all about. The same would hold for a person who doesn't know anything about meter but who is thrilled [by a poem]. . . . In music this is even more pronounced. (*LA*, sec. 17)[13]

Here the linkage between "knowing English" and "knowing meter" is telling. Inhabiting a culture (or at least engaging it fully) makes it possible to speak a language and, by extension, to recognize its metrical forms. In this sense, Wittgenstein implies, most of what passes for evaluation is really just description, the ability (or lack thereof) to call attention to what one sees. But, as he argues in part 2 of the *Philosophical Investigations*, *seeing as* is itself dependent on variables that are as cultural as they are individual. Consider the following propositions in the *Lectures on Aesthetics*:

> 25. The words we call expressions of aesthetic judgement play a very complicated role, but a very definite role, in what we call a culture of a period. To describe their use or to describe what you mean by a cultured taste, you have to describe a culture. What we now call a cultured taste perhaps didn't exist in the Middle Ages. An entirely different game is played in different ages.
> 26. What belongs to a language game is a whole culture. In describing musical taste you have to describe whether children give concerts, whether women do or whether men only give them, etc., etc. In aristocratic circles in Vienna people had [such and such] a taste, then it came into bourgeois circles and women joined choirs, etc. This is an example of tradition in music.

Art is, first and foremost, a cultural *practice*, dependent upon a particular time and place. "What made the ideal Greek profile into an ideal, what quality?" asks Wittgenstein in a 1932 lecture. "Actually what made us say it is the ideal is a certain very complicated role it played in the life of people. For example, the greatest sculptors used this form, people were taught it, Aristotle wrote on it" (*LEC*2, 36). We can never get at the causes of the phenomenon; what we can do is describe the language-game in which the "ideal" profile functions.

Does this mean that one can only understand the art of one's own tradition and culture, in Wittgenstein's case primarily the literature and music of nineteenth-century Germany and Austria on which he was raised? And if there is no larger theory of art, no overview of literary forms and genres that might apply, how can the reader avoid solipsism? These are difficult questions on which Wittgenstein scholarship has had little to say. [14]

When Rush Rhees asks Wittgenstein, "[I]s there tradition in Negro art? Could a European appreciate Negro art?" Wittgenstein responds frankly that he doesn't know. But he distinguishes between the English painter and sculptor Frank Dobson, who, according to Cyril Barrett, "was the first to bring to England the interest in African and Asian sculpture which characterized the work of Picasso and the Cubists" (*LA*, 9, n. 1) and the "educated Negro," who would have a "different appreciation altogether" (*LA*, 9). If this suggests an extreme cultural relativism, other of Wittgenstein's writings make clear that what he means is simply that, as he puts it in the *Investigations*, "the *speaking* of a language is part of an activity, or of a form of life," and that "[t]o imagine a language means to imagine a form of life." [15] This is as true of "religion" as it is of "art." "Christianity," for example, "is not a doctrine, not, I mean, a theory about what has happened and will happen to the human soul, but a *description of something that actually takes place in human life*. For 'consciousness of sin' is a real event and so are despair and salvation through faith. Those who speak of such things (Bunyan for instance) are simply describing what has happened to them, whatever gloss anyone may want to put on it" (*CV*, 28; my emphasis). And the "Remarks on Frazer's *Golden Bough*" make this point even more forcibly:

> I read, among many similar examples, of a Rain-King in Africa to whom the people pray for rain *when the rainy period comes.* But surely that means that they do not really believe that he can make it rain, otherwise they would do it in the dry periods of the year in which the land is "a parched and arid desert." For if one assumes that the people formerly instituted this office of Rain-King out of ignorance, it is nevertheless certainly clear that they had previously experienced that the rains begin in March, and then they would have had the Rain-King function for the other part of the year. Or again: toward morning, when the sun is about to rise, rites of daybreak are celebrated by the people, but not during the night when they simply burn lamps. (*PO*, 137)

Wittgenstein's surprising animosity to *The Golden Bough* was prompted by his objection to the inferences which Sir James Frazer drew from the texts in question: for example, how "primitive" it was to think prayer to a rain god could actually bring rain. Wittgenstein's own interpretation—that the "primitives" in question actually pray for rain at the beginning of the rainy season—a perfectly normal ritual gesture—is based on what we now call "close reading," that is, careful attention to verbal and grammatical detail. "Understanding," he says elsewhere in the "Remarks," "consists precisely in the fact that we 'see the connections' [*Zusammenhänge*]. Hence the importance of finding *connecting links* [*Zwischengliedern*]." And he continues,

> But a hypothetical connecting link should in this case do nothing but direct the attention to the similarity, the relatedness [*den Zusammenhang*], of the facts. As one might illustrate an internal relation of a circle to an ellipse by gradually converting an ellipse into a circle; *but not in order to assert that a certain ellipse actually, historically, had originated from a circle* (evolutionary hypothesis), but only in order to sharpen our eye for a formal connection [*Zusammenhang*]. (*PO*, 132,133)

The stress on *Zusammenhang*, on the "formal connections" (*Zwischenglieder*) between X and Y (here circle and ellipse) rather than on hypothetical causal or temporal explanation (the ellipse as a later variant of the original circle) has important implications for the art discourse Wittgenstein professed to despise. Relatedness (what Aristotle in the *Poetics* calls *to prepon* [fitness]) depends, in the case of narrative, on *ton pragmaton systasis* (the arrangement of the incidents, or plot);[16] it is such "arrangement" that separates poetic discourse from its cognates. Wittgenstein's own term for this "formal connection" is *grammar,* the actual arrangement of words in sentences or (in the case of poetry) in lines. Consider the following proposition:

> The limit of language is shown by its being impossible to describe the fact which corresponds to (is the translation of) a sentence, without simply repeating the sentence. (*CV,* 10)

Here, of course, Wittgenstein is talking not about a poetic unit of discourse but about any sentence. Still, the notion of untranslatability is crucial. For Wittgenstein, there is no such thing as "thought" expressible in a variety of verbal formulations. Rather, *"The limits of my language* mean the limits of my world" (*TLP,* 5.6) or again, "Language is not *contiguous* to anything else" (*LEC1,* 112). In the *Philosophical Investigations,* this formulation is applied specifically to the poetic:

> §531. We speak of understanding a sentence in the sense in which it can be replaced by another which says the same; but also in the sense in which it

cannot be replaced by any other. (Any more than one musical theme can be replaced by another.)

In the one case the thought in the sentence is something common to different sentences; in the other, something that is expressed *only by these words in these positions.* (Understanding a poem) [emphasis mine].

Poetry, in other words, is, for Wittgenstein, *irreplaceable language;* it is that which is said in the way it is said and in no other. In this emphasis on verbal autonomy, Wittgenstein is, consciously or not, very much a modernist aesthetician, akin, let us say, to such poets as Rainer Maria Rilke and such theorists as Roman Jakobson. For the implications of his proposition (which is no more than his proposition about language in general) is that there are no "ideas" outside of their linguistic expression, no "subject matter" to be discussed per se. Indeed, as Wittgenstein puts it in a proposition found in *Zettel,* "Do not forget that a poem, even though it is composed in the language of information (*der Sprache der Mitteilung*), is not used in the language-game of giving information (*das Sprachspiel der Mitteilung*)."[17]

Poetic discourse is thus untranslatable; a given poem allows for no verbal substitution; its saying takes precedence over the thing said. Consider an entry Wittgenstein made in a 1931 notebook with reference to a Frida Schanz *Rösselsprung* he came across in the newspaper. A *Rösselsprung,* so the note in *Culture and Value* tells us, is a variant of the crossword puzzle. "Each space is occupied by a separate syllable. These are joined together to form a meaningful passage by making transpositions according to the rules for the knight's move . . . in chess" (*CV,* 13). Here is the poem Wittgenstein makes of the puzzle:

> *Nebeltag. Der graue Herbst geht um.*
> *Das Lachen scheint verdorben.*
> *die Welt liegt heut so stumm,*
> *als sei sie nachts gestorben.*
> *Im golden roten Hag*
> *brauen die Nebeldrachen;*
> *und schlummernd liegt der Tag.*
> *Der Tag will nicht erwachen.*[18]

Wittgenstein writes: "I took this poem from a 'Rosselsprung' in which of course the punctuation was missing. So for example I don't know whether the word '*Nebeltag*' ('Foggy day') is the title or belongs to the first line, as I've written it. And it is strange how trivial the poem sounds when it doesn't begin with the word '*Nebeltag*' but with '*Der graue*' ('The gray'). The rhythm of the whole poem is changed accordingly" (*CV,* 13).

This may sound like no more than a trivial observation made by a man entertaining himself with word games, but it is a nice illustration of Wittgenstein's conviction that in poetry "something is expressed only by these words in these positions," that the placement of a single word matters, affecting, as it does, the rhythm (as well as the meaning) of the whole. One thinks of Wittgenstein's contemporary William Carlos Williams, rewriting "The Locust Tree in Flower" (first version, 1933), so as to "cut out everything except the essential words," and hence reducing his twenty-four-line lyric, which begins:

Among
the leaves
bright

green
of wrist-thick
tree

and old
stiff broken
branch

to half its size in the minimalist 1935 version: [19]

Among
of
green

stiff
old
bright

broken
branch
come

white
sweet
May

again

The *"Nebeltag"* example also relates to Wittgenstein's discussion of cultural practice. If, for example, one knows no German, the point about the poem's rhythm can't be made. *"Nebeltag"* is translated into English as "Foggy Day" or "Day of Fog," which makes the choice of placement (is it the title or the first word of the poem?) rather different. For one thing, an English translation cannot preserve the rhyme and trimeter of the original. But, more important, the capitalization (or lack thereof) of the second noun would tell us whether we are looking at a title or the opening line of the poem.

English critics have often rebuked Wittgenstein for caring little about the literature of his adopted country. F. R. Leavis, for example, remarked that Wittgenstein's "interest in literature had remained rudimentary." Aside from a little reading in Dickens, Leavis reports, "I never discovered that he took any other creative writing seriously. It may of course be that in German the range and quality of his literary culture were more impressive, but I can't give any great weight to that possibility."[20] Here Leavis reveals his own nationalist bias: If the tables were turned, one surmises, he would be judged the ignorant one. It is not, in any case, a question of goodwill. Wittgenstein, by his own account, simply didn't have the feel for the "connecting links" (*Zwischenglieder*) in English that would have allowed him to appreciate the poetry of, say, T. S. Eliot or even of Shakespeare, whose similes he pronounced "in the ordinary sense bad." "My failure to understand [Shakespeare]," Wittgenstein admits, "could be explained by my inability to read him easily. That is, as one views a splendid piece of scenery" (*CV,* 49). One senses here and in related remarks on Shakespeare[21] that language, in the literal sense, is not the only barrier for Wittgenstein, that, to an upper-class Viennese of his time, brought up as he was on the great Germanic poets, dramatists, and composers of the later eighteenth and nineteenth centuries, the cultural practices represented in Shakespeare's plays could hardly have been readily accessible.

Thus the limits of Wittgenstein's language *were* the limits of his world. At the same time, Leavis was quite wrong in assuming that his Cambridge friend didn't take "creative writing" seriously. For when the cultural practice in question was one where language was no barrier, he could be an extraordinary student of *textuality.* In a 1937 extract in *Culture and Value,* we find the following comment on the Gospels:

> Kierkegaard writes: If Christianity were so easy and comfortable, why should God in his Scriptures have set Heaven and Earth in motion and threatened *eternal* punishments? Question: But in that case why is this Scripture so unclear? If one wants to warn someone of a terrible danger, does one do it by giving him a riddle whose solution will be the warning?—But who says that the Scripture is really unclear? Isn't it possible that it was essential in this case to 'pose a riddle'? And that nevertheless a direct warning would have had the *wrong* effect? God lets four people recount the life of his incarnate Son, in each case differently and with contradictions—but couldn't one say: It is important, that this story have no more than average historical plausibility

precisely *so that* it not be taken as something essential and incontrovertible. So that the *letter* would not find greater faith than it deserves and the *spirit* would retain its due. I.e., what you should see cannot be communicated even by the best, most accurate historian; *therefore* an ordinary representation suffices; it is even preferable. For what is supposed to be conveyed to you, this one can also convey. (Roughly comparable to the way an ordinary stage set can be better than a more sophisticated one, painted trees better than real ones,—which might distract attention from what really matters.) (1937; *CV,* 31)

This is an eloquent brief against essentialism. Four versions of the Gospel are better than one because there cannot be one "right" version of the Christ story. "Truth" can never be singular. Wittgenstein's implication is that literary analysis is, at its best, comparative—a study of family resemblances—placing side by side the various versions of a story so as to understand, as well as possible, the intertextual "formal connections" as well as the cultural practices that are being represented.

Can we, then, as Bill Beckley puts it in my opening citation, "blame Wittgenstein for beauty's fall"? Is his seeming relativism (i.e., each of the four Gospels is as "good" or "beautiful" as the others, and there might be further versions that would be equally "good") antiaesthetic? Or does he simply replace aesthetic theory with a set of actual practices that can "work" in particular cases? And, if the latter, is Wittgenstein's a pragmatism in the William James tradition, the belief that the "truth" of a given proposition is a function of its ability to make the world a more inhabitable place than it now is? "What difference," asks James in "What Pragmatism Means," "would it practically make to any one if this notion rather than that notion were true? And further, *"ideas (which themselves are but parts of our experience) become true just insofar as they help us to get into satisfactory relation with other parts of our experience."*[22] Theories, holds a neopragmatist such as Richard Rorty, are ultimately justified by their instrumentality or the extent to which they enable people to attain their aims.[23]

Like the pragmatists, Wittgenstein rejected the claim that "truth" could be reached through deductive reasoning from a priori grounds; like them, he rejected what James described as "abstraction and insufficiency . . . fixed principles, closed systems, and pretended absolutes" (*WJ,* 379) in favor of the *pragma* or *practices* of our everyday lives. But in the end there are more differences than similarities between Wittgensteinian praxis and the pragmatism of James. Consider the following comment on "Pragmatic Theory" made in 1932 in response to a query about truth claims by the Oxford philosopher C. K. Broad:

Pragmatism. The hypothesis that there are electrons is taken as being true because in practice you can work as if it were the case. So also Einstein's

Theory of Relativity is accepted because it works in practice. Thus Euclidean space is used for everyday purposes, and relativity for immeasurable and astronomical distances. To decide between them would need a great deal of empirical evidence, and this is certainly the sense of truth we apply to them.

But we do also use the word true of a ruler, which is a sense not ascribable to any of the other examples given. Thus it is nonsense to try to find a theory of truth, because we can see that in everyday life we use the word quite clearly and definitely in these different senses. (*LEC1*, 76)

For Wittgenstein, pragmatism fails because it posits that if a proposition is judged to be "valid" in its production of desired results, it is then taken to apply in all instances—a conclusion he could not accept. More important, the notion of judging the value of an idea according to its practical consequences was completely alien to Wittgenstein. His is an inverted pragmatism: One begins by examining *use*—what is actually said and done by a given person or persons—and only then does one try to understand what this particular usage, this practice might mean in this instance. For Wittgenstein, ideas can never be justified by their instrumentality, because "use" is something that cannot be prescribed, that indeed is neither good nor bad. It merely is. "Philosophy, by clarifying, stops us asking illegitimate questions" (*LEC1*, 111).

In this sense, Wittgenstein's "practical" aesthetics is resolutely antipragmatist. Its sanctions, as in the case of the Gospels, "must lie outside the world" (*TLP*, §641). One doesn't read the Gospels for self-improvement, but, Wittgenstein would say, one—at least a Westerner—simply reads them, instinctively, inevitably, as a "form of life" that is part of our world. His interest is not in the consequences of such reading but—in line with formalist and poststructuralist theories of literature—in how they work *as texts*, how their language operates. As in the case of *"Nebeltag,"* "Our attention is drawn to a certain feature, and from that point forward we see that feature" (*LEC2*, 38). Wittgenstein's is thus a materialist perspective on art: not poetry, but this particular elegy by Goethe; not music, but the second movement of Beethoven's *Eroica*; not sculpture, but the profile of the Hermes of Praxiteles.

In *Philosophical Remarks* (1930), we find the following arresting proposition:

A searchlight sends out light into infinite space and so illuminates everything in its direction. But you can't say it illuminates infinity.[24]

Just so, a given "aesthetic statement" can shed light on the internal relations that make a particular work of art "beautiful," but it cannot generalize this statement into a theory of the beautiful. Does this spell the "death of beauty"? The equivalence between value judgment and the exclamation "Wow!" or the rubbing of place in his life," and then goes on to say that "aesthetic terms such as 'beautiful,' 'art,' or 'work of art,' are 'family-resemblance concepts.'" "There is no single condition," says Glock, "by virtue of which the artefacts of Beethoven, Beuys, Brecht, Cage, Giotto, Jandl, Praxiteles, Pollock and Warhol qualify as works of art" (31–35). All this is perfectly true but doesn't get around the fact that Wittgenstein did consistently make judgments about particular artworks.

15. Ludwig Wittgenstein, *Philosophical Investigations*, 3d. ed., trans. G. E. M. Anscombe (New York: Macmillan, 1958), §§23, 19. See, on this point, Stanley Cavell, "Aesthetic Problems of Modern Philosophy" (1965), in *Must We Mean What We Say?* (Cambridge: Cambridge University Press, 1976), 82–86. Discussing the reception of atonal music and the insistence on the part of many listeners that they do hear tonality in it, Cavell writes, "The language of tonality is part of a particular form of life, one containing the music we are most familiar with; associated with, or consisting of, particular ways of being trained to perform it and to listen to it. . . . No wonder we want to preserve the idea of tonality" (84).

16. See Aristotle, *Poetics*, trans. W. Hamilton Fyfe, Loeb Classics (Cambridge: Harvard University Press, 1960), 1455a and 1450a, and cf. the great sentence in 1460b, "the standard of what is correct is not the same in the art of poetry as it is in the art of social conduct or any other art."

17. Ludwig Wittgenstein, *Zettel*, ed. G. E. M. Anscombe and G. H. von Wright, trans. G. E. M. Anscombe (Berkeley: University of California Press, 1967), §160.

18. In Peter Winch's translation (*CV*, 12e), this reads:

Foggy day. Grey autumn haunts us.
Laughter seems tainted;
the world is as silent today
as though it had died last night.
In the red-gold hedge
fog monsters are brewing;
and the day lies asleep.
The day will not awaken.

19. For the two versions of "The Locust Tree in Flower," see A. Walton Litz and Christopher MacGowan, eds., *The Collected Poems of William Carlos Williams*, vol. 1, 1909–39 (New York: New Directions, 1986), 366, 379. For Williams's comment, see his 1952 note on 538.

20. F. R. Leavis, "Memories of Wittgenstein" (1973); reprinted in *Recollections of Wittgenstein*, ed. Rush Rhees (Oxford: Oxford University Press, 1984), 66.

21. See *CV*, 83–86. "I do not believe," says Wittgenstein in 1950, "that Shakespeare can be set alongside any other poet. Was he perhaps a creator of language

rather than a poet?" And again, "I could only stare in wonder at Shakespeare, never do anything with him."

22. William James, "What Pragmatism Means," in *The Writings of William James: A Comprehensive Edition*, ed. John J. McDermott (Chicago: University of Chicago Press, 1977), 377, 382; hereafter cited as *WJ*.

23. See Richard Rorty, "Introduction: Pragmatism and Philosophy," *Consequences of Pragmatism, Essays 1972–1980* (Minneapolis: University of Minnesota Press, 1982), xiii–xvii.

24. Ludwig Wittgenstein, *Philosophical Remarks*, ed. Rush Rhees, trans. Raymond Hargreaves and Roger White (Chicago: University of Chicago Press, 1975), 162.

In Which Henry
James Strikes Bedrock

R. M. Berry

In Stanley Cavell's account of Wittgenstein's later philosophy, everything we know depends upon what Wittgenstein calls "grammatical criteria." These criteria are what we go on when judging that something counts as an instance of our concept of, for example, "chair," "ardent love," or "headache." For the arts, Wittgenstein's focus on criteria leads in two, apparently opposite, directions. First, by making the activity of judging constitutive for language and culture, Wittgenstein makes aesthetics (or what is traditionally called aesthetics) a model for all philosophical activity. Determining the basis on which a phenomenon will count as an instance of any concept turns out to involve capacities that formerly seemed relevant only in cases of aesthetic judgment.

But Wittgenstein's focus on criteria also works against this centrality of aesthetics, for it makes an exceptional or limiting case of the art contemporary with Wittgenstein. According to Cavell, what modernist art reveals is that judging what counts as a novel, painting, or sculpture is no longer determined by grammatical criteria, or none to which we have access as we do our criteria for "chair," "ardent love," and "headache." This does not mean, or not quite, that nobody knows any longer what a novel is. It comes closer to meaning that the experience of modern art is of *finding out* what we know, what our criteria for sculptures, paintings, novels are. And it makes modernism the disclosure of a new artistic necessity: not merely to create a new work, but to create a new basis for work, a new *medium* for fiction. [1]

In what follows, my aim is to see how this necessity arises. My focus is on a particular period of Henry James's career, roughly from his review of George Eliot's *Middlemarch* in 1873 to his essay on Guy de Maupassant in 1888, a period that surrounds his now famous response to Walter Besant in "The Art of Fiction." I do not insist that this moment in James's career is a founding moment for modernist fiction. My only insistence is that whatever conditions do give rise to modernism—either for a whole culture or for an individual—they look like this moment.

1

Near the end of "The Art of Fiction," Henry James takes issue with Walter Besant (and the critic Andrew Lang) over the use of the word "story."[2] His stated provocations are, first, that Besant (in his lecture) has distinguished between "a part of a novel which is the story and part of it which . . . is not" ("AF," 178) and, second, that Besant and Lang (in his review of Besant's lecture) have made "adventure" a defining feature of any story ("AF," 179). James's procedure in the first case is to give examples of "the only [sense of 'story'] that I see" in which it can be spoken of as different from the novel as a whole. His procedure in the second case is to give examples of what constitutes an adventure "for me" (or what "I should say" is an adventure) and to confess that he is "utterly at a loss to see why" the plot of his own novella "An International Episode" does not count as an adventure if the other examples cited by Lang and Besant do. James gives no reasons why anyone *ought* to use the words "story" and "adventure" as he does. If we see senses of "story" other than the ones that James sees, if the fact that he is "utterly at a loss" makes no impression on us, or if we just do not care what Henry James considers adventurous, nothing he says seems designed to change our minds. His whole case rests on nothing stronger than the likelihood that in the circumstances he describes, we too will call or judge or find what he calls or judges or finds "a story," "an adventure," "exciting," and so on. If we don't, of course, we just don't, but the surprise is how often we do.[3]

Contrary to what James maintains, the problem with Besant and Lang's definition of "story" is not that it is "altogether arbitrary" ("AF," 179), or not quite. Words such as "story" and "adventure" are what Wittgenstein considers cousins ("If I teach anyone the use of the one word, he learns the use of the other with it").[4] If we recall the sort of stories from which we learned the word "adventure" (and the sort of adventures from which we learned the word "story"), we will encounter no special difficulty distinguishing "An International Episode" from, say, *Treasure Island* on this basis. James's plot contains no threats to survival, no exotic landscapes, no explicit violence, no extremes of vice or virtue, no calculated deceptions—in short, nothing sufficiently out of the ordinary that we would need to be *told* about it. James "tells" us about misunderstandings, frustrations, and disappointments that most of us know as well as he does. If humans *can* be told such things, that seems a significant fact about us, about telling, about our relation to what we know. If some of us cannot be—if, for example, Andrew Lang is incapable of seeing how "An International Episode" could be an instance of the same concept as *Treasure Island*—then teaching him to use the word "story" as we (for the most part) do could prove impossible. However, Besant and Lang complain of no such incapacity, and their disagreement with James never goes this deep. Besant's claim is that in calling something a story, we base our judgment on the features that distinguish *Treasure*

Island from an ordinary occurrence, and James's examples counter this claim to the extent that in certain circumstances we will use "adventure" to describe, for example, writing an article, making a new acquaintance, or disappointing a friend. If we agree that these ordinary occurrences can sometimes count as adventures, then Besant is simply wrong: We do not use the word "story" as he says.

If the disagreement in "The Art of Fiction" can be settled so easily, it seems trivial. Even five-year-olds know what a story is, and if the only issue between James and Besant is a word, then that hardly seems like an issue. However, if it is correct to say that a word is at issue in "The Art of Fiction," it is misleading to say that the issue is *only* a word. This latter expression might describe Besant and James's disagreement if their problem were how to classify an atypical work ("An International Episode"). In such a case, if there is doubt about what the work is, that just means there is doubt about which category fits it. Perhaps "An International Episode" crosses the boundary between two categories (i.e., it is partly a story, partly an analysis). Or it may be an exceptional instance of a category, a story with a difference.

Of course, disagreements about classification are not always trivial. If Lang does not consider "An International Episode" a story, he could be blind to something we care about. But if we observe him doing with James's novella the same things we do with stories—puzzling over a description, asking why an event occurs just here, seeing the point of a silence or gesture—then we are likely to feel that Lang sees everything we do. In that case, the issue is only a word.

In "The Art of Fiction," however, the problem is not to determine into which category "An International Episode" fits. In fact, the one point on which James, Besant, and Lang all seem to agree is that if "An International Episode" is not a story, it is simply nothing. There is no other category. Where the defining feature of "adventures" is at issue, Besant rules out any alternative by considering "fiction without adventure" to be "impossible."[5] Where distinguishing "story" from "novel" is at issue, James rules out the alternative by denying the intelligibility of the latter concept apart from the former ("AF," 178). What neither James nor Besant nor Lang attempts is to propose a new category for novels without stories, fiction without adventures. If the problem were how to classify "An International Episode," a new category would remove it.

The issue between James and Besant and Lang is not how but *whether* to classify James's novels (along with those of Howells, Flaubert, Maupassant, Turgenev, the Goncourt brothers, Zola, et al.). That is, the question is whether these objects succeed in entering our universe, whether they merit the attention that goes into calling them anything. If we wish to call this an aesthetic disagreement, then we will probably be using "aesthetic" in an expanded sense, one in which aesthetic judgments are not contrasted in the usual ways with epistemological assertions (and perhaps not with political acts). To call "An International Episode" a story is not to identify its category so much as to recognize its existence, where recognition is not what happens with an old acquaintance but what must happen (or not) with a new government. In such cases, recognition consists of establishing normal relations with the other, and the obstacle to this recognition is not the other's change, but the likelihood of our own. When James cites examples of what he "should say" is an adventure or of what is "exciting to me" or of what "strikes me" as a novel or what "seems to me" to contain "surprises," he is recalling to consciousness what our normal relations with stories consist in, what we (habitually or automatically) do in judging anything to be worth telling. In such a context, his comparison of Edmond de Goncourt's *Chérie* with *Treasure Island* ("AF," 180) stakes value more aggressively than his (conventionally aesthetic) judgment that *Chérie* is a failure and *Treasure Island* a success, for such a comparison stakes the basis on which *anything* counts as a story. If James's examples succeed, works like *Treasure Island* cease to be the norm. If they fail . . . well, it is difficult to imagine who we would be if they failed.

But there is another reason for not saying that the issue in "The Art of Fiction" is only a word: Henry James seems as confused about what a story is as Besant or Lang. For when Besant defines "story" on the basis of adventures, James responds, "Why of adventures more than of green spectacles?" To which the answer seems too obvious: Because it is a *story* (not a myopic redhead). James's points are that Besant's definition is "altogether arbitrary" and "that the good health of an art which undertakes so immediately to reproduce life must demand that it be perfectly free" ("AF," 169–70), by which word ("free") James sometimes means open to "experiments" ("AF," 166) and other times unregulated by moral cant or "dogma" ("AF," 179). But James seems unclear whether these points mean that a new basis for calling things stories needs establishing or that no basis for calling things stories *could* be established, "since it comes back in the last resort, as I say, to the preference of the individual" ("AF," 180). In the case of "adventure," James initially implies that adventures are as extraneous to narrative as "cholera, or hydropathy, or Jansenism" ("AF," 179), but a sentence later he alters his attack, treating the concept of adventure as relevant but trying to expand its application ("and what *is* adventure, when it comes to that . . . ?").

If recognizing the new fiction requires normalizing relations with it, this second line of attack seems more promising. It recalls, for example, that telling is related to venturing, that unrelated events are adventitious, and that the beginning of relations is an advent. When James calls the domestic mishap in "An International Episode" a "stirring" adventure, he counts on our knowledge of these affinities. However, when he objects to Besant's implication that only certain things in life "constitute stories" ("AF," 178), or when he says, "there is no limit to what (the novelist) may attempt" ("AF," 170), or when he recognizes sincerity as the "only condition" for a novel ("AF," 182), he seems to discount this same knowledge. If the use of "story" is as idiosyncratic as James implies, then what needs explaining is how his examples could succeed in countering Besant or Lang. If our use agrees with James's examples, then what needs explaining is how there could be so much agreement without any established basis.

2

For Wittgenstein, knowing a word, having a concept, is not a matter of knowing a definition. It is a matter of being able to use the word (apply the concept) in situations beyond those in which the word was learned. This means knowing which words can and cannot be joined with a word (i.e., we "summarize his story" and "doubt her story" but do not "summarize his painting" or "doubt her poem," at least not normally). And it means knowing how a word does and does not change when joined with other words (I can "follow her story" and "follow her orders" but if I "follow her story" in the way I "follow her orders," I will probably "lose the thread of her story"). And it means knowing which circumstances are right for joining specific words (only in particular circumstances can I mean the words, "I fail to see the point of your story," and if I am confused about these circumstances, I cannot even *lie* with these words). Wittgenstein's name for this knowledge is "grammar." When he says that agreement in language is agreement in "form of life" (*PI*, §241), he means that it is part of the grammar of the word "story" that we call certain acts "to summarize a story," "to doubt a story," "to lose the thread of a story," and so on. Knowing what a story is, knowing what "story" means, is knowing what counts as doing these things. We learn grammar by living in it.[6]

James's problem in "The Art of Fiction" is that he finds it perfectly natural to use the word "story" for works that wreck the grammar he and everyone else learned in learning the word. If *these* works are stories, then what he has called "to follow a story," "to criticize a story," or "to discount a story" no longer means "to follow a story," "to criticize a story," or "to discount a story." The problem is not that James does not know how to do these things with the new works. It is that when he does them, he is no longer sure what he and everyone else were doing with the old works. After all, calling *Tom Jones* or *Pride and Prejudice* a story was never a matter of having a definition. Such works seemed to *be* the definition. And following, criticizing, and discounting were simply what anyone did with them. But now these works are not functioning as norms. James cannot evaluate the success of the new novels by comparison with the old, because the terms of success and failure are precisely what is new, and treating either modern or traditional works as exceptions seems arbitrary: If *Chérie* and *Treasure Island* are both stories, then one is as much a story as the other. It is as if James were uncertain not whether the new works are stories but why *anything* is, so that what he is having to learn is the grammar of "story" all over again, on the basis of new instances. Wittgenstein describes such situations as ones in which "our normal language games lose their point" (*PI*, §142).

For James, this situation becomes unavoidable after the publication of *Middlemarch* in 1872. When in his 1873 review he says that Eliot "sets a limit . . . to the development of the old-fashioned English novel,"[7] he may mean that *Middlemarch* is the ultimate achievement for an unquestioning time or that the achievement of *Middlemarch* is to have ended that time, but either way, this novel signals a break. What forces the break is Dorothea Brooke, the novel's "great achievement" ("M," 49). For James, appreciating Dorothea's character and predicament—what he calls her tragic dignity or "weight"—means becoming dissatisfied with fiction's traditional medium. Wherever Eliot follows traditional procedures, she tends to undermine her achievement, to "make light of the serious elements of the story and to sacrifice them to the more trivial ones" ("M," 50). That is, she gives to Dorothea's experiences "a narrower part" ("M," 50) or to Mary Garth's "love problem" a "higher" place ("M," 49) than the reader feels is due them, or she makes Dorothea's conflict "factitious" by the use of devices like the "codicil" to Casaubon's will. James's examples of the problem have to do with Eliot's episodic plot, her stance as a voluble "rural historian," and her romantic resolution of Dorothea's conflict. Yet he never explains why the failure of these devices in *Middlemarch* has such far-reaching consequences. Why do Eliot's shortcomings imply a limit on *all* traditional novels, not just on traditional novels with a character like Dorothea Brooke in them?

At or near the climax of *Middlemarch*, Dorothea sees—or believes that she does—that the one in whom she has placed her faith, Will Ladislaw, has betrayed her with Lydgate's wife. Dorothea endures a night of violent grief and the next morning undergoes a transformation. She considers Lydgate's loss in the light of her own and begins to think how she might act on his behalf. As Dorothea looks out her window, Eliot tells us, "She felt the largeness of the world and the manifold wakings of men to labour and endurance."[8] Following the story at this point is difficult, in part, because the feeling attributed to Dorothea does not seem very specific. That is, distinguishing this precise feeling from, say, a general feeling of expansiveness, a feeling of solidarity with working people, or just that very good feeling we have some mornings may not be anything we normally do. We may not even believe that we *can* do it, that words will differentiate feelings so precisely. At the same time, we are probably confident that whatever feeling this is, we would not feel it in Dorothea's situation. That is, Dorothea feels the world's largeness and humanity's energetic stirring in circumstances where we would expect to feel the world's smallness and our strength's depletion, or where we would expect to feel the vastness of our hopes but the narrowness of our chances, or where we might puzzle over the world's largeness precisely because we could no longer *feel* it. Feeling the largeness of the world and the manifold wakings of men to labor and endurance is Dorothea's response to betrayal and the loss of first love.

What counts as following here? That is, what counts as staying with Dorothea's experience as opposed to "sacrificing" it to a more "trivial" one? Normally, a feeling will be *of* what we take it to be *of* only in certain circumstances. Only in certain circumstances will a feeling be a feeling of ardent love, not of ordinary lust or momentary infatuation (*PI*, §583; *CR*, 104–8), and only in certain circumstances will a feeling be a feeling of expectation, not a feeling of hope or fear mistaken for it (*PI*, §581), and only in certain circumstances will an experience that feels just like understanding be, in fact, understanding (*PI*, §§154–55, 179). Knowing these circumstances is a matter of knowing what comes "before and after" such feelings (*PI*, §35). If Dorothea's circumstances at this point in her story are not of the kind in which the largeness of the world is to be felt—and they certainly do not look like that kind—then, regardless of how open-minded or tolerant we may be, we will not recognize her experience as a normal instance of this feeling. We may conclude that she has undergone an unusual psychological episode ("She was so exhausted from grief and sleeplessness that the next morning she felt herself to be having one of those breakthrough experiences"). Or we may consider her merely young and understandably confused ("It was a horrible disappointment, and in her innocence she imagined that she had recovered in a single night"). Or we may conclude that her feeling is a normal instance of the feelings characters in novels have ("Where else do people 'feel' the 'largeness' of 'the world'?"). But we will not do what we would do if we were following an account of a feeling of the largeness of the world.

Following Dorothea's story, not a more traditional one, requires recognizing the sequence of realizations, acknowledgments, transformations, achievements, and desires that would make her situation the following morning one in which, given what we normally call "the largeness of the world," Dorothea's feeling would be a feeling of exactly that. And it also requires recognizing the subsequent decisions, actions, rejections, and satisfactions that would confirm that Dorothea's feeling has in fact been a feeling of exactly that. And the obstacle to our recognizing all this will be our unconsciousness of the sequence of realizations, refusals, decisions, and actions by which we make our own circumstances into ones in which only the smallness of the world can be felt. Following Dorothea's story means recognizing the limits of fiction as my doing.

3

What seems right about James's resistance to Besant and Lang in "The Art of Fiction" is that as long as nothing counts as our *normal* relation to stories, formulating definitions amounts to codifying self-imposed limits. In such straits, the last thing we need (literally) is rules. The first thing we need is perfect attention to stories ("Don't think, but look!" [*PI*, §66]), in particular, to the novels that have produced our desire for (and fear of) rules. For confusion in such cases results from nothing hidden (*PI*, §126) but from conditions these works have made newly perspicuous (*PI*, §122). James's examples of what he would call (judge to be) a story are initial efforts to meet our need, and his reviews and criticism take the effort deeper.

But if something seems right about James's resistance to Besant and Lang, there is something wrong too, or wrongheaded, and James's difficulties with the word "story" are partly results of this wrongheadedness. For if works such as *Middlemarch* have required James to project his concept of a story into new contexts, they have also provided him with a basis for doing so. Making the required judgments will be establishing those regularities—rules, norms, conventions, and so forth—on which James and our continued life with stories depends. If James nevertheless wants to cast doubt on these regularities—either because no generalization seems exact enough ("AF," 171) or because every generalization seems arbitrary ("AF," 179) or confining ("AF," 170)—then a picture holds him captive (*PI*, §115), one he has inherited from Besant's lecture. To see his cage, we need to look at the situation in which James finds rules unsatisfactory.

When James says, "He would be a clever man who should undertake to give a rule—an index expurgatorius—by which the story and the no-story should be known apart" ("AF," 179), the question I feel like asking is: Who *needs* this rule? Normally, the person who needs rules to identify a commonplace object is a cultural novice—say, a child or a foreigner. If such a person asks for help ("How come it's a story, Uncle Henry?" or: "What are these 'stories' of which you speak?"), a clever man or woman may be better at giving help, but most native speakers can make a stab at it: "Well, stories are usually something somebody tells or listens to or reads." Or: "If somebody asks what happened, the answer is usually a story." Or perhaps: "We use 'story' the way you use *histoire*, only we have another word for the kind of books Michelet wrote." Needless to say, such rules will not account for every case, but cultural novices rarely need rules for *every* case, and whether a more exact rule is needed (whether any rule could be more exactly what is needed) depends on the circumstances provoking the question.

James's dissatisfaction with rules, however, is not related to any situation of this kind. When he says, "It is impossible (to me at least) to imagine any such rule which shall not be altogether arbitrary" ("AF," 179), he does not mean that he would say to a bewildered child, "A story can be anything or everything, my dear," or to a nonnative speaker, "English speakers employ this word arbitrarily." The situation in which James finds rules unsatisfactory is one in which telling a story from a "no-story" is a matter of identifying a "subject" or *"donnée"* for a work of art. What James means is that no rule can help out the artist who, "as the time for 'sending in' his picture looms in the distance, finds himself still in quest of a subject" ("AF," 178–79). But it is difficult to imagine any (modern) artist who *expects* rules to help in such straits. James describes the artist's quest for a subject as the search for what will "speak to us" ("AF," 179), and if artists imagine that what speaks to them can be found by following rules, then that probably explains why they cannot find a subject. When Wittgenstein says, "If language is to be a means of communication there must be agreement not only in definitions but also (queer as this may sound) in judgments" (*PI*, §242), he means that we have rules, norms, and conventions only insofar as things do "speak to us," and until something does, there is nothing for a rule, norm, or convention to be a rule, norm, or convention of. For the artist to whom nothing "speaks," the rules are not arbitrary, inexact, or confining. They are nonexistent. And when something does "speak," nothing justifies its "speaking," not even the universal agreement of humankind. That (some) things just do (sometimes) speak to artists is the bedrock (*PI*, §217) of art. If we ask why they do, satisfactory explanations rapidly come to an end (*PI*, §1).

If rules can be formulated in any situation where rules are really needed, and if rules become problematic only in situations where they are extraneous, then we have good reason to suspect that James's dissatisfaction results from a false requirement. What we need to ask is: According to what picture of rules do rules become inexact, confining, and arbitrary in *every* situation? And the answer is: according to the picture in Besant's brief apologia for "the story."[9] In this paragraph from his lecture, Besant counters the "new school" of novelists (Howells, James, et al.) by presenting his rules for writing fiction as logical requirements of the concept "novel": "Fortunately these new theorists contradict themselves, because they find it impossible to write a novel which shall not contain a story, although it may be but a puny bantling. Fiction without adventure—drama without a plot—a novel without surprises—the thing is as impossible as life without uncertainty."[10] Besant's requirements operate independently of what particular novelists (the "new theorists") judge to be worth telling, and this autonomy makes the traditional or popular novel into an inescapable limit on the development of the art. It is as if, regardless of whether stories spoke to "novelists" or not, "novelists" would continue writing them, as though compelled by the grammar of a word.

James has little difficulty showing that these requirements are illusory. They are too vague to be rules because "novel" and "story" are being defined only by each other. They are arbitrary prescriptions, not logical necessities, because we just do and will use the word "story" for works markedly unlike traditional or popular novels. And they are confining because . . . well, because Besant *wants* them to be confining (*"Fortunately* these new theorists . . . find it impossible"). But what this shows is not, as James seems to imagine, that the novel has "so few restrictions" in comparison with the other arts ("AF," 182). It shows that not everything in traditional novels is necessary, that we have not recognized what has been essential at any moment to something counting for us as a story, so that what we have taken to be the conventions of the art of fiction just aren't.

It is *this* concept of a rule, one that would subordinate judgments to grammar, that James means to oppose by insisting that the art of fiction is idiosyncratic ("AF," 170) and without limit ("AF," 182). The problem his insistence creates for James is not that it makes him treat personal impressions as if they already were stories (and never melodies, dance movements, still lifes) or as if, no matter what a novelist wrote, so long as it met the conditions of interest ("AF," 170) and sincerity ("AF," 182), we would call it a novel (never a dialogue, prose poem, parable, satire, or polemic). The problem is that James's resistance to rules rules out what, in his examples of stories and adventures, he is trying to establish: a basis for his art.

4

The conclusion of "The Art of Fiction" comes in the late novels and "Prefaces," where James identifies the workings of consciousness as his new medium for fiction, but his difficulties with "the story" culminate much earlier, in his 1888 essay on Maupassant.[11] James's stated intention in this essay is to do justice to a writer whose moral skepticism poses a problem for him similar to that which his own work posed for Besant and Lang. However, his efforts to recognize Maupassant's positive achievement are continually vitiated by a Besantlike worry over all that Maupassant's fiction *lacks*. James initially praises the French writer's perceptiveness but cannot forbear noticing "a certain absence of love" ("GM," 204), and when admiring Maupassant's "hardness of form," James attributes it not to artistic integrity but to "the touch of softness that he lacks" ("GM," 198). The fact that Maupassant's fiction contains "no account of the moral nature of man" is attributable not to "artistic scruples" but to Maupassant's personal "limitations" ("GM," 206), and his "mastery" is simply the result of having omitted from his work "the whole reflective part of his men and women" ("GM," 219). Although James wants to substitute "clearness" for realism as his term of criticism ("GM," 199)—thereby to preserve Maupassant's "point of view" ("GM," 203)—he still accuses Maupassant of leaving out much with which "our imagination, and I think it ought to be said our observation, is familiar" ("GM," 212), and he complains that there is a "want of correspondence" between the world as represented in Maupassant's fiction and "our own vision of reality" ("GM," 213).

What makes this essay noteworthy is not its recognition of Maupassant's achievement. It is hardly about Maupassant's achievement. It is noteworthy because, in the midst of its catalog of Maupassant's omissions, James pauses over "a remarkably interesting experiment" ("GM," 215)—the novel *Une vie*. His attention to *Une vie* seems so striking because, unlike the other Maupassant stories James praises, *Une vie* is not an exception to his case against the French writer. On the contrary, in this work Maupassant has "eliminated excessively," suppressed "arbitrarily," and hardly arranged his material at all ("It is almost an arrangement of the history of poor Mme. de Lamare to have left so many things out of it"; "GM," 216). The central figure, Jeanne, has "no moral spring, no active moral life, none of the edifying attributes of character" ("GM," 217). What James calls "the miscellaneous *remplissage* of life" (friends, phases, episodes, chances, etc.) is "wholly absent" ("GM," 216–17). This means that James has as much trouble saying why *Une vie* is so "remarkably interesting" as he has saying what makes Maupassant's oeuvre a genuine achievement. Initially he explains that despite a "minimum of arrangement," *Une vie* still gives "an impression of truth," but this description does not take him or us very far. Either it makes the work a feebler version of a Jamesian novel (the "impression of truth" would have been "still better" if Maupassant had not "eliminated excessively"; "GM," 216), or the description is circular: the "impression of truth" is simply that Maupassant has arranged minimally ("his effort has been to give the uncomposed, unrounded look of life, with its accidents, its broken rhythm"). Either way, we have no explanation why this minimal arrangement is more interesting than a grocery list or other minimal arrangements, that is, interesting in the way *novels* are interesting, or why, among all novels, this one is so "remarkable."

In one sentence, however, James offers an altogether different reason for appreciating *Une vie*: "It is especially to be recommended to those who are interested in the question of what constitutes a 'story,' offering as it does the most definite sequences at the same time that it has nothing that corresponds to the usual idea of a plot, and closing with an implication that finds us prepared" ("GM," 217). James's idea is that in reading *Une vie*, we find ourselves following an action (there are "definite sequences") in the absence of that structure of action ("a plot") that we had thought (since Aristotle) we were following. There is movement but no direction: Trains of events "start but don't arrive" ("GM," 216). Nothing of consequence follows from what the main character does ("Jeanne is absolutely passive"; "GM," 217). But this does not mean that the outcome is random or unpredictable. On the contrary, the conclusion "finds us prepared": no surprises, no sudden reversals, no unexpected discoveries. There is nothing we are able to tell at the end that was not clear from the start, except that fact itself. For James, this does not mean what Besant might take it to mean, that Maupassant has attempted the impossible (i.e., to write a novel without a story in it). It means that James has followed a story in circumstances that he never dreamed possible. We read *Une vie* to find out what, apparently, never required telling. All that is bewildering is that this constitutes a novel.

If "clearness" is James's term of criticism, then Maupassant would seem to be his exemplary case. The French writer's achievement is to have revealed *more clearly* than did earlier nineteenth-century writers what we do in relating events. He reveals this in part by undoing the prior schemes or "pictures" that captivate us (*PI*, §115), that distract attention from "the aspects of things that are most important for us" (*PI*, §129). His continuous exposure of these aspects ("in despite of an urge to misunderstand them" [*PI*, §109]) establishes sequences in the absence of surprises, reversals, enigmas, or resolutions. This continuous exposure is what we follow to no end. However, after James's one-sentence appreciation of this achievement, he says nothing more about it. He notes "a certain purity" about *Une vie* yet attributes it not to Maupassant's clarity but to his emergent conscience in the work ("He almost betrays a sense of moral things"), and when James praises the author's handling of "renunciation" ("GM," 217), he cites the *protagonist's* renunciation, not Maupassant's.

If we ask how James could fail to recognize an achievement so suited to his categories, two answers suggest themselves. The first is that in the case of *Une vie*, what James has always called "recognizing the achievement of a story" no longer means "recognizing the achievement of a story." Unlike *Middlemarch* or James's own novels, the importance of *Une vie* is not a function of the importance of its characters or their experiences. If we say that *Middlemarch* is to be recommended to those interested in the question of what constitutes an "epic life" for a modern "Saint Theresa," we mean that Dorothea Brooke models such a figure, that her struggles represent or figure this life (often ironically). But if we recommend *Une vie* to those "interested in the question of what constitutes a 'story,' " we do not mean that Maupassant's characters model storytellers or that their actions figure reading, writing, and following. What makes *Une vie* remarkable is something closer to us: that it is a story, that we *have* followed it, as if this were now an achievement.

What counts as recognizing this achievement is not obvious. Perhaps we could provide a description of the experience of *discovering* that *Une vie* is a story: in particular, a description showing why it *required* discovering, why this knowledge comes as a *revelation*, why it is acquired in *following*. But such a description would call for a discipline as exacting as Maupassant's, and anyone who missed it in *Une vie* could still miss it. The problem of recognizing Maupassant's achievement comes down to this: In a sense not equally true of *Middlemarch*, knowing it is seeing it.

Which brings us to the second reason James fails to recognize Maupassant's achievement: He does not want to recognize it. In addition to the aim of doing justice to Maupassant, James's other stated aim in the essay is to "circumvent" ("GM," 204) or find "a legitimate way round" ("GM," 219) him. To this end, Maupassant's clearness is the obstacle James must get past. Where Maupassant prefers "the simple epic manner" over character analysis, James warns us to mistrust such "sharp distinctions" ("GM," 204); where Maupassant emphasizes differentiation, James speaks out on behalf of resemblance and "unconscious" originality ("GM," 206–7); and where Maupassant's theoretical statements are extraordinarily clear,

James admits that he would prefer them to be less so: "It would put us more at ease to find that if the fact with him (the fact of execution) is so extraordinarily definite and adequate, his explanations, after it, were a little vague and sentimental" ("GM," 198). What James never does is identify any artistic problem to which Maupassant's renunciations are a fully satisfactory solution, any obstacle that only a "clearness" as uncompromising as his could remove.

All of which points to the oddest feature of James's one-sentence appreciation of *Une vie:* It leaves in doubt whether James is himself among "those who are interested in the question of what constitutes a 'story.'" Of course, if we consider the "Prefaces," we may feel that James's interest goes without saying. There he insists that after "the story of one's hero" one still has "the story of one's story itself," and according to James, his own "bag" is "only half-emptied" by the "mere telling" of the former.¹² If we have in mind "The Art of Fiction," however, we may feel less certain. There James seems to distrust this kind of abstraction. If "the story" means anything different from the novel, it is just the novelist's initial idea, and "since in proportion as the work is successful the idea permeates and penetrates it," a story and its telling become inseparable ("AF," 178). It seems unclear how the novelist's bag could be only half emptied unless his novels were only half full, or why James's interest in, for example, Lambert Strether is not exhausted by *The Ambassadors* itself. All that James's sentence makes certain is that his interest in the "'story'" is different from his interest in a "plot" or in "sequences." For in his appreciation of Maupassant's achievement, James continues his practice from "The Art of Fiction" and other late writings of singling this word out with quotation marks. The implication is that "'story'" is *quoted,* that it appears through the agency of another, that it is not James's word.

Notes

1. For Cavell's account of Wittgensteinian criteria, see Stanley Cavell, *The Claim of Reason* (Oxford: Oxford University Press, 1982), part 1; hereafter cited as *CR*. For Cavell's comparison of judgment in Wittgenstein's philosophy and in art, see Stanley Cavell, *Must We Mean What We Say?* (Cambridge: Cambridge University Press, 1976), 73–96; hereafter cited as *MW*. For Cavell's account of the failure and recovery of grammatical criteria in modernist art, see *MW*, 213–24. For Cavell's notion of a "medium" of art, see *MW*, 220–21. Cavell's most extended discussion of the modern necessity to discover a new medium of art occurs in Stanley Cavell, *The World Viewed* (Cambridge: Harvard University Press, 1979), especially chapters 2, 5, 14, 15.

2. Henry James, "The Art of Fiction," in *The Art of Criticism: Henry James on*

the *Theory and Practice of Fiction*, ed. William Veeder and Susan M. Griffin (Chicago: University of Chicago Press, 1986), 165–83; hereafter cited as "AF." For the circumstances of James's disagreement with Besant and Lang, see Veeder and Griffin's commentary in the same volume, 178–80.

3. On the capacity of native speakers to say what *we* (who speak the language) call something, see *MW*, 1–43. For Cavell's discussion of Wittgenstein's reliance on what *we* say, see *MW*, chapter 2, especially 56–70, and also *CR*, chapter 1, especially 17–22.

4. Ludwig Wittgenstein, *Philosophical Investigations*, 3d ed., trans. G. E. M. Anscombe (New York: Macmillan, 1968), §224; hereafter cited as *PI*, with Wittgenstein's numbered paragraphs, or "remarks," indicated by the symbol §.

5. Walter Besant, "The Art of Fiction," *Writer* (August 1899): 123.

6. For an elaboration of this account of Wittgensteinian grammar, see *CR*, chapter 4, "What a Thing Is (Called)," especially 70–72. On knowing a word as the capacity to apply (or "project") it into new contexts, see *CR*, chapter 7, "Excursus on Wittgenstein's Vision of Language."

7. Henry James, "Middlemarch," review of *Middlemarch*, by George Eliot, in *The Art of Criticism: Henry James on the Theory and Practice of Fiction*, ed. William Veeder and Susan M. Griffin (Chicago: University of Chicago Press, 1986), 54; hereafter cited as "M."

8. George Eliot, *Middlemarch*, ed. Bert G. Hornback (New York: Norton, 1977), 544.

9. Besant, "Art of Fiction," 123.

10. Ibid.

11. Henry James, "Guy de Maupassant," in *The Art of Criticism: Henry James on the Theory and Practice of Fiction*, ed. William Veeder and Susan M. Griffin (Chicago: University of Chicago Press, 1986), 197–220; hereafter abbreviated "GM."

12. Henry James, *The Ambassadors*, in *The Art of Criticism: Henry James on the Theory and Practice of Fiction*, ed. William Veeder and Susan M. Griffin (Chicago: University of Chicago Press, 1986), 365.

"The Accomplishment of Inhabitation": Danto, Cavell, and the Argument of American Poetry

Gerald L. Bruns

In memory of Sherman Paul

1. Toward a Poetics of Nonidentity

Modern poetics begins with the French poet Stéphane Mallarmé's belief that poetry is made of words, not of ideas. That is, a poem is made of language but is
not, strictly speaking, a use of it. Poetry is made of words but not of any of the
things that we use words to produce—concepts, meanings, propositions about
the world, narratives, expressions of feeling, and so on. This does not mean that
the poem lacks these things. It is only that the poem is no longer reducible to them;
its definition can no longer be located in one or more of them. In other words, the
poem is no longer reducible to other sorts of discourse; it cannot be made a branch
of something else—part of an organon, for example, or a species of philosophy or
rhetoric. In poetry, language is no longer a form of mediation. So what is it, then?

The problem is how to tell that a piece of language is poetic. What is it that
separates the poem from the nonpoem? Mallarmé tried to answer this question
with an analytical distinction between poetic and ordinary speech, where the
one is a formally self-contained system of relations, a beautiful work of art that
occupies a space of its own—the white space of the printed page or, alterna-
tively, the "poetic universe"—while the other is, well, just talk. Various traditions
of rhetorical, romantic, and formalist-structuralist poetics have tried to clarify a
distinction of this sort, not always successfully. As if denying the possibility of any
such distinction, the American poet William Carlos Williams says, "A poem can be
made of anything," even newspaper clippings.[1] Poetry is *internal* to the discourse of
everyday life; it is not the product of a logic of exclusion but is conceptually, and
therefore aesthetically, nondifferentiated.[2]

Williams's *Paterson* (1946–58), for example, is a poem made out of every sort
of discourse imaginable, not all of it of Williams's own composition. Here is an

excerpt from book 5, section 2 (which also contains a poem by Sappho and a letter from Ezra Pound):

(Q. Mr. Williams, can you tell me, simply, what poetry is?

A. Well . . . I would say that poetry is language charged with emotion. It's words, rhythmically organized. . . . A poem is a complete little universe. It exists separately. Any poem that has worth expresses the whole life of the poet. It gives a view of what the poet is.

Q. All right, look at this part of a poem by E. E. Cummings, another great American poet:

```
(im)c-a-t(mo)>
b,i,l:e
FallleA
ps!fl
Oattumbll
sh?dr
IftwhirlF
(Ul) (IY)
&&&
```

Is this poetry?

A. I would reject it as a poem. It may be, to him, a poem. But I would reject it. I can't understand it. He's a serious man. So I struggle very hard with it—and I get no meaning at all.

Q. You get no meaning? But here's part of a poem you yourself have written: " . . . 2 partridges / 2 mallard ducks / a Dungeness crab / 24 hours out / of the Pacific / and 1 live-frozen / trout / from Denmark" Now that sounds just like a fashionable grocery list.

A. It is a fashionable grocery list.

Q. Well—is it poetry?

A. We poets have to talk in a language which is not English. It is the American idiom. Rhythmically it's organized as a sample of the American idiom. It has as much originality as jazz. If you say "2 partridges, 2 mallard ducks, a Dungeness crab"—if you treat that rhythmically, ignoring the practical sense, it forms a jagged pattern. It is, to my mind, poetry.

Q. But if you don't "ignore the practical sense" . . . you agree that it is a fashionable grocery list.

A. Yes. Anything is good material for poetry. Anything. I've said it time and time again.

Q. Aren't we supposed to understand it?

A. There is a difference of poetry and the sense. Sometimes modern poets ignore sense completely. That's what makes some of the difficulty. . . . The audience is confused by the shape of the words.

Q. But shouldn't a word mean something when you see it?

A. In prose, an English word means what it says. In poetry, you're listening to two things . . . you're listening to the sense, the common sense of what it says. But it says more. That is the difficulty.)[3]

What counts as poetry when poetry is no longer discernible from a grocery list? Williams says that the answer is how we listen. As if there were more to a grocery list than the items that compose it.

It will be useful to enlarge our field of examples. Consider the famous case of David Antin's "talk poetry," as in the following from *Talking at the Boundaries*:

> "what am i doing here?"
> what is it that im doing here?　im trying to find out　how i
> could find out　and what im trying to find out is by
> essentially doing what i think talking does　that is
> talking and thinking may not be the same thing　but i see
> thinking as talking i see it as talking to a question　which
> may give rise to another question　and it may open up some
> terrain and lose some terrain and answers come up but theyre not
> the same answers[4]

The "talk poem," Stephen Fredman says, "challenges us to conceive of poetry, criticism, and philosophy as a single activity. Antin performs a talk poem by standing up in front of an audience and improvising speech around a certain intellectual territory, combining critical questions about the nature of poetry or art with philosophical speculations about the way language influences our behavior and thought, complementing these ideas by often humorous anecdotes about himself, his family, and friends."[5] And of course he also talks about what he is doing, inserting the claim that (at least this) talk counts as a poem:

> i mean if i were to come and read to you from a
> book you would consider it a perfectly reasonable form of behavior
>   and its a perfectly respectable form of behavior generally
> thought of as a poetry reading   and it would be a little bit like
> taking out a container of frozen peas   warming them up and
> serving them to you from the frozen food container   and that
> doesn't seem interesting to me because then i turn out to be a cook
>   and i dont really want to be a cook   i don't want to cook
>   or recook anything for anybody   I came here in order to make a
>   poem   talking   to talk a poem   which it will be   all
> other things being equal[6]

Philosophy distinguishes itself jealously from what is "just talk." But, on Antin's showing, not so poetry, which cannot or maybe just does not distinguish itself from mere talk. Yet by what sort of argument or line of thought could we begin to understand Antin's talk as poetry?

At a climactic moment in his *In Search of the Primitive*, Sherman Paul records his exchange of letters with George Butterick concerning David Antin's talk poetry. Paul and Butterick had been discussing the splendid moment at a symposium at the Library of Congress when Marjorie Perloff gave a paper on Antin that caused an outraged Harold Bloom to storm from the room.[7] Without exactly siding with Bloom, or in other words granting that Antin is not just to be brushed aside with a superior gesture, Butterick had wondered if there wasn't, nevertheless, a moral that Bloom was trying to point:

> He [Antin] sure is on the right track: the primacy of story. I mean the
> guy's irrepressible. Imagine him in the CCNY cafeteria, circa 1952. But: Is
> it poetry? Need it be called such? Can't we reserve the term for something
> more formal (says the exponent of polymorphism)?

To which Paul responded:

> I don't want the last word and this isn't the last word, by any means. *Is it
> poetry?*, lower case *p*, and less *formal*, or form-ridden, than the privileged upper
> case variety. How hard it is to come into the open, to cling to the advance,
> as Williams said. How much talk is still needed at the boundaries!

Ever since Emerson, whose lectures on all accounts are *his* poetry, American poetry has tried to get beyond fixity and determinism, to destroy arbitrary boundaries, in order to release the energy and impulse of creation and restore the self's place in the world. It has questioned both the sovereignty of mind and the closure of the universe, demanded an ever greater inclusiveness ("the common and low"), and favored an art of individual experience, witness, and truth. It has sometimes been performative. It has respected speech. I can imagine Emerson, whose trial as a poet was so severe, listening appreciatively to Antin in the CCNY cafeteria, gladdened again by the advent of another New York poet.[8]

So in the spirit of Emerson one might ask: What would poetry be if it were just the thing of which it is made (language, speech, talk) and not, so far as one could tell, something else (something set apart as Poetry and nothing else)? This is the question posed by much of modern and contemporary American poetry—perhaps initially by Gertrude Stein in *Tender Buttons* (1912) but with true theoretical aggression by the "language poets" (or L = A = N = G = U = A = G = E poets), whose texts are frequently composed of the common locutions of everyday life—yet composed in such a way that one imagines that ordinary language has grown conscious of itself without, however, showing any philosophical desire to be anything else (anything but ordinary, everyday talk).[9]

Here are three lines (yes, three) from David Bromige's poem "Lines" (1984):

yes i do resent it

_____

when you use that word[10]

Or, again, take Tina Darragh's poem, "Raymond Chandler's Sentence" (1984)—which is about the poet's absorption in Raymond Chandler's remark that "I had to learn American just like a foreign language." ("Who doesn't?" an immigrant, even a child of immigrants, might be tempted to ask; but Chandler was from England, and, in order to write mystery novels set in the seedier or ordinary reaches of Southern California, he had to sound the way people talk in these places, or perhaps the way they are made to talk in Hollywood movies from the 1930s.)

In "Bay City Blues"
the detective is caught in a frame
& tries to escape
by climbing into the next room and dressing
in someone else's clothes,
even affecting another's voice
But C has the tough cop spot
him anyway & say
"get dressed, sweetheart & don't fuss with your necktie.
Places want us to go to them."[11]

Language poetry is, let us say, language about language, that is, not conceptually about language but (how should one say?) morally and politically responsive or receptive to the language in people's mouths—how people talk, come what may. A poem can be made of anything, depending on how one listens, which means that there is (in principle) nothing that cannot be counted as poetry. Poetry, unlike philosophy, is nonexclusionary. One might think of calling this a poetics of nonidentity.

Such a poetics might pose a problem for a philosophy deeply committed to the idea of art as something (necessarily) discernible—something, for example, discernibly different from reality. Arthur Danto, a philosopher who doubles as an art critic, has tried to clarify a problem of this sort. "My thought," Danto says, "is that philosophy begins to arise only when the society within which it arises achieves a concept of reality." But this can happen "only when a contrast is available between reality and something else," and it appears that in the West the philosophical function of art is to constitute this something else.[12] Art gives reality something to contrast itself with, but unfortunately this in turn gives art the power to empty the concept of reality of its force, or detach it from its application, just by being the thing it is to be contrasted with. The classic example would be Marcel Duchamp's *Fountain*, which not only looks like but is, for all the world, a urinal.[13] A showing of Duchamp's work would occasionally look like a hardware store, and it seems important to acknowledge that he is not alone in this sort of thing but is simply giving definition to a whole culture of art, one in which art does not so much mirror the world as appropriate objects from its socioeconomic environment (Danto's favorite example is Andy Warhol's *Brillo Box*). Danto has some good lines that remind us of how "Picasso was famous for transfigurations of the commonplace. He had made the head of a chimpanzee out of a child's toy; a goat's thorax out of an old wicker basket; a bull's head out of bicycle parts; a Venus out of a gasjet—and so why not the ultimate transfiguration, an artwork out of a thing?" (*TC*, 46). What counts as art when the work of art is the very thing it pictures itself as being? Or when it is made up of things that are the very things it is supposed to be different from? Or, for that matter, the same as—Danto imagines a painter who loves a painting so much that he paints it, the way he does his mistress or his favorite rural scene in France (*TC*, 38).[14]

Here we seem to arrive at some sort of cognitive limit, perhaps more than one sort of limit. One cannot tell a work of art from a real thing just by looking at it, because the question is not what a thing looks like, nor even what it is, but how it is situated, and how taken. Every work of art presupposes an "artworld," in Danto's famous expression, which is a world constituted by concepts, theories, and narratives as to what counts as art. "What in the end makes the difference between [Andy Warhol's] Brillo box and a work of art consisting of a Brillo box," Danto says,

is a certain theory of art. It is the theory that takes it up into the world of art, and keeps it from collapsing into the real object which it is (in a sense of *is* other than that of artistic identification). Of course, without the theory, one is unlikely to see it as art, and in order to see it as part of the artworld, one must have mastered a good deal of artistic theory as well as a considerable amount of the history of recent New York painting. It could not have been art fifty years ago. But then there could not have been, everything being equal, flight insurance in the Middle Ages, or Etruscan typewriter erasers. The world has to be ready for such things, the artworld no less than the real one. It is the role of artistic theories, these days as always, to make the artworld, and art, possible. It would, I should think, never have occurred to the painters of Lascaux that they were producing art on those walls. Not unless they were neolithic aestheticians.[15]

Warhol's *Brillo Box*, like Duchamp's *Fountain* before it, is a type of art of which not every Brillo box or urinal is a token. Danto puts this by saying that art is not a natural kind but a historical event, meaning that the essence of the thing is internal to the social and cultural (or institutional) space in which it is produced. All art, like all politics, is local and contingent.

Danto frequently cites Heinrich Wölflin's motto, "Not everything is possible at every time"—that is, "certain artworks simply could not be inserted as artworks into certain periods of art history, though it is possible that objects identical to artworks could have been made at that period" (*TC*, 44). So eventually debris from Etruscan or Jericho dump sites ends up as artifacts in museums. What is decisive between art and rubbish is the (Kripkean) concept of "causal history." When Duchamp, on what looks like a whim, pops into the local plumbers' supply for his latest composition, he disrupts the causal history of urinals and causes an ordinary thing to be art. "Transfiguration" is Danto's name for this. An ordinary urinal remains ordinary by getting left behind in the causal history of mere urinals (urinals not purchased by Duchamp: urinals whose causal history ends with their manufacture, purchase, and urinary use, not with the end of the history of art). The ordinary urinal lacks, so to speak, the self-consciousness that Duchamp's urinal, whose causal history sets it apart in a studio rather than a men's room, achieves (*TC*, 48–49)—as if ordinary things could have uncommon destinies (and why not?). There comes a time in the history of art when we know better than to treat all urinals alike. It is no trouble to imagine or experience a word or an object, say a urinal, turning up in a form of life in which it is not thought to belong, but where, against all reason, it fits, it catches on. In ancient rhetoric this event is called a metaphor or transfer from one context to another. In *The Claim of Reason* Stanley Cavell calls it "projecting a word," which he takes to be one of the ordinary things that goes on in ordinary language.[16]

However, it is a nice question whether, alongside urinals and soup cans, there is any room in Danto's aesthetics for a poetry made of language (just language). In the *Poetics*, for example, Aristotle famously set aside language (*lexis*) as an inessential ingredient of poetic structure, and in this he has been followed by almost all philosophers and literary critics (but, at least since Wordsworth's time, by very few poets).[17] Something about the embedment of literature in language makes Danto want to affirm his Aristotelian ancestry, and so in an essay called "Philosophy as/and/of Literature," he defends the basically Aristotelian principle that literature is still part of the organon or logic of propositional discourse—still a branch of semantic theory and therefore made of things, not words (still mimetic after all these years). "Semantical theory," Danto says, "does the best it can to connect literature to the world through what, after all, are the only kinds of connections it understands: reference, truth, instantiation, exemplification, and the like, and if this means distorting the universe in order that it can receive literary representations, well, this has never been reckoned a heavy price to pay—has not been reckoned a price at all but a creative opportunity—and it remains to the credit of this enterprise that it at least believes that some connection between literature and the world is required" (PD, 145).

Semantics here means "possible-world" semantics, or modal realism, which does strike some philosophers as distorting the universe in literature's direction. "My contention," Danto says, "is that philosophical semantics renders literature true of possible worlds . . . in such a way that it would be history for any of them if actual instead of ours. As Gulliver's Travels would be just anthropology for a world in which there are Lilliputians instead of Melanesians" (PD, 154). In possible-world semantics, works of fiction are not false (not *not* factual, not *merely* fantastic, however fantastic); they are simply true of worlds different from our own. If I understand David Lewis, there is no warrant for saying that these other worlds don't exist. They are as real as ours (the one we inhabit); it's just that they aren't ours.[18] Danto says that works of fiction connect up with our world by way of their readers, which is pretty much the same idea as Paul Ricoeur's looking glass theory of the text, where understanding a text does not mean going around behind it to retrieve some originating intention; rather, Ricoeur thinks of the literary text as projecting a possible world in front of itself and that understanding means entering into this project, this space in front of the text, making it one's own. The reader's task, our task, is to reconnect text and world by appropriating the world in front of the text, that is, putting it, in some sense, into play, say by intervening in our world in order to change it in the text's direction (instead of changing the text in our direction, translating into our language, integrating it into our order of signification, which is how allegory moves).[19]

This is good hermeneutics but doubtful poetics, because it reduces language (or literature) to its semantic or narrative function, whereas the poet is someone who is obsessed with what is irreducible in language (or literature). The poet Michael Davidson gives a straightforward narrative account of such an obsession:

I have a kind of naive idea of what a fact is. To paraphrase Wittgenstein, it's a point of departure for further investigation. I think it began with my interest in lists. At one point the idea of a list was a sort of ultimate autistic [artistic?] construct, because it would create the illusion of a random series that would relate immediately to my life. I would be able to go through my day and check off items on the list. They were words after all, but the syntax of the list was my activity [i.e., my daily life]. In that sense, it was a hermeneutic of reading the list. And then I began to realize that I wanted to tell stories; I wanted to describe events. And the problem, of course, occurred in the first few words: as I began to describe the event I was faced with my own language staring me back in the face. I simply couldn't describe. I found myself involved in the forms of mediation that were constantly coming up in front of me.[20]

Davidson writes as if language were both the form and the limit of mediation. Danto shows us a brief glimpse of his irrealist, non-Aristotelian side when he remarks in passing on the material aspects of artworks. "It is because," he says, "of these palpable features in excess of the features which make for semantical analysis that a work of art, even when straightforward narrative, cannot be collapsed into its content: there is something in the telling of the story which is more than the story told. It is for these reasons that even when a work of art is, as critics and literary theorists loosely say, 'referential,' it is never merely referential. For these reasons I speak of works of art as semiopaque objects" (PD, 79). Can we make sense of the thought that poetry might be the irreducibility of language to its semantic features?

In analytic philosophy, opacity is less a concept than a covering term for whatever gets in the way of the perception of logical form or interferes with the unpacking of deep structures. In this tradition natural languages are conventionally described as opaque (or, more rigorously, incoherent and opaque). The language poets encourage us to think of poetry as a discourse that takes responsibility for the native opacity of everyday language, that is, for its native resistance or irreducibility to the logical functions of mediation that characterize our use of it. Naturally one thinks of famous cases, sometimes imaginary, like Flaubert's dream of "a book about nothing," a work from which the features that make for semantic analysis would have to be completely eliminated; but actual cases will serve— Tristram Shandy, Mallarmé's poetry, James Joyce's Finnegans Wake, Maurice Blanchot's récits, the later poems of Paul Celan. What is interesting about so many of the language poets, in contrast to these famous cases, is that they seek to remain within the opacity of natural language, neither to thicken nor to reduce it by art but to write a poetry of the surface, a poetry of what otherwise—say, in the making of art objects, or of narratives, or of concepts—is overcome or subsumed through mediation. In general the language poets affirm the opacity of natural language against what Lyotard calls "the ideology of communicational transparency" that goes hand in hand with the commodification of art, knowledge, experience, and so on.[21] (So Theodor Adorno says that "the slick connoisseur who knows art like the inside of his pocket is the worst offender here because he distorts art, turning it into a completely transparent thing, which it is not.")[22] In "My Poetry" David Bromige writes of "the profound vocation of the work of art in a commodity society: not to be a commodity, not to be consumed."[23] This theme is sounded obsessively among the language poets—for example, in Charles Bernstein's "Three or Four Things I Know about Him" and Ron Silliman's "Disappearance of the Word, Appearance of the World."[24] Poetry contests the ideology of transparency, that is, it contests (under various names) an Aristotelian poetics that would assimilate poetry to the idea that language is reducible to its functions of mediation. As Bernstein says in his ars poetica "Artifice of Absorption,"

> The *thickness*
> of words ensures that whatever
> of their physicality is erased, or engulfed, in
> the process of semantic projection,
> a residue
> tenaciously in-
> heres that will not be sublimated
> away. Writing is not a thin film
> of expendable substitutions that, when reading, falls
> away
> like scales
> to reveal a meaning. The tenacity of
> writing's thickness, like the body's
> flesh, is
> ineradicable, yet mortal.[25]

"Writing," Stanley Cavell says in *The Senses of Walden*, "must assume the conditions of language as such; re-experience, as it were, the fact that there is such a thing as language at all and assume responsibility for it—find a way to acknowledge it."[26] What is it to take responsibility for language, that is, not just for the meaning of one's words but for the whole of them? If we imagine the materiality of language as a kind of flesh, then perhaps we can begin to understand the complexity of the claim to which the language poets are responding.

In "The Chinese Notebook" Ron Silliman says that "there is no useful distinction between language and poetry."[27] So how do we tell that a thing is a poem? We should imagine Silliman turning this question back at us: What makes us ask?

Silliman's idea is that the question expresses nothing so much as a consumer's anxiety. We can imagine him saying that our relation to a poem isn't one of knowing (for sure) that it is one. We might know, of course, or we might not, but what sort of knowledge are we talking about, and what sort of person has such knowledge? Knowledge or ignorance of this sort seems to presuppose a certain kind of culture, an aesthetic culture or a culture of connoisseurship (compare Hugh Kenner on Andy Warhol and other counterfeiters)—call it a culture of experts charged with monitoring the art world to make sure that nothing gets passed off on the buying public.[28] What could be worse than a fake poem? But what would a fake poem look like? Implicit here is a concept of authenticity, but in what sort of world does this concept have application? For Silliman, language poetry throws its weight against the application of such concepts. And so he and his colleagues write (as Williams wrote) in such a way so as to situate us at the limits of knowing or, even more radically, outside the site of the knowing subject, outside our concepts, no longer in a position to say that the text at hand is authentic, faithful to criteria.

The result seems very close to what Stanley Cavell had in mind when, in "Music Decomposed" (1965), he made the observation that "the possibility of fraudulence, and the experience of fraudulence, is endemic to the experience of contemporary music. . . . I do not see how anyone who has experienced modern art can have avoided such experiences. . . . [The] dangers of fraudulence, and of trust, are essential to the experience of art. . . . Contemporary music is only the clearest case of something common to modernism as a whole, and modernism only makes explicit and bare what has always been true of art"—and that truth is that our relation with works of art is more like a relation with a person than with an object.[29] We have to have a life with contemporary music in order to experience it as music. What is having a life with a work of art (as if it were a person)?[30] According to Cavell's famous distinction, it is not a relation of cognition, grasping a thing by means of concepts, but one of responsiveness and acknowledgment—a distinction, Cavell's argument goes, that registers "the moral of skepticism": namely, that our relation to the world is not one of knowing it but rather one of inhabiting it.[31]

Imagine poetry withdrawing itself from our aesthetic gaze, not to say from our concepts, concealing itself in the obviousness rather than in the uniqueness, strangeness, or difference of its language. Language poetry teaches us that poetry is not an object for us. It is poetry that alters—displaces—the traditional site from which we approach it. It is not so much language that is recontextualized within the history of poetry (although Danto's analysis of transfiguration holds for language poetry as for Duchamp's urinal). It is rather that we as connoisseurs of poetry are recontextualized outside the world of aesthetic differentiation.

Many years ago the French philosopher Emmanuel Levinas remarked that, "paradoxical as it may seem, painting is a struggle with sight. Sight seeks to draw out of the light beings integrated into a whole. To look is to be able to describe curves, to sketch out wholes in which the elements can be integrated, horizons in which the particular comes to appear by abdicating its particularity. In contemporary painting things no longer count as elements of a universal order which the look would give itself, as a perspective. On all sides fissures appear in the continuity of the universe. The particular stands out in the nakedness of its being."[32] This thought sheds light on what language poets seem to be trying to find a place for in their work, namely, that which ordinarily gets excluded from poetry within the domain of aesthetic differentiation: call it the obviousness of language, or what we are poetically deaf to. In his *Philosophical Investigations* Wittgenstein writes that "the aspects of things that are most important for us are hidden because of their simplicity. One is unable to notice something—because it is always before one's eyes."[33] One might take this as the motto of language poetry, which is not so much a poetry of sight as a poetry of recognition, of listening and responding.

This comes out in an important essay, or talk, by Ron Silliman called "The New Sentence" (1979), which is in part about our inability to say what a sentence is or to take any interest in it—or even to notice it. Silliman assembles a dossier of quotations in which experts from Saussure to Quine say that the sentence is external to language and so should be excluded from linguistics, literary criticism, and philosophy of language, where the sentence is always somehow less than the sum of its parts (is, e.g., not the same as a proposition, whose meaning is analyzable exactly into the meaning of each of its constitutive terms).[34] This suggests some common ground between poetry and the sentence (both inhabit the region of exiles). It is true that French structuralists such as Emile Benveniste and Roland Barthes showed some interest in the sentence, which they took to be a unit of integration whose integration into units higher still suggested the possibility of a linguistics of the text. In such a linguistics, however, the sentence remains a poor relation, occupying an empty space. In a similar way the sentence is external to the poststructuralist condominium—there is no such thing as a sentence when it comes to the textuality of the text, where there is only traversal and slippage. The sentence is simply the path of linearity that textuality disrupts. The sentence is indistinguishable from the fragment.

Now language poetry is, in so many of its versions, a poetry of sentences. Not of words or lines or texts but of sentences, as in Barrett Watten's "Complete Thought" (1982)—consult your first-grade grammar: What does a sentence express?

XIII
Connected pieces break into name.
Petrified trees are similar.

XIV
Everyday life retards potential.
Calculation governs speech.

XV
Rules stand out as illustrations.
People climb over piles of rock.

XVI
I am speaking in an abridged form.
Ordinary voices speak in rooms.

. . . .

XXXVIII
A straight road is unconvincing.
Not to kill the hero is a crime.

. . . .

XLIV
Candles stand up to icons.
Science gives feature to the world. [35]

Here is an excerpt from Lyn Hejinian's "My Life" (1980):

The coffee drinkers   The traffic drones, where drones is a
answered   noun. Whereas the cheerful pessimist
ecstatically   suits himself in a bad world, which is
    however the inevitable world, impossible of improvement. I close one
eye, always the left, when looking out into the glare of the street. What
education finally serves us, if at all. There is a pause, a rose, something on
paper. The small green shadows made the red jump out. Such displacements
alter illusions, which is all-to-the-good. Now cars not cows on the brown
hills, and a stasis of mobile homes have taken their names from what grew
in the valleys near Santa Clara. We have all grown up with it. If it is personal,
it is most likely fickle. The university was the cultural market but on Sundays
she tried out different churches. [36]

Is it poetry? It is, at all events, indistinguishable from prose—a feature or
condition that is basic to the Williams tradition, as Stephen Fredman explains
in *Poet's Prose*. Fredman's book is indispensable here because it studies the crucial
difference between "poet's prose" and prose that is poetic or arty: poet's prose is not

prose poetry. It may be indistinguishable from bad prose. It may even get boring at times. (Silliman writes in "The Chinese Notebook": "If this bores you, leave.")[37] The point is to keep the sentence from disappearing, from getting excluded from poetry, and if this means extending the concept of the poetic so that nothing is excluded from it, well, *that* is what the "poetics" of the Williams tradition had been trying for from the start.[38]

Silliman explains that what is new about "the new sentence" is the way it resists totalization. It is *not* a unit of integration but resists our desire for paragraphs that are organized logically into so many conceptual orders or woven into fabrics of belief. "The sentences are all sentences," he says, "the syntax of each resolves up to the level of the sentence." But there is always a twist somewhere (Silliman calls it "torquing") that shifts the movement of the sentence away from totalities of one kind or another toward the singularity of the sentence itself. There are endless ways of "torquing," many quite simple—as simple as joking—as in the following from Bob Perelman's *a.k.a.*:

I was left holding the bag. I peered into it.[39]

This illustrates nicely the idea that there is no useful distinction to be made between language and poetry. Language itself is the poem.

Of course, Mallarmé thought no less. But among contemporary language poets, language means ordinary language, whereas for Mallarmé it meant something quasi-transcendental: language as radically outside, not just purified of everyday use but outside all subjectivity and objectivity, outside culture and its discourses. Silliman, however, says that torquing "endows works of the new sentence with a much greater capacity to incorporate ordinary sentences of the material world."[40] So David Bromige, as if in a tribute to Williams, borrows from a Sonoma newspaper to write "One Spring." Elsewhere, as in the line from *a.k.a.* just quoted, poetry remains at the level of the idiomatic expression. Silliman's own poetry is notoriously made of the locutions belonging to his everyday environment, and the point to mark is that the language is not external to the environment, not "about" it, but is internal to the stuff of everyday life:

I run into Watten in a lumber yard. When you get near the bottom the newspaper droops. The dog is happy rolling in the dirt. I am rapidly running out of lines. Small stainglass frog hands in the window. Meat by-products. Education designs the brain. Education redesigns the brain. Dry petfood is cereal. Ibid. A man tunelessly whistles, lugging garbage down three flights of backstairs. Jars, cans & spray-bottles sit in a kitchen window. I slap my hands clean. What you determine from the sound of unseen traffic is the general size of vehicle. Old broomsticks rotting on porch. Think of stitching as a mode of margin. Children scavenging crushed cans as a scout project. One million pennies from the National Endowment. Chickenwire on the fencetop to prevent entry.[41]

There is, one can see, something vaguely naturalistic about this poetry. It is documentary writing of a sort, but what it documents is the language of the everyday, that is, the language that *goes with* the everyday, where "[d]ry petfood is cereal." "A man tunelessly whistles, lugging garbage down three flights of back-stairs": whistle while you work, say the Seven Dwarfs. "I slap my hands clean." And of course that's exactly what one does, and exactly what one would say, as if slapping one's hands clean were an idiomatic gesture or, say, a piece of everyday practice that only the idiom can register. So the whole of the everyday is, in effect, drawn into the poem. Our contemporary form of life, in all of its gritty, commercial debris, is internal to the poem's horizon.

2. The Proximity of Poetry

Earlier I cited Danto's thesis that the difference between a work of art and a real thing from which it is indiscernible "is a certain theory of art. It is the theory that takes it up into the world of art, and keeps it from collapsing into the real object which it is. . . . Of course, without the theory, one is unlikely to see it as art, and in order to see it as part of the artworld, one must have mastered a good deal of artistic theory as well as a considerable amount of the history of recent New York painting." In "Aesthetic Problems of Modern Philosophy" (1965), Stanley Cavell takes up the question of atonal music, whose strangeness appears to extend the concept of music beyond anything known or knowable as music. What counts as music when there are rival and seemingly incompatible claims to being the thing itself? How does one settle such a question? Appealing to formal criteria is of no help, because criteria are already internal to the world (or worlds) which the rival musics presuppose. What Danto calls an "artworld," Cavell calls "a form of life," as in "To imagine a language is to imagine a form of life" (*PI*, §19). Between an artworld and a form of life there might be this difference, that our relation to a form of life is not theoretical:

The language of tonality is part of a particular form of life, one containing the music we are most familiar with; associated with, or consisting of, particular ways of being trained to perform and to listen to it; involving particular ways of being corrected, particular ways of responding to mistakes, to nuance, above all to recurrence and to variation and modification. No wonder we

want to preserve the idea of tonality: to give all *that* up seems like giving up
the idea of music altogether. I think it *is*—*like* it.

I shall not try to say why it is not fully that. I shall only mention that it
cannot be enough to point to the obvious fact that musical instruments, with
their familiar or unfamiliar powers, are employed—because *that* fact does not
prevent us from asking: But is it music? Nor enough to appeal to the fact that
we can point to pitches, intervals, lines and rhythm—because we probably
do not for the most part know what we are pointing to with these terms.
I mean we do not know *which* lines are significant . . . and which intervals
to hear as organizing. More important, I think, is the fact that we may see
an undoubted musician speak about such things and behave toward them in
ways similar (not, I think, more than similar) to the ways he behaves toward
Beethoven, and then we may sense that, though similar, it is a new world
and that to understand a new world it is imperative to concentrate upon its
inhabitants. (*MW,* 84)

The problem is, hermeneutically, the same as the anthropological one of
trying to understand an alien culture: Within the writing of poetry, as within the
composition of music, there are multiple and heterogeneous forms of life among
which agreement as to what counts as poetry or music or art cannot occur, that
is, they are not reducible to one another or to some common ground or set of
criteria; no translation manual will give us access to the thing itself. There is no
overarching theory; rather, theory is internal to local times and places.

This is as much as to say that there is no essence of poetry or of music or
art, only local, contingent, heterogeneous practices of writing and composition
distributed horizontally across the anarchic plane of "anything goes" rather than
vertically in a canonical order of classical models that one learns to imitate (in order
perhaps to supersede). Or, in other words, our relation to poetry or music is not
determined by the legislation of our concepts; rather, it is one of acknowledgment
or recognition that comes from living with the thing, belonging to its world or,
say, to its histories. As Cavell says, our counting the new music as music, our
accommodating it, amounts to "naturalizing ourselves to a new form of life, a new
world" (*MW,* 84). So the question of what counts as poetry that Antin and the
language poets raise resolves itself into the question of what sort of migration
we are being urged to undertake. What sort of conversion or transformation of
ourselves are we facing? It is as if the main question as to what counts as art were
not "What must one know?" but "How must one live?"[42]

The beginning of an answer to this question might be that what seems to characterize language poetry is that its poets reject, or at all events seem to interpret
in marvelously ironic and satiric ways, the aesthetic principle of the ontological
peculiarity of the work of art, or the idea, formulated flawlessly by Danto, that the

work of art is necessarily, logically, external to the world. Doubtless Danto could find an argument that language poetry is still (in his sense) external to reality, but it is part of the uncanny realism of the language poets that they take such pains to situate their writing within the horizon of the ordinary, where things are not set aside as art. Thus the language of the language poets is internal to the situations in which it is learned; its projections are always, in Cavell's sense of the word, "natural" (not transfigurations of the commonplace but acknowledgments of it).[43]

Another way to put this would be to say that the materiality of the language of language poetry is not a product of art, as it is in the case of Mallarmé or Joyce's *Finnegans Wake*, or indeed as in the case of most poetry from almost any tradition, where writing consists in doing something to the language to set it apart from the everyday; rather, as per Williams's *Paterson*, for example, language registers the materiality of everydayness itself.[44] Only we shouldn't be misled by this "itself": Everydayness is an open-ended category (or, in other words, not so much a category as a direction). As Marjorie Perloff suggests in her essay "Poetry and the Common Life" (1984), the common life is not a common denominator—not something to work down to: not a foundation and a norm.[45] Her essay is in part a reply to the poet Louis Simpson, who seems to want to think of the common life as foundational, like Wordsworth's "real language of men." The common life, Simpson thinks, is what poets like John Ashbery ignore (he forgets that Ashbery has a terrific poem about Daffy Duck). Perloff quotes Simpson's "26th Precinct Station," where the common life turns out to be a product of naturalism (a distinctively European aesthetic):

> One night Jake telephoned
> to say, "Mike has stabbed Lorna."
> He wanted me to call his lawyer . . .
> couldn't do it himself, he was tied up.
> I called the lawyer, who had just come in
> from seeing *Kismet*. We shared a taxi.
> All the way down to the station
> he kept humming "And This Is My Beloved."
> Lorna recovered, and wrote a novel.
> Mike married and went to live in Rome.
> Jake Harmon died. But I remember
> the 26th Precinct Station.
> A black woman in yellow wig,
> a purple skirt, and stiletto heels;
> a pickpocket; a cripple
> arrested for indecent exposure.
> The naked light bulb; the crack in the wall

that loops like the Mississippi at Vicksburg;
the shadow of the cockroach
under the baseboard, lurking, gathering his nerve.[46]

Here the common life seems sketched, as by a naturalist, that is, by a purely ascertaining observer, a maker of documents; whereas in the Williams tradition the common life is inhabited, not described. Perloff suggests roughly this sort of distinction when she opposes to Simpson's poem some poems by that unforgettable old beatnik Kenneth Rexroth. Here is Rexroth's "The Signatures of All Things" (1950):

When I dragged the rotten log
From the Bottom of the pool,
It seemed heavy as stone.
I let it lie in the sun
For a month; and then chopped it
Into sections, and split them
For kindling, and spread them out
To dry some more. Late that night,
After reading for hours,
While moths rattled at the lamp—
The saints and philosophers
On the destiny of man—
I walked out on my cabin porch,
And looked up through the black forest,
At the Swaying islands of stars.
Suddenly I saw at my feet,
Spread on the floor of night, ingots
Of quivering phosphorescence,
And all about were scattered chips
Of pale cold light that was alive.[47]

The title of Rexroth's poem is borrowed from Stephen Dedalus ("Signatures of all things that I am here to read"), but his poem is a constant allusion to Thoreau's *Walden*, and it inscribes Cavell's moral (in *The Senses of Walden*) that our relation to the common, the mean, and the low is not one of observing, as with a Joycean "scrupulous meanness." So poetry is, in this context, not incompatible with a sort of realism—not, to be sure, realism as an alternative to nominalism: not philosophical realism or realism as an aesthetics of correspondence or as a claim about art's cognitive power over empirical reality, but rather realism in the sense of not being sealed off from one's environment (think of a realist as one who has been exposed to reality; or think of realism in Cavell's sense of "taking an interest in one's experience"). [48]

Realism from the site of habitation, not observation and description.

Thinking of Cavell, one is inclined to quote the following, from a poem by Gerald Burns, whose name is not misspelled (although mine frequently is). The poem is called "Letters to Obscure Men" (1975):

> The quality of forties light
> in B detective films
> always coming through venetian blinds
> the extra care with which they photographed
> telephones as if they mattered
> whether they rang or not
> may be due, I thought, to German light men
> growing up in small towns with gas lamps
> and I've thought when Poe was on
> the Broadway Journal shadows
> must have been interesting in New York
> but now I think that watching forties films
> is not like watching fifties films
> because we now ignore
> the surface noise coming off the sound track
> when nothing audible is on the screen
> whereas when I was growing up
> I loved to hear that sound
> because it told me if you listen hard
> the sound duration makes is audible
> as we all watched the telephone
> and heard it not ring. [49]

A poem about listening! But as if with Thoreau's, or John Cage's, or even Heidegger's ear: the sort of ear that language poetry calls for, as in Michael Davidson's "After the Dancers," from *The Prose of Fact* (1981):

> He had a hearing fault,
> a near ache
> is that what you said?
> he lost his left foot
> they walked on the right side
> the good one
> they had a run through

or didn't, it didn't matter
one of their sides was missing
but present in the wings,
he heard them breathing
as a kind of wall
like light bulbs
always necessary
when they turned them on
it didn't matter
but made a small clicking sound
like an ear clearing[50]

Imagine being connected to the world by way of the ear rather than as purely ascertaining observers. This was Heidegger's idea, namely, that we are in the world not as spectators but as belonging (*gehören*), where "belonging" is also the word for "listening"—"We have heard [*gehört*] when we belong to [*gehört*] what is said," says Heidegger.[51] Moreover, listening is how Heidegger characterizes thinking, that is, at the end of philosophy the task of thinking can no longer be adequately conceived as conceptual representation or calculative reasoning, nor even as questioning, but as openness and responsiveness—an idea that Cavell picks up on when he links together Heidegger and Emerson: "the idea of thinking as reception . . . seems to me a sound intuition, specifically to forward the answer to skepticism [which Emerson meant it to do]. The answer does not consist in denying the conclusion of skepticism but in reconceiving its truth. It is true that we do not know the existence of the world with certainty; our relation to its existence is deeper—one in which it is accepted, that is, received. My favorite way of putting this is to say that existence is to be acknowledged" (*SW,* 133).

The difference between Heidegger and Emerson (and Cavell) is that there are hardly any people in Heidegger's world. Heidegger sides with Heraclitus in saying, "You never hear properly so long as your ears hang upon the sound and flow of a human voice in order to snatch up for yourselves a manner of speaking. Heraclitus [rejects] hearing as nothing but the passion of ears."[52] By contrast, in the tradition Cavell is trying to recover for American philosophy, listening, reception, and acknowledgment are social, political, and ethical concepts. The ear connects us up with a world of other people. This seems to be the connection that is registered in language poetry, which is distinctive not so much for its voice as for its ear. But the poet's ear does not simply listen empirically in order to reproduce the world's sounds in the sounds of language (onomatopoeia). Rather, the idea seems to be that whereas the speaking subject moves consecutively along syntactic lines, the listening subject is, like Tristram Shandy, nonlinear, open to distraction, indeed in a constant state of interruption, because a world organized according to listening is a world of simultaneous events that, unless one is ready to exclude most of what happens, one is bound to sort out into lists rather than into narratives and propositions, as in Ron Silliman's *What*:

> Over breakfast, three sisters
> speak at once. Sound truck
> on Fifth Ave is unintelligible
> in midday traffic, tho signs read
> Stop Union Busting Now.
> I hear finches sing
> in the magnolia while a blackbird
> runs in the grass, dotted
> with the white flower of clover.
> An old man comes down
> the stairs slowly,
> putting one foot onto the next step,
> then the other, both hands
> on the railing. It's fathers flirt
> with their infant daughters,
> that's where that's learned.
> Let's rake puns.
> Big robin light on the branch and stares.
> Cars pass. I sit
> on an old porch swing,
> held by chains
> which are thoroughly rusted[53]

In his "Artifice of Absorption" Charles Bernstein lays down what seems to me a poetics of the ear (just to call it that) when he says that

> In my poems,
> I frequently use opaque & nonabsorbable
> elements, digressions &
> interruptions, as part of a technological
> arsenal to create a more powerful
> ("souped up")
> absorption. . . .[54]

Absorption is how the ear works, as against the selective eye that can focus things in and out of its world or simply close itself off. Eye contact is something one has to learn, whereas the ear is exposed to perpetual interference. A mote in the eye obliterates everything, but what sticks in the ear is something one cannot get out of one's head. Speaking several languages at once means speaking with the ear, as in the pun, a species of nonexclusionary discourse.

At all events, a running theme in language poetry is that our relation to language is not by way of linguistic competence or the propositional attitude or as expressive agents. So writes the Canadian poet Steve McCaffery:

> It is sound more so than meaning binds
> the body to language[55]

The ear registers the excessiveness of language, or what McCaffery calls "the elsewhere of meaning," namely, that which otherwise gets excluded by the operations of deep structure—grammar, syntax, but also logic, rhetoric, and poetics, which are artifices of elimination that work to bring discourse under control.[56] Whereas language poetry, as Cavell says of Emerson's writing, is "the exercise not of power but of reception" (SW, 135).

Naturally poetry that is porous and receptive with respect to its environment is likely to pose special problems of reading; that is, how one responds to such poetry will depend in large part on how one stands with respect to its social and cultural environment. On this point readers seem to fall roughly into two groups. Thus, in his essay "Postmodernism, or the Logic of Late Capitalism," Fredric Jameson hears in the language poets the schizophrenic logic of an over-flushed capitalist nation-state. Likewise the poet Eliot Weinberger, reviewing Ron Silliman's anthology of language poets, In the American Tree, hears a narrow self-obsessed nationalism indifferent to European or multicultural aesthetics ("it is rare in the extensive critical writings of the 'language' poets to encounter any reference to foreign poetry outside of Russian futurism").[57] Not surprisingly, readers of language poetry frequently register the cultural shock that occurs whenever cosmopolitanism confronts the peculiar temporality, the randomness or fragmentation, of American culture, particularly the way this culture is foregrounded in California (an obviously mad place, an anti-Republic from which it is impossible to exclude anything: Los Angeles is what Plato must have foreseen, to his horror, in the Athenian refusal of metaphysics). California has always inspired apocalyptic arm waving, as in Adorno's and Horkheimer's famous polemic against the "culture industry" ("the idolization of the cheap involves making the average heroic"), which is a nice tract to read before taking up Cavell's Pursuits of Happiness. Whereas Horkheimer and Adorno link Hollywood with Hitler's Germany, Cavell links it with philosophy, or at least philosophy of a certain Emersonian sort. Here purely ascertaining observation is put aside in favor of "taking an interest in one's experience," meaning also one's everyday (as against once-in-a-lifetime) cultural inheritance; for example, Cavell does not hesitate to link up Frank Capra with

Immanuel Kant as a way of introducing a discussion of the transgression of limits in *It Happened One Night.*[58] Cavell is here coherent with the Williams tradition, with its self-conscious refusal of cosmopolitanism—a refusal that situates Williams alongside Cavell's Emerson ("I embrace the common, I explore and sit at the feet of the familiar, the low. Give me insight into today, and you may have the antique and future worlds. What would we really know the meaning of? The meal in the firkin; the milk in the pan; the ballad in the street; the news of the boat . . .").[59] Compare the prologue to "Kora in Hell," with its idea of a museum of everyday paintings—

> I wish Arensberg had my opportunity for prying into jaded households where the paintings of Mama's and Papa's flowertime still hang on the walls. I propose that Arensberg be commissioned by the Independent Artists to scour the country for the abortive paintings of those men and women who without master or method have evolved perhaps two or three unusual creations in their early years. . . . Carefully selected, these queer products might be housed to good effect in some unpretentious exhibition chamber across the city from the Metropolitan Museum of Art.[60]

Williams suggests that that which gets excluded from the canon of authentic productions itself could constitute a canon of inauthentic productions, and so on without end, with every event inspiring not a consequence but an alternative definition of what counts as art.

When Cavell asks, in *The Senses of Walden,* "Why has America never expressed itself philosophically?" (*SW,* 33), this might sound, to the global ear, like your basic hundred-dollar-a-plate jingoism, but in fact the question is an acknowledgment of historicalness, like Emerson's "Self-Reliance," which sounds like an isolationist tract ("the wise man stays at home") but which is in fact about America's difference from European culture, its discontinuity within the history of the West, its refractoriness and uncontainability not just with respect to English or Continental categories but with respect to categorical operations as such, or, in other words, its failure to be one thing and whole. American difference from European culture has always been a foundational theme in American literature and criticism, which is inclined to figure this culture horizontally as an anarchic distribution of communities and cultural centers rather than as a capitalist entity or European-like nation-state controlled from the top down. Gordana P. Crnković makes the interesting argument that for Eastern Europeans America has always been imagined as a utopia constructed anarchically as a horizontal series, in contrast to the Eastern European experience of a unitary, vertical culture in which questions of what counts as poetry or music are settled from instituted power centers.[61] If this Eastern European picture is, arguably, *merely* utopian, it is nevertheless symmetrical with the utopia projected by American poetry itself.

This is the upshot of Stephen Fredman's argument in *The Grounding of American Poetry: Charles Olson and the Emersonian Tradition*. For American poets, "ground" has always meant a surface to be traversed rather than a position to be occupied or a foundation on which vertical structures (churches, states, universities) are to be raised.[62] Hence the enormous premium, mounting to an obsession, in American poetry and criticism (as in Williams's *Paterson*, or Charles Olson's Gloucester poems) on the "sense of place," where place is an open-ended list from which nothing can ever be excluded: beach town and border town, mountains and desert, middle border and high plains, tidewater and backwater, sun belt and rust belt, main streets and mean streets, loops and beltways, Chinatowns and barrios and neighborhoods in various stages of cultural transfer—but also Mexico, Vancouver, not to mention the endless places of American exile. Walt Whitman taught us to make poetry out of lists of places, on the principle that the list is our only recourse in a world where space is more surface than container, where master narratives and deep structures have no application—a world that resists the analytic frame of mind, as if made for traveling rather than penetrating—

Under the bluffs of Oroville, blue cloud September skies, entering U.S. border, red red apples bend their tree boughs propt with sticks—
    At Omak a fat girl in dungarees leads her big brown horse by the asphalt highway.
    Thru lodgepole pine hills Coleville near Moses' Mountain—a white horse standing back of a 2 ton truck moving forward between two trees.
    At Nespelem, in the yellow sun, a marker for Chief Joseph's grave under rilled brown hills—white cross over highway.
    At Grand Coulee under leaden sky, giant red generators humm thru granite & concrete to materialize onions—
    And grey water laps against the grey sides of Steamboat Mesa.
    At Dry Falls 40 Niagras stand silent & invisible, tiny horses graze on the rusty canyon's mesquite floor.
    At Mesa, on the car radio passing a new corn silo, Walking Boogie teenager's tender throats, "I wish they could all be California girls"—as black highway curls outward.[63]

—which is to say that how one reads a list like this depends on how one is situated, or how one moves. The cosmopolitan intellectual who writes essays like "Disneyland: A Degenerate Utopia" identifies one familiar site.[64] For the Jamesian expatriate, who is still something of a cultural norm for the American intellectual, each item on this list represents a closed or isolated world where writing becomes the natural language of exile.[65] My favorite version of this is Willa Cather's theory of Nebraska, whose hostile plains destroy the sensitive artist in a twinkling (*My Antonia*). For the Emersonian, by contrast, each place is an invitation to its own separateness and whimsy, and the question is whether it is an invitation one can bear to accept.

It is against this (problematic) cultural background that Cavell, in *The Senses of Walden*, writes:

> Study of *Walden* would perhaps not have become such an obsession with me had it not presented itself as a response to questions with which I was already obsessed: why has America never expressed itself philosophically? Or has it—in the metaphysical riot of its greatest literature? Has the impulse to philosophical speculation been absorbed, or exhausted, by speculation in territory, as in such thoughts as Manifest Destiny? Or are such questions not really intelligible? They are, at any rate, disturbingly like the questions that were asked about American literature before it established itself. In rereading *Walden*, twenty years after first reading it, I seemed to find a book of sufficient intellectual scope and consistency to have established or inspired a tradition of thinking. One reason it did not is that American culture has never really believed in its capacity to produce anything of permanent value—except itself. So it forever overpraises and undervalues its achievements. (*SW,* 32–33)

One of Cavell's own ways of interpreting this is to say that what Americans share is not a common culture; that is, "nothing of high culture is common to us," meaning that, among other things, "no text is sacred," no law is law of the land, no criteria are settled, the term "canonical" has no special application, as if American culture, whether philosophical, literary, utopian, or popular, were underived, without ground (without why), existing only in its versions, each of which would have to be studied, well, anthropologically.[66] The charge to look and see compels us to attach ourselves to the individual case, that is, it takes us out of the holistic attitude in which we deal with ideologies and conceptual schemes and forces us to consider things in their irreducible singularity, as one damn thing or place after another in no coherent order, where our task is not so much to represent and construe as to be open and receptive in the Cavellian (also Heideggerian) sense of "thinking as the receiving or letting be of something, as opposed to the positing or putting together of something" (*SW,* 152).

In "Thinking of Emerson" Cavell says that "Emerson's and Thoreau's relation to poetry is inherently their interest in their own writing. . . . I do not mean their interest in what we may call their poems, but their interest in the fact that what they are building is writing, as it realizes itself daily under their hands, sentence by shunning sentence, the accomplishment of inhabitation, the making of it happen, the poetry of it. Their prose is a battle, using a remark of Nietzsche's, not to become poetry [presumably poetry with a capital P]; a battle specifically to remain in conversation with itself, answerable to itself" (SW, 134). A decently trained American scholar would have no trouble translating this into Charles Olson's line of thinking about composition in the open, or composition by field as against linear or period composition, where one abandons the closed forms of literary tradition, sometimes called "closed Eurocentric forms," that do your speaking for you, and risks instead "a whole series of new recognitions" that refuse the legislation of our concepts and so might look like anything but poetry. As Olson says: "from the moment [the writer] ventures into FIELD COMPOSITION—puts himself in the open—he can go by no track other than the one the poem under hand declares, for itself."[67] No saying what happens next. "Whatever gets written," says Charles Bernstein, "gets written in a particular shape, uses a particular vocabulary & syntax, & a variety of chosen techniques. . . . Sometimes this process takes place intuitively or unconsciously (the pull of influence comes in here since somewhere in the back of your mind are models for what looks natural, personal, magical, mystical, spontaneous, automatic, dream-like, confessional, didactic, shocking). Sometimes it is a very conscious process. Anyway, you're responsible for what turns up."[68] "The accomplishment of inhabitation"—suppose we gloss this happy phrase as follows, partly summarizing Cavell: Skepticism says you can't tell the difference between poetry and talk, poetry and language, poetry and prose, good poetry and bad, art and nonart, art and reality, or (indeed) poetry and philosophy. Your criteria are without foundation; they float and drift across multiple horizons (the frontier in America is not a boundary but an opening). Whatever claim you make on behalf of whatever text (or canon) cannot be supported by an appeal to criteria. A poem can be made of anything.

To which Cavell might be imagined to respond: What you say is not to be refuted. A poem can be made of anything (translated into philosophy, this means that the extension of the concept of poetry cannot be closed by a frontier)—only it does not follow therefore that anything goes, or that everything collapses into aporia. If we cannot distinguish between poetry and talk, poetry and prose, poetry and philosophy, this does not mean that they are indiscriminate or identical. What you say about criteria is true: They float and drift and fail to settle things once and for all, but all this means is that they do not decide for us independently of where we stand or where our history places us. The idea that not everything is possible at any time is simply a reminder that I am always situated, always historical, always the inheritor of certain parameters of poetry writing or the making of artworlds. These parameters are my responsibility, and I express this responsibility by drawing them, these parameters, perhaps in defiance of the fear of exclusion or the threat that others, seeing me draw (or write), will say that I have merely transgressed them to no purpose, that what I have done is not poetry or art. But my writing is not (before everything) answerable to them, and so I might have to give up the name of poet (capital *P*) in order to write what I do, much the way David Antin gives it up when he says that if Robert Lowell is what a poet is, then he (Antin) is not a poet.[69] Cavell likes to quote Emerson's "Self-Reliance" to this effect: "I would write on the lintels of my door-post, *Whim*" (*SW*, 137).

So, to bring the point home, we may imagine poetry writing by analogy with walking. In *Conditions Handsome and Unhandsome* Cavell writes:

> Suppose one day I start sliding my feet one after another rather than lifting them (lots of people more or less do that now), or start skipping or hopping or goose-stepping or whirling once around on the toes of each foot in succession. If you question me about this perhaps I answer: "I've always meant to do this, you just did not know," or, "I didn't know what moving along the ground could be until now, the inclination is powerful and the results are wonderful." But suppose I answer: "I don't know what has come over me, I don't want this, the inclination is not mine, it mortifies me." Or just: "I'm doing the same as I've always done, the same as you do, making measured moves in a given direction under my own steam. I am not moving faster than walking, we are comfortably keeping up with one another—not like our acquaintance far back there who takes a step once a minute and calls that walking." Wittgenstein's comment seems in place here: "It would now be no use to say: 'But can't you see . . . ?'—and repeat the old examples and explanations" (§185). That is, I surely know everything about walking that you do. What you respond to as deviant behavior in me is a threat to me; what I do smacks a little of insanity and I will soon be kept, at least, out of most public places. You might put tremendous pressure on me to conform—do you think I do not know intolerance? I know very well the normativeness of the way things are done—and not just in this society (as though the normativeness were merely something justified by custom or morality); I know of no society that enjoys, or deplores the fact that it engages in, walking as I do, though I might explore for one.[70]

Compare Robert Creeley's "Was That a Real Poem or Did You Just Make That Up Yourself?"[71] No explanation, no theory, can account for the way one walks, which means that in walking we always risk ourselves, expose ourselves, for example, to stares or ridicule or even arrest—picture the race-walking style at the Easter parade.

> God help him then
> if such things can.

That risk
is all there is.[72]

"I know of no society that enjoys, or deplores the fact that it engages in,
walking [writing poetry] as I do, although I might explore for one." My thought is
that the language poets give us a sense of what this might mean. In "Canons and
Institutions: New Hope for the Disappeared," Ron Silliman takes up the problem
of poets who disappear "from the public discourse and consciousness of poetry"—
really the ancient or once and future problem of the unacknowledged poet. What
counts as acknowledgment? The question of poetry finally comes down to this.
Silliman attacks the edifice of a vertical culture—that is, the idea is that there is, or
has been at least since the 1950s, a "process of public canonization" that is tied to
the university study of literature and is therefore in the control of people like Helen
Vendler, whose *Harvard Book of Contemporary Poets* has become oddly expressive of
the poets it notoriously excludes—Charles Olson and Robert Duncan, for example, whom Silliman identifies as "outsider poets" who "perceived their own poetry
as part of a larger project of constructing a new public canon, not necessarily more
heterodox than that which they confronted [e.g., the old Oscar Williams *Little
Treasury of American Poetry* widely used in the 1950s], but rather utterly different and
extending well beyond the borders of poetry, the ultimate purpose of which was
to have served as the foundation for a new paradigm of knowledge and agency in
social life itself."[73] The important point is that "a new poetic canon, an alternative
tradition," is not reducible to a new style or a set of recognizable formal features
that enable us to tell (just by looking) that what we are looking at is a poem as
such or a poem of a certain species; rather, it comes down to the construction
of a (local) poetic culture, a social grouping of poets who not only write but
also read or listen to and study one another and, as in the case of the language
poets, publish one another's work—and who provide, in their exchanges with one
another, a discursive background against which their poems can be understood. So
the poem is no longer a commodity that can be shipped anywhere but is internal
to a collective or social achievement of habitation. Silliman's argument is that it is
not enough for "outsider poets" to produce alternative anthologies (like Silliman's
own *In the American Tree*) to counter those anthologies that carry the imprimaturs
of university presses and large commercial publishing houses. There are plenty of
anthologies. Likewise, the point is not to win for the language poets recognition
from critics like Vendler. To be sure, for Silliman the problem of the unrecognized
poet is institutional. He takes it as analogous to the problem of radical or opposi-
tional politics with respect to the Democratic Party—how to get the institution to
acknowledge what is external to the legislation of its concepts. But as Silliman well
knows, universities cannot be a substitute, and only rarely can they be an occasion,
for poetic communities (San Francisco, Black Mountain, New York, Iowa City) in

which the question of what counts as poetry can be addressed in a nontrivial way, namely, as Adorno might say, as a type of utopian social practice.

But then there will always be superb poets whose lack of recognition derives from a kind of antique or Jamesian restlessness, the exiles, wanderers, misfits, whose audiences require a long time to form themselves, and perhaps never do, there being almost too much to know: for example, John Matthias, an American poet who, although formally very much in the tradition of open form that gives us language poetry—

> E. has written to me once a year for eight years straight. This year it's about my poems. And his. His muse grows younger (he is over sixty-five) as mine begins to age. My attraction to quotation, commentary, pastiche: exhaustion? or the very method of abstention [from solitary singing?] that he recommends. Many days I'd be a scribe, a monk—and I, like monk and scribe, am permitted to append the meanings that my authors may have missed. "He abandoned himself to the absolute sincerity of pastiche": on Ekelöf, Printz-Pahlson. Otherwise? Poets know too much. We bring things on us. There is always an extra place at the table: the poem, as Ernie says, arranges it. . . .[74]

—nevertheless stands outside all the familiar "poetic communities." No doubt this is due to his having been expropriated (there seems no other word for it) by the British countryside, among other places, whence his sense of place is expressed by a kind of Brownian movement back and forth between Suffolk, England, and Indiana (a movement described in what he calls his "mid-Atlantic poems," the "Stefan Batory Poems," and the "Mihail Lermontov Poems," named after the ships that shuttled him between England and the United States). Matthias's poems are as much the product of the difficulty as of the achievement of habitation, which is perhaps why they are full of itineraries, trails, rivers, turns, crossings, explorers, traders, missionaries, pilgrims, not to mention modern exiles, drifters, refugees, lost friends, fugitives, poets hounded by authorities, and, in general, people violently out of place ("Alexander Kerensky at Stanford"; "Paul Verlaine in Lincolnshire").[75]

It is worth a moment's reflection on how far poetry (American poetry in particular, where the metaphor of the open is foundational) is inspired by a terror of confinement—confinement, not, perhaps, as in Eurocentric theory, within history or the prison houses of language, culture, and ideology, but, quite the contrary, confinement as being sealed off, as in confinement to a self that, Descarteslike, lacks embodiment, or to a place that, say, to the eye of a purely ascertaining observer, is blank, forbidding, uninhabitable, innocent of speech—a condition that forms the subject of Emerson's "Experience," with its reference to "this yet unapproachable America."[76] Whereas the language poets consult their ears, Matthias's difficulty of habitation is mediated by the names, the lore, and the layers of historical narrative and encyclopedic detail that attach to the places he crosses (from the Midwest to East Anglia to Scandinavia to Poland, and back again). So a place is, once more, a surface across which one moves rather than a container of objects; and, again, the surface is traversable only through its language—language in the sense of the words of other people, language aroused by reading and listening, whence the need for quotation, commentary, pastiche: The poem is the reception of this language, hence of the place it embodies. Matthias's collection of three long poems called A Gathering of Ways, for example, is an archaeology of the multilanguaged discourse surrounding the waterways and trails (called "ley lines") used since Neolithic times by travelers in East Anglia, the American Midwest, and Provence. The second of these poems, "Facts from an Apocryphal Midwest," is a pastiche of geography, geology, history, and local legend about American ley lines and rivers, for example, the Old Sauk Trail and the Saint Joseph—Kankakee Portage, and, besides the Kankakee and Illinois, the Saint Joseph River near which Matthias lives but to which, all by himself, or as if (just) in his own voice, he could never belong.

> Never having walked a foot along the banks of the St. Joseph river, I now followed [Francis] Parkman—who must have trudged virtually through my back yard on his visit to the area in 1867—followed La Salle who followed his Indian guide along the portage trail to the Kankakee marsh. With respect to the self, the solution seemed to be this: that I, who had little feeling for the place I would evoke and engage, should embody myself in a figure who had great feeling for it, who in turn embodies himself in the figure who initially explored the place, contended against it, and had perforce to fit his mind to the external world to survive and the external world to his mind to prevail.[77]

This is Matthias's way of reading himself into his own poem, where Parkman is characterized as follows:

> The man who followed him [the explorer La Salle] in many ways was like him, and read his words, and read the words and followed all the trails of others who had passed this way before he did himself, but after him who was the first to come and was the object of his search. Charlevoix he read, and La Hontan. Tonty's own account, and Hennepin's, and all of La Salle's letters both to Canada and France. Transcripts, depositions. He too knew about insatiable ambition, pride and isolation, subduing all to an inflexibility of purpose. When his chronic and mysterious illness made his head swim and his joints swell, made his eyes so sensitive to light he could not read, his nights so sleepless that he could not even dream his shattered double's

thousand mile trek from the lower Illinois back to Montreal, he had his friends read *to* him, tried to comprehend their strange pronunciations of the language of the texts and maps and manuscripts *de la France Septentrionale* which he followed to the Kankakee or Seignelay and then beyond.[78]

The self in this event is no longer the sealed-off punctual ego or purely ascertaining observer who monitors the lifeworld; it is a self embodied in another's words, as if there were no getting into the world—or, in other words, as if there were neither self nor a world for it—except through the mediation of other voices, other people, which is a nice interpretation of the moral of skepticism. And so it no longer makes sense to speak of a separate realm of subjective validity; rather, this validity is now socially mediated as by an open, porous subject given as much to listening as to speaking. The special turn given to this line of thinking by John Matthias is that, like poetry, the self is excessive with respect to its boundaries: Its habitations are on the way.

Notes

1. William Carlos Williams, "Kora in Hell: Improvisations" (1920), in *Imag-inations*, ed. Webster Schott (New York: New Directions, 1970), 70.

2. The term "aesthetics of nondifferentiation" belongs to Hans-Georg Gad-amer, who argues that "the being of art cannot be defined as an object of aesthetic consciousness," that is, one cannot tell whether a thing is art just by looking at it. There are no formal features that set the work of art apart from nonaesthetic objects; the work is not external to the world that it represents. A good deal of contemporary North American poetry and poetics can be read as, in effect, the working out of Gadamer's critique of aesthetics: "The work of art cannot simply be isolated from the 'contingency' of the chance conditions in which it appears, and where this isolation occurs, the result is an abstraction that reduces the actual being of the work. It itself belongs to the world to which it represents itself" (Hans-Georg Gadamer, *Wahrheit und Methode* [Tübingen: J. C. B. Mohr, 1975], 111; *Truth and Method*, 2d rev. ed., trans. Joel Weinsheimer and Donald G. Marshall [New York: Crossroad, 1989], 116–17). As Gadamer remarks in passing, his analysis leaves open the question of what counts as art. Gadamer doesn't try to close this question but rather takes it as a pretext for developing a nonobjective conception of art in which art is no longer a work but an event in which we are caught up as in the playing of a game. Art history, in Gadamer's view, is just such a game in which the artist is often so far in advance of our ability to play that we are frequently left not knowing what art is.

3. William Carlos Williams, *Paterson* (New York: New Directions, 1963), 261–62.

4. David Antin, *Talking at the Boundaries* (New York: New Directions, 1976), 20.

5. Stephen Fredman, *Poet's Prose: The Crisis in American Verse* (Cambridge: Cambridge University Press, 1983), 135.

6. Antin, *Talking at the Boundaries,* 211–12.

7. Antin builds a talk poem around this event. See David Antin, "What it Means to Be Avantgarde," *Formations* 2, no. 2 (1985): 53–71; reprinted in David Antin, *What It Means to Be Avant-Garde* (New York: New Directions, 1993), 41–64.

8. Sherman Paul, *In Search of the Primitive: Rereading David Antin, Jerome Rothenberg, and Gary Snyder* (Baton Rouge: Louisiana State University Press, 1986), 62.

9. See Fredman, *Poet's Prose,* 140–48; Fredric Jameson, "Postmodernism, or the Logic of Late Capitalism," *New Left Review* 146 (1984): 53–92; Marjorie Perloff, "The Word as Such: L = A = N = G = U = A = G = E Poetry in the Eighties," in *The Dance of the Intellect: Studies in the Poetry of the Pound Tradition* (Cambridge: Cambridge University Press, 1985), 215–38; Lee Bartlett, "What Is Language Poetry?" *Critical Inquiry* 12 (1986): 741–52; George Hartley, *Textual Politics and the Language Poets* (Bloomington: Indiana University Press, 1989); Jeffrey Nealon, "Politics, Poetics, and Institutions: 'Language Poetry,'" in *Double Reading: Postmodernism after Deconstruction* (Ithaca, N.Y.: Cornell University Press, 1993), 132–59.

10. David Bromige, "Lines," in "The L = A = N = G = U = A = G = E Poets," ed. Charles Bernstein, *Boundary* 2 14, nos. 1–2 (fall 1985–winter 1986): 70.

11. Tina Darragh, "Raymond Chandler's Sentence," *Striking Resemblance: Work, 1980–86* (Providence, R.I.: Burning Deck, 1989), 32.

12. Arthur Danto, *The Transfiguration of the Commonplace: A Philosophy of Art* (Cambridge: Harvard University Press, 1981), 78; hereafter cited as *TC*. Danto developed his arguments further in the essays collected in his *The Philosophical Disenfranchisement of Art* (New York: Columbia University Press, 1986); hereafter cited as *PD*. See particularly the title essay, 1–22.

13. See William Camfield's account of the short, possibly violent career of Duchamp's *Fountain*, "Marcel Duchamp's *Fountain*: Its History and Aesthetics in the Context of 1917," in *Marcel Duchamp: Artist of the Century,* ed. Rudolf E. Kuenzli and Francis M. Naumann (Cambridge: MIT Press, 1989), 64–94.

14. Williams, in his prologue to *Kora in Hell,* has this wonderful anecdote: "We returned to Arensberg's sumptuous studio where he gave further point to his remarks by showing me what appeared to be an original of Duchamp's famous 'Nude Descending the Staircase.' But his, he went on to say, is a full-sized pho-

tographic print of the first picture, with many new touches by Duchamp himself" (*Imaginations*, 8–9).

15. Arthur Danto, "The Artworld," *Journal of Philosophy* 61, no. 19 (October 1964): 581.

16. See Stanley Cavell, *The Claim of Reason: Wittgenstein, Skepticism, Morality, Tragedy* (New York: Oxford University Press, 1979), 180–90.

17. This supposition was articulated very straightforwardly years ago by the Chicago Aristotelian Elder Olson: "In the order of our coming to know the poem, it is true, the words are all-important; without them we could not know the poem. But when we grasp the structure we see that in the poetic order they are the least important element; they are governed by everything else in the poem. We are in fact far less moved by the words as mere words than we think." William Empson, "Contemporary Criticism, and Poetic Diction," *Critics and Criticism*, ed. R. S. Crane et al. (Chicago: University of Chicago Press, 1952), 34.

18. See David Lewis, "Truth in Fiction," *Philosophical Papers*, vol. 1 (New York: Oxford University Press, 1983), especially 266–70.

19. See Paul Ricoeur, *Hermeneutics and the Human Sciences*, trans. John B. Thompson (Cambridge: MIT Press, 1981), especially 141–44. See the discussion of Ricoeur's hermeneutics in my *Hermeneutics Ancient and Modern* (New Haven, Conn.: Yale University Press, 1992), 229–46. Cf. Fredric Jameson's Marxist and utopian hermeneutics as developed in *Marxism and Form: Twentieth-Century Dialectical Theories of Literature* (Princeton: Princeton University Press, 1971), especially 116–59, and *The Political Unconscious: Narrative as a Socially Symbolic Act* (Ithaca, N.Y.: Cornell University Press, 1982), especially 74–75. Like Habermas, Ricoeur, et al., Jameson draws the line at discourse that interferes with the project of world making. See Fredric Jameson, "Postmodernism, or the Cultural Logic of Late Capitalism," *New Left Review* 146 (July/August 1984): 53–91, where Jameson compares the writing of language poets to schizophrenic discourse. For Jameson, narratives are forestructures for understanding the world, where understanding means entering the world and changing it. Marxism, on Jameson's account of it, is the forestructure in which texts are approached in this way, call it the "right" way of getting into the hermeneutic circle. So a text is not (not just) a piece of ideological recital to be excoriated or burned but a window or threshold onto the future: a looking glass. Reading on this view is not consumption but action (action turns texts into prophecies, as the ancients knew). Danto thinks that the reason why the history of art is the history of censorship is that every work of art stands the chance of coming true if enough people act on it: The work of art is a project that opens the future in a certain way by projecting possibilities, and so at the very least it gives us a standpoint that cannot help being critical with respect to the world we inhabit (now, at this moment). See the title essay in *PD*, especially 5–18.

20. Michael Davidson, "The Prose of Fact," *Hills* 6–7 (spring 1980): 166.

21. Jean-François Lyotard, *The Postmodern Condition*, trans. Geoff Bennington and Brian Massumi (Minneapolis: University of Minnesota Press, 1984), 5.

22. Theodor Adorno, *Aesthetic Theory*, trans. C. Lenhardt (London: Routledge and Kegan Paul, 1984), 179.

23. David Bromige, "My Poetry," in *In the American Tree*, ed. Ron Silliman (Orono, Maine: National Poetry Foundation, 1986), 217.

24. See Charles Bernstein, *Content's Dream: Essays, 1975–1984* (New York: Sun and Moon Press, 1986), 13–33, and Ron Silliman, *The New Sentence* (New York: Roof Books, 1987), 7–18.

25. Charles Bernstein, "Artifice of Absorption," *PaperAir* 4 (1987): 63–64, reprinted in his *Poetics* (Cambridge: Harvard University Press, 1992), 86–87.

26. Stanley Cavell, *The Senses of Walden: An Expanded Edition* (San Francisco: North Point Press, 1981), 33; hereafter cited as *SW.*

27. Ron Silliman, "The Chinese Notebook," in *The Age of Huts* (New York: Roof Books, 1986), 49.

28. See Hugh Kenner, *The Counterfeiters* (Garden City, N.Y.: Anchor Books, 1973), 57–90.

29. Stanley Cavell, *Must We Mean What We Say? A Book of Essays* (Cambridge: Cambridge University Press, 1969), 188–89; hereafter cited as *MW.*

30. Behind this link between the work of art and a person is Wittgenstein's notion that a thing (e.g., a word) is meaningful if it has a place in our life. Cora Diamond has a nice account of how this is to be understood in "Rules: Looking in the Right Place," in *Wittgenstein: Attention to Particulars; Essays in Honour of Rush Rhees,* ed. D. Z. Phillips and Peter Winch (New York: St. Martin's Press, 1989), 12–34. One might think of language poetry as a way of responding to the place words have in our lives.

31. See *CR,* 241. Compare *MW,* 324: "The world is to be accepted; as the presentness of other minds is not to be known, but acknowledged." On the concept of acknowledgment, see also Stanley Cavell, *In Quest of the Ordinary: Lines of Skepticism and Romanticism* (Chicago: University of Chicago Press, 1988), 8 [hereafter cited as *IQ*]: "I do not propose the idea of acknowledging as an alternative to knowledge but rather as an interpretation of it"—a way of taking knowledge differently: no longer as grasping something but now as responding to something; no longer as possessing something but now as being with something.

32. Emmanuel Levinas, *De l'existence à l'existant* (Paris: Fontaine, 1946), 90; *Existence and Existents,* trans. Alfonso Lingis (The Hague: Martinus Nijhoff, 1978), 56.

33. Ludwig Wittgenstein, *Philosophical Investigations,* trans. G. E. M. Anscombe, 3d ed. (New York: Macmillan, 1968), §129, hereafter cited as *PI,* with Wittgenstein's numbered paragraphs, or "remarks," indicated by the symbol §.

34. Silliman, *The New Sentence,* 63–93.

35. Barrett Watten, "Complete Thought," in *In the American Tree,* ed. Ron Silliman (Orono, Maine: National Poetry Foundation, 1986), 43–47.

36. Lyn Hejinian, "My Life," in *In the American Tree,* ed. Ron Silliman (Orono, Maine: National Poetry Foundation, 1986), 51.

37. Silliman, "Chinese Notebook," 50.

38. Adorno, in *Aesthetic Theory,* speaks of the "open form" underwritten by aesthetic nominalism, or the idea that form is always singular and unrepeatable, that it can never be objectified but is always internal and specific to the individual work—in short, the rejection of the universal or what Fredric Jameson, in a happy phrase, calls "single-shot" definitions of the work of art (Fredric Jameson, *Late Marxism: Adorno, or, the Persistence of the Dialectic* [London: Verso, 1990], 159). Aesthetic nominalism not only "spells the end of any universal aesthetics or doctrine of aesthetic invariables, the tendency even goes so far as to challenge the very conception of aesthetic unity and of the closure of the work itself" (160). Hence the appeal of the Williams tradition to the metaphor of the open. For Jameson, language poetry is an example of aesthetic nominalism invading subjectivity itself and producing a kind of schizophrenia. See Jameson, "Postmodernism," 53–92. From the standpoint of traditional aesthetics, Williams, Charles Olson, and the language poets would be aesthetic nominalists who think that "the work of art is supposed to organize itself from below rather than submit to ready-made principles of organization foisted on it from above. But this [says Adorno] is impossible. No work that is left to its own devices has the power of self-organization and self-limitation, and the attempt at endowing it with such powers must end in fetishism. In aesthetics, nominalism unchained is destructive of all forms. . . . It literally ends in facticity, which is irreconcilable with art," that is, the distinction between art and nonart, or in other words the whole Kantian idea of aesthetic differentiation, becomes now impossible to uphold (Theodor Adorno, *Aesthetic Theory,* ed. Gretel Adorno and Rolf Tedemann, trans. Robert Hullot-Kentor [Minneapolis: University of Minnesota Press, 1997], 313–14). The language poets might be thought of as taking up the challenge of a nominalist poetics. Language poets are in love with facticity.

39. Bob Perelman, *a.k.a.* (Great Barrington, Mass.: Figures, 1984), 1.

40. Silliman, *The New Sentence,* 90.

41. Ron Silliman, *Tjanting* (Berkeley, Calif.: Figures, 1981), 201.

42. As if ethics constituted the limits of reason (Levinas).

43. See *CR,* 177: "In 'learning language' you learn not merely what the names of things are, but what a name is; not merely what the form of expression is for expressing a wish, but what a wish is; not merely what the word for 'father' is, but what a father is. . . . In learning language, you do not merely learn the pronunciation of sounds, and their grammatical orders, but the 'forms of life' which make those sounds the words they are, do what they do—e.g., name, call, point, express a wish or affection, indicate a choice or an aversion, etc." See also 189–90.

44. See Williams, *Paterson*, 164. Daniel Tiffany would disagree: "Language poetry," he says, "should . . . be understood as a belated contribution to a persistent, modernist rhetoric of materiality, whose utopian desire is to extract the word from its semiotic and ideological matrix, in order to plunge it into the jouissance of pure materiality." See Daniel Tiffany, "The Rhetoric of Materiality," *Sulfur* 22 (1988): 203. But perhaps a good example of the materiality I have in mind is Charles Bernstein's "I and The," in *The Sophist* (Los Angeles: Sun and Moon Press, 1987), 59–80, a poem (he says) that "was compiled from *Word Frequencies in Spoken American English*," by Hartvig Dahl (Detroit: Verbatim/Gale Publishing, 1979). Dahl's sample was based on transcripts of 225 psychoanalytic sessions involving 29 generally middle-class speakers with an average age in the late twenties. These speakers, 21 of whom were men, used a total of 17,871 different words in the session. In the poem, frequency is presented in descending order"—beginning with:

> I and the
> to that you
> it of a
>
> know was uh
> in but is
> this me about
>
> just don't my
> what I'm like
> or have so . . .

and ending with:

> plain joke carried
> future ground hang
> help picking nine
>
> blow value advantage
> closer attempt silence
> park punishes cousin
>
> relevant independence shot
> glasses support magazine
> courses pardon results

45. Marjorie Perloff, "Poetry and the Common Life," *Sulfur* 12 (1984): 160–64.

46. Louis Simpson, "26th Precinct Station," quoted in Perloff, "Poetry and the Common Life," 162.

47. Kenneth Rexroth, "The Signatures of All Things," quoted in Perloff, "Poetry and the Common Life," 163.

48. Stanley Cavell, *Pursuits of Happiness: The Hollywood Comedy of Remarriage* (Cambridge: Harvard University Press, 1981), 41.

49. Gerald Burns, "Letters to Obscure Men," in *Letters to Obscure Men* (Quincy, Ill.: Salt Lick Press, 1975), 2.

50. Michael Davidson, "After the Dancers," in *The Prose of Fact* (Berkeley, Calif.: Figures, 1981), 34.

51. Martin Heidegger, "Logos (Heraclitus Fragment 50)," in *Early Greek Thinking*, trans. David Farrell Krell and Frank A. Capuzzi (New York: Harper and Row, 1975), 66. See Heidegger, *Being and Time*, trans. John Macquarrie and Edward Robinson (London: SCM Press, 1962), especially §26 on "being-with" as a description of our relation to the world and to others in it: "The world of Dasein is a *with-world* [*Mitwelt*]. Being-in [the world] is *Being-with* Others" (155). In §34 Heidegger says that discourse (*Rede*) is a mode of being-in-the-world, and that listening and keeping silent are as much modes of discourse as speaking. In particular: "Listening to . . . is Dasein's existential way of Being-open as Being-with for Others" (206). Similarly, in §§31–32, Heidegger characterizes our relation to the world, or being in it, as one of understanding (*Verstehen*), where understanding is a mode of practical involvement rather than theoretical cognition capable of being laid out in statements and descriptions from an observer's standpoint.

52. Heidegger, *Early Greek Thinking*, 67, but contrast *Being and Time*, §34, where Heidegger characterizes listening in terms of "hearing the voice of the friend" (206).

53. Ron Silliman, *What* (Great Barrington, Mass.: Figures, 1988), 66.

54. Bernstein, "Artifice of Absorption," 38.

55. Steve McCaffery, "Lyric's Larynx," in *North of Intention* (New York: Roof Books; Toronto: Nightwood Editions, 1986), 178. See my *Heidegger's Estrangements: Language, Truth, and Poetry in the Later Writings* (New Haven: Yale University Press, 1989), 144–46.

56. Ibid., 170.

57. Eliot Weinberger, review of *In the American Tree*, by Ron Silliman, ed., *Sulfur* 20 (1987): 196–97. Interestingly, Weinberger complains that language poetry does not (often) include translations from poetry in other languages. In the same way, perhaps, what might fail to survive the translation of a language poem into another tongue would not be anything linguistic; that is, if a language poem is untranslatable, it would not be for the reasons normally given for untranslatability of poetry, for example, the ineffability of it, or that its meaning is so embedded in its words that it cannot be transported apart from them. What is not transportable

is context: language poetry foregrounds the speech of its own everyday environment, which is to say a form of life that, as H. L. Mencken would say, is not English, nor does it exhibit any recognizable intellectual or cultural refinement that would lift its better portion to a more accessible plane—it seems unredeemed in every sense: The unmemorable, entirely forgettable, erasable locution is what is most likely to make its way into a language poem, as if in defiance of the very idea of criteria. This doesn't have to mean that language poetry is confined to its environment. See Marjorie Perloff, "*Traduit de l'américain:* French Representations of the 'New American Poetry,'" in *Poetic License: Essays on Modernist and Postmodernist Lyric* (Evanston, Ill.: Northwestern University Press, 1990), 53–69. Heidegger, in his Aristotelian period, would have put it that language poetry, being "mere talk" (*Gerede*), mere "gossiping and passing the word along," is "inauthentic" because nothing is disclosed in such talk, nothing matters to it, nothing is worth taking to heart. ("And indeed this idle talk is not confined to vocal gossip, but even spreads to what we write, where it takes the form of 'scribbling' [das 'Geschreibe']") (*Being and Time,* 212). Imagine language poetry trying to express the genius of inauthenticity.

58. See Max Horkheimer and Theodor Adorno, *Dialectic of Enlightenment,* trans. John Cumming (New York: Seabury Press, 1972), 156; and Cavell, *Pursuits of Happiness,* 41–42, 73–80.

59. Quoted by Cavell, *SW,* 142.

60. Williams, "Kora in Hell," 9.

61. Gordana P. Crnković, "Utopian America and the Language of Silence," in *John Cage: Composed in America,* ed. Marjorie Perloff and Charles Junkerman (Chicago: University of Chicago Press, 1994), 167–87, especially 168–69. It is precisely the verticality of American culture that the language poets attack in their writings—and of course not just the language poets, as the ongoing controversies surrounding the National Endowment for the Arts make quite plain.

62. Stephen Fredman, *The Grounding of American Poetry: Charles Olson and the Emersonian Tradition* (Cambridge: Cambridge University Press, 1993), especially 139–49.

63. Allen Ginsberg, "Beginning of a Poem of These United States," in *Fall of America* (San Francisco: City Lights, 1972), 1.

64. See Louis Marin, "Disneyland: A Degenerate Utopia," in *Glyph,* vol. 1 (Baltimore: Johns Hopkins University Press, 1977), 50–66, and especially 54:

Disneyland is the representation realized in a geographical space of the imaginary relationship which the dominant groups of American society maintain with their real conditions of existence or, more precisely, with the real history of the United States and with the space outside of its borders. Disneyland is a fantasmatic projection of the history of the American nation, of the way in which this history was conceived with regard to other peoples and to the natural world. Disneyland is an immense and displaced metaphor of the system of representations and values unique to American society.

65. "For a man who no longer has a homeland, writing becomes a place to live." Theodor Adorno, *Minima Moralia: Reflections from a Damaged Life,* trans. E. F. N. Jephcott (London: New Left Books, 1974), 87.

66. So Wittgenstein: "What is common to them all?—Don't say: 'There must be something common, or they would not be called "games"'—but *look and see* whether there is anything common to them all.—For if you look at them you will not see something that is common to them *all,* but similarities, relationships, and a whole series of them at that" (*PI,* §66). See *IQ,* 13.

67. Charles Olson, "PROJECTIVE VERSE," in *Charles Olson: Selected Writings* (New York: New Directions, 1966), 16. See Robert Creeley, "A Note on Poetry," in *A Quick Graph: Collected Notes and Essays* (San Francisco: Four Seasons Foundation, 1970), 26: "The sonnet says, in short, we must talk, if you want, with another man's mouth, in the peculiar demands of that 'mouth,' and can't have our own."

68. Bernstein, *Content's Dream,* 17.

69. Antin, *Talking at the Boundaries,* 1.

70. Stanley Cavell, *Conditions Handsome and Unhandsome: The Constitution of Emersonian Perfectionism* (Chicago: University of Chicago Press, 1990), 85.

71. Robert Creeley, *Was That a Real Poem and Other Essays* (Bolinas, Calif.: Four Seasons Foundation, 1979), 106.

72. Robert Creeley, "Waiting," in *The Collected Poems of Robert Creeley* (Berkeley: University of California Press, 1982), 270.

73. Ron Silliman, "Canons and Institutions: New Hope for the Disappeared," in *The Politics of Poetic Form: Poetry and Public Policy,* ed. Charles Bernstein (New York: Roof Books, 1990), 150, 156.

74. John Matthias, "The Stefan Batory Poems" ("Five: the library"), in *Crossing* (Chicago: Swallow Press, 1979), 81–82. *Crossing* has this bibliographical note appended to it: "I am indebted, as in *Turns* and *Bucyrus* [Matthias's earlier volumes], to an odd assortment of books and authors for facts, fancies, passages of verse or of prose, translations, information, scholarship and scandal which I have had occasion in these poems to quote, plagiarize, willfully ignore, tactfully modify, stupidly misconstrue, or intentionally travesty" (121). There follows a list of about fifty or so texts which form the discursive background to *Crossing.*

75. See John Matthias, *Turns* (Chicago: Swallow Press, 1975), 57; Matthias, *Crossing,* 48–49. A difficulty of habitation is what Maurice Blanchot thinks of as poetry's "originary experience": "The poem is exile, and the poet who belongs to it belongs to the dissatisfaction of exile. He is always lost to himself, outside, far from home; he belongs to the foreign, to the outside which knows no intimacy or limit, and to the separation which Hölderlin names when in his madness he sees

rhythm's infinite space." See Maurice Blanchot, *The Space of Literature*, trans. Ann Smock (1955; reprint, Lincoln: University of Nebraska Press, 1982), 237.

76. See Stanley Cavell, *This New Yet Unapproachable America: Lectures after Emerson after Wittgenstein* (Albuquerque, N.M.: Living Batch Press, 1989), 91: "Why is this new America said to be unapproachable? There are many possibilities"—the first being that one dwells there, "but is unable to experience it."

77. John Matthias, "Places and Poems: A Self-Reading and a Reading of the Self in the Romantic Context from Wordsworth to Parkman," in *The Romantics and Us: Essays on Literature and Culture*, ed. Gene W. Ruoff (New Brunswick, N.J.: Rutgers University Press, 1990), 54.

78. John Matthias, *A Gathering of Ways* (Athens, Ohio: Ohio University Press, Swallow Press 1991), 43–44.

Cavell and Hölderlin
on Human Immigrancy

Richard Eldridge

. . . beginning no doubt with the strangeness of oneself.
—Stanley Cavell, *A Pitch of Philosophy*, xv

Describing the ambition of ordinary language philosophy and taking it as his own, Stanley Cavell remarks that the ordinary language philosopher's "problem [in proceeding from what is ordinarily said] is to discover the specific plight of mind and circumstance within which a human being gives voice to his condition."[1] This ambition can be variously pursued in autobiographical writing, in poetry, and in criticism, as well as in ordinary language philosophy.

One way to pursue it would be to arrive, or to claim to arrive, at a final discovery of the human condition: to announce, for example, that we are immortal souls capable of eternal knowledge, in substantial union with a mortal, material body; or that we are nothing but congeries of atoms; or that we are made in the image of a God of justice and love, thence to take one's bearings from that announcement. This is roughly the way of dogmatic philosophy, in seeking final results—ultimate characterizations of our condition, vouchsafed to us from an encounter with the dictates of reason alone, or with reality as such, material or divine, as the case may be.

One does not have to be a hyperbolic skeptic to be suspicious of this ambition, articulated and worked out in this way. What are the criteria of an encounter with reason or reality alone? How might any such announcement, even to oneself, be trusted? But there is another, more distinctly critical way to follow this ambition, proceeding, as it were, from within the continual having of it. This latter way eschews the ultimacy of any discovery of our condition in favor of tracing—and sharing in—swerves between self-composure and self-abandonment on an eccentric path: as though one found oneself along with other human beings whose expressions of their plight one might read as neighbors to one's own, always in medias res between nothingness and at-homeness with oneself, others, and the world, in living composedly according to reason and the nature of things. Here the ambition to discover our condition so as to take one's bearings persists, but this condition is experienced as a continuing plight within which one comes to voice and judgment, rather than as an object of knowledge that voice and judgment might master.

This latter way of thinking within a continuing ambition of human self-discovery is not easy to articulate. (Any characterization of how one might or must so think itself uneasily verges on dogmatism.) The claim that this way of thinking is appropriate to what we are cannot be justified by any argument that would satisfy anyone committed to standards of demonstrative proof independent of any appeal to a transfiguration of perception. Some might see that this is how things are—that we always live thus in medias res—and some might not. But there can be no demonstrative rational proof of the ultimate correctness of this critical view.

This perception of our condition can, however, be filled in persuasively by elaborating readings of various responses to that condition.[2] Such elaborated readings might invite acknowledgment, even if they are unable to command it, and in doing so might serve to keep open lines of reflection and conversation with others and within oneself, rather than short-circuiting them into avoidance and repression. Or they may not. That there is at least a way of thinking philosophically and poetically and critically, through the elaboration of readings of our condition, aiming at acknowledgment, and that this way of thinking is a distinctive and potentially valuable realization of philosophy and of our condition are things that I will try to suggest by juxtaposing some Wittgensteinian thoughts about the strangeness of language as our almost habitation, Cavell's diagnoses of philosophy's motives, and some pieces of Friedrich Hölderlin's philosophy and poetry. Such a juxtaposition might help fill in a distinctively romantic shape of thinking so conceived, pointing toward romantic articulations of our mindedness—at once philosophical, poetic, and critical—under which we might acknowledge ourselves to fall and which we might come to see to be in play in literature, in criticism, and in human life.

1

When we are not thinking philosophically, or otherwise not overcome by wonder at the sheer existence of the world before us, we find words to be familiar objects of use. They come to the tongue and hand as thought comes to the mind. But it is also possible, when in the grip of philosophy or wonder, for words to strike us as strange. Wittgenstein notes this experience of the strangeness of words: "Suppose I had agreed on a code with someone; 'tower' means bank. I tell him. 'Now go to the tower'—he understands me and acts accordingly, but he feels the word 'tower' to be strange [*fremdartig*] in this use, it has not yet 'taken on' the meaning." Or the effect of strangeness can be produced by simply repeating a word: you would be missing something "if you did not feel that a word lost its meaning and became a mere sound if it was repeated ten times over."[3] What are the sources and meanings of this joint familiarity and strangeness?

Spoken and written words are there in one's early childhood environment as aural and visual stimuli if not yet as objects of recognition as words, before one comes to master any of them. They circulate among others who are in control of their own bodies and who attend to their own needs. A dim half recognition—not yet voiced and conceptually structured—of one's dependence on these others inhabits this not yet conceptually conscious quasi experience of one's environment. (Cavell, in describing this condition in which speech and conceptual thought are yet beyond and above us, notes with approval Rousseau's remark that the first encounter in the state of nature with another human being will "produce the name 'giant.'")[4]

Then, after a time, speech and thought come, at first haltingly and in specific domains and then with an astonishing rapidity of fluency and generality. What has happened? One has come to share with others—in part at least, and mysteriously—a world of speech, thought, and recognitive perception. Wonder at the joint familiarity and strangeness of words is bound up with wonder at this accomplishment. How have I, by trafficking in unseen ways, with these sounds and marks—how have I come to do this thing? If I concentrate on these sounds and marks as sounds and marks, then they seem awkward and inert. If I simply use them in accomplished speech and writing and thought, then a grasp of the basis of their life passes me by, as I am caught within their flow. Just how and how far do I share a world of speech and writing and thought with others? What have I done?

One way to respond to this primitive perplexity—the way of dogmatic philosophy, or of what Cavell calls "skepticism"—is to attempt to settle it intellectually: to articulate and confirm rationally an exact account of the nature and limits of this achievement, so as to still any latent anxieties. (A second way is simply to repress this perplexity. This is not always or even often dishonorable, but it involves giving oneself over wholly to conventions of thought and language. These conventions might prove untrustworthy, or one might feel one's life in subscribing to them not to be the fruit of one's own will.) This intellectual effort has a natural appeal. If we could know how we, and others, have come to language and thought, and we could know how far we share conventions, and how apt those conventions are to the world and to our thinkings, then the risks we run in speaking would be diminished, even settled. Instead of facing moments of repudiation and misunderstanding as we venture forth in words ("That is not it at all, / That is not what I meant, at all"),[5] we might speak and think in full assurance that all is in order in our speech and thought, in their relations with the world and with others. Dogmatic philosophy, or skepticism, by raising questions about how we come, or might come, to thought and language, keeps open the primitive quasi experience of our accession to language in which, it may well seem, we all share. This accession remains marked by unsureness about its nature and anxiety over its potential repudiability. In Cavell's phrasing, skepticism "names our wish (and the possibility of our wishing) to strip ourselves of the responsibility we have in meaning (or in failing to mean) one thing, or one way, rather than another."[6]

To the extent—and how shall this extent be measured? from what position and perceptions?—that our perplexity with language and with our own thinking is primitive and that skepticism and dogmatic philosophy arise out of it, they are unavoidable unless we repress them. The human experience of coming to language and thought moves us toward querying their bases philosophically in hopes of perfecting away our risks. In Cavell's formulation,

> there is inherent in philosophy a certain drive to the inhuman, to a certain inhuman idea of intellectuality, or of completion, or of the systematic . . . that exactly because it is a drive to the inhuman, it is somehow itself the most inescapably human of motivations. The quest for the inhuman is an essential part of the motivation to skepticism. And it is a reason why . . . skepticism is forever an inherent aspiration of the thing we know as human.[7]

The philosophical effort to discover in something given (intellect, or matter, or God) the bases of language and thought emerges here as an all too human "attempt to convert the human condition, the condition of humanity, into an intellectual difficulty, a riddle" (CR, 493), something to be solved and done with. Sometimes this effort will take the form of positing a power of inner recognition, prior to all instructions and stimuli—a fantasy of a private language. "This may be seen as part of philosophy's denial of my powerlessness (over the world, over others, over myself, over language) by demanding that all power seem to originate with me, and in isolation." Or sometimes it will take the form of seeing actions and utterances as nothing but materially caused events, caught up in nature's own meaningless course. "It may be seen as philosophy's denial of my power (such as it may be) by sublimizing the power of the world, or say nature" (PP, 112–13).

Either way, and whether or not the philosophical effort is worked out in any specific, articulate shape, it may well seem that we live caught between fantasies of perfect power in thought, action, and speech, on the one hand, and of freedom from responsibility and escape into powerlessness by way of acceptance of or submission to the world, on the other. If one has this perception of our "betweenness" in exercising our powers in the world—our immigrant not quite at-homeness, not quite homelessness—then it may seem important not to deny this perceived fact of the continuance of fantasies, drives, ambitions, wishes, and frustrations: "I say this struggle with skepticism, with its threat or temptation, is endless: I mean to say that it is human, it is the human drive to transcend itself, make itself inhuman, which should not end until, as in Nietzsche, the human is over."[8]

It seems impossible to escape the sways of context and the ways of others in having words that are there before one. Without those sways and ways, there are no criteria of recognition, no chances of thought speaking only to itself alone. There is no room to insert thought between the world and these sways and ways. "[I]t *makes no sense* at all to give a general explanation for the generality of language, because it makes no sense at all to suppose words in general might not recur [—in actual usages—], that we might possess a name for a thing (say 'chair' or 'feeding' and yet be willing to call *nothing* (else) 'the same thing'" (CR, 188). This means, among other things, that the risks of misfiring in attempting to extend words to new things as others do are, even if necessarily rarely realized (at least in extreme forms), necessarily also perennial. "[I]f utterances *could* not fail, they would not be the human actions under consideration, indeed not the actions of humans at all" (PP, 85).

Nor, however, are we given over wholly to powerlessness and to unthinking submission to the natural. We bear responsibility, to ourselves and to others, for how we extend our words and how we think and act. There arises for us a question about what we ought to do or desire, or what it is best for us to do or desire, no matter what we in fact do or desire. (Thus Heidegger: "*Dasein* is an entity which does not just occur among other entities. Rather it is ontically distinguished by the fact that, in its very Being, that Being is an *issue* for it.")[9] In this questioning (or its suppression), and in the bearing of responsibility, the self displays itself "as a thing existing in perpetual relation to itself . . . as a thing of cares and commitments, one which to exist has to find itself." In thinking and speaking, as things that we do and for which we bear responsibility, we find ourselves caught up in the "self's judgmental forming of itself, as something to be further possessed or overcome." To be so caught up is to be cast always en route toward the perfection of action and responsibility, toward a kind of horizonal, fully expressive action, in which thought and gesture inform one another wholly, in transparency to each other, to oneself, and to others, to be cast on a "journey to freedom."[10]

Between self-standing, perfect power and abandonment to powerlessness, there is the fact—if it is a fact—of human immigrancy, as we ever seek at-homeness in the world, in our bodies, in our actions, in our thoughts: seek perfect expressiveness. "[T]he human necessity of the quest for home and the human fact of immigrancy are seen together as aspects of the human as such" (PP, 47).

2

Within this conception (or perception) of the standing immigrancy of the human, a critical path in reading and thinking will involve trying to find "ways to prevent [the impulse to self-scrutiny] from defeating itself so easily" (CR, 176), either in complacent intellectual revelation or in self-dramatizing intellectual skepticism.

Instead of arriving at final results that would either cure our immigrancy or absolutize it skeptically so as to kill our ambition to overcome it, thinking must rather come to terms with it, in what Cavell describes as "the achievement of the unpolemical, of the refusal to take sides in metaphysical positions. . . ." Managing this achievement will involve *reading* the texts and lives of others, and one's own texts and life, as expressions of this immigrancy and of the motives with which we inhabit it. In this perception philosophers—and poets, and critics, and people generally—"have left us with a trail of images of themselves preparing for philosophy or recovering from it" (*PP*, 22, 3) These images can be read in the discernment of the ambitions, wishes, strategies, and frustrations that motivate them.

Reading these images, and doing so in awareness of one's own participation in the human motives that animate them, will differ from any interpretive procedure controlled by a definite method that yields predictable results. It will be unlike de Manian deconstruction, which finds always the same aporias and indeterminacies and so theatricalizes our positions as readers and subjects by calling attention to ourselves rather than to the specific play of motives and pursuits in the text and subject under consideration. "To conclude that such issues are undecidable . . . theatricalizes the threat, or the truth, of skepticism."[11] It will be unlike some sorts of New Historicist criticism, those which reduce texts to reflections of a social life with an independent logic, involving power dynamics independently laid down and of which the interpreter is master. Instead, both social life and one's own stances in reading will be seen to involve plays of motives and fantasy that are already present, or present under transformations, in the text under study. And it will be unlike formalism or New Criticism in connecting the paradoxical self-crossings and self-reference of literary form with plays of human motives to pursue freedom and expressiveness rather than taking texts as self-standing objects of purely absorptive-perceptual interest. One will see not only the form but the human subject—that is, oneself—in the form and in its expression of one's own motives.

Reading in discernment of the human motives that give birth to philosophy, motives in which one shares, will mean adopting a stance *next* to the text, between sheer submission to it and sheer control over it. It will mean both noting and oneself reenacting the play of energy and limit in the text, thus revealing it as a precursor of one's own response to it. Unlike method-driven criticism, it will involve suspending one's sense of what the answers to philosophical questions must be, keeping open the space of the unpolemical expression of our plight. "[T]he reader would have to ask himself or herself 'Do I know what philosophy can—and cannot—do?' "[12]

Yet criticism or reading here will also be more than a collection of scattered and unrelated aperçus. While the (philosophical) motives to freedom, expressiveness, and the subliming away of responsibility that are under discernment are tangled and self-criticizing, for they involve commitments both to independence and common attachment, and while the fruits that their pursuits may lead to remain unclear, they are nonetheless, in this perception, not accidental. They are essentially connected—and so this way of reading both perceives and reenacts—with our lives as subjects, as creatures who are minded and in possession (we know not how) of language. (It is Wittgenstein's sense of his having a share in these motives that, for Cavell, finally distinguishes his writing from Austin's.)[13] Hence the thought arises, when, in reading, one shares in these essential motives, "that the human is representative, say, imitative, that each life is exemplary of all, a parable of each" (*PP,* 11).

What one may variously call motives to philosophy, or to freedom, or to expressiveness, or to intimacy wedded to independence, or to a kingdom of ends, are worked into the very structure of our conceptual consciousness, into our being *able* to reflect on our own judgmental activity and to deliberate. These motives have to do with "the formation of moral consciousness as such,"[14] indeed with the formation of judgmental consciousness as such, where judgments are always among our deeds, hence bound up with matters of responsibility and possibilities of reflective assessment. We have the sense of ourselves as both in need of and open to guidance, as we assess or can assess our doings. This is enough for philosophy, as a way of both thinking about and sharing in the terms of these assessments of what we do freely and what dully, or under constraint, or without interest, to get started. "[P]hilosophy begins with . . . and may at any time encounter an aspiration toward . . . a sense of itself as guiding the soul, or self, from self-imprisonment toward the light or instinct of freedom."[15]

Insofar as we share in these tangled motives to freedom, or to philosophy, there is for us "no assurance of, or only relative finality to, human identity" (*PP,* 121) as possessors of rational and deliberative capacities and capacities for a free life. We are cast, both with others and with ourselves, between acknowledgment and avoidance, between accepting the common as our home and aversively asserting our own independence. (This is perhaps the place to remark that Cavell almost follows Hegel's great turning point, in which the desire to know is seen as absorbed into a prior desire for a free life with oneself and with others. It is no accident that a central term for human achievement in both Cavell and Hegel, in seeing problems of knowledge as the obverse face of problems of human relations, is "acknowledgment" [*Anerkennung*]. The difference is that, for Cavell, the desire for a free life remains an ideal that is irrepudiable, but less than clearly fully satisfiable, so that the desire for a free life is continually threatened with collapse back into a desire to know how to lead a free life that is not yet present.[16] The threat or truth of skepticism cannot be evaded by a turn to the practical.) Lacking more assurance than this, but not simply despairing of finding any, we will find ourselves asking the questions that Cavell asks and that, within this perception, the most serious writers will be seen to find inevitable as they go about their recountings: Am I known (to myself and to others)? What have I done? How am I now to go on?[17]

3

So much can be gleaned from a Wittgensteinian vision of language and mind in conjunction with a Cavellian reading of it. Is it convincing? There can be, again, no neutral, demonstrative argument in favor if it, independent of the focusing or transfiguring of a perception of our condition. But it may help to elaborate the depth and imaginative appeal of this vision of our immigrant condition to see how much it shares with Hölderlin's philosophical romanticism and its consequences in Hölderlin's poetic practice. The following features are central to both a Cavellian-Wittgensteinian and a Hölderlinian understanding of the immigrancy of human conceptual consciousness.

First, there is a specific inheritance of and responsiveness to Kant's critical turn, in particular to Kant's sense that there are human rational powers whose possession calls us from within our mindedness toward a somehow free and elevated life. The apt exercise of these powers is, however, betrayed by any effort to guide them by reference to some given external reality to be discovered. Instead, the possession of these powers is to make us capable of a certain orientation toward and with one another and the world, from within our having of them. Cavell notes that

> In Kant's interpretation of a fundamental Platonic picture, the individual self has as it were internalized the sensuous and the super-sensuous worlds— Plato's unreal and real realms. These are now two "standpoints" which it is the condition of being human to be able to adopt in succession, in opposition to each other. . . . In Kant's *Foundations* the turn from one realm to the other takes place in every moral judgment each time you stop to think, to ask yourself your way. . . . [A]fter Kant, the journey to freedom has been cut short—to a half step—you see how to take it, and where it lies, or you do not. (*PP,* 143)

Similarly, Hölderlin describes in his letters his own sense of the importance of Kant's intimation of possibilities of elevation from within, both for himself and for his culture.

> The new circumstances in which I live are now the best ones imaginable. I have much leisure for my own work, and philosophy is once again my almost exclusive occupation. I have taken Kant and Reinhold and hope to collect my

spirit in this element which was dispelled and weakened by fruitless efforts of which you were a witness. . . . Kant is the Moses of our nation who leads it out of the Egyptian apathy. . . .[18]

Second, there is a sense of mixed fallenness from and elevation out of nature, a sense of an arche-separation from self-enclosed nature in the having of conceptual-judgmental consciousness and deliberative capacities. For Cavell, there is no general explanation—no philosophical explanation over and above the humdrum facts of teaching and training and imitating and, mostly, going on from them—of how we come to possess language and to be distinctively minded in that possession. Once that happens, we are both cursed with partiality, or not quite at-homeness in our mindedness in language and culture, and blessed with possibilities of perfection. For Hölderlin, "*Judgment*. In the highest and strictest sense, is the original separation of object and subject . . . that separation through which alone object and subject become possible, the *arche*-separation."[19] Despite its pains, this arche-separation dimly enables us to do something, to live freely and in celebration of our mindedness in nature, if we can but learn to express aright what is highest, to live religiously, in Hölderlin's poetic sense of the term. "Here there can yet be spoken about the uniting of several religions into one, where each one honors his god and all together honor a communal one in poetic representations; where each one celebrates his higher life and all together celebrate a communal higher life, the celebration of life [as such]."[20]

Third, in bearing the possibility and problem of a higher, free life, there is a specific sense of wandering. Our reorientation is to arise from the release of our latent capacities and possibilities, but these capacities and possibilities are crossed or tangled, admitting of no ready, univocal expression guided by knowledge of an external object. Cavell holds that "we live lives simultaneously of absolute separateness and endless commonness" (*PP*, vii). In consequence, attachment or reattachment to the common can come as either a balm for painful isolation or a confinement that compromises independence; assertions of apartness can either mark out a new and vital expressive path or enact a fall into narcissistic emptiness. There is no way to know specifically how to go forward fruitfully—no criterion of a life of freedom that is vouchsafed to us by external objects—independently of trying one's powers in a mixture of engagement with and departure from the common, and then waiting. (The truth of skepticism names our wish to know, and our impossibility of knowing, in advance how to go forward fruitfully, with absolute assurance.)

Hölderlin holds that "the infinite, like the spirit of the states and of the world, cannot be grasped other than from an askew perspective."[21] The infinite, the spirit of the world, cannot be seen straight on so as to yield direct and reliable knowledge of how to enact it. We are cast, always, on "an eccentric path,"[22] in pursuit simultaneously of love and selfhood, community and autonomy. In Dieter Henrich's memorable summary of Hölderlin's sense of human life,

> Conscious life is at once shaped and unbalanced by the basic conflicting tendencies orienting it. And the formative process of life aims at finding a balance and a harmony amid this strife, in which no one tendency is entirely suppressed or denied in its own right. The preface to the fragment of *Hyperion* already identifies the highest and most beautiful state humanly attainable as the ability to withstand what is greatest, and yet to be humbled by what is smallest. . . . [Man] is bound to a world that, like himself, originates in opposition. For the sake of unity he strives actively beyond each of its boundaries. Yet in it he at once confronts the beautiful—an anticipation of the unity that is lost to him and that he seeks to restore. As he embraces the beautiful, the complete truth, which lies at an infinite distance, is realized for him within limits. He is thus captivated by it, and for good reason. But he must not forget that his active nature is called upon to overcome the finite. In the conflict of love and selfhood he runs his course, either errantly or with self-understanding. [23]

An eccentric path moves jaggedly about a self-divided center—the longed-for unification of love and selfhood; the common and the individual; the passional and the reflective—drawn by it into abrupt movements, as a moth is drawn to a flame, but never mastering or possessing it.

4

What would it be to move along such an eccentric path, or to run one's course, with *understanding?* There can be no univocal and formulable answer to this question. Any univocal and formulable answer would have to rest on a complete conceptual grasp of the self-divided center that draws yet escapes us. A univocal and formulable answer would put an end to our wandering or immigrancy. In the romantic vision of our condition as always in medias res, always on an eccentric path, any claim to have arrived at a final conception of how to live with understanding must appear as a piece of hubristic dogmatism that is belied by the fact of our movement. Instead of answers, there can at best only be enactments, or expressions, or acknowledgments, of our immigrancy and of the possibilities that we bear and that captivate us. At best, these might know themselves, or those who give birth to them might know them to be enactments, expressions, or acknowledgments of a subject's position on a path, rather than items of external knowledge. How might such a piece of self-knowledge show itself?

Here is one short, poetic fragment of Hölderlin's—"The fruits are ripe . . . [*Reif sind . . .*]"—that seems to me to show such self-knowledge. It comes from a collection of fragments reconstructed by D. E. Sattler in editing the Frankfurt edition of Hölderlin's works and given the title *Aprioritat des Individuellen,* [24] as though this collection of fragments addressed the question of what necessities govern any individual human life. Here is the entire fragment:

Reif sind . . .
Reif sind, in Feuer getaucht, gekochet
Die Frücht und auf der Erde geprufet und ein Gesez ist
Das alles hineingeht, Schlangen gleich,
Prophetisch, träumend auf
Den Hügeln des Himmels. Und vieles
Wie auf den Schultern eine
Last von Scheitern ist
Zu behalten. Aber bös sind
Die Pfade. Nemfich unrecht
Wie Rosse, gehn die gefangenen
Element' und alten
Geseze der Erd. Und immer
Ins Ungebundende gehet eine Sehnsucht. Vieles aber ist
Zu behalten. Und Noth die Treue.
Vorwärts aber und rükwärts wollen wir
Nicht sehn. Uns wiegen lassen, wie
Auf schwankem Kahne der See. [25]

The fruits are ripe . . .
The fruits are ripe, dipped in fire, cooked
And tested here on earth, and it is a law,
Prophetic, that all things pass
Like snakes, dreaming on
The hills of heaven.
And as
A load of logs upon
The shoulders, there is much
To bear in mind. But the paths
Are evil. For like horses
The captive elements
And ancient laws
Of the earth go astray. Yet always
The longing to reach beyond bounds. But much

To be retained. And loyalty a must.
But we shall not look forward
Or back. Let ourselves rock, as
On a boat, lapped by the waves.

Against the background of the post-Kantian (Hölderlinian, romantic, Wittgensteinian-Cavellian) conception of mind and language, it is fairly straightforward to parse much of this fragment. Our lives are lived out amid already afforded ways of culture—ripe fruits—that are themselves formed somehow by both natural processes (growth and ripening) and self-conscious agency (dipping and cooking). Present human action and speech are further natural-agentive refigurings (ripenings and cookings) of these affordances. They have no pure, self-present origin in either nature alone or culture alone but instead arise both naturally and culturally out of already past interplays.

Both prior cultural affordances and present actions pass away or go under (*hineingeht*), into the earth like snakes, or into oblivion. There is no possibility of present immortality for us, in and through our actions in culture. It is chastening to recognize this. This recognition is a burden (*Last*) to be borne in mind, or kept (*zu behalten*). Though the burden is heavy, holding it fosters humility.

We cannot, however, simply stand and hold the burden. There are paths—ways of culture—on which we are always already in motion. Only to stand and wait, quietistically, is also to act, as long as one bears conceptual consciousness and the possibility of attitudes toward the world. To go on these paths—to take up and modify one cultural affordance rather than another—is to move in a specific cultural direction. This has its costs, in ignoring both others outside one's specific cultural orbit and aspects of oneself that might engage with those others. A life of universal, reciprocal freedom and acknowledgment is not to be attained from within individual modifications of culturally afforded specific patterns of action. Playing the cello, organizing for better housing, working in a soup kitchen, participating in communion, raising one's children, telling jokes, comforting the sick, seeking and offering forgiveness—none of these activities is free from partiality; none is a sure and straight road toward human freedom: toward community and independence, love and selfhood. Hence the paths are "evil." That is to say (*nemlich*), they go astray, or are not right, or are unsuitable (*unrecht*), like horses we cannot control. What we have managed to build and accomplish on these paths (the captive elements) fails to match or express the deeper necessities and possibilities of freedom (the ancient laws of earth). Or our accomplishments are informed by the ancient law of their partiality, their one-sidedness that will lead them to go under. There is no perfect remembrance and enactment of freedom along these paths of culture.

Yet still we wish for our lives in culture to be straightened, informed wholly by what is eternal, so that they are rationally transparent and in good order, to ourselves and to others. We wish to act on standing good reasons that can be endorsed reflectively by everyone, no matter what: "always the longing to reach beyond bounds." In this too there is much to be retained, held: the facts of human desire for rational transparency and of the limits in fulfilling that desire that lie along its tangled, crossed paths. These facts now present themselves as facts of conceptual consciousness as such, as facts of our lives with thought and language as we inherit and extend them. We must retain, hold, both the fact of our partiality and the fact of our standing desire to overcome it.

In this condition, it will be necessary to trust certain ways of culture as the best, the most sure vehicles for the expression and cultivation of freedom that one has to hand (*Und Noth die Treue*). One should not step back from cultural engagements—from cello playing, political organizing, feeding the poor, telling jokes—into an empty, skeptical-solipsistic rejection of the value of anything that is present. Yet we cannot quite help doing this sometimes, in our awareness of the rational one-sidedness of any cultural affordances and present actions.

In this necessity and impossibility of trust of the common lies the difficulty and accuracy of the fragment's final three lines. What does the *wollen* at the end of the fifteenth line mean? The translator offers "shall," and this captures one sense of *wollen*: to be about to do something or to be on the point of doing it. This reading captures a sense of resoluteness in acceptance of the common, of what is already culturally afforded, as at least of partial value: We shall let ourselves be rocked by it, carried by it out of our skeptical resistances. It is unavoidable. Yet *wollen* also carries an even stronger sense of wanting, willing, or wishing. We want to let ourselves be carried by culture, want not to look forward or backward but instead to abandon ourselves to the common, or even to allow ourselves to be swept away by an unusual destiny in a blue sea of August: anything to move out of mere onlooking, alone. This sounds less honorable, as the skeptical voice has always intimated. Perhaps we should rather owe loyalty also to the fact of our desire to reach beyond bounds, to our possibilities of judging and refiguring the present. Though we want not to look forward and back and want instead only to drift over the infinite of the sea, we must also hold and retain our desire to go down into the infinite, to hold our present ways to account.

So which is it, and what are we to trust—the ways of culture as they present themselves to us in their partial value or our powers of assessment and refiguration, of looking forward and backward and accepting and pursuing agentive control? It is Hölderlin's special and difficult expression of the post-Kantian sense of our mindedness to have posed these alternatives in the very same words, thus letting us see the appeal of each mode of trust as we swerve between the sense of each reading. It is this enactment of our mindedness, I want to say, to which our immigrancy in mind and language and culture comes. But, if this is right, then that is not something for anyone simply to say.

Notes

1. Stanley Cavell, "Knowing and Acknowledging," in *Must We Mean What We Say?* (New York: Scribner's, 1969), 240.

2. The critical, as opposed to dogmatic, epistemological significance of juxtaposed readings of our condition, amounting to a perspicuous representation of it, is the main theme of my "Hypotheses, Criterial Claims, and Perspicuous Representations: Wittgenstein's 'Remarks on Frazer's *The Golden Bough*,'" *Philosophical Investigations* 10 (1987): 226–45.

3. Ludwig Wittgenstein, *Philosophical Investigations*, 3d. ed., trans. G. E. M. Anscombe (New York: Macmillan, 1958), pt. 2, p. 214e. Throughout this short summary of Wittgenstein on the physiognomy of words, I rely on Stephen Mulhall's discussion in sections entitled "The Experience of Meaning" and "The Physiognomy of Meaning" in his *On Being in the World: Wittgenstein and Heidegger on Seeing Aspects* (London: Routledge, 1990), 35–45.

4. Stanley Cavell, *A Pitch of Philosophy: Autobiographical Exercises* (Cambridge: Harvard University Press, 1994), 161 [hereafter cited as *PP*], citing Rousseau's *Essay on the Origin of Language*.

5. T. S. Eliot, "The Love Song of J. Alfred Prufrock," reprinted in *The Norton Anthology of English Literature*, 3d. ed., vol. 2, ed. M. H. Abrams et al. (New York: Norton, 1974), 2167.

6. Stanley Cavell, "Being Odd, Getting Even: Postscript A—Skepticism and a Word Concerning Deconstruction," in *In Quest of the Ordinary: Lines of Skepticism and Romanticism* (Chicago: University of Chicago Press, 1988), 135.

7. Stanley Cavell, in James Conant, "Interview with Cavell," in *The Senses of Stanley Cavell*, ed. Richard Fleming and Michael Payne (Lewisburg: Bucknell University Press, 1989), 50. Compare Cavell, *The Claim of Reason* (New York: Oxford University Press, 1979), 207 [hereafter cited as *CR*]: "[Wittgenstein] never underestimated the power of the motive to reject the human: nothing could be more human. He undertook, as I read him, to trace the mechanisms of this rejection in the ways in which, in investigating ourselves, we are led to speak 'outside language games,' consider expressions apart from, and in opposition to, the natural forms of life which give those expressions the force they have."

8. Stanley Cavell, *This New Yet Unapproachable America: Lectures after Emerson after Wittgenstein* (Albuquerque, N.M.: Living Batch Press, 1989), 57.

9. Martin Heidegger, *Being and Time*, trans. John Macquarrie and Edward Robinson (New York: Harper and Row, 1962), 32.

10. *PP*, 142, 150, 143. See also the discussion of expressive freedom in Richard Eldridge, *Leading a Human Life: Wittgenstein, Intentionality and Romanticism* (Chicago: University of Chicago Press, 1997), 6–7.

11. Cavell, "Being Odd, Getting Even," 135.

12. Stanley Cavell, "A Conversation with Stanley Cavell on Philosophy and Literature," in *The Senses of Stanley Cavell*, ed. Richard Fleming and Michael Payne (Lewisburg: Bucknell University Press, 1989), 3, 14.

13. See, for example, *PP*, 113.

14. *PP*, 142. See also Eldridge, *Leading a Human Life*, 8–9 and 17–20, on the essential connection between conceptual consciousness and moral consciousness.

15. *PP*, 4. On how a commitment to freedom is worked into the structure of conceptual consciousness according to Kant, see Onora O'Neil, "Reason and Autonomy in *Grundlegung* III," in *Constructions of Reason* (Cambridge: Cambridge University Press, 1989), 51–65, especially 63, and more generally, Richard Velkley, *Freedom and the End of Reason* (Chicago: University of Chicago Press, 1989).

16. Hegel announces the great "turning point" [*Wendung*] in *Phenomenology of Spirit*, trans. A. V. Miller (Oxford: Oxford University Press, 1977), para. 177, 110. See the discussion of this turning point in Eldridge, *Leading a Human Life*, 27–33.

17. Apropos of passages in Cavell's autobiographical *A Pitch of Philosophy* that voice versions of these questions, I have in mind pages 6, 22–23, 56–57, and especially 169. On how these questions animate Wordsworth's *Prelude*, in specific responsiveness to a felt sense of having possibly done or been nothing, see Richard Eldridge, *On Moral Personhood: Philosophy Literature, Criticism, and Self-Understanding* (Chicago: University of Chicago Press, 1989), 106–11. On how responses to these questions remain conjectural and require tendentious narrative revisions of one's course so as to bring out its reasonableness, but in being revisions remain haunted by their erasures, see Richard Eldridge, "Wordsworth and 'A New Condition of Philosophy,'" *Philosophy and Literature* 18 (1994): 50–71.

18. Friedrich Hölderlin, Letter No. 117 to Immanuel Niethammer, 14 February 1796, and Letter No. 172 to his Brother, 1 January 1799, both in Friedrich Hölderlin, *Essays and Letters on Theory*, ed. and trans. Thomas Pfau (New York: SUNY Press, 1988), 131, 137.

19. Friedrich Hölderlin, "Judgment and Being," in Hölderlin, *Essays and Letters on Theory*, 37.

20. Friedrich Hölderlin, "On Religion," in Hölderlin, *Essays and Letters on Theory*, 94–95.

21. Friedrich Hölderlin, "Remarks on *Antigone*," in Hölderlin, *Essays and Letters on Theory*, 116.

22. Dieter Henrich, "Hegel and Hölderlin," trans. Taylor Carman, in *The Course of Remembrance and Other Essays on Hölderlin*, ed. Eckart Forster (Stanford, Calif.: Stanford University Press, 1997), 124. Henrich has drawn the phrase "an eccentric path" out of the preface to the "Fragment of *Hyperion*."

23. Henrich, "Hölderlin in Jena" and "Hegel and Hölderlin," in *The Course of Remembrance and Other Essays on Hölderlin*, ed. Eckart Forster (Stanford, Calif.: Stanford University Press, 1997), 112, 127–28. I cannot forbear noting the specifically Emersonian sound of Henrich's phrase "to withstand what is greatest, and yet to be humbled by what is smallest."

24. See the editor's note to this fragment in Friedrich Hölderlin, *Hölderlin, Hyperion and Selected Poems*, ed. Eric L. Santner (New York: Continuum, 1990), 300.

25. Hölderlin, "The fruits are ripe . . . [*Reif sind . . .*]" in Hölderlin, *Hölderlin, Hyperion and Selected Poems*, 274–77.

Moonstruck, or How to Ruin Everything

William Day

There are any number of reasons for taking an interest in popular films, but what gets us thinking about them, now or ever? That question, however presumptuous, comes easily, thinking of *Moonstruck* (1987; written by John Patrick Shanley and directed by Norman Jewison), not only because of the striking absence of thoughtful writing about it since its initial, generally favorable reviews[1] but because *Moonstruck* itself seems to raise the question: What gets us thinking about a film? Or more simply: What gets us thinking, and what keeps us from thinking? My aim in what follows is to show that *Moonstruck* raises some such question. It is not a question every film will raise. That may seem obviously true about what you might call a bad film; it may be equally true about a film that wears its greatness on its sleeve, so that it prompts thought about itself but not yet about the question of what gets thinking going. Consider Werner Herzog's *Fitzcarraldo* (1982), like *Moonstruck* a dark romantic comedy inspired by an idea of the opera. There is no mystery to why we begin thinking about *Fitzcarraldo*; it is enough to be reminded of its central visual metaphor (art exacts from the artist an exertion as momentous as carrying a ship over a mountain). Herzog's film contains scenes of dialogue that address explicitly philosophical themes, as well as moments of sublimity—thinking for example of the moment we learn why the aborigines have cut the boat loose—that are nothing if not philosophically sublime.

It is not my intention to compare *Fitzcarraldo* and its relation to opera to *Moonstruck* and *Moonstruck's*. But to see how *Moonstruck* could be an instance of superior filmmaking, it helps to see how a film can have depth without making the explicit concerns of its characters serve (as they do in *Fitzcarraldo*) as a conduit for the audience to descend to those depths. *Moonstruck* prompts thinking much the way dreams do, through a structure that conceals as much as it reveals and by a peculiar juxtaposition of the familiar and the bizarre. In this more or less familiar tale of romance, what can strike one as bizarre is, for beginners, the slightly echoing repetition of some of the words ("death," "luck," "cold," "snow," and the question "How long must I wait?") and the offbeat cadence of parts of the dialogue (for instance: "Rose. Rose. Rose. *Rose.*"—"Who's dead?"). There are also certain visual repetitions: the recurring full moon, naturally, and the gloved hands reaching for and taking hold of one another, first shown on stage at the Met, in the snow scene from *La Bohème*, and repeated in the cold outside Ronny's apartment, where Ronny offers the warmth of his wooden hand to Loretta. And there are the musical repetitions, from Puccini's opera ("Che gelida manina," "Donde lieta uscì," "O soave fanciulla," "Quando m'en vo'") and from American popular music ("It Must Be Him," "That's Amore"), each heard more than once over the course of the film. Perhaps one does not make anything of these repetitions initially, but one does notice them eventually. They function much the way that repetitions and variations in music do, initiating and advancing their own discourse, establishing their own logic. It is the logic and the attractiveness or attraction of this film, an attraction that we will see is not unlike the gravitational pull of the moon.

First, though, here is a review of the story line of *Moonstruck*. Loretta (Cher), an Italian-American widow from Brooklyn in her late thirties, is engaged to marry Johnny (Danny Aiello), an Italian-American man in his midforties who is not, we sense, a serious candidate for marriage because of his continuing devotion to his mother. When he calls Loretta from his mother's deathbed in Palermo, he reminds her to call and invite his brother Ronny (Nicolas Cage) to the wedding. Johnny and Ronny have not spoken to each other for five years. Loretta calls Ronny, but he hangs up on her, so she goes to his bakery. There she learns about the accident that maimed him five years ago: he lost his hand in a bread slicer while he was cutting up some bread for Johnny, and shortly thereafter Ronny's fiancée left him. Loretta asks Ronny if she can talk with him alone. Up in his apartment she makes him some coffee, cooks him a steak, and (as she puts it) tells him his life—in particular that he is a wolf and that he is afraid of that part of himself now. He responds by overturning the kitchen table in a fury, kissing her passionately, and taking her to his bed; she yields in a mixture of resignation and desire.

The next morning, awakened by the light of day and still in Ronny's bed, Loretta blames "bad luck" for her succumbing to him and says that they must never see each other again. He tells her that he loves her but that he will leave her alone forever if she will go with him that night to the opera. It is a surprising invitation coming from a large, young, tattooed baker, and we are only a little less surprised that Loretta accepts. She goes off to church and the confessional, but then she finds herself walking into the Cinderella Beauty Salon to get her hair done, the gray taken out, nails manicured, eyebrows plucked . . . and she buys herself a new evening dress and accoutrements. That evening Loretta and Ronny meet outside the Metropolitan Opera House. They go in and take their seats, and the opera begins. We are shown the moment in act 3 of *La Bohème* when Mimi and Rodolpho agree to part. It is winter, and they have met outside the tavern. We see Mimi offer her gloved hand to Rodolpho as she sings, "Goodbye, Goodbye—no bitterness!"; here Rodolpho takes her hand and squeezes it. We are shown Loretta moved to tears.

Walking home, Loretta tells Ronny that they are both guilty for what has happened between them; she then finds to her surprise that they have arrived at his apartment. Loretta makes a speech about how she is able now to take control of her life. She tells him that she is going to go home—she says she is freezing to death. Ronny counters with a speech about how love ruins everything, including our ability to take control of our lives. He tells her that he wants her to come upstairs and get in his bed. We see Ronny offer his wooden, gloved hand to Loretta as he says "Come on! Come on"; here Loretta takes his hand and squeezes it. She then follows him into his apartment.

Loretta arrives home the next morning. Shortly thereafter, Ronny arrives—to meet the family. The family and Ronny are seated at the kitchen table when Johnny, who returned from Palermo the night before, comes to call on Loretta. Johnny tells Loretta and everyone assembled two things: (1) His dying mother recovered right after he told her that he was getting married; (2) he cannot marry Loretta because then his mother would die. Ronny then asks Loretta to marry him, and she says yes, whereupon everyone drinks a toast to the family.

My outline takes the repetition of the clasped hands as the film's central moment, tied as it is to the scene that Loretta and Ronny saw on stage at the opera and framed, there as here, by the snow and the cold of winter. Immediately the scene outside Ronny's apartment raises several questions: What is wrong with Loretta's speech about taking control of her life? What is right about Ronny's speech? Why is Loretta freezing to death? Whose hand gets warmed by whose? How are the speeches and the freezing cold and the warming of hands understandable as the consummation of a night at the opera? And how do we understand our position as witness both to that scene from the opera and to this consummation of it? In the course of answering these questions I want to align *Moonstruck* with certain Hollywood film comedies of the 1930s and 1940s, those Stanley Cavell calls comedies of remarriage.[2] So I begin by saying a word or two about those comedies in order to explain and motivate the reading of *Moonstruck* that is developed in the first half of the essay. The second half turns to some aspects of Emerson's writing, in particular his interest in our relation to heroes, or to human greatness generally, and his coinciding interest in our relation to the words of a text. My intent is then to show how the procedures of *Moonstruck* inherit these Emersonian interests.

1

The Hollywood films Cavell identifies as comedies of remarriage (including *His Girl Friday* [1940], *The Philadelphia Story* [1940], and *Adam's Rib* [1949]) bear comparison to Shakespearean romantic comedy in their emphasis on the heroine over the hero, particularly in showing her somehow transformed or restored. But these films follow a different track from Shakespeare's comedies in taking as their romantic concern not the joining of a young couple in the first throes of love but the rejoining of a somewhat older couple who find their familiar love threatened from within, despite themselves. Their problem is not that they have grown apart so much as that their marriage has led them to discover marriage's age-old limitation: its inability, as Cavell says, to ratify its pairing of the sexual and the social,[3] what could also be called the crossing of nature and convention. To restore the couple's marriage turns out to require conversation, or to require what conversation requires: a willingness (typically the woman's) to be instructed, a willingness (typically the man's) to be seen as a fool, a willingness to exchange active and passive roles, the ability to yield to another without betraying yourself, the ability to make a claim on another without demanding acquiescence. There are other features of the genre's overarching mythos that are either features of these films or in some way compensated for in each film's particular realization of the mythos, features such as the sympathetic, midwifish role of the woman's father, the marked absence of the woman's mother, and the presence and nature of the romantic couple's romantic rivals.

Moonstruck can be located, and in some ways locates itself, as a descendant of these film comedies, meaning first and foremost that it is concerned with the form of conversation that characterizes them—a conversation such as Ronny and Loretta have outside Ronny's apartment, which could be seen as the culmination of Loretta's instruction at Ronny's hands, or hand. But it would be a large undertaking to consider all of the points of similarity and contrast between *Moonstruck* and these earlier films, as for example (to note a point of similarity) how Johnny, the romantic hero's brother and rival, matches the rival figures in the earlier films by satisfying the woman's half-conscious wish to put her sexual desire to sleep. Or to note a point of contrast, how the not-to-be-expected presence of the woman's mother, Rose (Olympia Dukakis), is compensated for by her showing herself to be still subject to the threats and joys of marriage, which suggests that she is still justified in imagining she knows what her daughter desires and so still qualified to serve as a model for her daughter of how best to preserve that desire. We see Rose's vitality in her unwillingness to acquiesce to her husband's avoidance of her and in her brief but promising flirtation with Perry, the professor she encounters in the restaurant and converses with over dinner and a walk home.

There is, however, one point of comparison that cannot be overlooked if we wish to align *Moonstruck* with the films of this genre. We can name it by asking why we ought to think of Loretta and Ronny as seeking or requiring remarriage. If we want to claim that the mythos of remarriage offers the best picture of Loretta's and Ronny's relation to each other and to their desire, then we are obligated to show how they already share a life, or that they somehow share a past, as the film begins. There are at least intimations that they do. Parts of the dialogue seem to identify

Ronny with Loretta's first husband, as when Ronny asks Loretta why she didn't wait for the right man again, since she waited for him the first time. Loretta answers, "You're late," thereby conceding that she was waiting for him, as if in anticipation of his return, but at last could wait no longer. There is also the apparent visual identification of Ronny and Loretta's first husband by means of a bus: the bus that ran over the husband (that he was hit by a bus is virtually all we know of him) with the bus that twice appears in the orientation shot of Ronny's bakery and apartment. One can notice this detail without imagining that the bus counts as an element of this film in the same sense that, for example, Ronny's wooden hand does however we come to read the latter's significance. But once you notice it, it is hard not to imagine that the bus is an element of that shot.

More immediately, however, the compensation which the genre predicts, given that Loretta and Ronny begin as strangers, is provided through their alarming, almost clairvoyant knowledge of each other's deepest secrets—the knowledge each expresses by claiming that, at bottom, the other is "a wolf" (or as Ronny says to Loretta, "You run to the wolf in me, that don't make you no lamb"). Any reading of this film must take on itself the task of spelling out what that accusation, both titillating and frightening, amounts to. We begin by recalling, apropos of our thinking of Ronny and Loretta as working through a marriage rather than toward one, that we first hear the accusation (that so-and-so is a wolf) entered against an older, married man by his wife. This is the couple who run the Sweetheart Liquor Store where Loretta stops on her way home from the airport, near the beginning of the film. Further, it seems fair to say that we understand that accusation, which we overhear with Loretta as if by chance, to be part of an ageless quarrel, part of the universal but private conversation of marriage.

When the accusation is remembered and repeated by Loretta up in Ronny's apartment, it punctuates an exchange strewn with sexual imagery, specifically with two or three figures for genitalia that the film borrows from Freud, or perhaps from Howard Hawks.[4] I mean the head and the hand (or foot). *Moonstruck's* play with these associations comes to a head at the culmination of that scene, in the final exchange between Ronny and Loretta before they go off to make love:

Ronny: Why are you marrying Johnny? He's a fool!
Loretta: Because I have no luck.
Ronny: He . . . he made me look the wrong way and I cut off my hand. He could make you look the wrong way, you could lose your whole head!
Loretta: I'm looking where I have to to become a bride.
Ronny: A bride without a head!
Loretta: A wolf without a foot!

Are we to hear these as warnings or as allegations? Perhaps as both warnings and allegations. But of what? *Must* we say "castration"? And having said it, is it obvious what we are to make of it? One way to pursue this is to ask how we should read Ronny's wooden hand when he first reveals it to Loretta and to us (in the bakery oven room scene). It appears to be wooden, but it is nonetheless a hand—he uses it in some of the ways that a hand is usually used. That is why its unveiling, to return to words used earlier, is both frightening and titillating. This is how the scene in the oven room unfolds: Ronny asks Loretta, "Do you know about me?" A young woman who works at the bakery interrupts him in shock or embarrassment, as if she knows what he is about to reveal or expose. He silences her and says, "Nothing is anybody's fault, but things happen. *Look.*" Then he peels off his white work glove finger by finger, as if doing a striptease. What is he revealing—that he lacks a male organ or that he has one? (What fact about a man is not anybody's fault exactly? What does he think a woman who would get engaged to his brother Johnny might not know about someone like him—that is, about a man?)

What Ronny is revealing is that he has a wooden hand: his organ is petrified. After he unveils it he says, "It's wood. It's fake." But if a hand is wooden, which already tells us there is no blood coursing through it, what does saying "It's fake" add, and about what? It tells us, it would seem, that the look of wood is deceptive. Ronny is fixated on the moment of his parting from his bride-to-be, a moment he represents to himself as the parting of his male part, which in turn is represented by the severed hand, as when he exclaims, "I lost my hand! I lost my bride!"—the one following the other in accordance with some familiar bit of logic. We see him reliving the moment of parting when he plays a recording for Loretta of the act 3 parting scene from *La Bohème*—the very scene Ronny lends further weight to later on at the Met, when he kisses Loretta's hand at the scene's climax. Why is he showing Loretta all this? In order to reveal something and conceal something. What he means to reveal to her, as suggested before, is that his organ is petrified—that is, he has a male organ, but since losing his bride he has become afraid to use it. Loretta interprets what he shows her as an attempt at concealment, reversing his logic when she tells him that *first* he wished to escape his bride, *therefore* he dismembered himself—which suggests that his fear of using his male part is as old as the having of it. (Perhaps this is the quintessentially modern male fear; perhaps it is the old fear of forming attachments.) What Ronny attempts to conceal from himself as well as from her, Loretta says, is that he is a wolf. ("You don't see what you are, and I see everything. You're a wolf.") So we ask again: What does that accusation amount to?

There is the suggestion, first of all, that being a wolf is something one tries to conceal from oneself and from others, or pretends not to know—something that shuns publicity. But in fear of what? Dismemberment? And yet here with Ronny we see that the willingness to dismember oneself can be taken as *evidence* that one is a wolf. Shunning publicity and prompting concealment might suggest that being a wolf is unnatural—something either beyond or below the human. Yet the wife behind the counter in the Sweetheart Liquor Store says, "I seen a wolf in everybody I ever met." So Ronny's concealment is meant to represent a more widespread suppression. Why hesitate to identify being a wolf with having a libido, and the domestication of our wolfishness with the institution of marriage, so that Loretta's picking up the charge and accusing Ronny with it is no more than her expressing her insight into his unnaturally dormant sexual life, as well as an indirect invitation to revive her own, which leads eventually to their finding in one another a fit partner for marriage? It is because that line of thinking, however true it may be to facts about us, seems to me false to an experience of the film. That is not to deny that *Moonstruck* is about a romantic couple who are at first intent on repressing the sexual—as in Ronny's pretty clear sublimation, and therefore expression, of his sexual desire by (as he says) "shovel[ing] this stinking [bread] dough in and out of this hot hole in the wall." But *Moonstruck* treats the repression of sexual desire as itself an expression or image for something else, for the suppression of something buried no less deeply in the human, like a potential we have but fail to realize.

2

Here it will prove helpful to turn to the thought of Emerson, which Cavell locates behind the genre of remarriage comedy and which I find especially pertinent to the experience of *Moonstruck*. It is a familiar fact that Emerson's writing is guided by an interest in self-trust or self-reliance, where the self in question is not myself as I now stand but the one in trusting which, or by trusting which, I remain true to myself. Emerson speaks of this as my next self, my higher self, and my unattained but attainable self. One image for it is as something to be discovered, like a new world, whose paradigm is an idea of America—what Emerson in "Experience" calls "this new yet unapproachable America I have found in the West."[5] A complementary image is as something to be recovered, like a primal memory, modeled for Emerson in Plato's myths of the netherworld and the soul's recollections, modeled for us perhaps in the practice of psychoanalysis. But it might be more helpful, rather than multiply images, to place Emersonian self-trust in opposition to some of its natural and commercial debasements—which urge me, for example, to be all that I can be or to heed my inner child. Emersonian self-trust, in contrast to these, is not a state I might occupy or an attitude I arrive at, as if once and for all; nothing, at least nothing of interest, is to be perfected or settled. "I unsettle all things" is how Emerson says this in the essay "Circles" (*CW,* 2:188). Nor does self-trust involve a course of action I map out for myself, as if in readiness to take control of my life. That understanding of relying on the self, to anticipate, is one which Loretta in *Moonstruck* finds she must unlearn. And critically, Emersonian self-trust does not preclude trust in others, at least so long as trusting others means something short of conforming to them. While Emerson recognizes with Thoreau, and with Plato and Nietzsche, that one's progress away from one's disappointment with oneself may generate a critique of society as it stands, and while that may leave one at a distance from society (as if to get a better look), it does not entail one's withdrawal from society. For Emerson, the way to the next self communicates with the selves of others. Ideally this means all others; practically, or for now, it means one's friends, those Aristotle first called another self.

The importance to Emersonian self-trust of friendship for mutual guidance or instruction[6] is reflected in Emerson's nearly lifelong preoccupation with prompting his readers to a next self by inviting them to work through their relation to their mentors or teachers, a relation he pictures sometimes as friendship's double, sometimes as its antithesis. Emerson's name for these teachers, who may be living or dead, or texts, or works of art, is typically, "great men." Here are two familiar Emersonian remarks on the relation of humans to human greatness:

> In every work of genius we recognize our own rejected thoughts; they come back to us with a certain alienated majesty. ("Self-Reliance," *CW*, 2:27)

> It is remarkable that involuntarily we always read as superior beings. ("History," *CW*, 2:4–5)

Notice that between these two sentences the ascription of our attitude or mood toward the greatness of others gets inverted. The sentence from "Self-Reliance" says that the thoughts of genius are no more than our (supposedly common) thoughts estranged and raised; to paraphrase Emerson's conclusion, we read in shame. The sentence from "History" says that the (supposedly superior) thoughts we read, certainly no less here than before our rejected thoughts, raise us and ours. It may not be news to suggest, as I take this pairing of remarks to suggest, that our relation to our mentors or teachers is best characterized as one of ambivalence. Here the ambivalence is between exhilaration and depression; more generally it will be an ambivalence between attraction and repulsion, love and hate. An ambivalence between reverence and fear is at work in that section of Hegel's *Phenomenology of Spirit* called "Lordship and Bondage," in the internal struggle of the bondsman that follows his life-and-death struggle with the one who in winning becomes his master.[7] It is this internal battle between reverence and fear of the master, which gets worked out in the bondsman's work, that finally prompts his nascent self-consciousness, what Hegel also calls his independence. Ambivalence, of course, characterizes the patient's relation to the psychoanalyst, an ambivalence which gets worked out in the revelation and acknowledgment of the analyzed transference. Cavell argues that the structure of transference is the best image for or picture of the redemptive powers of reading[8]—as if reading were its own therapy, provoking readers at its best to think through their attitude toward the text, meaning here especially their dependence on it. In a moment we will see that a redemptive or transfigurative reading is the aim of Emerson's prose, as it is of certain other exemplary philosophical writing, and that it is in sharing this aim that *Moonstruck* claims the interest of philosophy. But the moral I wish to draw from the present line of thought, which has traveled from ambivalence through work and transference to reading, is this: although an Emersonian self-trust recognizes the dangers of overinfluence and the need to recover oneself from the sway of others, it sees equally the need to recover oneself in, or to lose oneself in, others. In his essay "Uses of Great Men," Emerson warns of the threat of overinfluence and yet is able to conclude: "A more generous trust is permitted. Serve the great" (*CW*, 4:17). This is not an endorsement of self-enslavement but a call for self-abandonment. If we are bound, our bond is our abandon.

Emerson's trust in the moment of abandonment, when one gives oneself over to the one who reveals one's aspirations, is pertinent to both the explicit and implicit intentions of *Moonstruck*. Explicitly, we can identify what *Moonstruck* calls our wolflike nature with the human capacity to ravage and abandon one's present self—or as Ronny says, to ruin ourselves, to make of our present selves ruins, the first task in remaking or upbuilding ourselves. That is what Ronny, struggling to find words, is able to recall to Loretta in his speech about how "love ruins everything." Thinking back to the scene in the Sweetheart Liquor Store, where a wife accuses her husband of being a wolf, we might recall that that scene's sinister aspect is dissolved only when the woman's husband says to her, "You know what I see in you, Lotte? The girl I married." He does not *deny* that he is a wolf. On the contrary, by suggesting that the eyes with which he looks at other women are the eyes with which he looks at her, and that this look has not changed, that it is in fact the same look with which he first gave himself over to her, he is telling Lotte in effect that it is she who brings out and sustains the wolf in him. And Lotte accepts this and is touched by it—as is Loretta, as is anyone who has eyes. Thus *Moonstruck* joins other remarriage comedies in portraying marriage as an arena for abandonment and recovery, a recovery of the self from something this film calls death. (Loretta pleads with Ronny, "I'm freezing to death"; her mother explains to Perry, "Why do men chase women? . . . I think it's because they fear death.")

If proposing such an ideal of marriage is the explicit intention of *Moonstruck*, its implicit intention is to show that film is itself a potential site for abandonment—not exactly or simply the way art in general might be but specifically by virtue of film's capacity to project a world of larger-than-life human beings, men and women transfigured by the camera, the forms of life we christen with the exquisite name "movie stars." Our relation to human greatness is one of the natural themes and persistent concerns of film, a special version of film's interest in our relation to film itself. One might put this by saying that part of the task of explaining our fascination with and attraction to movies is to explain our attraction to and fascination with movie stars. And that requires our coming to understand why movie stars look great on film, where "looking great" identifies conditions and prospects distinct from those of looking handsome or beautiful. Howard Hawks, thinking of Walter Brennen, said that the camera likes "personalities";[9] Cavell says it creates "individualities."[10] The thought is that while you and I may have some of one or the other, chances are neither of us has their *looks*. But then what the greatness of movie stars teaches is that human greatness is neither predicted by nor precluded by particular traits, or features; rather, it insists on human particularity itself, on the expression of an identity.

Moonstruck's interest in the heroic or representative possibilities of film is shown through its insisting not only that its female star declare her identity (as other remarriage comedies do)[11] but that she enact before the camera its trans-formation of her, beginning at the moment we see Loretta Castorini step into the Cinderella Beauty Salon and ending at the moment we see Cher step out of a cab in front of Lincoln Center. (Tom Hanks enacts a similar transformation in John Patrick Shanley's later film, *Joe Versus the Volcano* [1990].) Still, one may feel that this transformation of Loretta Castorini that culminates in the vision of Cher's singular attractiveness has nothing to teach us beyond the fact of our separateness from it, as from the projected world that creates it. The silver screen screens its world from me, Cavell says;[12] the world I converse with in the city and in the farms is not the world I eye, Emerson almost says. (He says it is "not the world I think" ["Experience," *CW*, 3:48].) We sometimes say that movies offer an escape from the world; but that expression fails to capture the otherness of the projected world, and especially the fact that we cannot go there—as we can go, even escape, to Acapulco. That is not to deny the sense in which the projected world is the same as our world; what other world does a film camera film? But then one is not denying that Cher's body is the same as ours—I mean, is human—if one confesses that gazing at her up on the screen is not the same as looking at someone across the breakfast table, even when that someone is Cher. The greatness of movie stars on the screen is in part a function of the otherness of their world. Think of that as an instance of the fact that the greatness of others is in part a function of their otherness, their separateness. (The majesty of our rejected thoughts is a function of their alienatedness.) Then how can some other represent to us our unattained but attainable selves?

Consider as a candidate feature of the best texts and works of art, and so of the best teachers, their care to declare or remind us of their otherness—that we cannot become them, or that *they* are unattainable, or that the path to a next self leads us not just to them but past them. For a movie to teach this would be something. *Moonstruck* does, again in Ronny's speech to Loretta, at the part that begins, "We aren't here to make things perfect. The snowflakes are perfect." When now—as we see the first flakes of perfect, cinematic snow, and hear the first notes of "Che gelida manina," and cut to the first and only close-ups of Nicolas Cage in this sequence—when now Ronny continues, "The *stars* are perfect. Not us. Not us! We are here to *ruin* ourselves," he is naming the necessary and sufficient distance between those screened images of light (what "Cher" means, what "Nicolas Cage" means) and the one who gazes, the one whose ruins are the only building blocks for any attainable self.

But even if this is correct, what if any difference does it make? The unapproachable distance between our worlds seems to militate against communication. We gaze unaffected. Both invisible and absent to the projected world on the screen, we experience an involuntary skepticism. But then this is only an emblem of the skepticism we live with respect to ourselves as we gaze, or read, or otherwise meet our rejected thoughts and doubt our own majesty, which is to say our freedom. The best that any film or text can do to overcome this distance is to offer some compensatory gesture. Its task is not somehow, fantastically, to eradicate the distance between us; distance or separateness is one of communication's conditions. The task is rather to remove the barrier between ourselves and our viewing, so that we come to think of our viewing as a gazing inward. A good film or text will try to make us self-conscious, or to re-create self-consciousness, perhaps not by instilling in us an absolute fear of death as Hegel's lord does his bondsman but by naming us in ways that arrest our thoughts, like an invitation out of the blue. To return to the language of the opening pages: The challenge, for a film or text that takes this to be its challenge, is not so much to make us think as to make it possible for us to be struck by thought (as if thought were essentially an experience). It tries to prepare us for the inception of thought as for a spectacle or revelation.

This is what is at work in such passages of Emerson's writing as the following, again from the essay "History":

> These hints, dropped as it were from sleep and night, let us use in broad day. The student is to read history actively and not passively; to esteem his own life the text, and books the commentary. Thus compelled, the muse of history will utter oracles, as never to those who do not respect themselves. I have no expectation that any man will read history aright, who thinks that what was done in a remote age, by men whose names have resounded far, has any deeper sense than what he is doing to-day. (*CW*, 2:5)

I read "history" as naming "History," the essay we are reading, so that by "the muse of history" Emerson names himself, or rather his muse, what in "Self-Reliance" he calls his genius and Whim (CW, 2:30). Then his way of writing "in broad day" is to indicate beneath or beyond the surface of his words both how he should be read ("actively," that is, by one who "esteem[s] his own life the text, and books the commentary") and why he feels "compelled" to write thus indirectly. And his reason seems to be that he wishes not only to protect and possibly offend those who are not ready or willing to hear what he has to say, but also to address more convincingly and intimately those who are. All of that, and seeing it all, if you will, is the "deeper sense" of "what he is doing to-day," that is, what Emerson's reader is doing here and now, reading "History."

Nothing, of course, compels readers to go along with this, or to imagine that they are reading the utterances of a muse. But then such is the etiquette or logic of an invitation, especially of one to esteem one's life a text and so regard the transfiguration of a word ("history" into "History") as commentary on the transfigurative possibilities of one's reading, of oneself in reading. Emerson can no more argue (philosophy's favored mode of persuasion) for an experience of conversion than he can demand it. So like Plato and Augustine before him, he takes another tack, endeavoring to animate the reader's conversion to a new mode of life not only by representing it somehow in the work of writing but by founding it in the act of reading. When such writing succeeds, reading becomes not only a means to knowledge but a form of knowing. If this is philosophy, it suggests that the experience of reading certain philosophical texts is as integral to (at least one rendering of) philosophy's aspirations as the experience of a performance is to the aspirations of music and the theater, or the experience of a screening to the aspirations of film.

To recognize the comparable, invitatory moment in Moonstruck requires seeing that one of the film's images for itself, the image for its serving as a site of abandonment, is the recurring full moon, that heavenly body at which wolves are known to howl. But to see the full significance of this image requires more than noticing the similarities between moonbeams and screened images, between reflected and projected light. It requires seeing that—as the Old Man, Loretta's grandfather (Feodor Chaliapin), says in conversation over a grave—"the moon brings the woman to the man, capisce?"; seeing, that is, how the film declares through this image its ability to transport us.

The place to look is again at the scene outside Ronny's apartment which culminates in Ronny's offering his hand to Loretta, a gesture that repeats Mimi's offer of her hand to Rodolpho in the act 3 scene from La Bohème that we see on stage at the Met. Although one hand echoes the other here, the music gets displaced: Instead of Mimi's melodramatic aria of parting, "Donde lieta uscì," we hear Rodolpho's act 1 aria of courtship, "Che gelida manina." The tenor enters as Ronny first commands, then invites Loretta, who says she is freezing to death, in from the cold. The words to Rodolpho's aria run like this:

Che gelida manina,
se la lasci riscaldar.
Cercar che giova?
Al buio non si trova.
Ma perfortuna
è una notte di luna,
e qui la luna
l'abbiamo vicina.

What a frozen little hand,
let me give it back its warmth.
What's the use of looking?
In the dark we'll find nothing.
But by good luck
it's a night of the moon
[it's a moonlit night]
and here the moon
is a near neighbor. [13]

Putting aside certain themes or figures that are taken up by the film (being frozen; having luck; finding a near neighbor), I mention only that Loretta takes Ronny's proffered hand at the precise moment we hear Rodolpho sing his first *luna* ("moon"). It is Ronny's wooden or petrified or frozen hand, and so the hand that is missing—call this the hand that guides the plot, the hand that made these images and this film. A moment earlier we saw this hand raised and extended more or less toward us, intercut with a close-up of Loretta looking at it pensively. When Loretta reaches for this hand, her hand comes from our direction. And after her hand takes his, she seems virtually to step into the film, as if accepting the invitation for us, as if enacting our conversion.

Moonstruck seems to acknowledge the impotency of this gesture, its inability to compel the viewer, through the detail of casting Ronny's petrified member as stand-in for the film's makers. But having said that, we ought to add that its makers claim to be masters at making the petrified or emulsified "look better than they did in real life." That is the implication of these opening words of the film spoken by an undertaker ("I am a genius!") as he exits what we might call the wake room of his funeral home, a kind of theater, where the corpse he has embalmed is on display before an admiring crowd of mourners. If the mourners, whom we hear but who are not visible, fairly represent our condition as viewers as the film begins, then *Moonstruck's* culminating scene is meant to show how we are represented no less by the visible, transfigured shades up on the screen, and so how we might not only learn to mourn ourselves but undertake our abandonment.

Notes

1. Harriet Fraad has written a short essay, "Personal Life as Problematic: A Comparison of Woody Allen's *September* and Norman Jewison's *Moonstruck*," *Rethinking Marxism* 1 (1988): 169–74. But her essay is less an opening for thought into these films than a reminder of the straitjacketing of thought that late middle-aged Marxism has become.

2. Stanley Cavell, *Pursuits of Happiness: The Hollywood Comedy of Remarriage* (Cambridge: Harvard University Press, 1981).

3. Ibid., 31.

4. Ibid., 118; William Rothman, *The "I" of the Camera: Essays in Film Criticism, History, and Aesthetics* (Cambridge: Cambridge University Press, 1988), 101–2.

5. Ralph Waldo Emerson, *The Collected Works of Ralph Waldo Emerson*, 5 vols., ed. Robert E. Spiller, Alfred R. Ferguson, et al. (Cambridge: Harvard University Press, Belknap Press, 1971–), 3:41; hereafter cited as *CW*, followed by volume and page numbers.

6. For a discussion of this aspect of Emerson's thought in the context of a tradition of thinking that Stanley Cavell calls "moral perfectionism," see his *Conditions Handsome and Unhandsome: The Constitution of Emersonian Perfectionism* (Chicago: University of Chicago Press, 1990); hereafter cited as *CH*.

7. G. W. F. Hegel, *Phenomenology of Spirit*, trans. A. V. Miller (Oxford: Oxford University Press, 1977), see 117–19 (§§194–96).

8. Stanley Cavell, "The Politics of Interpretation," *Themes Out of School: Effects and Causes* (San Francisco: North Point Press, 1984), 52–53; cf. *CH*, 57.

9. Joseph McBride, *Hawks on Hawks* (Berkeley: University of California Press, 1982), 106.

10. Stanley Cavell, *The World Viewed: Reflections on the Ontology of Film*, enl. ed. (Cambridge: Harvard University Press, 1979), 33.

11. Cavell, *Pursuits of Happiness*, 63–64, 105–7.

12. Cavell, *World Viewed*, 24.

13. Puccini, Giacomo, *La Bohème*. Libretto by Giuseppe Giacosa and Luigi Illica. Trans. Peggie Cochrane, modified by author. London OSA 1299.

Beginning at the Beginning in Genesis

Kenneth Dauber

Why does the Torah begin with 'In the beginning'"? Rabbi Yitzhak's well-known question, quoted in the first Rashi,[1] the most important Jewish commentary on the Hebrew Bible, fittingly inaugurates a mode of dispersal of inaugurations everywhere present in rabbinic thought. "When do we say the evening Shma," as the first mishna, the oral companion to the Torah, asks, not what is this "Shma" which the Torah tells us to say. "Why does the mishna begin with 'When,'" as the first gemorrah, the most important investigation of the mishna, wonders, not what is the evening, the "when," which the mishna is concerned to define.[2] As the rabbis' procedure seems to indicate, beginnings proliferate everywhere. You must not presume to know where the center of the matter is. You do not charge brazenly up to it, but sidle around the corners. Maybe, even, there is no center of the matter. Maybe there are only corners. Or, at least, the corners themselves, an important Torah concern—of face ("do not mar the corners of your beard" [Lev. 19:27]), in field ("do not harvest the corners of your field" [Lev. 19:9]), on garments ("they shall make fringes on the corners of their garments" [Num. 15:38])—are always to be given an independent attention, are as important as the center. As we might say, reading as method what, in the rabbis, has surely not separated out as anything different from matter, translating into theory what remains practical, theory itself should be practical. You need to approach it from a territory whose approaches require approaching, as well. Before you ask your question, you need to know where your question reaches, what application its answer might have, the world in which it might signify.

Rabbi Yitzhak is on the firmest of grounds here. His world, we might say, *is* the world, or the world raised to a kind of ideal of itself: the significance of the statement he questions for the world in which it is given, the conditions which define the sort of statement it might be. "It should have begun with 'This month is for you the first of months' [Exod. 12:2]," God's first commandment to the people to whom the Torah was given, after all, *as* a commandment, as Rabbi Yitzhak goes on to say. No wonder Rashi, himself concerned with the p'shat, the plain meaning of the commandments, begins with Rabbi Yitzhak. No wonder, to this day, students taking the traditional course of Torah study begin not with "In the beginning" altogether, but with Leviticus and God's command, *Vayikrah el Moshe*, "And [God] called to Moses" (Lev. 1:1), giving him the laws of the sacrifices. For Rabbi Yitzhak is concerned with where he is, not where he came from. He seeks his life, not the life prior to his life. Accordingly, if "In the beginning" remains, stubbornly, the Torah's beginning, we might pause to consider Rabbi Yitzhak's heroism, his struggle *to* live, its costs and its pathos.

This is the rabbinic agon, Rabbi Yitzhak's agon, and if Rabbi Yitzhak is, as some believe, Rashi's father (for "Rashi" is an acronym meaning "Rabbi Shimon, son of Yitzhak"),[3] it is Rashi's agon, perhaps even the agon of the Torah itself, that mutual product of God the father and man his sons. It is the agon of sons wrestling with their father for his recognition of them *as* sons, so much greater than Harold Bloom's adolescent agon of the son's struggle to *be* the father, or that postagonism of faithless Derridean rabbinism with its despair of the condition of sons and father alike. It is the agon of men struggling to be men, not God, and struggling to win from God his recognition of them *as* sons, with all the limitation of their power that that implies. Or better, it is the struggle to win from God the power of limitation itself, in faith believing all the while that that is what God has really desired.

"Shall not the judge of all the earth do justice?" (Gen. 18:25), as Abraham asks God, struggling with God for the life of Sodom and Gomorrah. And indeed, has not God anticipated the struggle, called for it, when he bends to Abraham, remarking, "Shall I hide from Abraham what I am about to do?" (Gen. 18:17). "Why should [you let] the Egyptians say . . . ?" (Exod. 32:12), as Moses asks God, struggling for the preservation of his status as one of *b'nei Yisroel*, the sons of Israel, rather than as the father of a nation that God would make of him in acting on his intention to destroy Israel. And does not God own Moses "the servant of God" (Deut. 34:5), "more humble than any other man" (Num. 12:3), as he calls him, for the very arrogance that insists that man's humility is just what God must own? For this, if anything, is the meaning of that special relation that Israel claims with God, as, though it acknowledges him as the God of all people, it yet insists on the specialness that can come only from the limitation of being a "peculiar" people (a better translation than the King James's "chosen" people), of knowing not the truth that man, returned to his origin before peoplehood, might know as God knows it but knowing instead what men, in all their variety, in the variety indeed that comes from the blocking off of origins, even origins in God, can in fact know.

This, too, Rabbi Yitzhak says, as he answers his question, "Why does the Torah begin with 'In the beginning'": "So that if the peoples of the world, say . . . we may respond. . . ." For there is a worldliness in Jews, too, who belong to the peoples of the world, a worldliness that in its refusal of the limitation of peculiarity, that in its arrogance without humility, demands transcendence rather than peculiarity, the unity of all people which means the obliteration of peoples. And the Torah will indulge that worldliness, perhaps as a concession to the limitation of man's ability to accept limitation. But it will indulge it only so far, and then it will humble it, as when the people of Babel go too far, when their desire to be one people in one world with one language becomes, inevitably, the desire to build a tower to Heaven, to be "like God" and not a people after all.

For, as we may say, Rabbi Yitzhak fears what the Torah has already anticipated, the pulling down of the world's creator through elision of the world he created, the arrogation to man of the voice of the Bible's author through elision of the Bible he authored, and he would return us, as the Bible would return us, to the world in which the Bible, beginnings and all, is to function. It is man's world, though given to him by God, just as the Bible, as the rabbis tell us, is spoken in man's language, though spoken by God. For, as we might put it, the world to which the Bible would return us is the world *of* man's language, a world "all before us," in Milton's phrase, not a world before the world before us. It is not a world of which our language is some vague representation or picture, whose focus, to understand what it pictures fully, we need only learn to correct. But it is a world our language presents directly, as it were on our own recognizance. It is the world of a language we know already, an ordinary language world, the responsibility of which knowing Genesis is everywhere at pains to make clear.

1. Genealogy

"In the beginning, God created the heavens and the earth." It is a commonplace that in the Bible we may find the origin of our history, indeed the origin of our very idea of history, which is to say a beginning in beginnings, in causes and, through a long chain, their effects even until the very end. Still, as the idea of an end to history is a late idea in the Bible, consolidated as it is in Revelation, which owes much to a Hellenistic culture in which "causes" were not merely efficient but material, final, and especially—the ultimate expression of Greek aesthetics—formal as well, it is worth pondering the meaning of a beginning without end, of a causality that is ceaselessly, even ruthlessly, efficient alone. The further consequences for man's actions, what is required of him *as* man by such a notion of causality, is something to which we will return in greater detail later. Without final cause, there are no ends to excuse one's means. Without material cause, means lose their character of neutrality, their existence as mere techne. Without formal cause, means and ends cannot even be identified as such. Form and content, purpose and action collapse, and agency, the efficient agent, is left naked before what it has wrought.

For now, however, we may note that without the idea of an end, causes and effects will appear not as a chain but as a network and not even as a network but as a set of reciprocal and overdetermined influences impossible to get behind. Without an end to recast the beginning as the beginning of an end, that is, beginnings will occur not only in the beginning but over and over again at every moment, in each and every action. Beginning loses its temporality. Everything becomes, as it were, a beginning of everything else simultaneously, and even genealogy, that most seemingly deterministic of histories, will present to us not the certainty of existence well placed, but the burden of placing ourselves instead.

A remnant of this sense of genealogy may be found in the opening of even so late a text as Matthew. There is no genealogy at all in the two other synoptic Gospels, and the Gospel of John will Hellenize the idea of genealogy almost totally, as we shall discuss. But as the most Jewish of the Gospels, Matthew offers a genealogy that might be seen as a kind of midrash on the genealogies of Genesis, though designed to end all midrash. It is a kind of intertextual revision, that is, in keeping with the rabbinic proliferation of beginnings, but accordingly heterodox not simply for the revisionary nature of its dogma but for the objectification it attempts, the sloughing off of the origin of its revisionism onto something other than its own exegetical activity. It is a revolution cast as revelation, a sort of conservatizing of its radical revisionism through the deus ex machina of a virgin birth:

> The book of the generation of Jesus Christ, the son of David the son of Abraham. Abraham begat Isaac; and Isaac begat Jacob; and Jacob begat Judas and his brethren; And Judas begat Phares. . . . And Eleazar begat Matthan; and Matthan begat Jacob; And Jacob begat Joseph the husband of Mary of whom was born Jesus, who is called Christ. So all the generations from Abraham to David are fourteen generations; and from David until the carrying away into Babylon are fourteen generations; and from the carrying away into Babylon unto Christ are fourteen generations. (Matt. 1:1–17)

The last verse takes steps to prevent that enabling doubt that an efficient causality rather insists upon. Working to make straight the very crookedness that requires of man that he act in the first place, the neat symmetry of three sets of fourteen generations each is a formal binding together of a chain of "begat"s that, the longer it extends, as evident even in the foreshortened excerpt we have quoted, the less certain it seems. The nonlinked link, in particular, which relates Jesus to the Davidic line through the nonfather Joseph, though he is the husband of Mary, is especially notable in this respect as suggesting just how powerful the doubt is before which Matthew retreats. As Stanley Cavell has remarked, the father's historical inability to know conclusively whether his child is, in fact, his child is a fitting image not only of skepticism about genealogy but of skepticism in general,[4] or to amend Cavell slightly, the child's inability to know conclusively who either his father or mother is universalizes the analogy to men and women alike. And yet, if the link between King David and Jesus is thus weak, it is also precisely what gives the birth of Jesus its revolutionary moment. Without spaces between the links to raise questions about the continuity of the chain, what space is there for something to occur that is not merely there already in its first link? To speak theologically, without room for skepticism, what possibility is there of faith? Matthew is not willing to entertain too much skepticism. The burden of making a revolution is great. Knowing that what you know is only what you know, that others might disagree and that only on you and on those who agree with you rests the responsibility for such consequences as come from what you have decided to know, is a burden not easily shouldered. A sign from above, dissolving agency into its act, settles all questions: the miracles or the "Spirit like a dove" hovering over Jesus in Mark (1:10) in the place of Matthew's genealogy; or the "perfect understanding of all things from the very first," the eyewitness account of what requires no exegesis in the same place in Luke (1:3); or the quasi-ontological proof on which rests the Logos of John; or even the rabbinic midrash of how Abraham came to know God—if men worship the sun, yet who made the sun[5]— a kind of rudimentary proof of what will become, in the Middle Ages, God as the prime mover. And so in Matthew, though with more ambivalence, that the new birth is the birth not of a new man but of God and that the birth gives us at least retrospectively a formal, even symmetrical, patterning of births objectifies his faith, rendering it supererogatory. Matthew, as it were, sublimes his doubts and so cedes some of the power of doubting. He minimizes his skepticism and so makes his faith something passive. Yet this is because he resists what he understands almost too well is the radicalness of the injunction of skepticism against passivity. It is because what he resists is skepticism's injunction *to* the efficiency of agency, an injunction Genesis rather makes in the strongest possible terms.

This is the reason why, while genealogies are ever present in Genesis, it is nevertheless man who determines what his genealogy is. God promises Abraham a son, but it takes Sarah, to whom God himself tells Abraham to listen, to make clear to Abraham which son, Ishmael or Isaac, is the one intended. Genealogy offers no assurances. That Isaac is born less than a year after Sarah is taken for a wife by Abimelech, who does not realize that she is already married to Abraham, is no mere matter of history. It is not, say, some scandalous gossip acknowledged only that it may be controverted. Rather, as we might say, in an old structuralist vein, the origin of Israel is neither in the nature of Israel nor in its culture but in the redoubling of its culture on its nature.[6] In biblical terms, if God chooses that Abraham be the father of a great people, yet the people must choose God simultaneously for God to choose them.[7] And, indeed, again and again, though primogeniture is a command of the Bible, it is the second son, the nonnatural inheritor, who inherits the father's portion—Isaac; then, of Isaac's children, Jacob instead of Esau; then of Jacob's children, Joseph and Judah more than Reuben and Simon; and even of Joseph's children, Ephraim before Menassah. It is almost as if a certain reversal occurs, as if the point of genealogy is not to establish continuity but to assure us that such newness and discontinuity as the line from Abraham to Ephraim represents are continuous enough. Or, to take genealogy more seriously, genealogy is what is given. It is the given that God gives, what is—nature, let us say—outside of man's determination. That is why the Bible represents primogeniture as being commanded in the first place. Materiality is acknowledged as the real, after all. But its reality becomes a cause only as man causes it to be his cause. It is his beginning only as he begins it. So that if he does not begin it, it is what is not a beginning, of which he is the cause as well.

As we might put it, in somewhat Kantian terms, causality in Genesis is universal but subjective. It is a matter of matter, of the real and not the fantastic. Yet for all its reality, it inheres not *in* matter but in whom it matters *to*, so that the subliming of subjectivity into objectivity can do nothing but erase causality altogether. As the Bible will insist over and over again—when Adam and Eve attempt unsuccessfully to conceal themselves from God in the bushes (Gen. 3:8), when God puts a mark upon Cain (Gen. 4:15), even when Moses buries the Egyptian he has killed, for wholly good reasons, in the sand only to find he has been observed anyway (Exod. 2:12)—there is no place in which a subject may hide. [8] There is nothing for which he is not responsible. He cannot plead ignorance, say Esau's ignorance that taking a Canaanite wife would invalidate his father's line (Gen. 27:46). He cannot plead sympathy, Esau's obvious love of his father, his occupying himself in bringing his father food while his blessing is stolen. He cannot plead self-interest, his cry, "Behold, I am at the point to die: and what profit shall this birthright do to me" (Gen. 25:32). Least of all can he plead the natural course of things, the fact that Esau is, after all, Isaac's firstborn son. For to sum up the lesson of biblical genealogies in general, though the son can inherit his father only as he is his natural son, he cannot inherit his father *because* he is his natural son. He is, as it were, responsible for his nature. Or to return to beginnings once again, you must, indeed, begin somewhere. But that is because somewhere is where you are, a somewhere, as we should say, not therefore anterior to you but the very where, as Genesis enjoins, that, to become your beginning, you must make begin. And this may explain the stylistic feature of the Hebrew Bible whereby, in a kind of genealogy of genealogies—a generalization of genealogy marking an attitude toward beginnings: beginning as an idea, as a philosophy, not simply a history—a general, and sometimes even particular, account of a series of events is given only to be followed by an account of one of the events in the series as if it were the beginning of a new series.

So we find God's creation of the world in the so-called second story of the creation after the first story of the creation has been finished. Or, even more remarkably, we find God's command to Abraham to leave Ur of the Chaldees for Canaan after Abraham's father, Terah, has already taken him from Ur of the

Chaldees toward Canaan (Gen. 12:1 and 11:31). As we might say, here God himself gives man a model of the beginnings he is to begin and, as in the story of the flood, perhaps even because he has learned such beginnings from man, a version of Rabbi Yitzhak's insisting to God on the very power of man's limitation, since God himself would seem to take such a limitation up. As Genesis puts it, when God decides on the flood, "And God saw that the wickedness of man was great in the earth, and that every imagination of the thoughts of his heart was only evil continually" (6:5). But as it virtually repeats, when God decides that never more will he destroy the earth, "and the Lord said in his heart: I will not again curse the ground any more for man's sake; for the imagination of man's heart is evil from his youth" (8:21).

The crucial word here is the second "for," in Hebrew *ki*. Its root meaning is "because," so that God would appear to decide against destroying man on the very same basis that earlier he had decided *to* destroy him. The Jewish Press Society smoothes out the problem by translating *ki* as "although," which is not implausible, in effect reading the clause "because the imagination of man's heart is evil from his youth" as a misplaced modifier that ought properly to have followed "I will not." In the thinking of Genesis, however, this is to make a distinction without any difference. "Because" and "although" are synonymous. "Despite the fact that" ("although") and "on account of the fact that" ("because") reduce merely to "the fact that," that is to say, a material given of responsibility, which makes it neither an excuse nor a direction.[9] And so, "The imagination of the thoughts of his heart is evil": in the first rendering, a rendering from the point of view of God, man's evil imagination is reason for acting against him. Objectivity is God's, and judging by the standards of such objectivity, man cannot measure up. But that the imagination of the thoughts of man's heart is evil in the second rendering is a rendering from the point of view of man, to which God rather accedes, establishing the limits of man's subjectivity as the measure of existence by which even God himself now agrees to judge.

2. Language

No wonder Genesis's account of the creation begins, alone among extant creation stories, with a word. Nor, as in John, is the word quite with God nor, certainly, is it God, but it is man's, behind which we never get. "In the beginning was the Word": this is a midrash bearing comparison with a well-known rabbinic midrash that has it that *B'reishit*, usually translated "In the beginning," is more properly translated "*With* the beginning" and so that the phrase really means that God created the world with the word "beginning." There is, that is, nothing anterior to the word. Language is no transparency opening onto something prior to it. It does not end in a thing but is the thing itself. As is implicit in the Hebrew word for thing, *davar,* which means also speech, words and things are one, though the perspicuousness of the King James translation often makes this difficult to see.

Yet John, retreating from such an absence of ends even more radically than does Matthew, turns the midrash back on itself, in effect reversing the trajectory it would seem otherwise to have opened up. For if, in John, there is nothing behind the word, finally there is nothing in front of it or alongside it, either. Anteriority is not eliminated, but hypostatized. The word becomes its own end, thus ending even before it begins. He therefore elides altogether the "generations" of the creation, as Genesis terms it (4:2), which Matthew, following the text of creation far more closely, had made sure to represent. Gone are the days and the stages—the creating: "And God said . . ."; the judging: "And God saw . . ."; the refashioning: "And God separated . . ."; the placing: "And God called . . ."—limited, as it were characteristically human activities with all their uncertainty, though God, in his infiniteness and his omniscience, would seem to affirm them in his own performance of them.

As John rewrites it:

> In the beginning was the Word, and the Word was with God, and the Word was God. The same was in the beginning with God. All things were made by him and without him was not any thing made that was made. (John 1:1–3)

The words circle around here, recollected from their proliferation to a unity at once prior to and after. In place of difference there is only "the same." In place of generation there is iteration. And as "the Word was made flesh" (John 1:14), the end is joined with the beginning, in effect objectifying begetting in the begotten, limitation in limitlessness, words—in a word—in *the* word. Here, there is no efficient causality, indeed hardly any causality at all, or rather cause becomes an emanation and efficiency dissolved into the material ("flesh"), the final ("the same was in the beginning"), and the formal ("the Word") all at once. Beginnings do not make their beginning. They are implicit in it. What words might be consequent on the word are never in doubt. They are the word itself, which is always the same word.

As we might say, in Wittgensteinian terms, what John elides is the difficulty of "going on," the difficulty, that is, in the absence of an antecedent referent to fix its meaning, of proceeding from one word to another, from one set of words to another set. The meaning of a word in John is not "meaning as," but what we might call meaning "of." That is, meaning is not the use to which a word is put, the way it consorts with other words to which it is made to relate. This is a conception of meaning that raises as a kind of ethical necessity the need to determine what words a word should be made to relate to, what words it relates to already, and thus a conception that enjoins on us, if we would know what a word might mean, the responsibility of knowing everything we can know and, since we cannot know everything, the responsibility of deciding what we will not know as well. But in John all words are but manifestations of the one word, referring always back to it, and so requiring of us, rather, an abandonment of all things for the one thing. To put it again in Wittgensteinian terms, the meaning of a word, here, is not the history of the education of the subject that enables him to use it, all the words he has experienced, in relation to which the word finds its significance. But it is the word as object itself, meaning beyond man's experience of it. It is meaning requiring no subject to make it mean—signification, but requiring, indeed, the subject's very silencing of himself.

Undoubtedly, John is working through a rigorously ontological logic of representation. God, after all, speaks the world into being. Surely, then, his speech must be more than subjective. It must be objectively real, the very thing itself, a referent, as it were one with that to which it refers. John's word, though it is a picture of itself, after all is yet a picture. Nevertheless, Genesis's representation of creation is quite other, quite antipictorial, as indeed all of Genesis is. And this is because in the metaphysics of that representation, to follow a remarkable suggestion of Jill Robbins by borrowing a slogan of Emmanuel Levinas, the ethics of God's speaking is prior to the ontology of what he speaks. [10] God, too, is a subject. This is why his speech is so insistently personal. The objects of his speech are not himself, and he must speak to them to convince them, to command them, to punish them, and so forth. As we may say, God's speech is the expression of an angle of vision, a will, a desire, a certain, let us even call it limited, point of view not general to the world but particular to God. It is only that the limit of this point of view is objectivity itself. And so, although he would speak creation into that objectivity— before the fact, as when his command creates; but after the fact, too, as when he chastises, say, or covenants—though he would keep his creations consonant with their reality, their nature, their essence, to use a traditional metaphysical language, he thus gives commanding and chastising and creating priority *over* nature, acting *over* being, and from the very first.

Accordingly, as we have said, there are at least four words for creation in Genesis, and they thus introduce even into God's originary fiat an ongoingness that becomes a kind of model for man:

> And God *said*, Let there be light: and there was light. And God *saw* the light, that it was good: and God *divided* the light from the darkness. And God *called* the light Day, and the darkness he called Night. And the evening and the morning were the first day. (Gen. 1:3–5)

It is difficult to parse these different words, difficult to know how different, in fact, they are, whether they describe the same or different acts. Ibn Izra, a medieval commentator roughly contemporaneous with Rashi, for example, takes "calling" to be the mechanism of God's "dividing," rather than something subsequent to it. Even if the words represent separate acts, moreover, the acts are not necessarily separate creations. This is the position of Nachmanides, a commentator who lived somewhat after Rashi and Ibn Ezra, who takes creation—genuine creation, ex nihilo—to be described only in Genesis's first verse, "In the beginning God created the heavens and the earth," which he understands as the creation of the primum materium, the Greek *hyle,* as he notes, or *tohu,* in Genesis's second verse, "Now the earth was tohu and bohu" ("without form and void"), so that the other acts are merely a matter of fashioning, of shaping and arranging the *hyle.*

Still, as we have said, the issue that Genesis addresses, what it wishes to determine, is not nature, or not, at any rate, the nature of nature, which only God can, in any case, know. But it addresses the subjectivity through which nature becomes a determination or, rather, how one shall determine nature's determinations. It is a subjectivity that the different words for creation open up as it were between God and himself, a gap as we may say *of* determination: "And God saw the light, that it was good: and God divided the light from the darkness" (Gen. 1:4). God must pause to decide even how he is to go on, how he is to go on even from what he himself has said. The space of a hesitation becomes the space of agency. The space of skepticism becomes the space of faith. That God's creation of light is to be the beginning of the world must be affirmed, and then it must be reaffirmed. Beginnings deliver us only unto new beginnings, which themselves must make what presumably determined them their beginnings in turn. And here, in fact, none of the classical Jewish commentators are in dispute at all.

Ibn Izra is the most straightforward, linking God's act of division to his determination of its value—"And God saw the light, that it was good"—quite literally. Rashi, a little more cautious about the implications of God appearing to be less than omniscient, nevertheless also, at a certain allegorical distance, affirms the link. As he puts it, God saw that the light, being good, should not serve evil people, and so he separated it out for the righteous in the world to come. Even Nachmanides, however, in accordance with his position about a single act of creation, and therefore even as he objects that the readings of Ibn Izra and Rashi would put God in the position of second-guessing himself, asserts that the meaning of "God saw that it was good" is that he "established" that it would exist so long as it remained good. For the whole point of Genesis, Nachmanides says—and here, like Rabbi Yitzhak, he too would seem to wrest from a story about the creation of the world a story about its continuation—is "to instruct us that their stability [the stability of the things God created] is a matter of his will." In Nachmanides' reading, that is, even nature, by remaining good, must determine itself. And even God must determine that the nature he has determined will remain determinative. So, for example, as we read when God establishes that he will no longer destroy the world with a flood, he puts his rainbow in the sky so that *he* will see it and remember and not man:

> I do set my bow in the cloud, and it shall be for a token of a covenant between me and the earth. And it shall come to pass, when I bring a cloud over the earth, that the bow shall be seen in the cloud. And I will remember my covenant, which is between me and you and every living creature of all flesh. . . . (Gen. 9:13–15)

Remembering, too, is creating, and if signs in Genesis are pictures at all, what they then picture is an intention not prior to signification but established only as it were *in* signifying.

To put it in other terms, signs in Genesis are not so much referents as performatives. Or, more formally, as performative theory itself would put it, the language of creation in Genesis is rather declarative than assertive. That is, as Gerda Elata-Alster and Rachel Salmon, following John Searle, distinguish in a seminal piece on biblical covenants, while assertives, as statements of reference, "never fully succeed in making the word fit the world," declaratives, by bringing word and world into being at the same time, do.[11] Assertives, that is, depend on just that anteriority of world to word that the language of beginnings in Genesis abolishes, while declaratives work on the basis of their simultaneity: "In the beginning was the word," as we have seen. It is only, as we must add, that in that case, as the rainbow shows, the declarative power of declaratives is possible only insofar as they are really rather yet a third kind of performative, what Elata-Alster and Salmon call "commissives," or statements committing their speaker to maintain what he or she declares—statements, in other words, where the fit between word and world must be renewed continually. For if ethics, in the creation represented in Genesis, is indeed prior to ontology, then it is the possibility for agency opened up by the very lack of the necessity of fit that sustains such fit as may be found. The fit between word and world—let us say the reality of words: God's as well as man's; God's words, indeed, as modeling man's—is never given but made, is not given but given over, to be begun in a beginning, as we have said, which thus begins again and again.

As Rashi and Ibn Ezra and many other commentators translate, *B'reishit barah Elohim et hashamayim v'et ha'aretz*: not "In the beginning God created the heavens and the earth," but "In the beginning *of* God's creation of the heavens and the earth," or, more simply, as the Anchor Bible and others render it, "When"—"When God began to create the heavens and the earth." This translation, linguistically more plausible than the traditional translation, lacks the traditional translation's originary punch. It does not quite satisfy our desire for certainty. Here the beginning of Genesis is not exactly the beginning of the world for which we might hope. Here, when God does begin to create the world with "Let there be light," he begins in medias res. So, even more radically than in Rabbi Yitzhak's dispersal of the beginning in other beginnings, the beginning disperses itself. Still, if we insist on "In the beginning" as, evidently, we will, if we insist, that is, on what Genesis would seem, precisely in the difficulty it presents for translating its opening verse, to anticipate that we will insist, then perhaps we should allow both translations and say that Genesis, even as Rabbi Yitzhak will do later, thus inserts the story of the creation of the world in which we might hope to rest into the story of the world in which there is no rest. And this is because, like Rabbi Yitzhak, it will not let us get beyond the world, will not, no matter how badly we may wish it, let us see prior to the time when there was time, prior to when there was a "when," but will maintain that the responsibility for creation lies with the created, in whose "when" God began to create, whose "when," that is, is always in the present. Or, to put it in the terms of that great story of the Fall of mankind into the world, the story of the Garden of Eden, there never was a time when man was not in the world, there never was a Fall, there never was a Garden of Eden. Or, rather, even the Garden of Eden was no Garden of Eden, though its history is given precisely to turn our demand for it to more productive use.

3. Ethics

We have already spoken of the way in which the history of the Garden of Eden is one example of the Bible's peculiar habit of beginning all over again in the very midst of a series that has begun already at an earlier point in the narrative. On this rebeginning, with its different order, its genealogy of man and the animals and nature reversing the order of the "first" creation, as is well known, modern biblical criticism founds itself. It should now be clear, however, that the reordering of creation—or this new creation of a particular world within the world already created, as some commentators hold[12]—is but a particular example of the way in which, though he has created it, God hands creation over to man for creating anew. "And every herb of the field had not yet grown, for . . . man was not yet there to till the ground" (Gen. 2:5). All depends on man. Man first and everything else later constitutes the ethically causative order all along implicit, as we have seen, in the material order presented previous to it. So "Let us make man in our image" (Gen. 1:26) becomes, in the incident of Adam's rib, man virtually causing himself to be made in his own image. "Be fruitful and multiply" (Gen. 1:28), whose great temptation is that it might be seen as merely referential, a kind of just-so story explaining how it is that man came to procreate, is ordered ethically as a performative, a command making man determinative of nature, placing man's objective nature as one who does procreate into the subjective power of man who, as one commanded, will procreate rather as a matter of will.

As we might say, the "When" of the first verse of Genesis is reconstituted, again midrashically, in order to open up to man's participation the rather internal deliberation of God with himself. We move from "And God saw. . . . And God called," as we have discussed it in relation to the goodness of light and its division from the darkness, to "And he [God] brought [the animals] to man to see what he [man] would call them" (Gen. 2:19). God still sees, but it is now man who calls, making man a partner in the dialogue in which the first creation was represented.

Once again, the translation is not without problems. "To see what he would call them": "them" would seem to refer to the animals. But its proper translation is really "him" or "it," a pronoun in the singular, which may make its antecedent the "all" or "every" of "every animal" which God has created in the phrase before, but which may also, perhaps more properly, be translated "to him" or "for him" (the pronoun is, in fact, in the dative), in which case Adam is naming the animals "to" or "for himself." As we have said, causation in Genesis is a subjective universal. It is a mistake, especially in light of the ambiguity of "them"/"for himself" to rest, as again we might like to rest, in the traditional notion that Adam's names, to speak again in a traditional metaphysical language, in some sense name the essences of the animals. On the other hand, neither are his names, say, simply rigid designators, in Saul Kripke's term, circumstantial, as it were arbitrary, references whose force is but as strong as historical contingency can make it. [13] Adam's names, that is, cannot be disconnected either from Adam or from the animals he names. They are neither real, in the sense of independent of him, nor arbitrary, in the sense of not really constituting what he names. Rather, their reality is their constitution of a world whose ethics Adam determines in using them. For, to put it once more in performative terms, if the story of Adam naming the animals is indeed a kind of reference, then like "Be fruitful and multiply" it too refers not as a just-so story refers, but within the context of an ethical relation. It refers as just the kind of reference that an ethics demands, naming the fact that none of the animals will serve as the helpmeet that Adam requires, a helpmeet that God will thus create for him because, this time, God sees not whether the animals are or are not good, but that Adam has determined the good that they are for him.

Now the performative by which that good is determined is the rather general injunction of God to Adam, "rule over them." This is an injunction that, with Noah and the multiplication of man into society, will need to be elaborated at levels of some particularity, as in the injunction after the flood not to eat of an animal while it is still alive (Gen. 9:3–5), or later, even more particularly, as in the injunctions to Israel not to cause animals pain (Exod. 23:5) or, as a matter of cultic practice, not to drink their blood (Lev. 8:26–27), to give a portion of animals slaughtered for sacrifice to the priests (e.g., Lev. 2:3,10), and so forth.

In the case of Adam, whose culture is a culture of one, no such particularization is necessary. "Rule over them" is equivalent to "be a ruler." It is the conferral on man of agency, the constitution of him as not a beast, the constitution, that is, of mankind as a subjectivity presocially in the case where there is only one subject and so where there is no need to distinguish subjects from each other but only to distinguish subjectivity as a whole from what is not a subject. This is the difference of Adam's language from languages post-Babel. If we wish, in order to mark its difference from the more arbitrary languages that become the lot of man when proper societies come into being, we may even call it a transcendental language, much though ideas of the transcendental have fallen today into disfavor, especially among those who prefer to see all language as political from the start. Post-Babel ethics, indeed, will require a politics: first, as we may suppose, for the adjudication of subjectivities in their variety of claims;[14] and second, as we have discussed, in order to prevent the objectification of any rules of adjudication beyond subjective limits. But then, we must also understand that such a politics must be held to account by ethics, too. For limitation is equivalent not to arbitrariness but, as we have seen, to responsibility, and if arbitrary limitation becomes necessary because mankind has failed to recognize his limitation himself, it then becomes necessary in order to restore to man the power of his subjectivity rather than to deconstruct it. That is to say, if man's language is marked as arbitrary as a way of preventing him from taking it for a language of essences, from taking it as naming what is transcendent or beyond man, then what man is returned to is what is rather transcendental than transcendent: the limited, if universal, condition of man as responsible subject. And this limitation, in its ethical universality, precisely, is just what the story of the Fall insists upon over and against our desire for a knowledge caught in the deconstructive binary of all or none, over and against our desire for knowledge beyond ethics altogether.[15]

Who does not know the meaning of the story of the Garden of Eden? It is the story of God's great plan, the whole contained in the particular, the ending already in the beginning. It is the resolution of the problem of evil in a world that God created, and said he created, as good, the explanation of all difficulties, all problems, all those impossible and not very good situations in which man in fact finds himself, comforting him with original sin, say, or the state of nature, his beginnings before he became what he is, a marplot but all the more a part of God's eternal plan. Accordingly, "And did you eat from the tree?" God asks Adam. And Adam replies, "The woman whom you gave me, gave me from the tree, and I ate." "What is this you have done?" God asks Eve. And Eve answers, "The serpent beguiled me, and I ate" (Gen. 3:11–13). From cause to cause to cause, the chain connects backward, answering why, and why, and why again, the questions of a child, of man in his adolescent quest for knowledge beyond the knowable, knowledge beyond the responsibility of man. And God is willing to meet man halfway, to play the interlocutor for him, to go on with him in his questioning. But God will go on only so far, and then he will stop. For God does not ask the snake why he beguiled Eve. He knows already: because he made the snake "more subtle than all the beasts" (Gen. 3:1), folding the chain back on itself, returning us all over again to the question of evil in a world God presumably made good. And so *arum*, the Hebrew word translated as "subtle," is also the very same word used to describe the state of Adam and Eve before they fell, though presumably to be translated there (Gen. 2:25) as "naked." For naked and subtle, innocent and cunning name not states of being but actions, according to which God created us neither good nor bad but responsible for both. And this is why Adam and Eve are responsible for eating of the fruit of the tree of the knowledge of good and evil even before, by eating of the fruit, they come to have the knowledge of good and evil. For good and evil are just what man knows in the only sense of knowing in which Genesis is really interested, nor does it excuse him to insist that first he must know that he knows them, which is all that eating of the fruit accomplishes.

As Wittgenstein put it, explanations must stop somewhere. As Genesis would say, beginnings must begin somewhere. As we have seen, that beginning is always now.

Notes

1. Gen. 1:1. Classical Jewish commentary proceeds verse by verse and is numbered accordingly. The translations are my own. Translations of biblical passages are from the King James and the Jewish Press Society or are my own, as the context requires.

2. Tractate Berachot 1a.

3. The medieval source is referenced in the Sifsei Hachamim, a commentary on Rashi. The Sifsei Hachamim speculates that Rashi wished to honor a father not known for his learning and therefore began by citing him, rather than someone more authoritative, a speculation that dovetails with my reading of the agon of fathers and sons, though it proceeds from the opposite direction.

4. Stanley Cavell, "Psychoanalysis and Cinema," in *The Cavell Reader*, ed. Stephen Mulhall (Cambridge, Mass.: Blackwell, 1996), 241ff.

5. Available most conveniently in English in Louis Ginzberg, *The Legends of the Jews*, 7 vols., trans. Henrietta Szold (Philadelphia: Jewish Publication Society of America, 1909–38).

6. Cf., e.g., the discussion in Claude Lévi-Strauss, *The Elementary Structures of Kinship*, trans. James Harle Bell and John Richard von Sturmer, ed. Rodney Needham (Boston: Beacon Press, 1969), on the "scandal" of the incest taboo,

which, because it is universal, he takes to be natural, but which, because it is legislated, he sees as simultaneously cultural, marking it as the beginning of culture, at least according to the thinking of structural anthropology. In a similar vein, in *The Second Treatise of Government*, John Locke analyzes the concept of "natural law." In keeping with his generally empirical disposition, Locke treats the development from natural to political communities as historical. But we might reconstrue the philosophically significant point of his analysis as the ethical one that, in what we might call political community, man chooses to follow that same law which, in what we call a natural community, he simply *does* follow.

7. Cf. Emmanuel Levinas, in *Nine Talmudic Readings*, trans. Annette Arono-wicz (Bloomington: Indiana University Press, 1990). See also Kenneth Dauber, "The Bible as Literature: Reading Like the Rabbis," *Semeia* 31 (1985): 27–48.

8. The case of the Levites is perhaps exemplary. Because they obey God and kill those of their brothers from other tribes who worshiped the golden calf, they are rewarded with the temple service originally designed to be the right of the firstborn throughout Israel. But they are also deprived of their portion of land among the other tribes. As the Bible will have to enjoin the tribes in a formulation, repeated in variant forms, that reveals the Levites' status, "Do not forget the widow, the orphan, and the Levite."

9. This is to understand materiality not as what determines will, as Hume understands it in his *Treatise of Human Nature*, but as what conditions it, that is to say from the point of view of the sort of radical skepticism we have been maintaining.

Cf. Sforno and Hizkuni, two more medieval Jewish commentators, who read *ki* as "because" and who also see it as introducing merely a condition, though they put this reading to other purposes.

10. Suggestion made by Robbins in conversation with the author. Thanks to Robbins, Levinas expert, author of *Altered Reading: Levinas and Literature* (Chicago: University of Chicago Press, 1999), and editor of *Is It Righteous to Be: Interviews with Emmanuel Levinas* (Stanford, Calif.: Stanford University Press, 2001). The phrase from Levinas is from *Existence and Existents*, trans. Alphonso Lingis (The Hague: Nijhoff, 1978).

11. Gerda Elata-Alster and Rachel Salmon, "Biblical Covenants as Perfor-mative Language," in *Summoning: Ideas of the Covenant and Interpretive Theory*, ed. Ellen Spolsky (New York: State University of New York Press, 1993), 27–28.

12. For a modern version, see Umberto Cassuto, *A Commentary on the Book of Genesis*, trans. Israel Abrahams (Jerusalem: Magnes Press, 1961–64). Other recon-ciliations abound. Most of the classical explanations are based on some version of the principle of rebeginning, usually understood as filling in the details of what has been stated earlier. Ibn Ezra, however, goes so far as to turn the principle into the further principle that "there is no early and no late in the Scriptures," an even more radical statement than we have ventured to offer.

13. Saul Kripke, *Naming and Necessity* (Oxford: Blackwell, 1980).

14. Cf. Levinas on justice, in Robbins, *Is It Righteous to Be*.

15. It is, I think, because of its pre-Babel concern with transcendentality, too, that the story of Cain and Abel does not specify what exactly Cain's sin is in offering God a sacrifice from the fruits of the ground he has tilled. God's admonition to him is, simply, "Why art thou wroth? and why is thy countenance fallen? If thou doest well it shall be lifted up, and if thou doest not well, sin lieth at the door; and unto thee is its desire, but thou canst rule over it" (Gen. 4:6–7). This is the equivalent of the injunction to Adam, "Rule over them." (Or it is almost the equivalent. There is another person in Cain's case, after all, Abel, whose sacrifice God accepts. Even in the story of Cain's murder of Abel, however, there is a corresponding vagueness. Asked where his brother is, Cain replies, "I know not; am I my brother's keeper" [Gen. 4:9], which would appear to be an attempt to deflect responsibility by requiring that action be grounded in a self-destructing theory of being. If God says yes, then he compromises the very agency on which responsibility depends. If he says no, then there is no responsibility in the first place. God does not take the bait. His response cuts to the chase: "And he said, What hast thou done? The voice of thy brother's blood crieth unto me from the ground" [Gen. 4:10]. See the following discussion of Adam.)

Afterword

Stanley Cavell

Ever since Kenneth Dauber and Walter Jost wrote to me describing their plans for a collection of essays meant to illustrate something to be called ordinary language criticism, I have, inescapably, wondered what would be made of that new phrase by the contributors to the volume, for since they are the first to exemplify the phrase, they are the initial proposers of its sense. Coming away from my first reading of the collection, I am of course gratified by the sustained level of distinction of the contributions and heartened by what the editors describe as the "varieties" of interests and texts they take up. I note that it is largely the editors who undertake to sketch something of a program meant to show connected promptings among the essays; the essays themselves, including those by the editors, tend fairly directly to settle down to a work of critical thinking at hand. Perhaps it is the idea of participating in such a volume that enables or occasions this directness, for it does seem true that of the major lines of work that have served to inspire thinking across the borders or channels between philosophy and literary study in the past three or four decades, Wittgenstein's has played the smallest, or least gaudy, role. So it is good that some action has been taken if only to counter a bit what to some of us has seemed a puzzling disproportion. But how do we understand the disproportion? Why doesn't, or hasn't, Wittgenstein exactly fit?

Philosophers used to speak of something like revolutions in twentieth-century philosophy. The names of Peirce, Dewey, Husserl, Heidegger, Carnap, Wittgenstein (early and later), Austin, Foucault, Derrida have been regarded (first, characteristically, by themselves) in such a light. (Whether Freud and Lacan are parallel or transverse to these developments is unclear to me.) We live in the aftermath of these revolutionary claims. No one of the claims is dead, but no one can any longer hold the field alone. (That may create the impression, if not exactly the possibility, of pluralism. The actuality is that no one—no single one known to or imagined by me—is equipped to do justice to the aggregate of demands of learning and practice these contenders for our reason put in place.) Revolutionary change creates exiles, new qualifications for advancement, new forms of address, new silences. Ordinary language criticism is invoked by the editors as an avenue of liberation from what were felt to be, let's say, conformities to system, ones having the effect of a kind of inhibition (perhaps in the form of a reactive excess) of reading, as though what was felt to be a fetishized response to texts had become transformed into a phobic response. I felt something of this sort of liberation on encountering Wittgenstein and Austin (not exactly on the first encounter, but eventually, and decisively), but, coming, I believe, from a different generation than any of the other contributors to this volume, and making a living from the profession of philosophy, unlike Kenneth Dauber and Walter Jost in literary studies, my experience has taken a different, in some ways opposite, course. A critical measure of the difference is that I had to understand not how my professional field had become overrun with events associated with, let's say, structuralist and poststructuralist developments in France, but why it was, and remains, largely unmoved by them.

On returning to the university in the late 1940s, a year after graduating college, and deciding that I had received next to no education for what I indistinctly felt would provide an intellectual existence for myself, my intellectual diet was made of two cuisines—formal courses in a first-rate philosophy department where pragmatism and positivism were old and new royalty, and isolated, avid, it seemed quite furtive, midnight reading of the famous literary/political quarterlies of those years (*Partisan Review, Kenyon Review, Hudson Review, Sewanee Review*, etc.) where in any season you might encounter the latest thoughts of, for example, Kenneth Burke, R. P. Blackmur, John Crowe Ransom, Lionel Trilling, William Empson, Paul Goodman as an outrider—readers, in a word, but with philosophical longings. I can hardly claim that there is a sensible reason for supposing that these two advanced representations of academic philosophy and of literary reflection should or could be put together, but to my mind they virtually shouted for one another, philosophy to be reminded that it should be discontent with (without renouncing) its professionalism, criticism to be reminded that the present of philosophy is to some inevitable and beneficial degree professionalized.

With some exceptions (for example, Empson's once taking on positivism's emotive theory of meaning, complicating a line of thought earlier introduced by his mentor I. A. Richards), the positions of mutual disregard between the revolutions associated with Vienna and those with New York and Nashville seemed to harden. Then in the 1950s came the translation of Wittgenstein's *Philosophical Investigations* from Cambridge and the rush of what was called ordinary language philosophy from Oxford, an outpouring of work from many talented hands, first among them, to my mind, those of J. L. Austin, who died in 1960 at the age of forty-eight. (It would be decades before I knew enough for it to count for me that Walter Benjamin died at the same age, under other circumstances, in 1940, the year Austin began his military service that would make him, according to good account, the leading expert in England on German military preparations.) Wittgenstein's and Austin's work put motion into the relation of philosophy and literature, if for no other reason than that their manner of writing, it seemed evident to me, entered into their thinking: The language of the street, or language shared with the street, was no longer, as with the philosophers they challenged, the enemy of philosophy, but its resource, and for that reason more difficult than ever to arrive at an understanding with.

But from what position could their manners of writing be assessed? Not from that of philosophy (as it stood), since that would seem to deny philosophy's seriousness, or change its subject; and not from that of literary studies, because that would require taking responsibility for the philosophy, and the philosophy was so hard to pick up, born as it was in fire.

Among the other convulsions of the late 1960s, the decisive arrival began of the events in Paris philosophy and psychoanalysis and linguistics whose apparently endless and exclusive reception of tributes here has most directly caused the call for the essays in the present volume. I said that my age gave a somewhat different valence to my difficulties with these developments. What their clamorous success seemed to reveal to me was that my wish for some, we could say, rapprochement between philosophical and literary studies was far more widely desired than I had dreamed. But the terms of rapprochement which others seemed to recognize in these forms and absorbed with pleasure were mixed with too high a cost for my rejoicing. The New Criticism as a movement of practice fell into virtual oblivion, for reasons not explained in any account I know of—for example not sufficiently explained by its own faults of, let's say, gentility. And philosophy in its analytical form, which is half the mind of philosophy as it now exists, and existed then, was unrecognized as a voice to contend with. An immediate cost of this continued shunning of (at least half of) philosophy was that it compromised the understanding of the work of Wittgenstein and that of Austin.

So it was with a renewed sense of intellectual isolation that I greeted the ensuing 1970s. No doubt that sense has sometimes caused my prose to screech and whine more than I would have liked, but it has also caused me to seek companionship in places I might not otherwise have sought so excitedly, in film for example, or Emerson and Thoreau, sometimes in stretches of the French reception that was having its frequently disheartening consequences.

Companionship and work bring me to the present occasion. At the end of the day (so they say these days; the transcendentalist in me would prefer speaking of the start of the day) what matters in these strifes of culture is the capacity and luck to produce work in faithfulness to one's desire. Handsome work is plain throughout these pages, and I hope they may inspire more. I am thankful for whatever role I have had in helping this to happen. I want particularly to say to those contributors whose efforts for these pages took them to readings made in explicit sympathy with or extension of ones of my own that I feel very well treated in them and grateful for it.

Notes on Contributors

Charles Altieri teaches twentieth-century literature in English at the University of California at Berkeley. His most recent books are *Subjective Agency*, *Postmodernisms Now*, and the forthcoming *Aesthetics of the Affects*.

R. M. Berry, a professor of English at Florida State University, is author of the novel *Leonardo's Horse* and the story collections *Dictionary of Modern Anguish* and *Plane Geometry and Other Affairs of the Heart*. His literary criticism has appeared in *Narrative*, *Philosophy and Literature; The Journal of Beckett Studies; Context; The American Book Review;* and various anthologies. He is publisher of the literary press Fiction Collective Two.

Gerald L. Bruns is the William P. and Hazel B. White Professor of English at the University of Notre Dame. He has written on subjects ranging from legal theory to the literary canon, and he is the author, among other books, of *Modern Poetry and the Idea of Language: A Critical and Historical Study; Inventions: Writing, Textuality, and Understanding in Literary History; Heidegger's Estrangements: Language, Truth, Poetry in the Later Writings; Hermeneutics Ancient and Modern;* and, most recently, *Tragic Thoughts at the End of Philosophy: Language, Literature and Ethical Theory*.

Anthony J. Cascardi is a professor of comparative literature, rhetoric, and Spanish at the University of California at Berkeley. His books include *Consequences of Enlightenment*, *The Subject of Modernity*, and *Literature and the Question of Philosophy*. He is the editor of *The Cambridge Companion to Cervantes* and is at work on the topic of aesthetics and agency.

Kenneth Dauber is a professor of English at the State University of New York at Buffalo. He is the author of *Rediscovering Hawthorne* and *The Idea of Authorship in America: Democratic Poetics from Franklin to Melville*. He is at work on a study of sentimentality.

William Day is an assistant professor of philosophy at Le Moyne College in Syracuse, New York, where he teaches aesthetics. He has worked on Wittgenstein, Emerson, and Leo Strauss and is coeditor of the forthcoming *Seeing Aspects in Wittgenstein*.

Edward Duffy is an associate professor of English at Marquette University. He is the author of *Rousseau in England: The Context for Shelley's Critique of the Enlightenment* and, more recently, of articles on Wordsworth, Raymond Carver, and Harry Potter.

He is nearing completion of a book tentatively entitled *The Constitution of Shelley's Writing.*

Richard Eldridge is a professor of philosophy and chair of the philosophy department at Swarthmore College. He is the author of *On Moral Personhood: Philosophy, Literature, Criticism and Self-Understanding; Leading a Human Life: Wittgenstein, Intentionality, and Romanticism; The Persistence of Romanticism;* and the forthcoming *An Introduction to the Philosophy of Art.* He is also the editor of the forthcoming *Beyond Representation: Philosophy and Poetic Imagination* and *Stanley Cavell.*

William Flesch is an associate professor of English at Brandeis University. He is the author of *Generosity and the Limits of Authority: Shakespeare, Herbert, Milton* and has written on topics ranging from Proust to light verse. The article in this volume is part of a book in progress on literary and philosophical approaches to quotation.

Garry L. Hagberg is the James H. Ottaway Professor of Philosophy and Aesthetics at Bard College, where he also chairs the division of social studies and directs the program in philosophy and the arts. His books include *Art as Language: Wittgenstein, Meaning, and Aesthetic Theory* and *Meaning and Interpretation: Wittgenstein, Henry James, and Literary Knowledge.* He guest-edited a special issue of *The Journal of Aesthetics and Art Criticism* on improvisation in the arts, and he is the coeditor of *Philosophy and Literature.*

Walter Jost is an associate professor of English at the University of Virginia. He is the author of *Rhetorical Thought in John Henry Newman* and *Rhetorical Investigations: Studies in Ordinary Language Criticism* and has coedited several volumes, most recently Blackwell's *A Companion to Rhetoric* (forthcoming 2003).

Stephen Mulhall is a fellow and tutor in philosophy at New College, Oxford. He is the author, among other books, of *Stanley Cavell: Philosophy's Recounting of the Ordinary* and, most recently, *Inheritance and Originality: Wittgenstein, Heidegger, Kierkegaard* and *On Film.*

Martha C. Nussbaum is the Ernst Freund Distinguished Service Professor of Law and Ethics in the undergraduate college, divinity school, law school, and department of philosophy at the University of Chicago. She is the author of, among other books, *The Fragility of Goodness: Luck and Ethics in Greek Tragedy and Philosophy; Love's Knowledge: Essays on Philosophy and Literature;* and, most recently, *Upheavals of Thought: The Intelligence of Emotions.*

Marjorie Perloff is the Sadie Dernham Patek Professor (emerita) in the humanities at Stanford University. She is the author, among other books, of *The Dance of the Intellect: Studies in the Poetry of the Pound Tradition; The Poetics of Indeterminacy: Rimbaud to*

Cage; The Futurist Moment: Avant-Garde, Avant Guerre, and the Language of Rupture; Wittgenstein's Ladder: Poetic Language and the Strangeness of the Ordinary; and, most recently, *21st Century Modernism: The "New" Poetics*. She was elected to the American Academy of Arts and Sciences in 1997.

Austin E. Quigley is a professor of English at Columbia University. He has also taught at the universities of Nottingham, Geneva, Konstanz, and Massachusetts. He is the author of *The Pinter Problem* and *The Modern Stage and Other Worlds*.